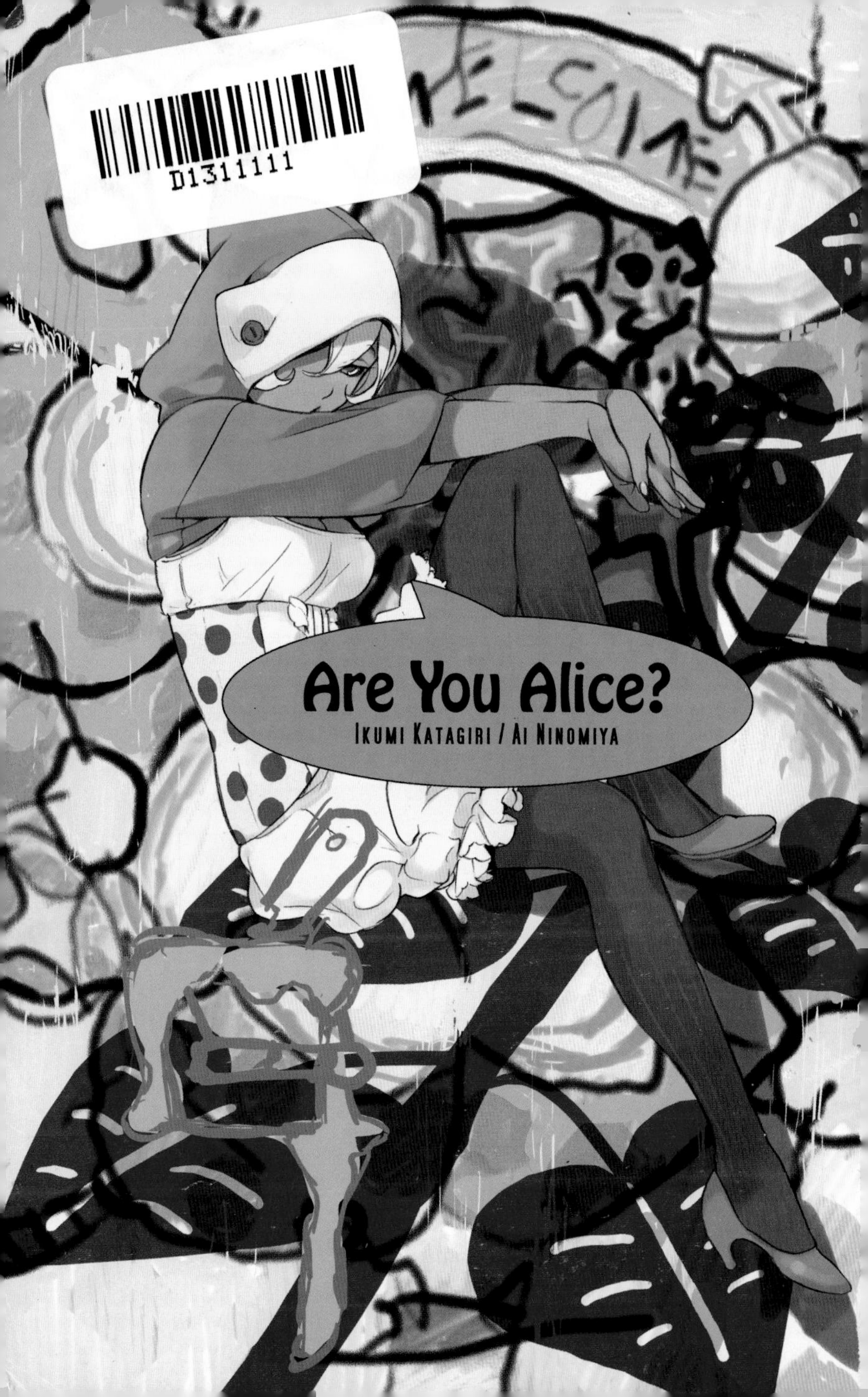
Are You Alice?
Ikumi Katagiri / Ai Ninomiya

Are You Alice?
4
CONTENTS!

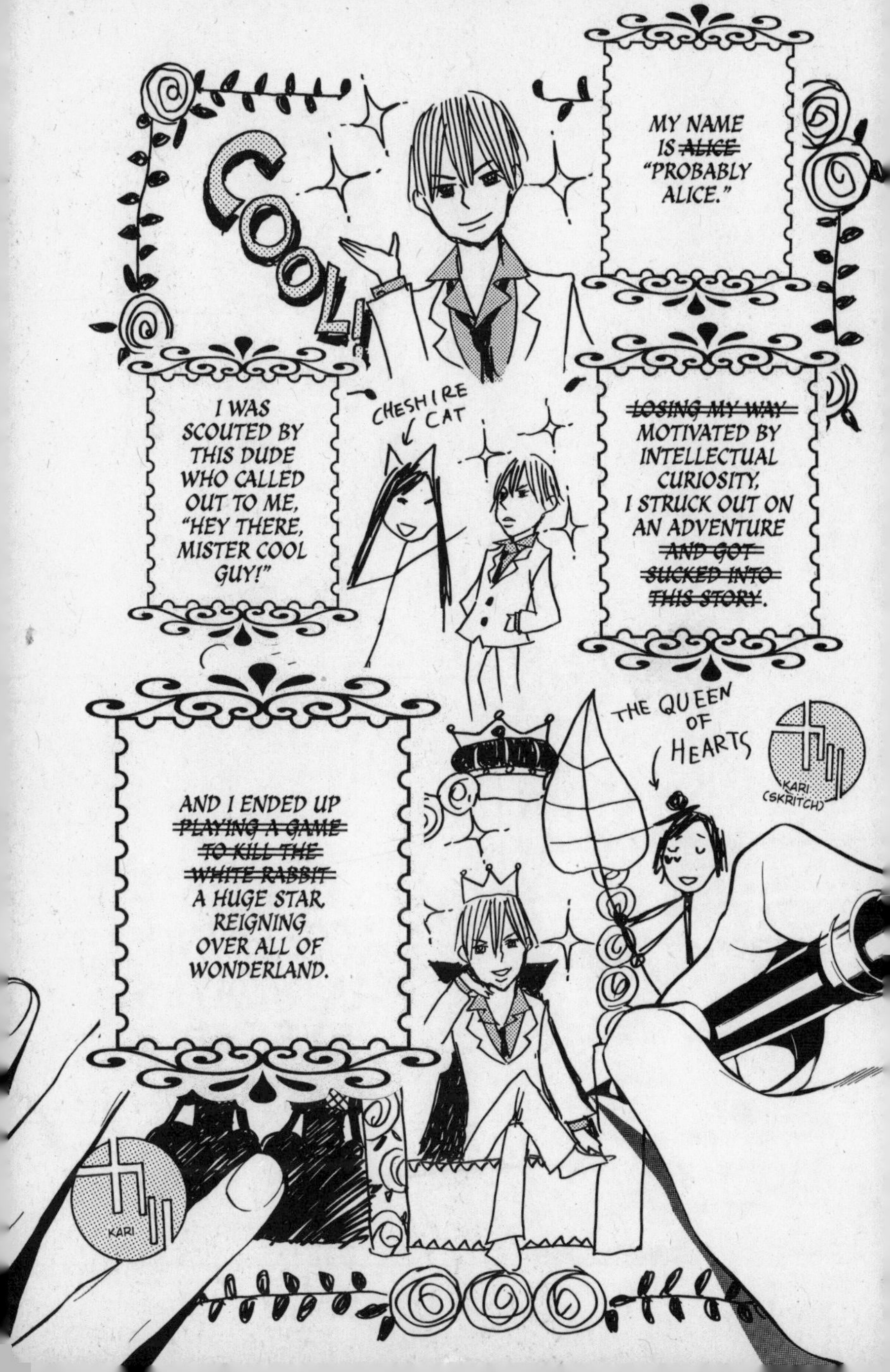
MY NAME IS ~~ALICE~~ "PROBABLY ALICE."
COOL!
~~LOSING MY WAY~~ MOTIVATED BY INTELLECTUAL CURIOSITY, I STRUCK OUT ON AN ADVENTURE ~~AND GOT SUCKED INTO THIS STORY~~.
CHESHIRE CAT
I WAS SCOUTED BY THIS DUDE WHO CALLED OUT TO ME, "HEY THERE, MISTER COOL GUY!"
THE QUEEN OF HEARTS
KARI (SKRITCH)
AND I ENDED UP ~~PLAYING A GAME TO KILL THE WHITE RABBIT~~ A HUGE STAR REIGNING OVER ALL OF WONDERLAND.
KARI

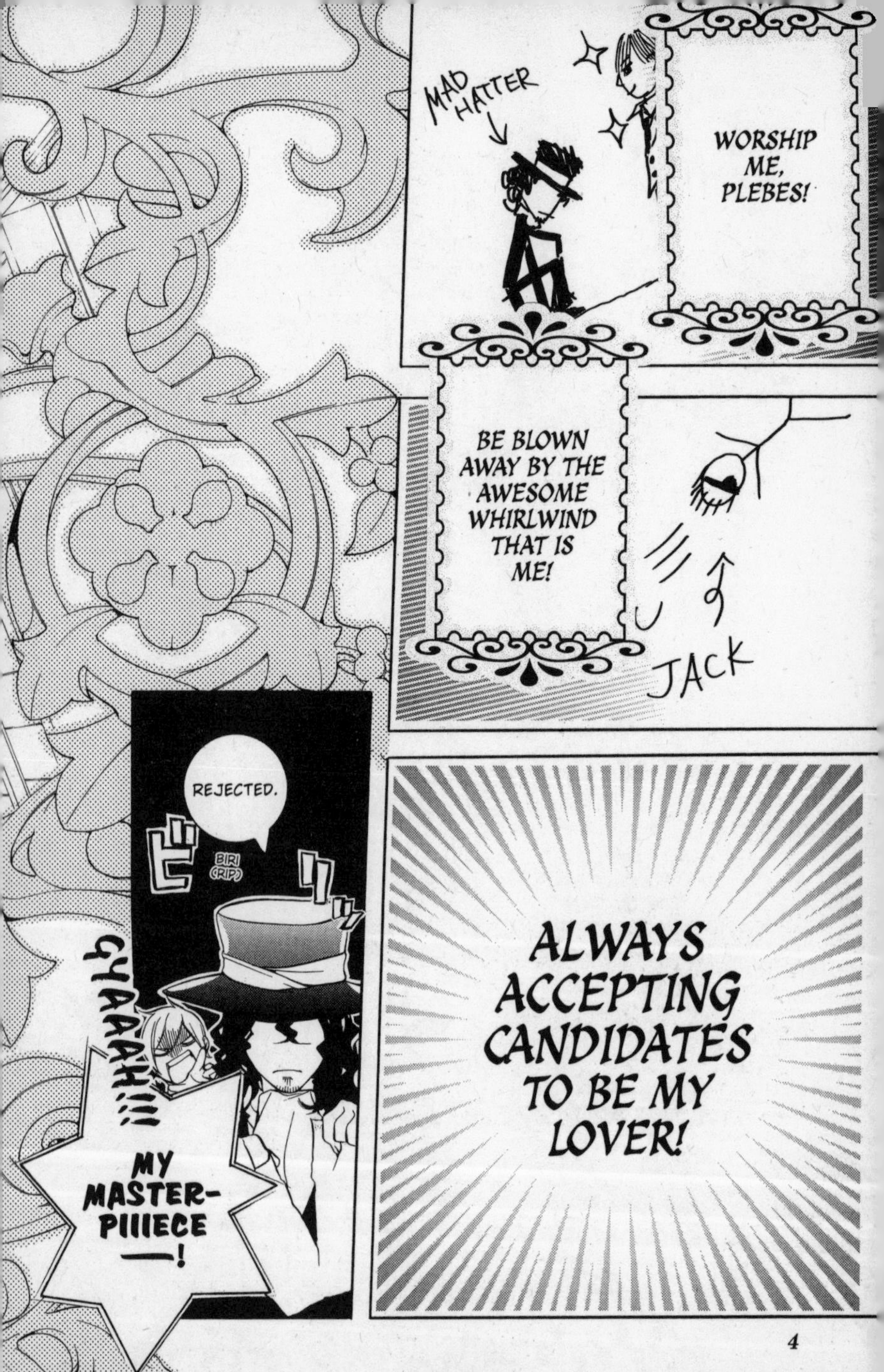
WORSHIP ME, PLEBES!
MAD HATTER
BE BLOWN AWAY BY THE AWESOME WHIRLWIND THAT IS ME!
JACK
ALWAYS ACCEPTING CANDIDATES TO BE MY LOVER!
REJECTED.
BIRI (RIP)
GYAAAAH!!!
MY MASTER-PIIIECE—!

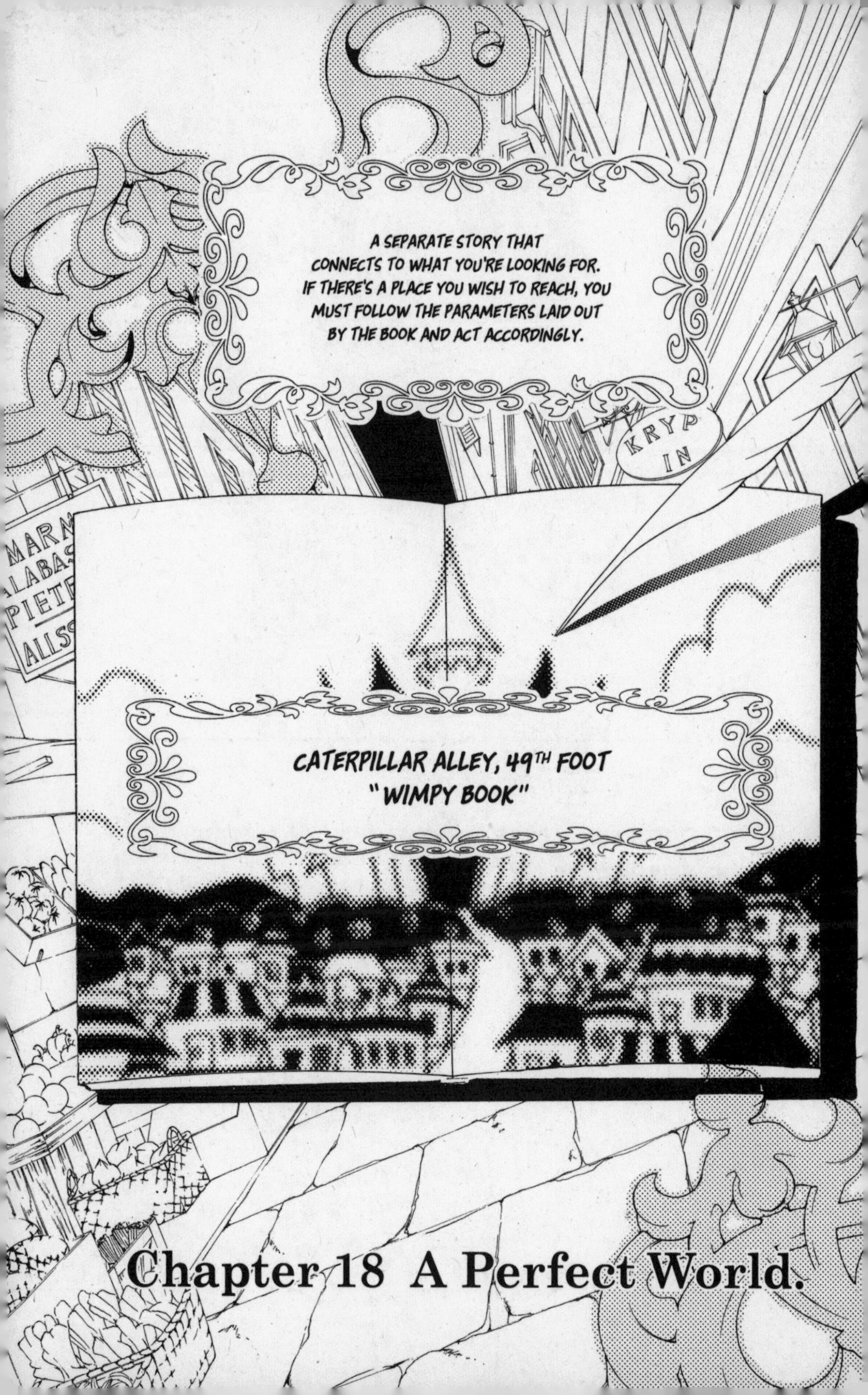
A SEPARATE STORY THAT CONNECTS TO WHAT YOU'RE LOOKING FOR. IF THERE'S A PLACE YOU WISH TO REACH, YOU MUST FOLLOW THE PARAMETERS LAID OUT BY THE BOOK AND ACT ACCORDINGLY.
CATERPILLAR ALLEY, 49TH FOOT
"WIMPY BOOK"

Chapter 18 A Perfect World.

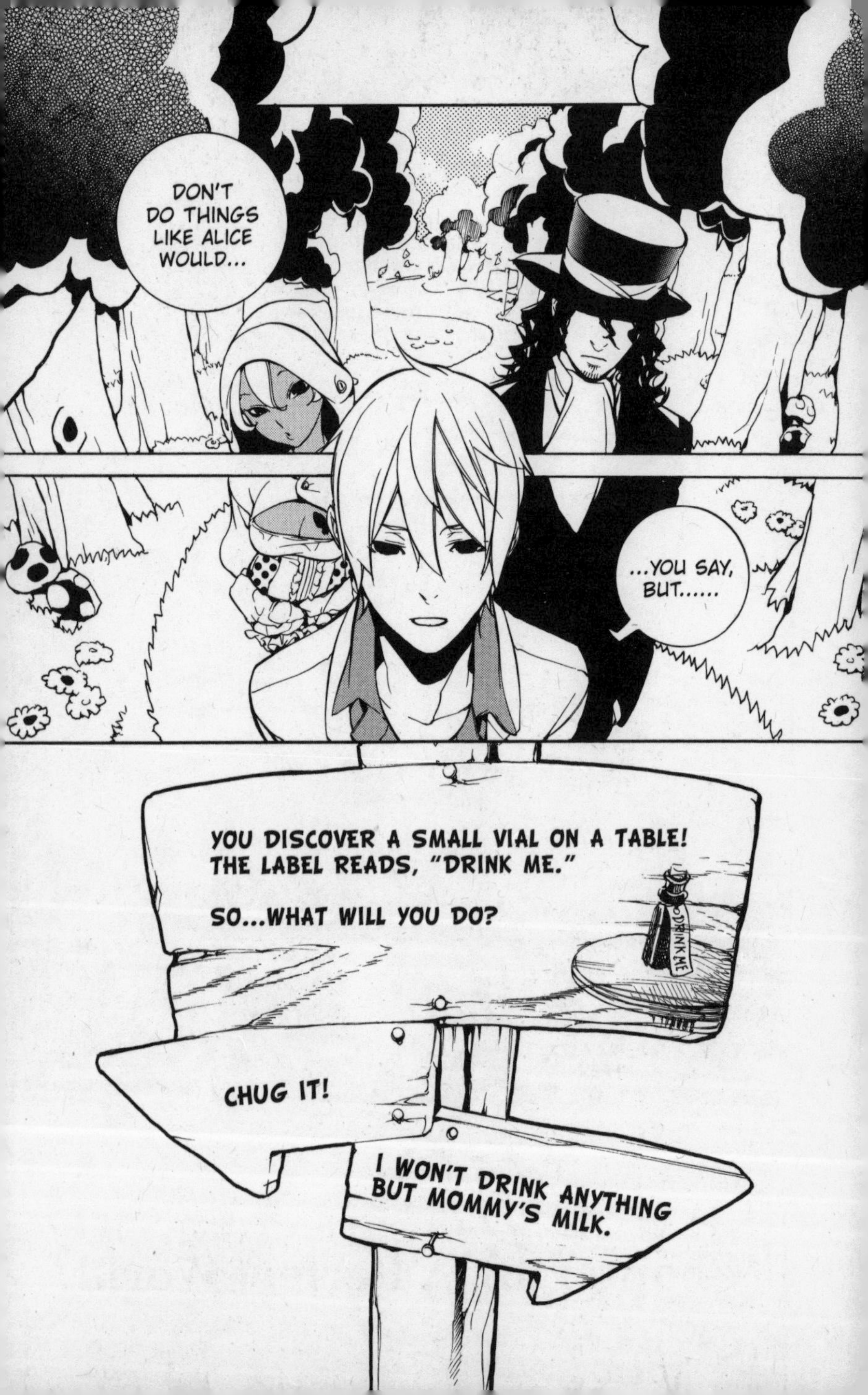
DON'T DO THINGS LIKE ALICE WOULD...
...YOU SAY, BUT......
YOU DISCOVER A SMALL VIAL ON A TABLE! THE LABEL READS, "DRINK ME."
SO...WHAT WILL YOU DO?
DRINK ME
CHUG IT!
I WON'T DRINK ANYTHING BUT MOMMY'S MILK.

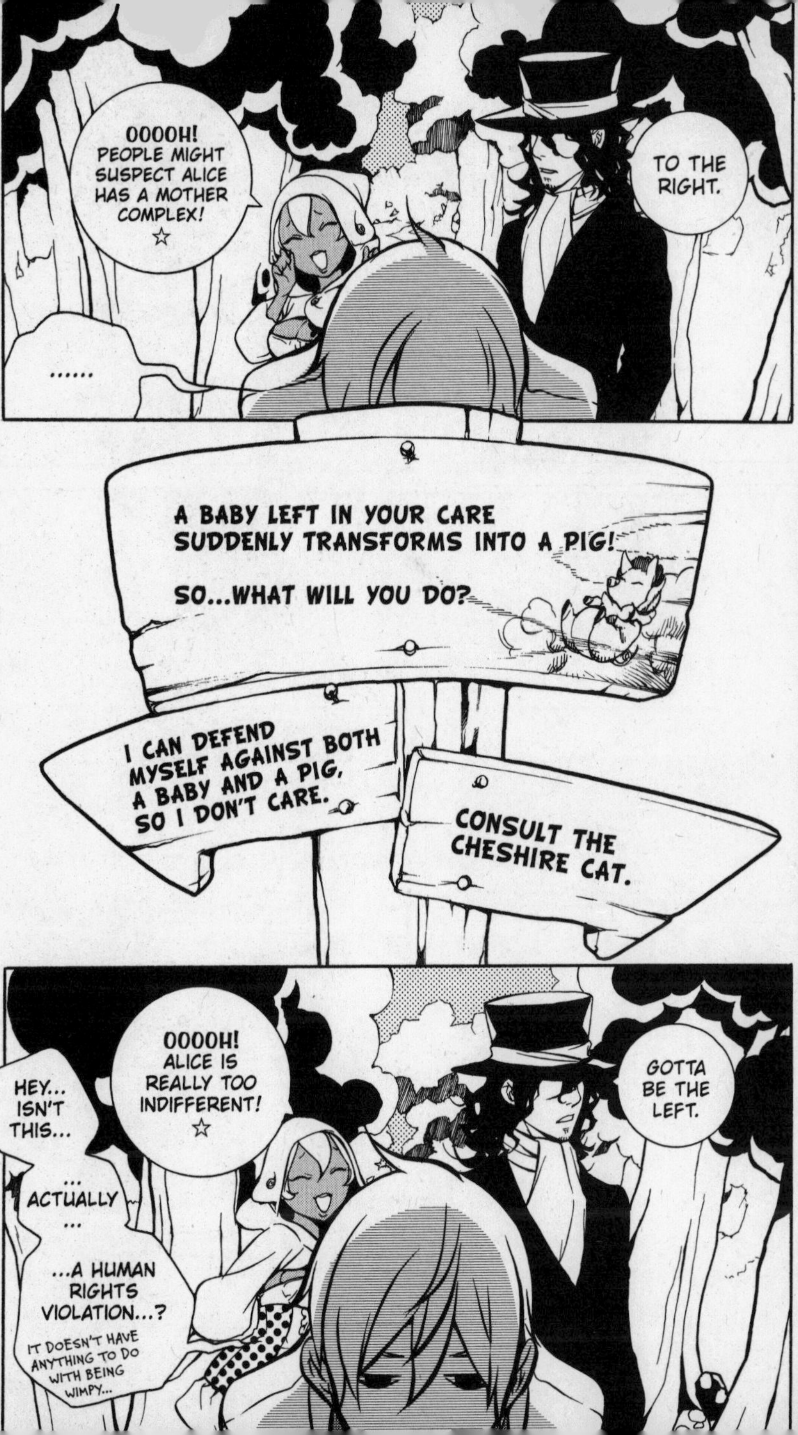
TO THE RIGHT.
OOOOH! PEOPLE MIGHT SUSPECT ALICE HAS A MOTHER COMPLEX! ☆
......
A BABY LEFT IN YOUR CARE SUDDENLY TRANSFORMS INTO A PIG!
SO...WHAT WILL YOU DO?
CONSULT THE CHESHIRE CAT.
I CAN DEFEND MYSELF AGAINST BOTH A BABY AND A PIG, SO I DON'T CARE.
GOTTA BE THE LEFT.
OOOOH! ALICE IS REALLY TOO INDIFFERENT! ☆
HEY... ISN'T THIS...
... ACTUALLY ...
...A HUMAN RIGHTS VIOLATION...?
IT DOESN'T HAVE ANYTHING TO DO WITH BEING WIMPY...

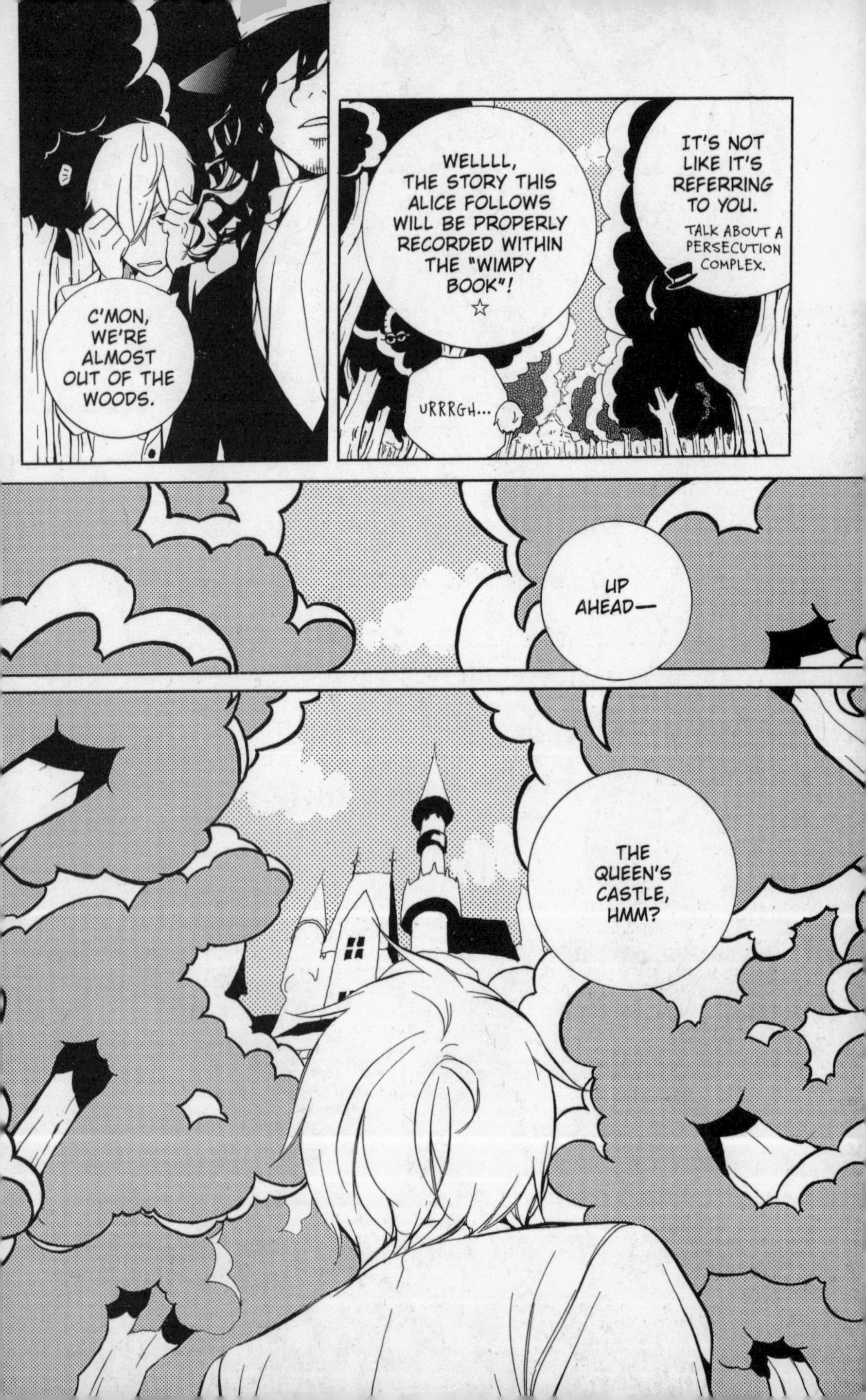
IT'S NOT LIKE IT'S REFERRING TO YOU.
TALK ABOUT A PERSECUTION COMPLEX.
WELLLL, THE STORY THIS ALICE FOLLOWS WILL BE PROPERLY RECORDED WITHIN THE "WIMPY BOOK"! ☆
URRRGH...
C'MON, WE'RE ALMOST OUT OF THE WOODS.
UP AHEAD—
THE QUEEN'S CASTLE, HMM?

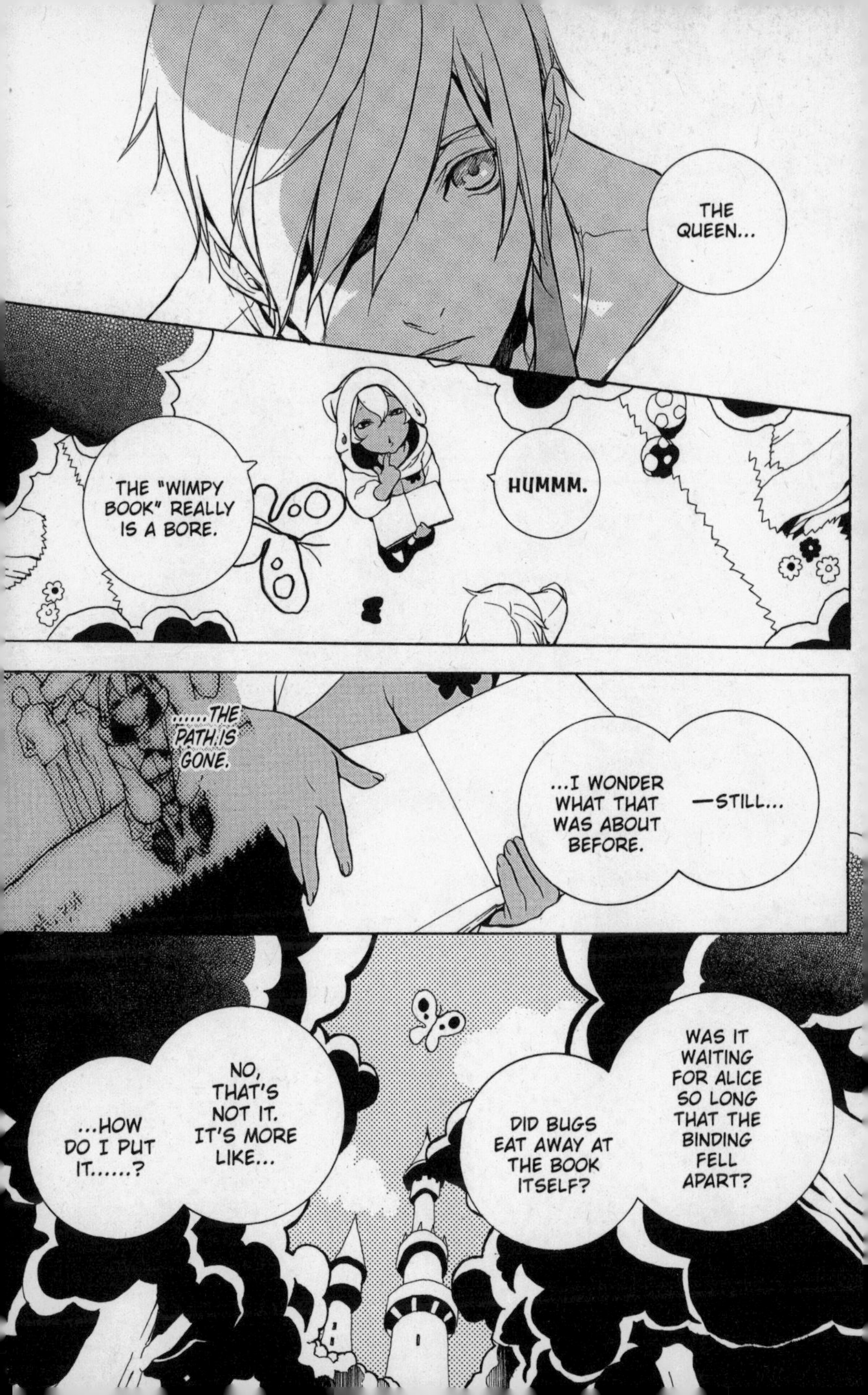
THE QUEEN...
HUMMM.
THE "WIMPY BOOK" REALLY IS A BORE.
—STILL...
...I WONDER WHAT THAT WAS ABOUT BEFORE.
......THE PATH IS GONE.
WAS IT WAITING FOR ALICE SO LONG THAT THE BINDING FELL APART?
DID BUGS EAT AWAY AT THE BOOK ITSELF?
NO, THAT'S NOT IT. IT'S MORE LIKE...
...HOW DO I PUT IT......?

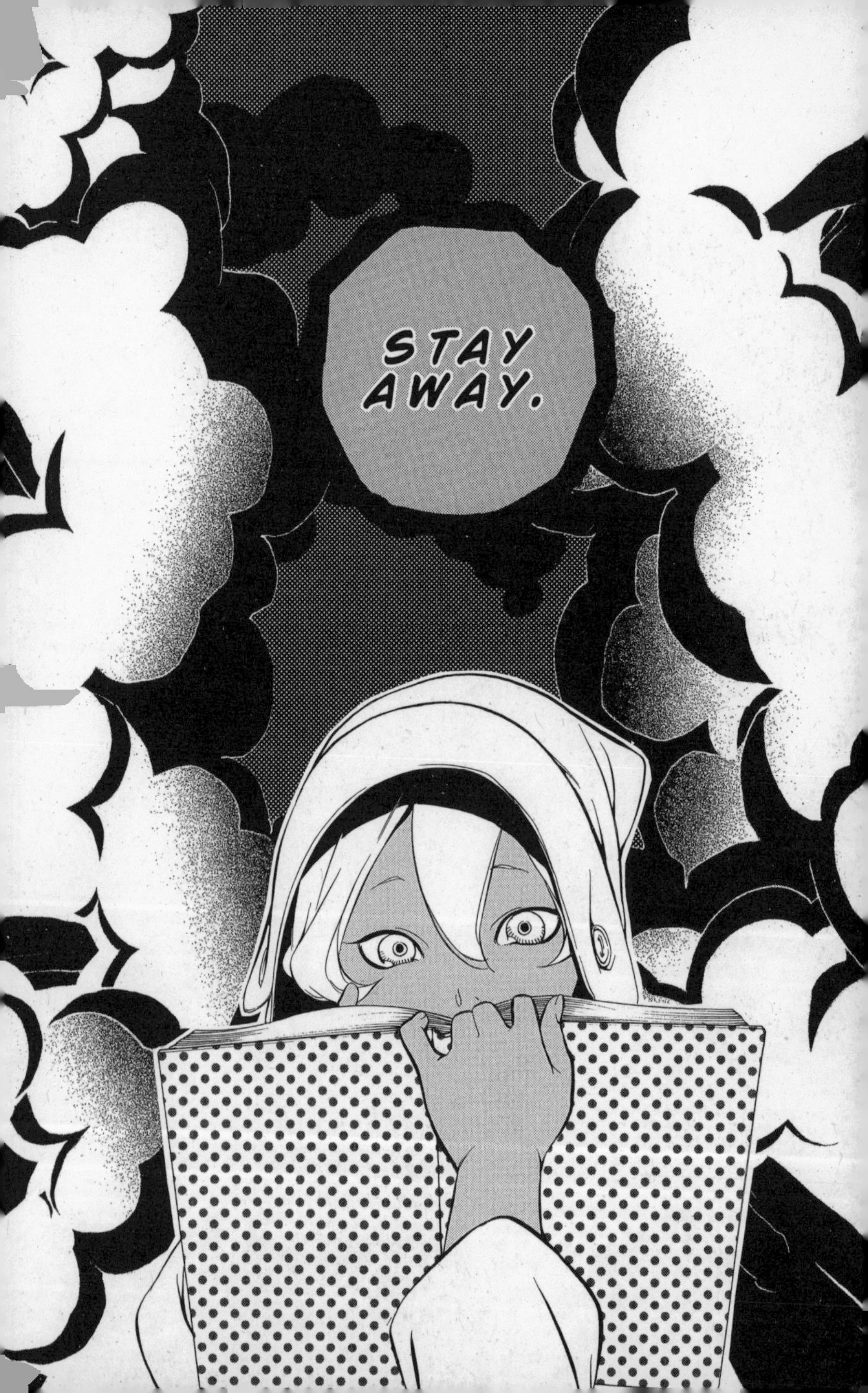
STAY AWAY.

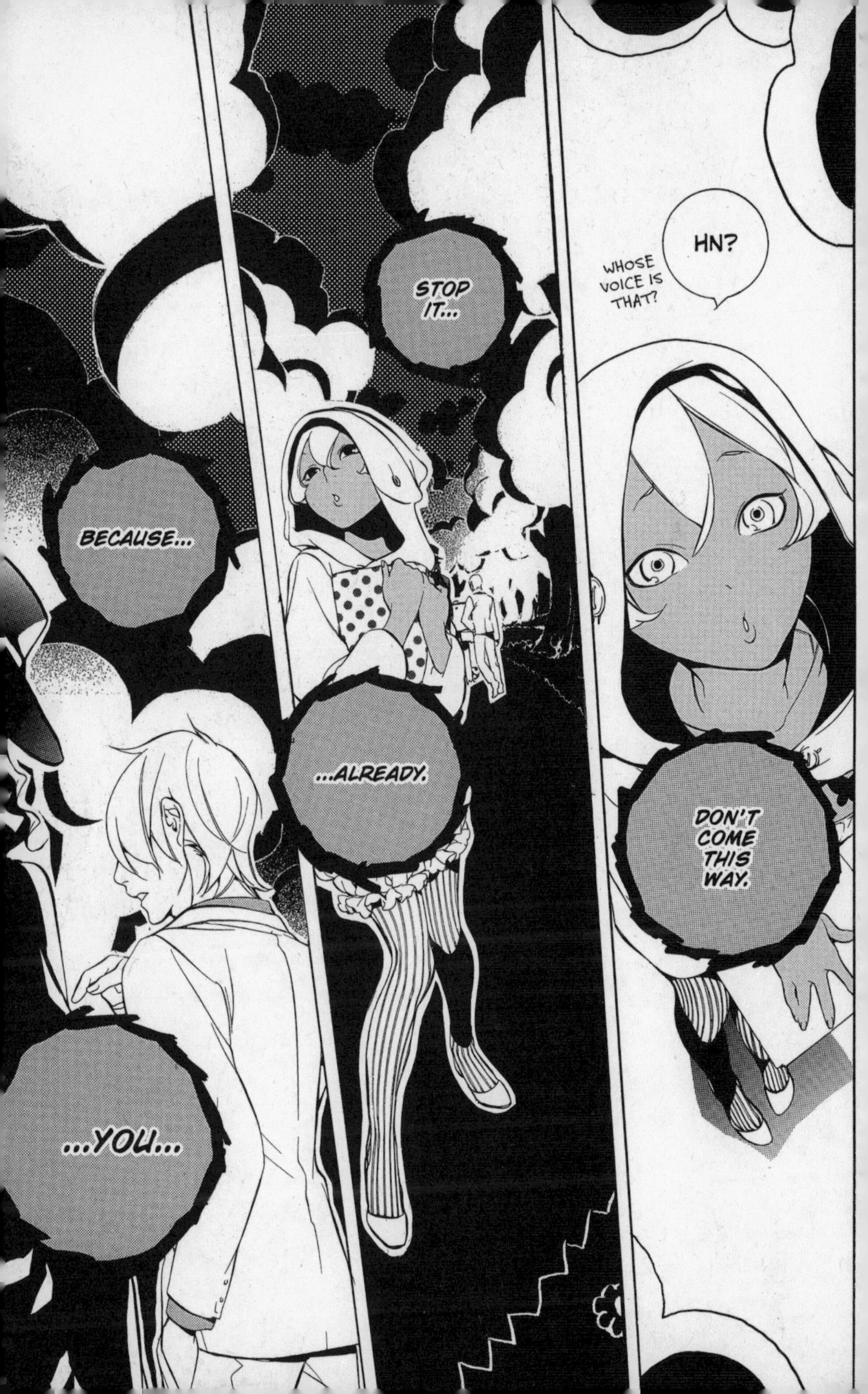
HN?
WHOSE VOICE IS THAT?
DON'T COME THIS WAY.
STOP IT...
...ALREADY.
BECAUSE...
...YOU...

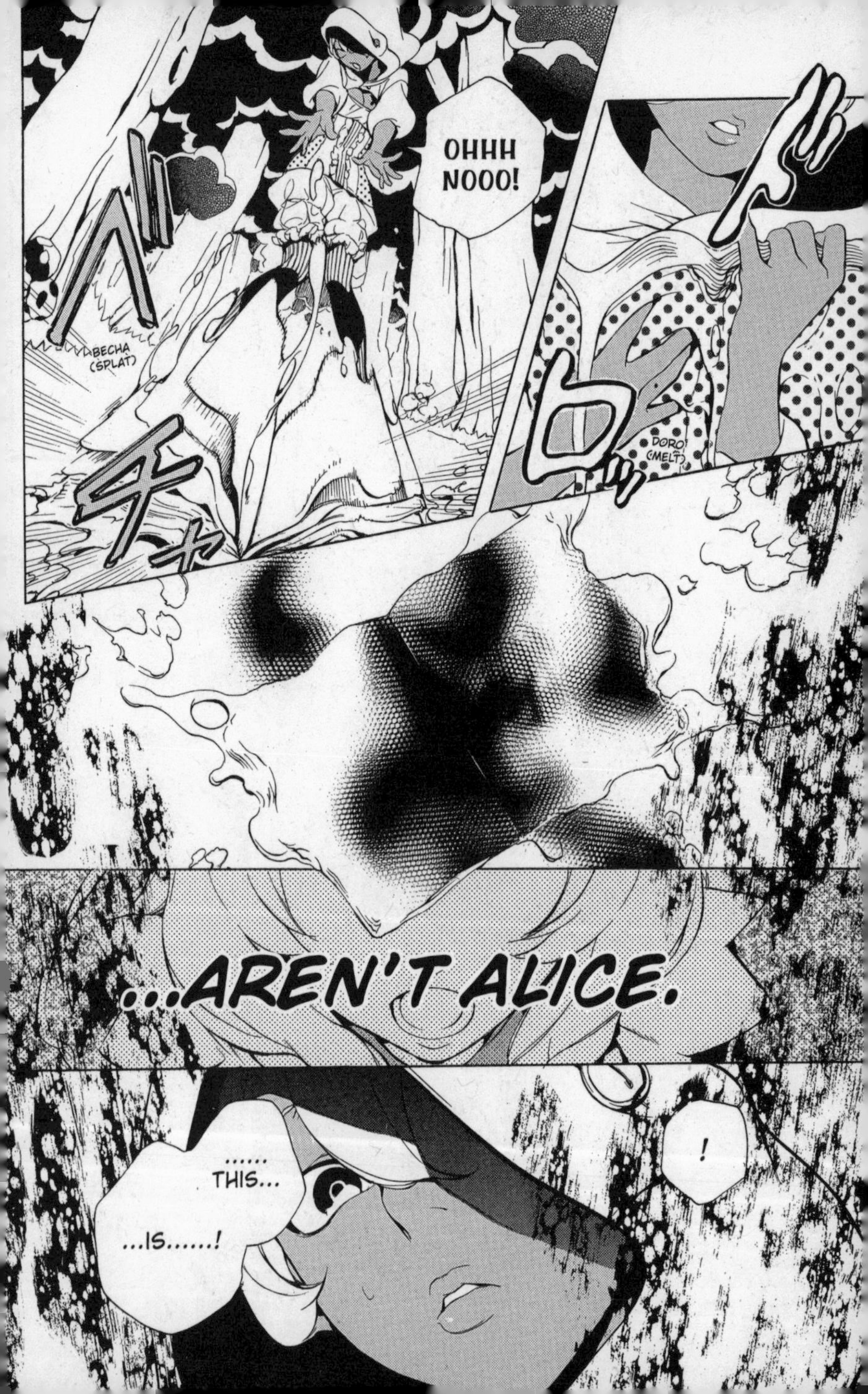
DORO (MELT)
OHHH NOOO!
BECHA (SPLAT)
...AREN'T ALICE.
!
...... THIS...
...IS......!

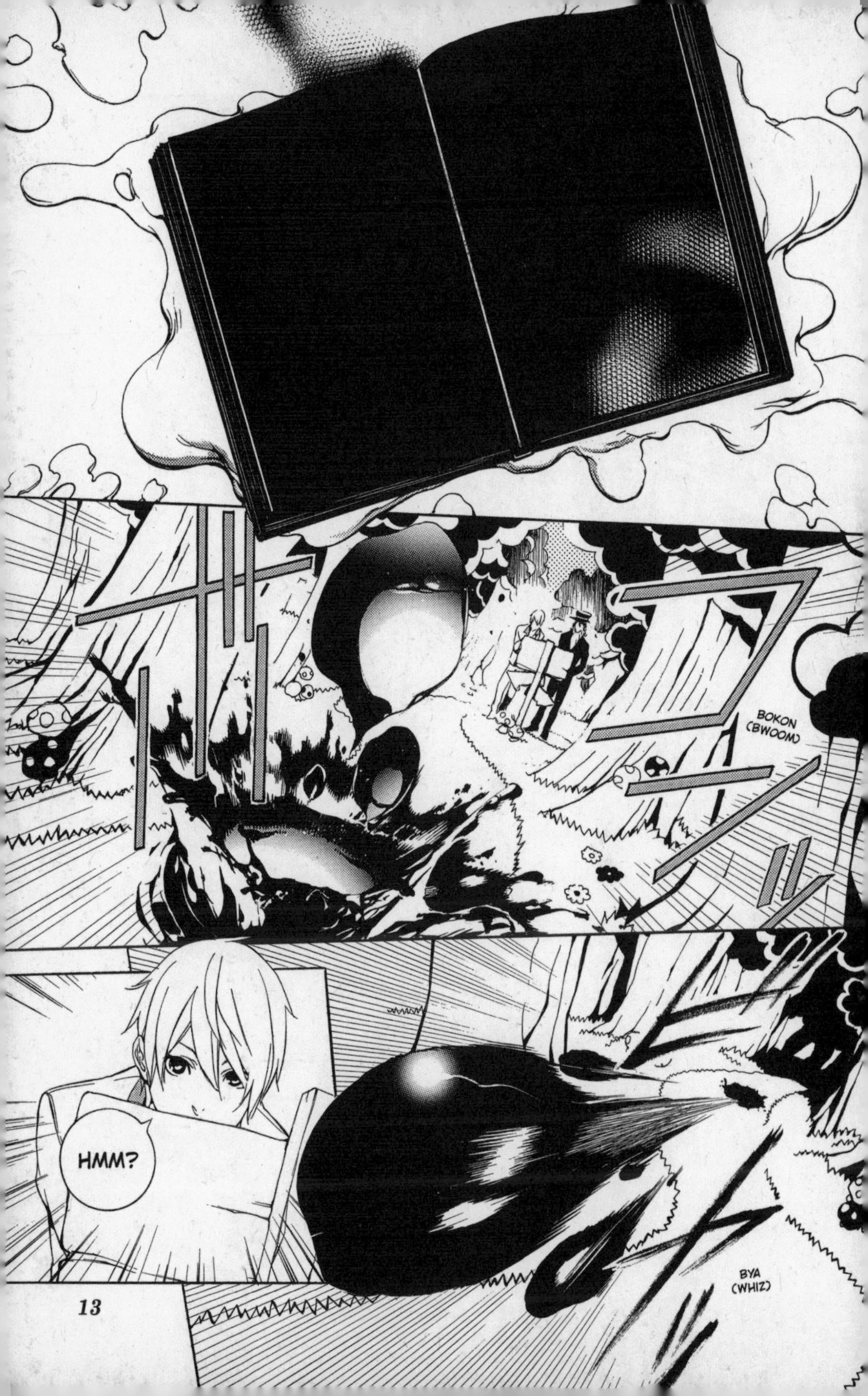
BOKON
(BWOOM)
BYA
(WHIZ)
HMM?

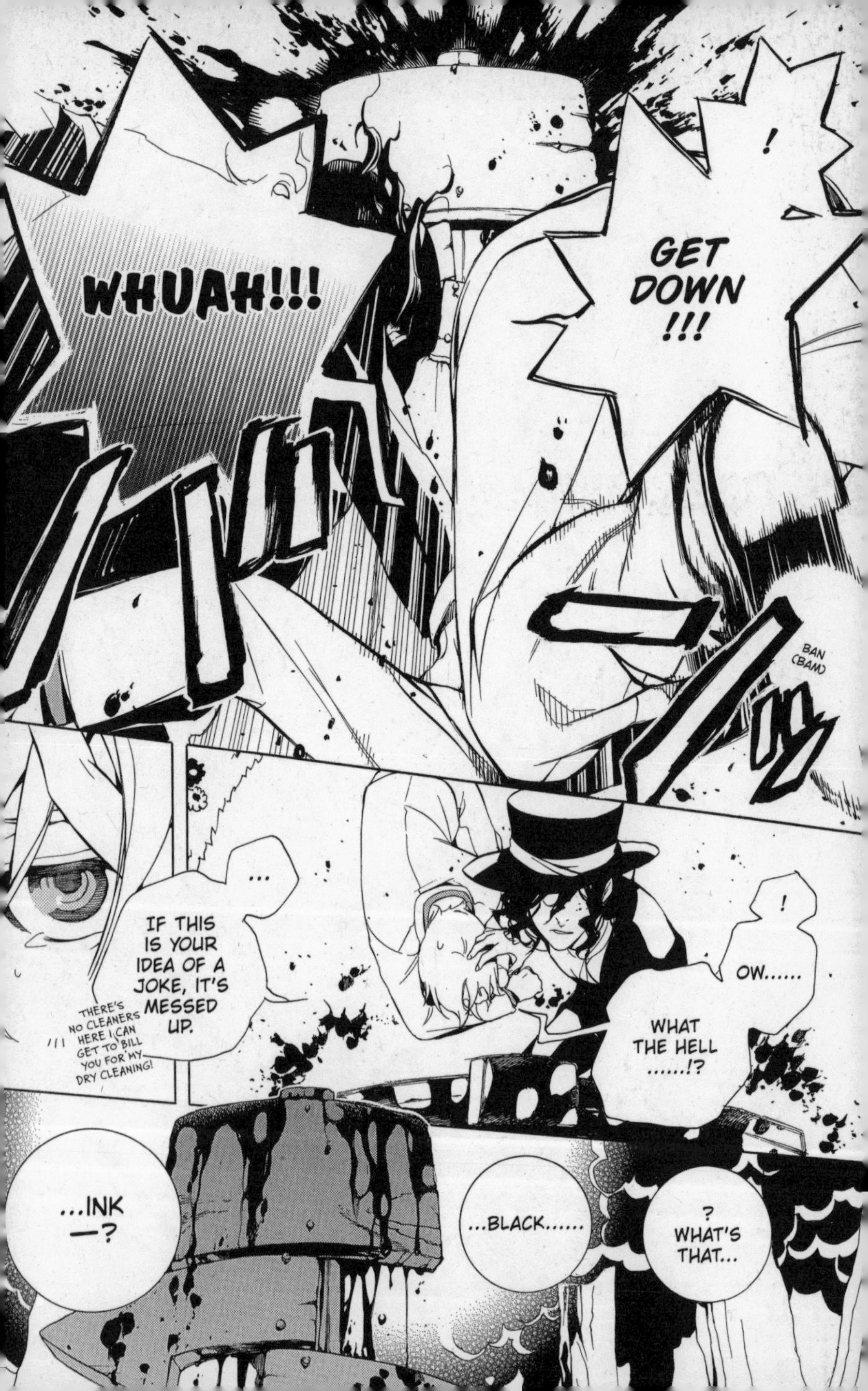
!
GET DOWN !!!
WHUAH!!!
BAN (BAM)
!
OW......
WHAT THE HELL ......!?
...
IF THIS IS YOUR IDEA OF A JOKE, IT'S MESSED UP.
THERE'S NO CLEANERS HERE I CAN GET TO BILL YOU FOR MY DRY CLEANING!
? WHAT'S THAT...
...BLACK......
...INK —?

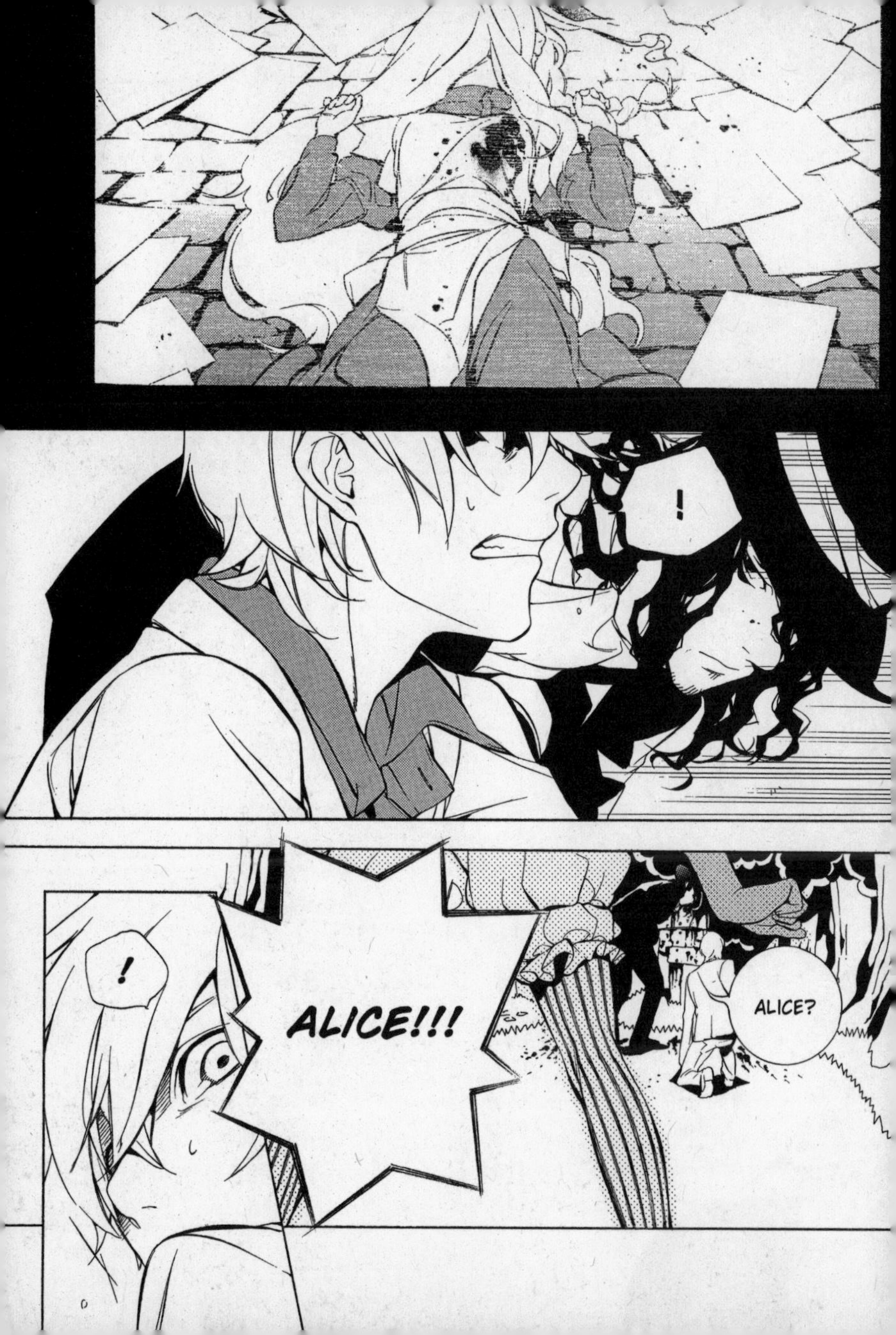
!
ALICE?
ALICE!!!
!

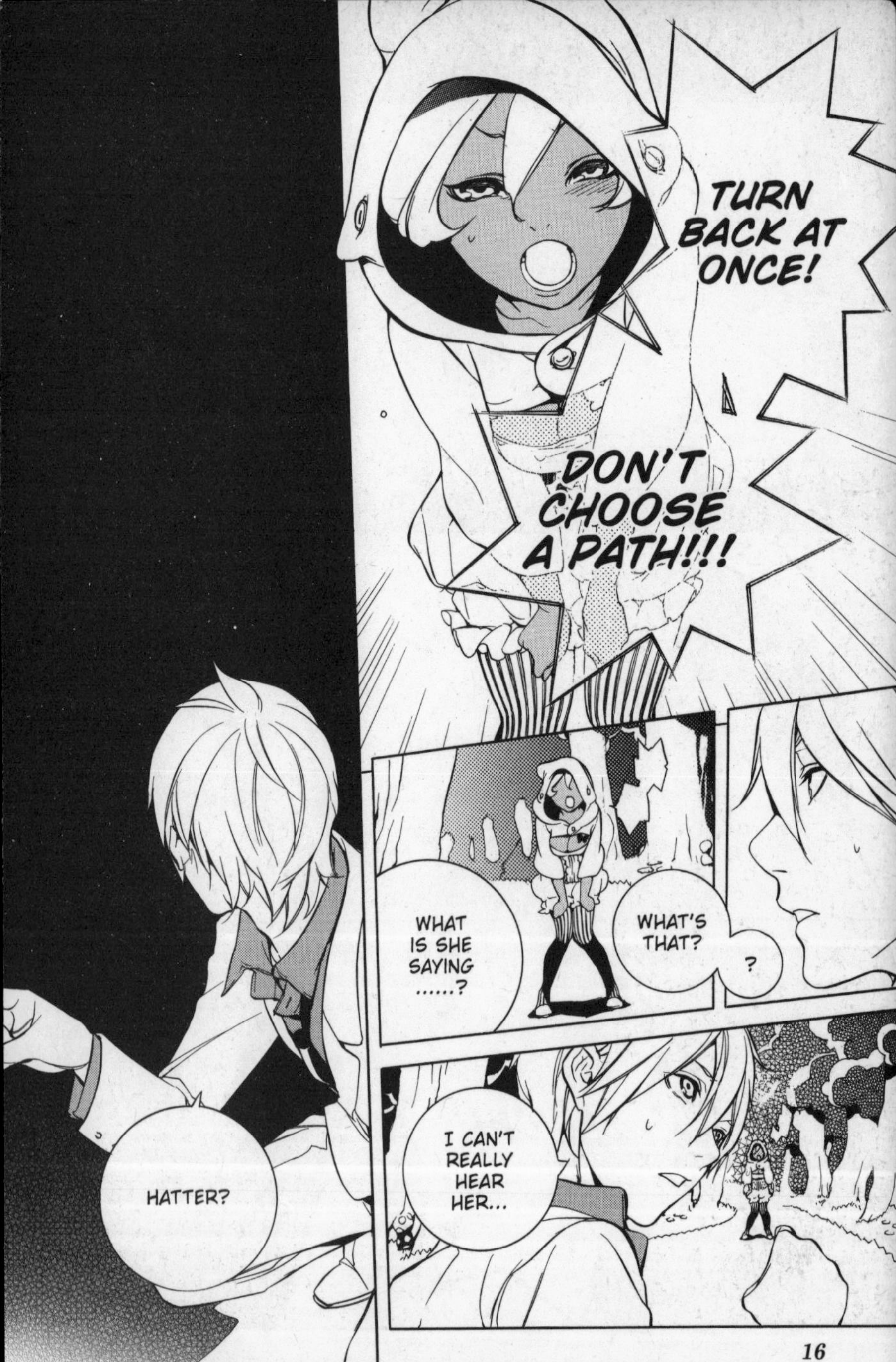
TURN BACK AT ONCE!
DON'T CHOOSE A PATH!!!
?
WHAT'S THAT?
WHAT IS SHE SAYING ......?
I CAN'T REALLY HEAR HER...
HATTER?

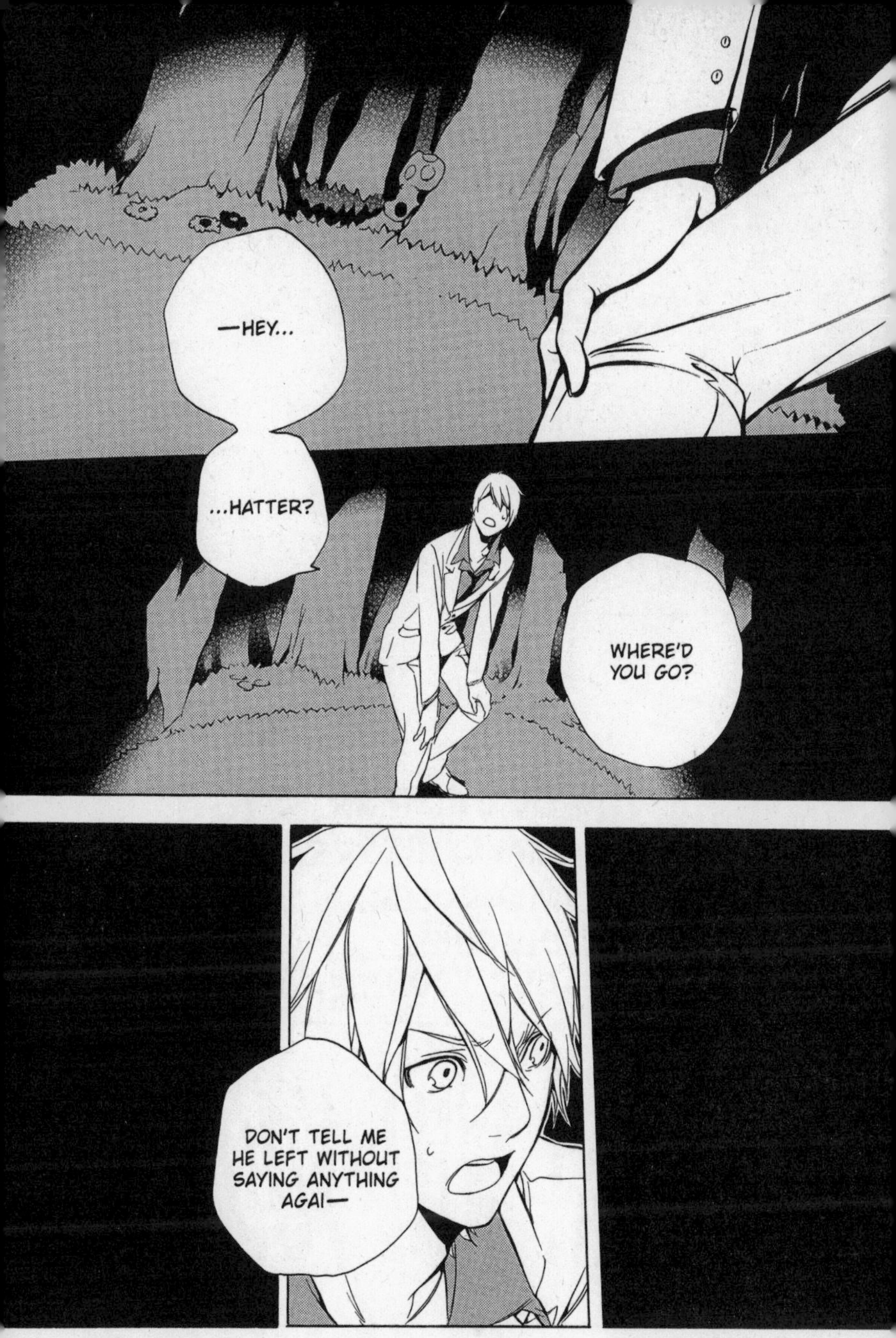
—HEY...
...HATTER?
WHERE'D YOU GO?
DON'T TELL ME HE LEFT WITHOUT SAYING ANYTHING AGAI—

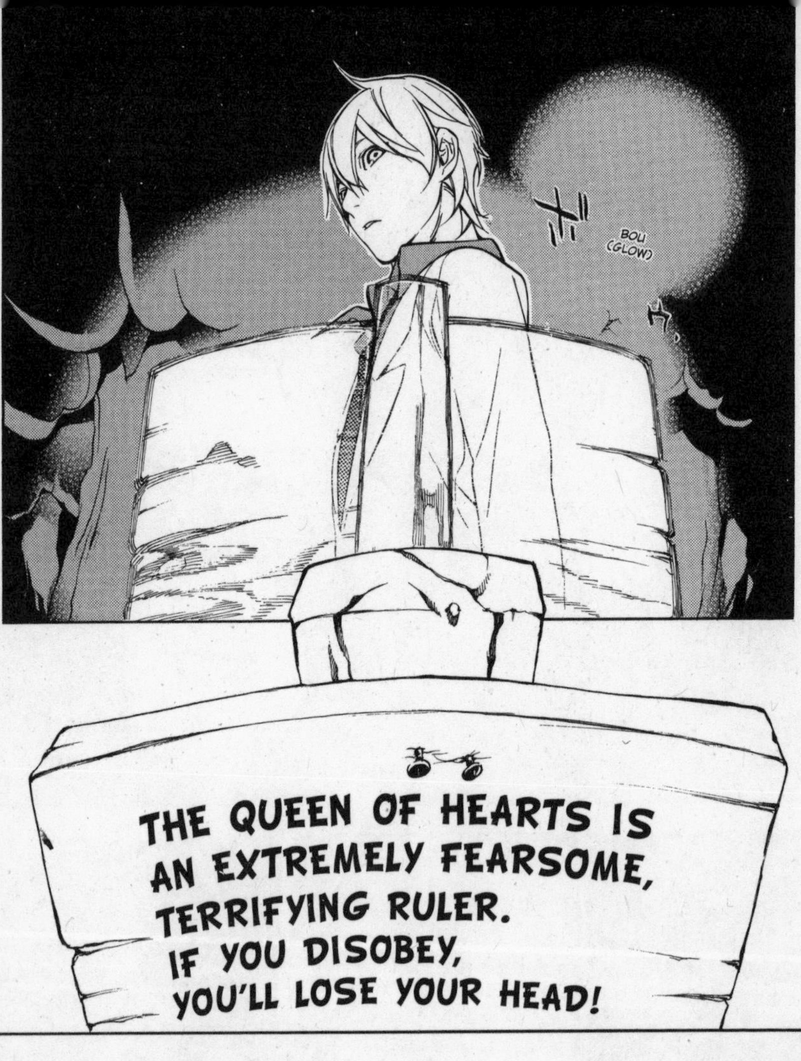
BOU (GLOW)
THE QUEEN OF HEARTS IS AN EXTREMELY FEARSOME, TERRIFYING RULER. IF YOU DISOBEY, YOU'LL LOSE YOUR HEAD!

SO...WHAT WILL YOU DO?

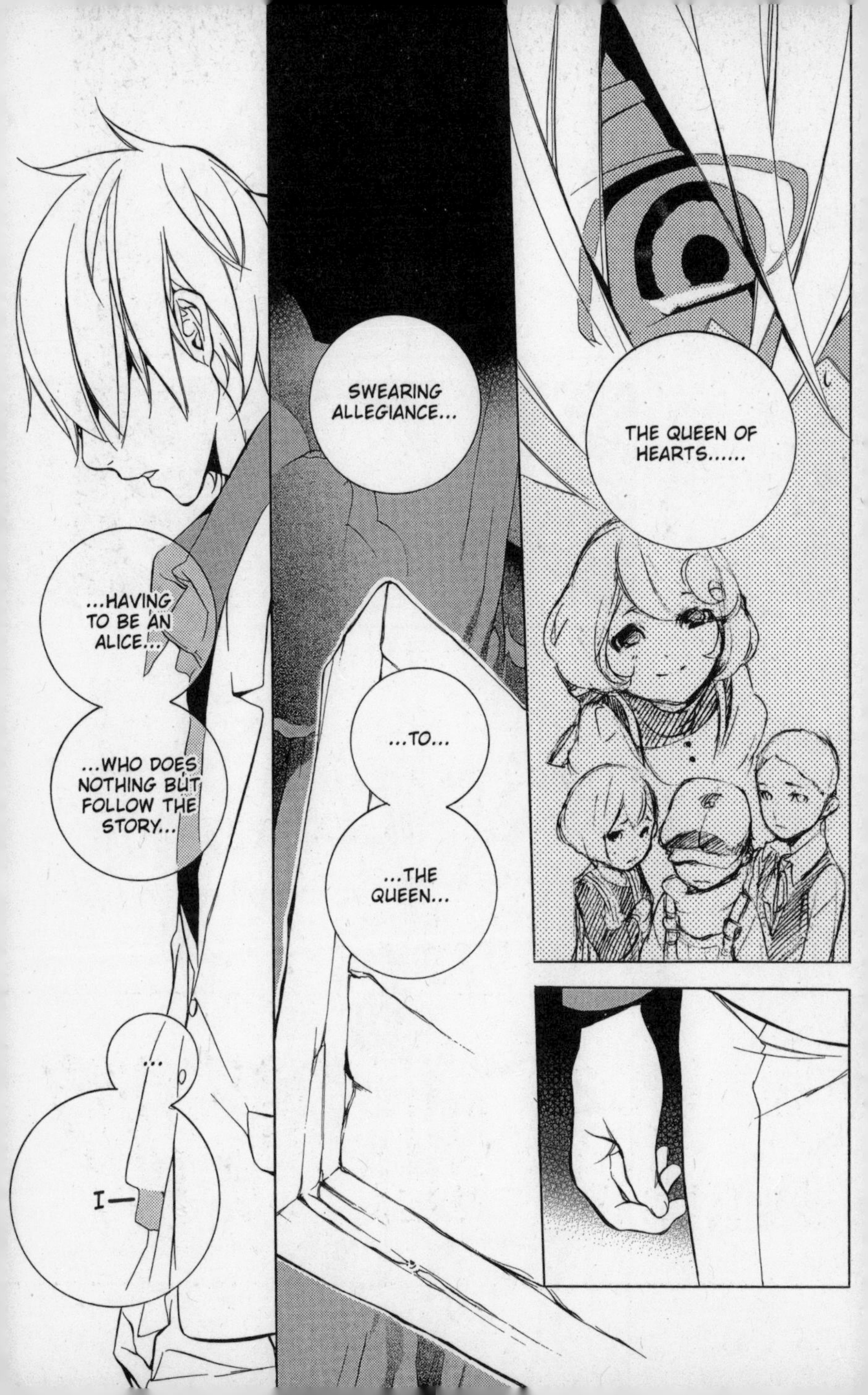
THE QUEEN OF HEARTS......
SWEARING ALLEGIANCE...
...TO...
...THE QUEEN...
...HAVING TO BE AN ALICE...
...WHO DOES NOTHING BUT FOLLOW THE STORY...
...
I—

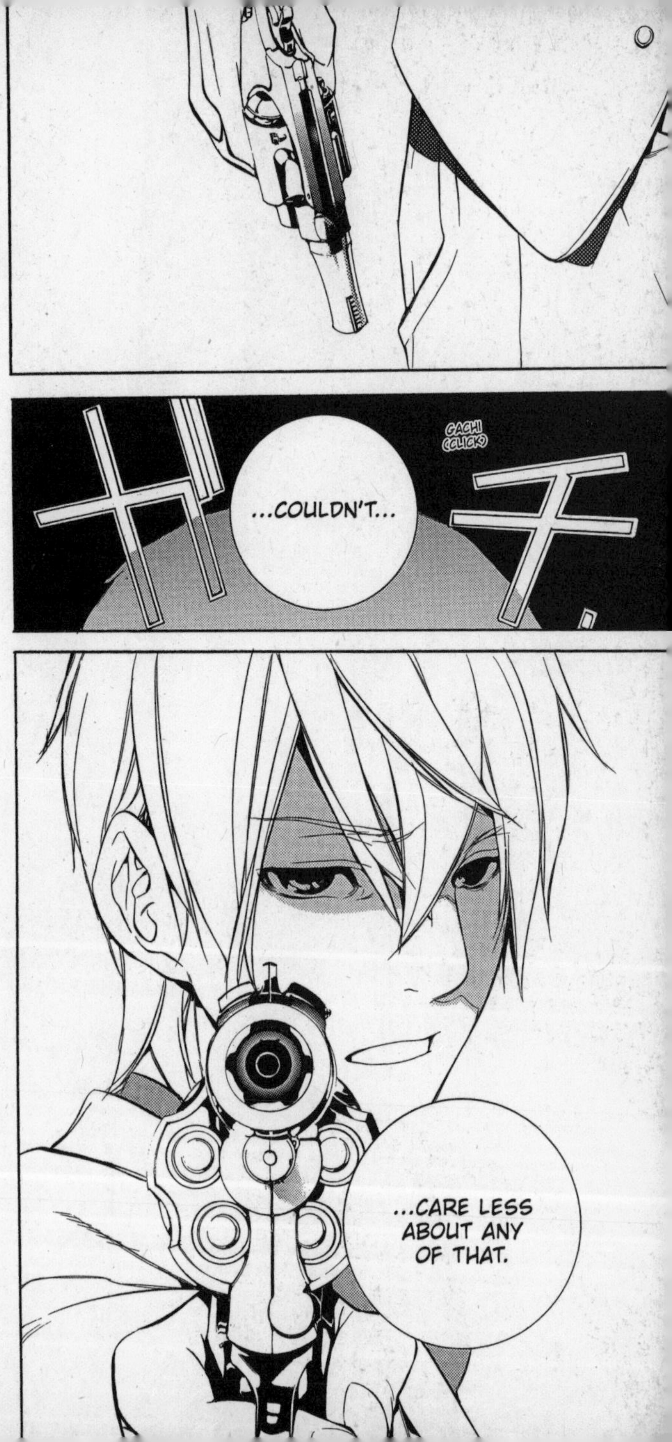
GACHI (CLICK)
...COULDN'T...
...CARE LESS ABOUT ANY OF THAT.

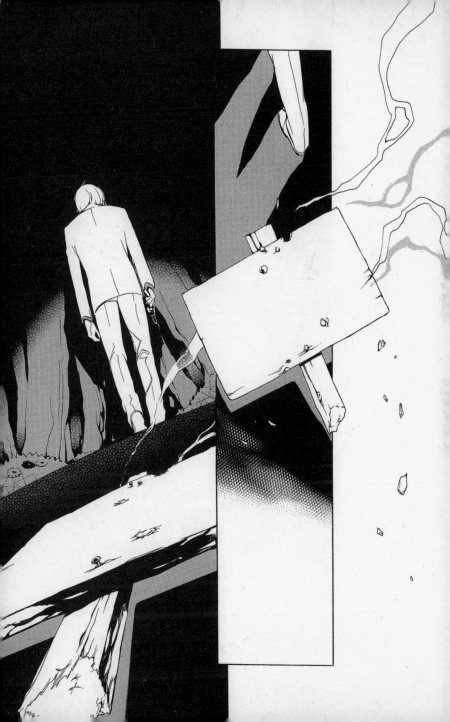

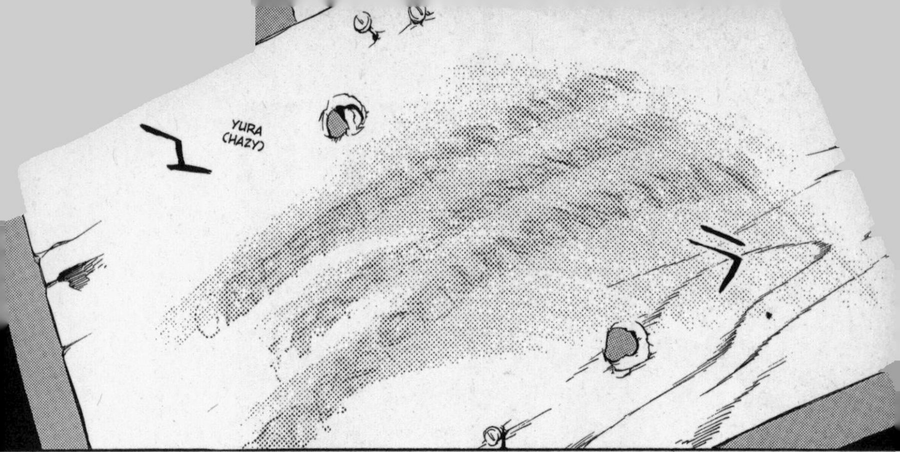
YURA
(HAZY)

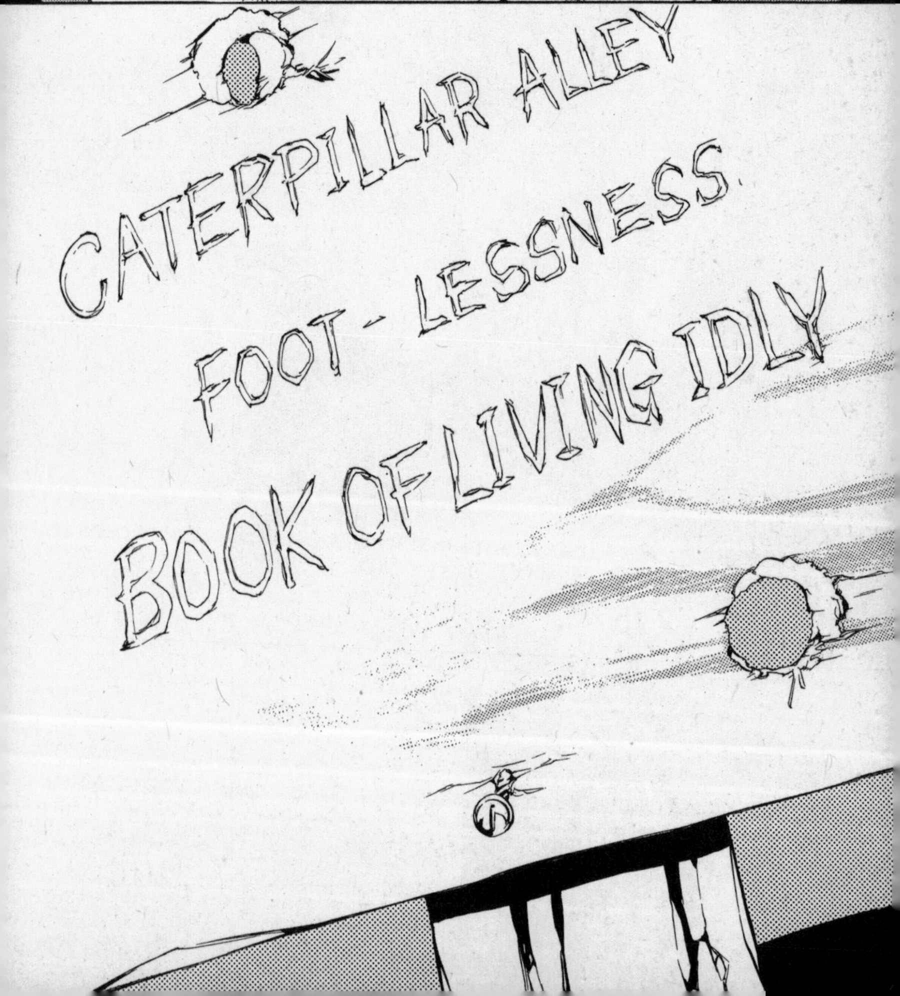
CATERPILLAR ALLEY
FOOT - LESSNESS
BOOK OF LIVING IDLY

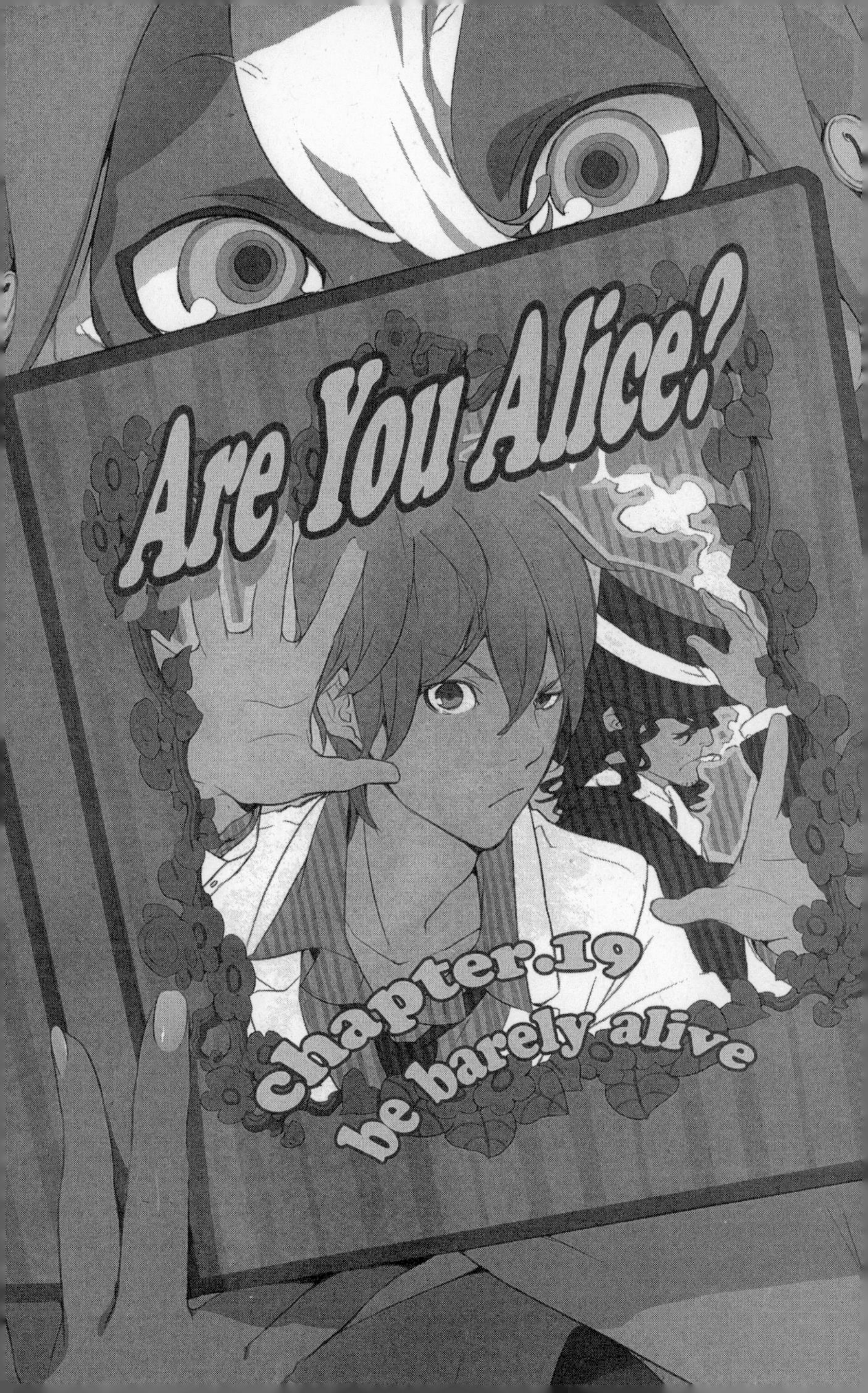
Are You Alice?
chapter.19
be barely alive

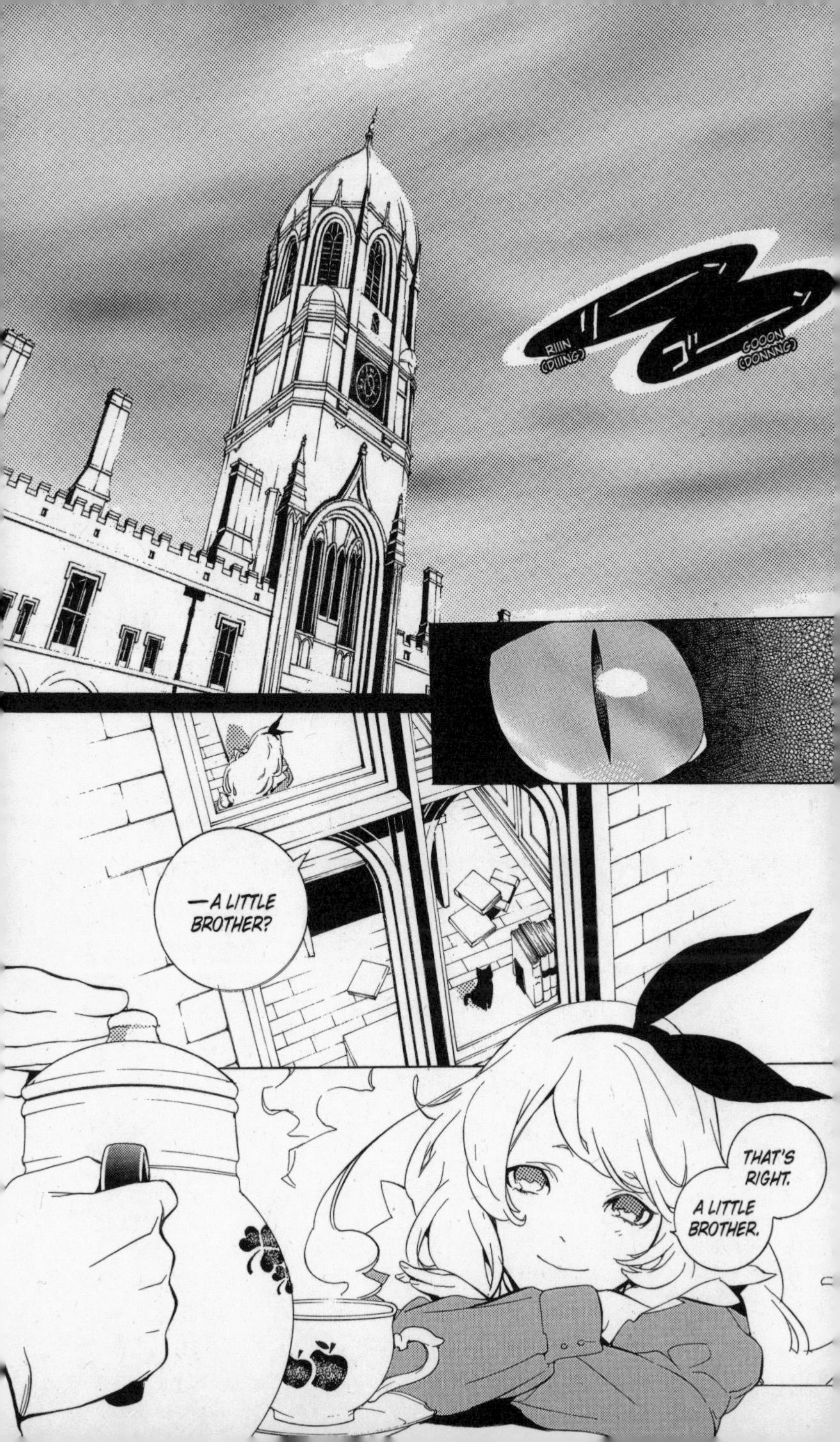
GOOON (DONNNG)
RIIN (DIIING)
—A LITTLE BROTHER?
THAT'S RIGHT.
A LITTLE BROTHER.

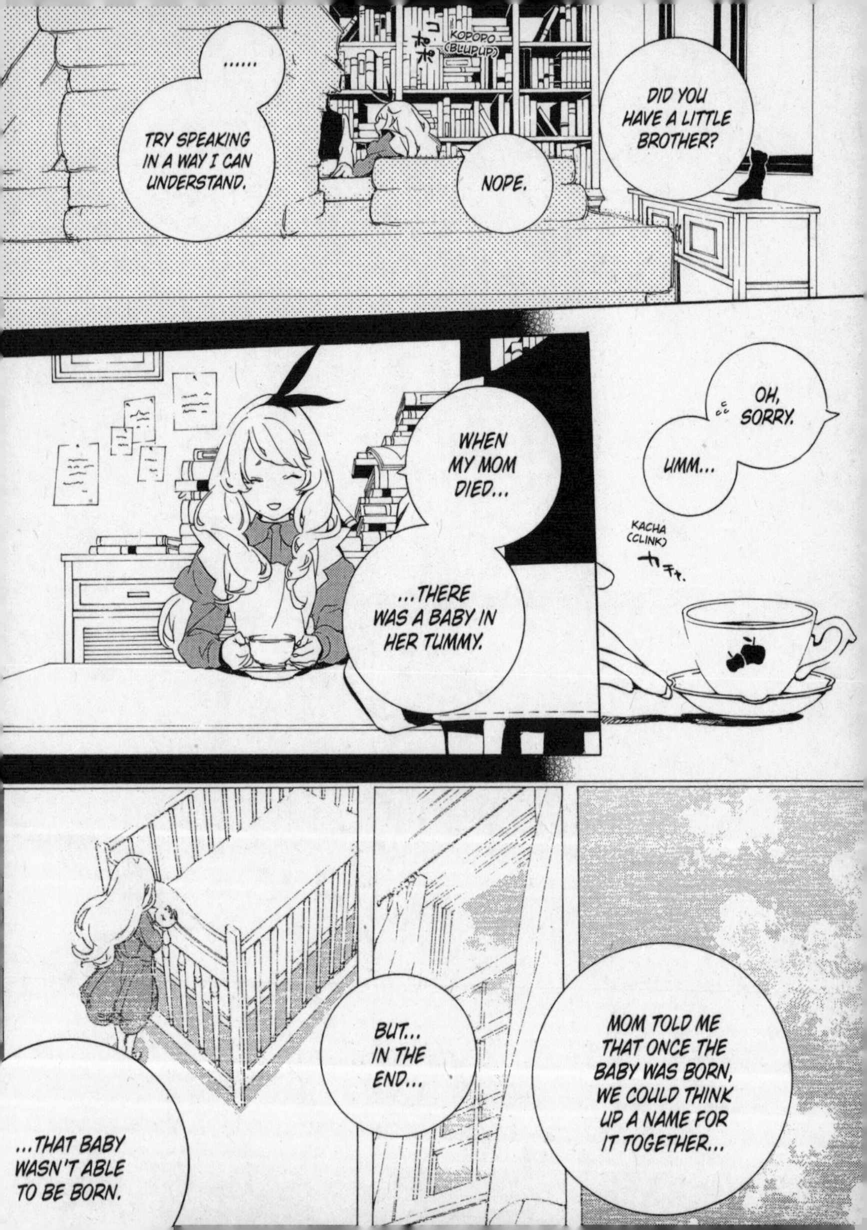
DID YOU HAVE A LITTLE BROTHER?
NOPE.
コポポ
KOPOPO (BLUPUP)
......
TRY SPEAKING IN A WAY I CAN UNDERSTAND.
OH, SORRY.
UMM...
KACHA (CLINK)
カチャ
WHEN MY MOM DIED...
...THERE WAS A BABY IN HER TUMMY.
MOM TOLD ME THAT ONCE THE BABY WAS BORN, WE COULD THINK UP A NAME FOR IT TOGETHER...
BUT... IN THE END...
...THAT BABY WASN'T ABLE TO BE BORN.

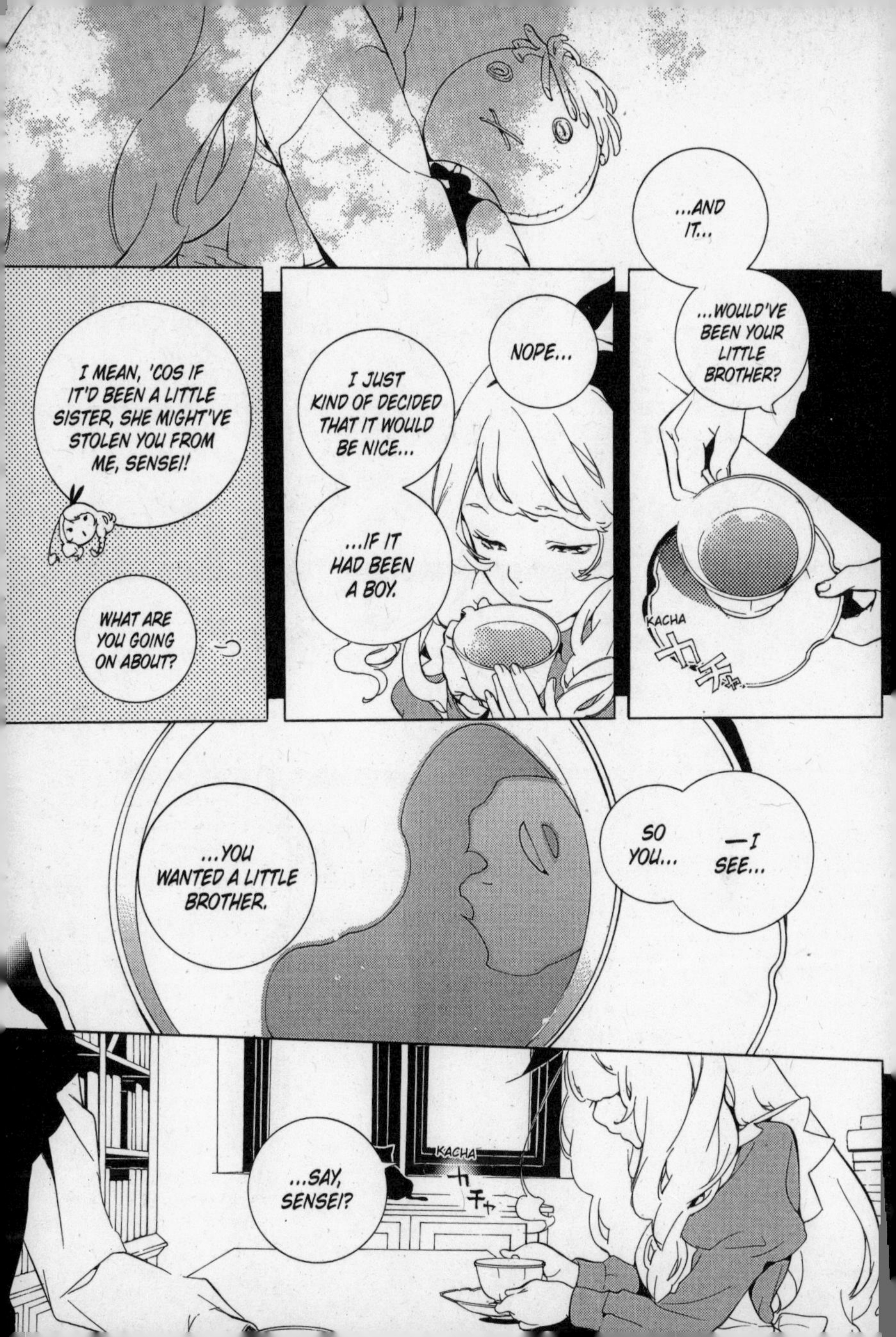
...AND IT...
...WOULD'VE BEEN YOUR LITTLE BROTHER?
KACHA
NOPE...
I JUST KIND OF DECIDED THAT IT WOULD BE NICE...
...IF IT HAD BEEN A BOY.
I MEAN, 'COS IF IT'D BEEN A LITTLE SISTER, SHE MIGHT'VE STOLEN YOU FROM ME, SENSEI!
WHAT ARE YOU GOING ON ABOUT?
—I SEE...
SO YOU...
...YOU WANTED A LITTLE BROTHER.
KACHA
...SAY, SENSEI?

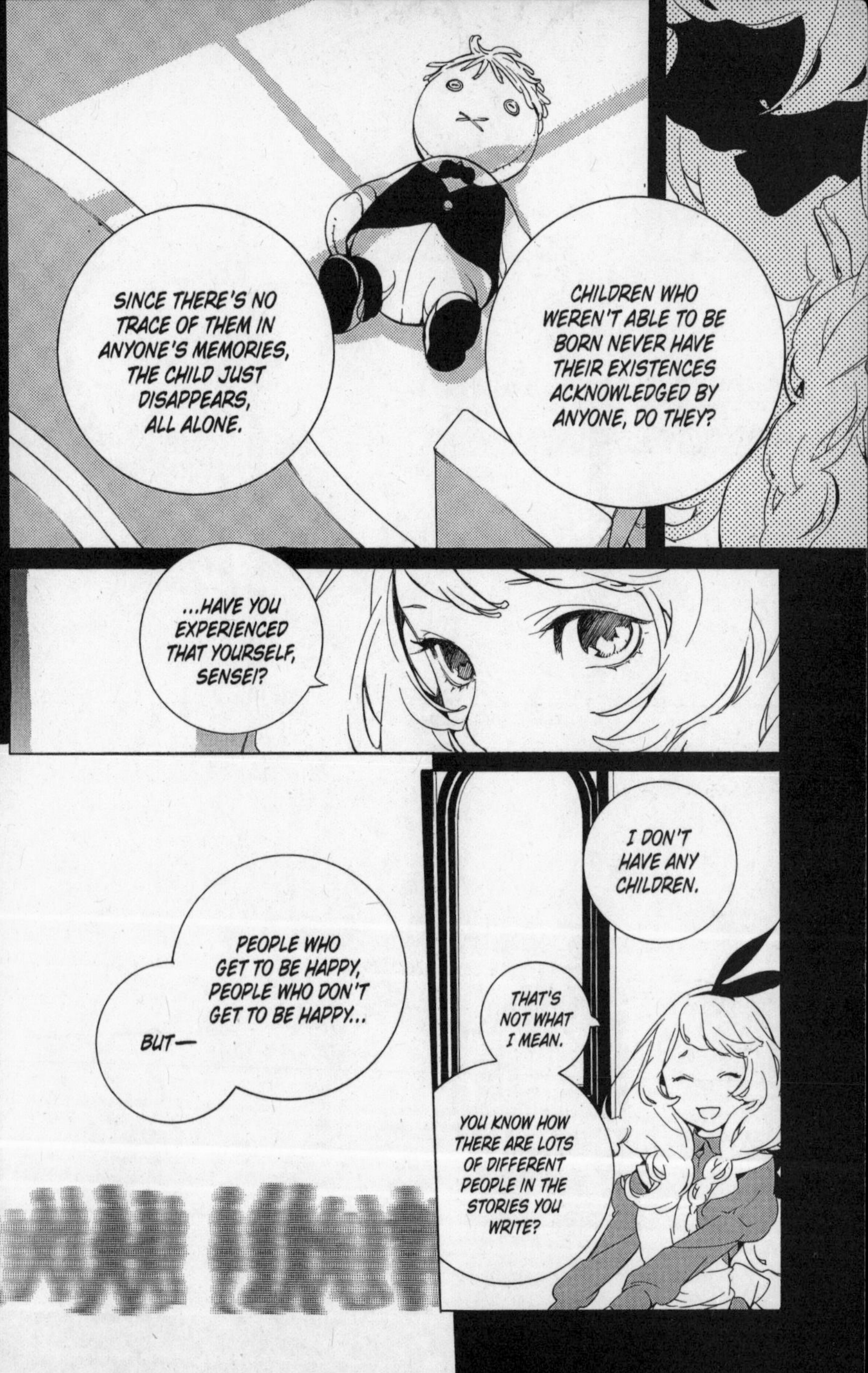
CHILDREN WHO WEREN'T ABLE TO BE BORN NEVER HAVE THEIR EXISTENCES ACKNOWLEDGED BY ANYONE, DO THEY?
SINCE THERE'S NO TRACE OF THEM IN ANYONE'S MEMORIES, THE CHILD JUST DISAPPEARS, ALL ALONE.
...HAVE YOU EXPERIENCED THAT YOURSELF, SENSEI?
I DON'T HAVE ANY CHILDREN.
THAT'S NOT WHAT I MEAN.
YOU KNOW HOW THERE ARE LOTS OF DIFFERENT PEOPLE IN THE STORIES YOU WRITE?
PEOPLE WHO GET TO BE HAPPY, PEOPLE WHO DON'T GET TO BE HAPPY...
BUT—

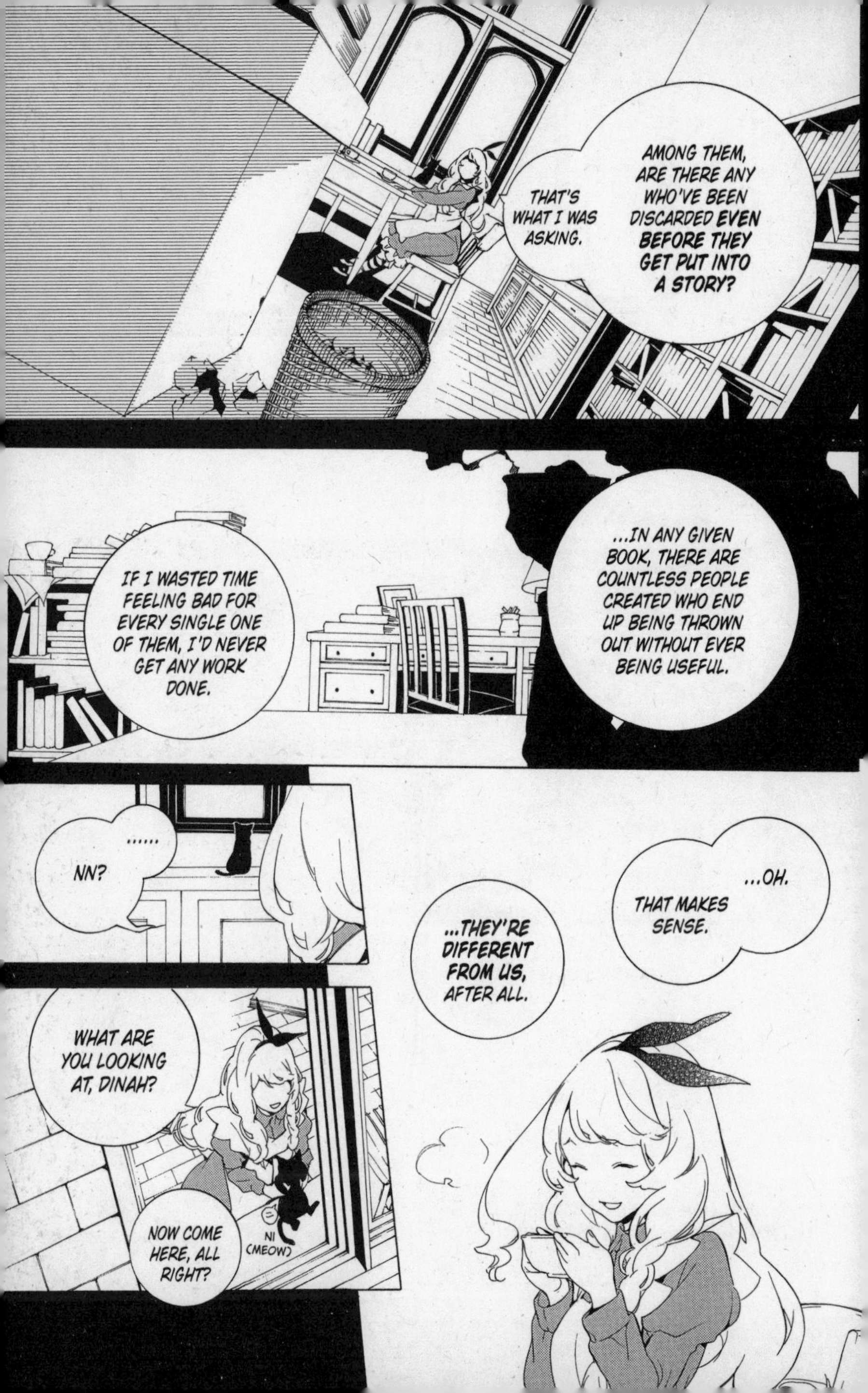
AMONG THEM, ARE THERE ANY WHO'VE BEEN DISCARDED EVEN BEFORE THEY GET PUT INTO A STORY?
THAT'S WHAT I WAS ASKING.
...IN ANY GIVEN BOOK, THERE ARE COUNTLESS PEOPLE CREATED WHO END UP BEING THROWN OUT WITHOUT EVER BEING USEFUL.
IF I WASTED TIME FEELING BAD FOR EVERY SINGLE ONE OF THEM, I'D NEVER GET ANY WORK DONE.
...OH.
THAT MAKES SENSE.
...THEY'RE DIFFERENT FROM US, AFTER ALL.
......
NN?
WHAT ARE YOU LOOKING AT, DINAH?
NI (MEOW)
NOW COME HERE, ALL RIGHT?

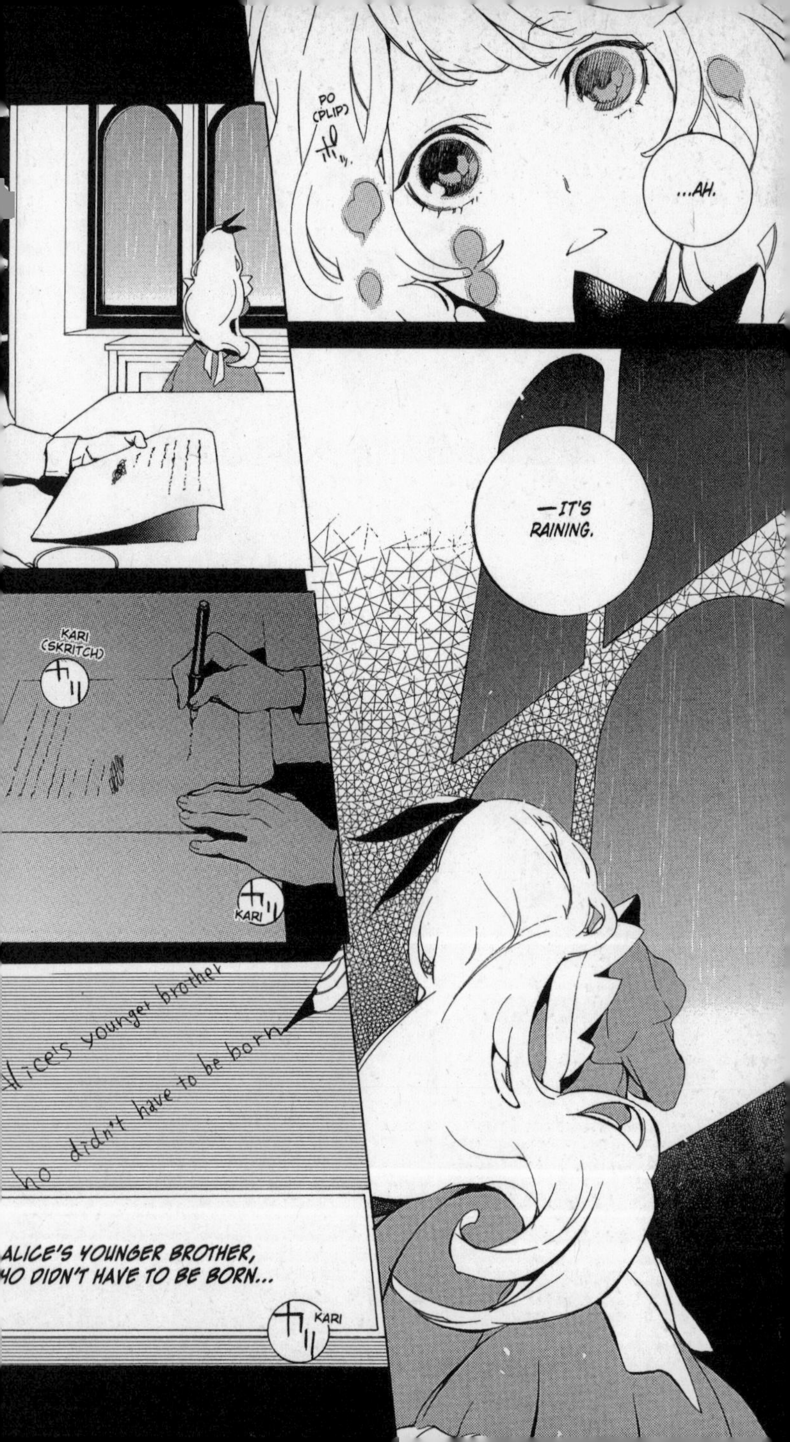
PO (PLIP)
...AH.
—IT'S RAINING.
KARI (SKRITCH)
KARI
lice's younger brother
ho didn't have to be born
ALICE'S YOUNGER BROTHER,
HO DIDN'T HAVE TO BE BORN...
KARI

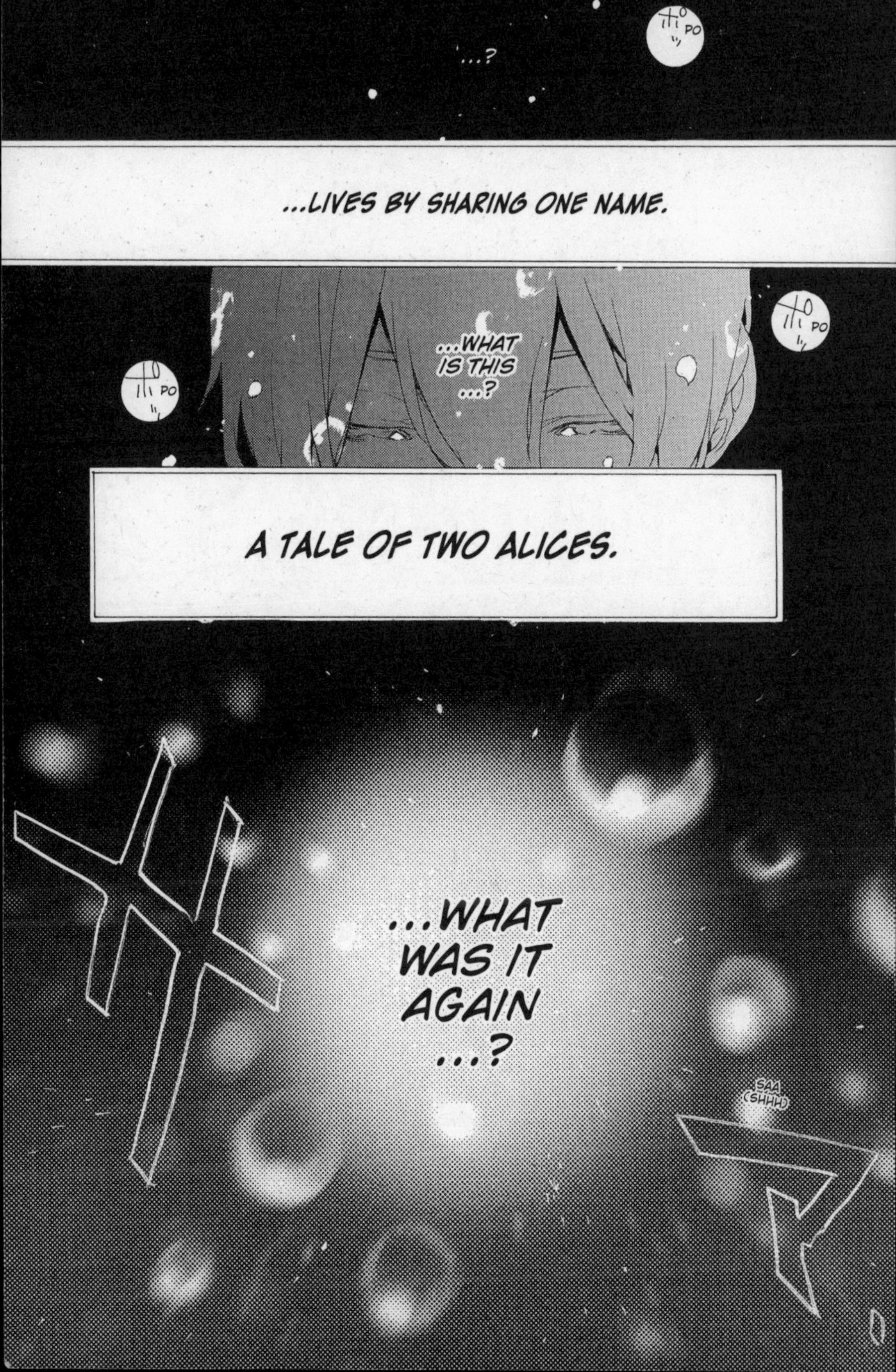
PO
...?
...LIVES BY SHARING ONE NAME.
PO
...WHAT IS THIS ...?
PO
A TALE OF TWO ALICES.
...WHAT WAS IT AGAIN ...?
SAA (SHHH)

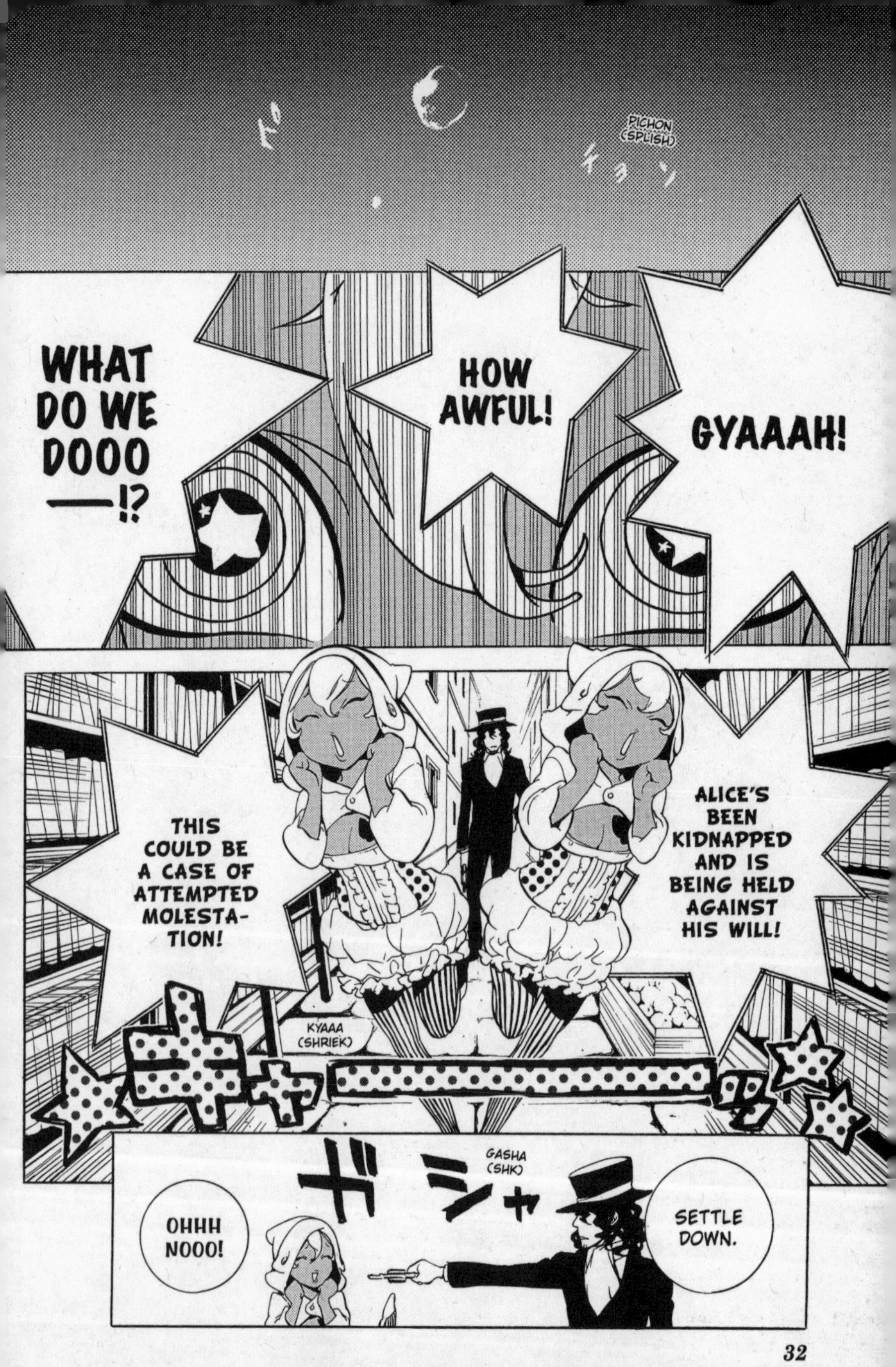
PICHON (SPLISH)
GYAAAH!
HOW AWFUL!
WHAT DO WE DOOO—!?
ALICE'S BEEN KIDNAPPED AND IS BEING HELD AGAINST HIS WILL!
THIS COULD BE A CASE OF ATTEMPTED MOLESTATION!
KYAAA (SHRIEK)
SETTLE DOWN.
GASHA (SHK)
OHHH NOOO!

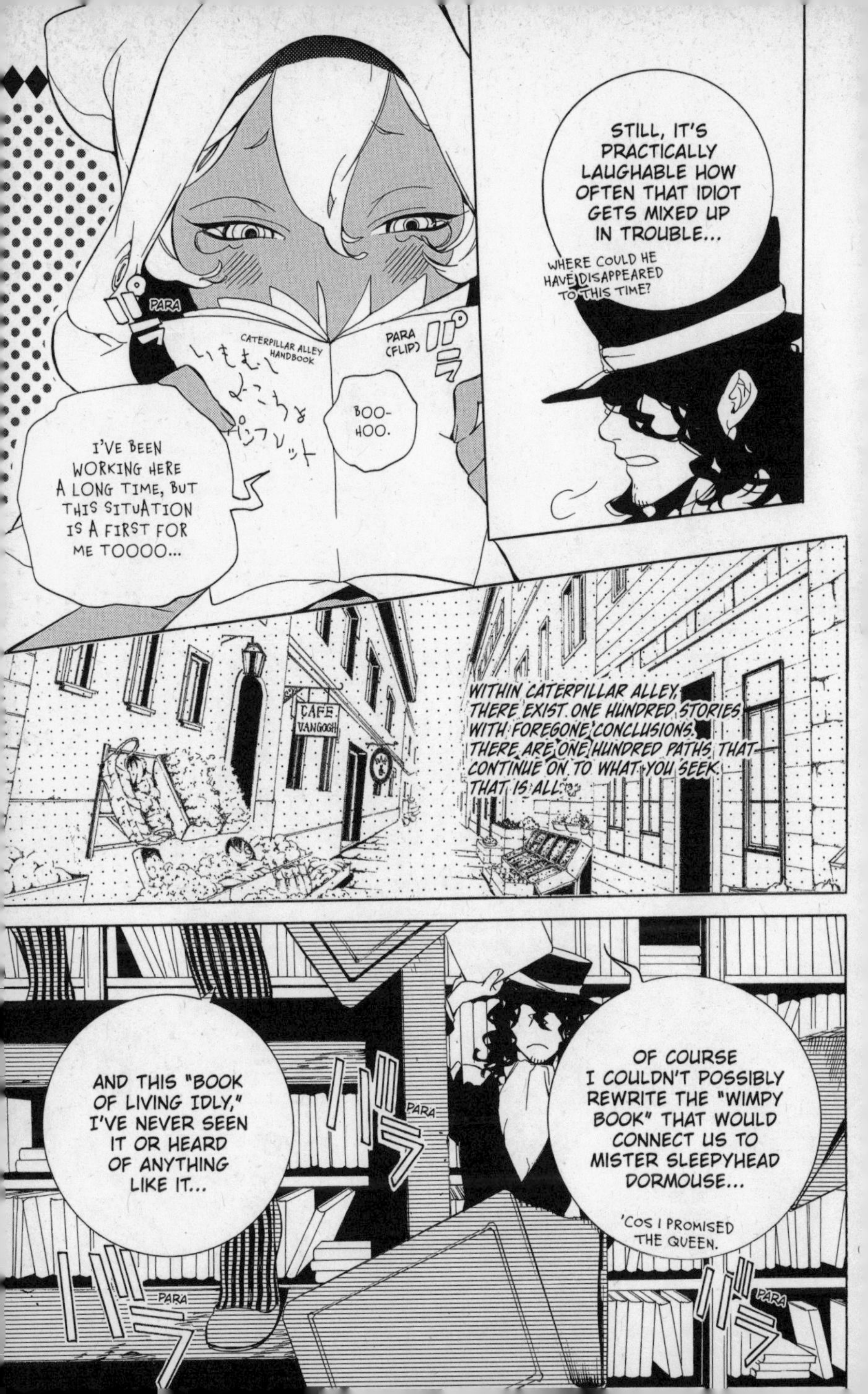
STILL, IT'S PRACTICALLY LAUGHABLE HOW OFTEN THAT IDIOT GETS MIXED UP IN TROUBLE...
WHERE COULD HE HAVE DISAPPEARED TO THIS TIME?
PARA
PARA (FLIP)
CATERPILLAR ALLEY HANDBOOK
BOO-HOO.
I'VE BEEN WORKING HERE A LONG TIME, BUT THIS SITUATION IS A FIRST FOR ME TOOOO...
WITHIN CATERPILLAR ALLEY, THERE EXIST ONE HUNDRED STORIES WITH FOREGONE CONCLUSIONS. THERE ARE ONE HUNDRED PATHS THAT CONTINUE ON TO WHAT YOU SEEK. THAT IS ALL.
CAFE VANGOGH
OF COURSE I COULDN'T POSSIBLY REWRITE THE "WIMPY BOOK" THAT WOULD CONNECT US TO MISTER SLEEPYHEAD DORMOUSE...
'COS I PROMISED THE QUEEN.
PARA
AND THIS "BOOK OF LIVING IDLY," I'VE NEVER SEEN IT OR HEARD OF ANYTHING LIKE IT...
PARA
PARA

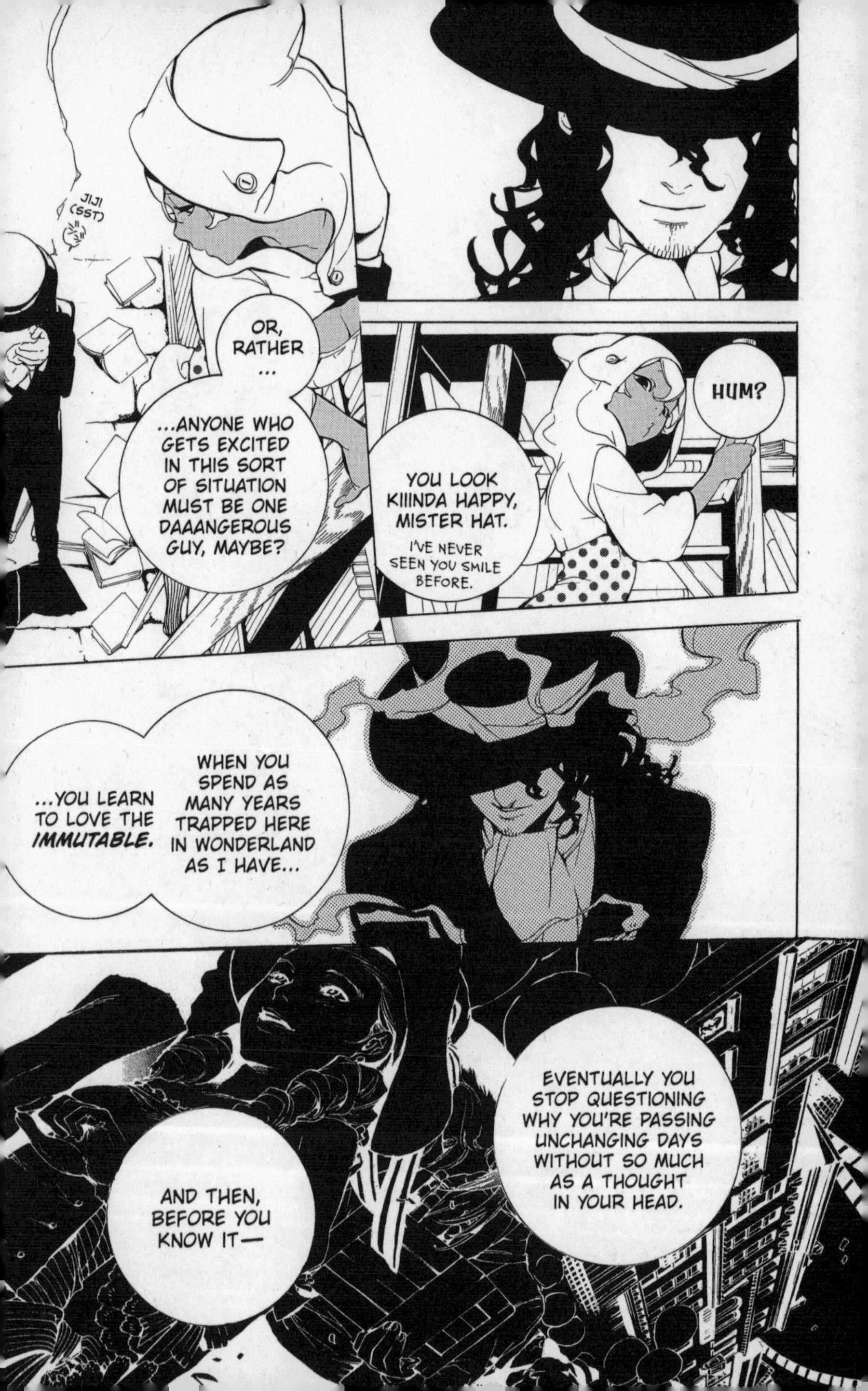

HUM?
YOU LOOK KIIINDA HAPPY, MISTER HAT.
I'VE NEVER SEEN YOU SMILE BEFORE.
OR, RATHER...
...ANYONE WHO GETS EXCITED IN THIS SORT OF SITUATION MUST BE ONE DAAANGEROUS GUY, MAYBE?
JIJI (SST)
WHEN YOU SPEND AS MANY YEARS TRAPPED HERE IN WONDERLAND AS I HAVE...
...YOU LEARN TO LOVE THE *IMMUTABLE.*
EVENTUALLY YOU STOP QUESTIONING WHY YOU'RE PASSING UNCHANGING DAYS WITHOUT SO MUCH AS A THOUGHT IN YOUR HEAD.
AND THEN, BEFORE YOU KNOW IT—

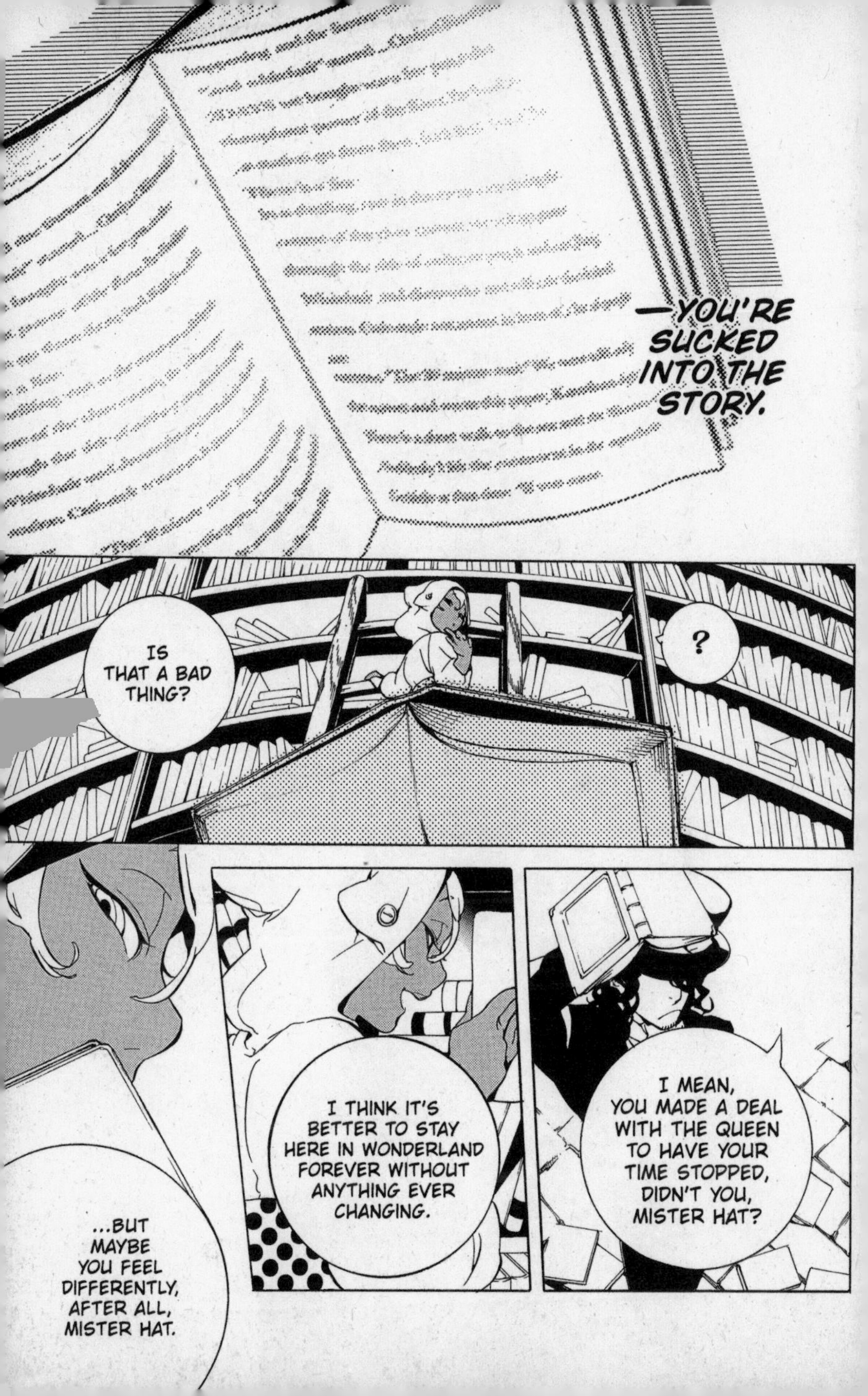
—YOU'RE SUCKED INTO THE STORY.
?
IS THAT A BAD THING?
I MEAN, YOU MADE A DEAL WITH THE QUEEN TO HAVE YOUR TIME STOPPED, DIDN'T YOU, MISTER HAT?
I THINK IT'S BETTER TO STAY HERE IN WONDERLAND FOREVER WITHOUT ANYTHING EVER CHANGING.
...BUT MAYBE YOU FEEL DIFFERENTLY, AFTER ALL, MISTER HAT.

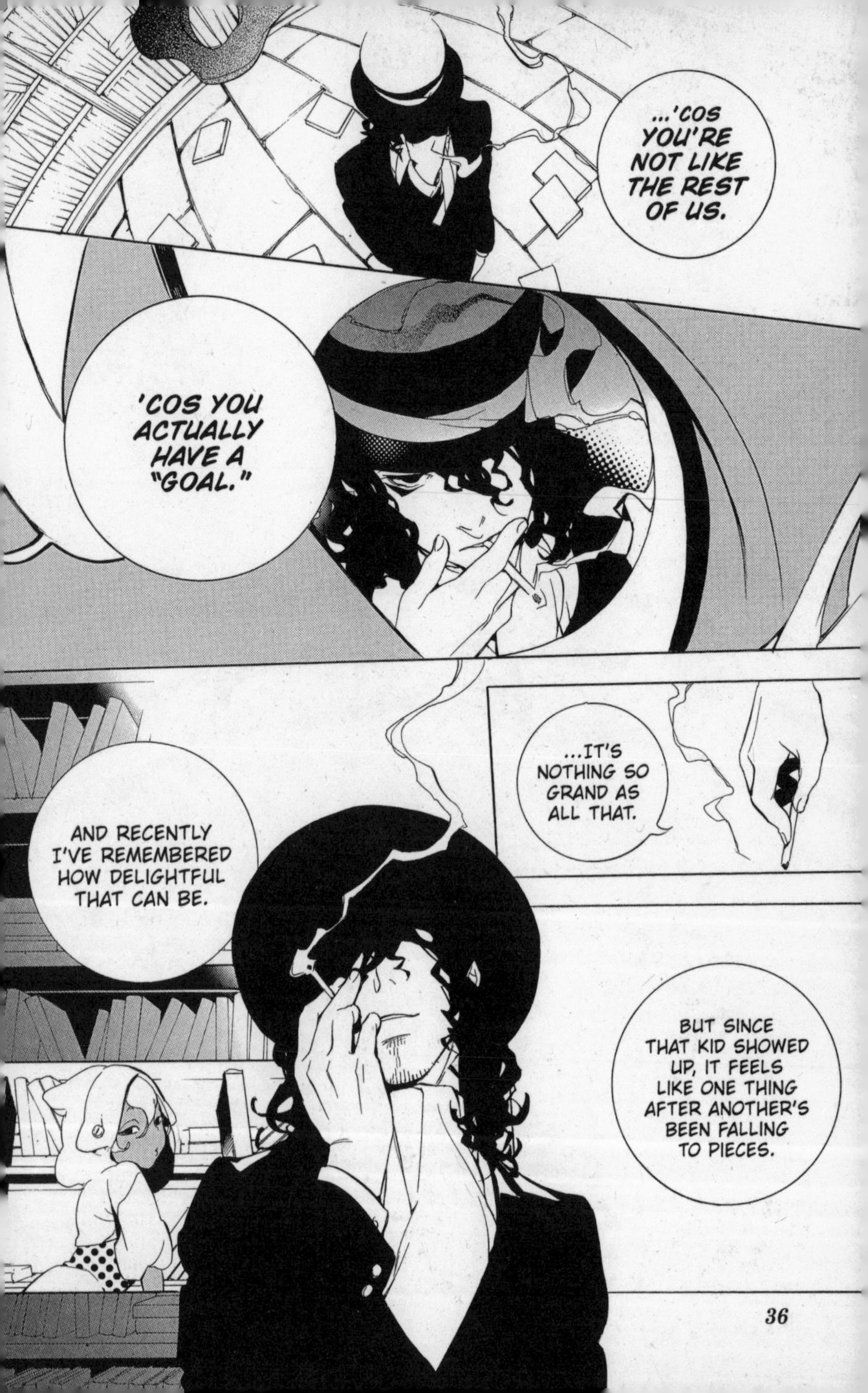
...'COS YOU'RE NOT LIKE THE REST OF US.
'COS YOU ACTUALLY HAVE A "GOAL."
...IT'S NOTHING SO GRAND AS ALL THAT.
BUT SINCE THAT KID SHOWED UP, IT FEELS LIKE ONE THING AFTER ANOTHER'S BEEN FALLING TO PIECES.
AND RECENTLY I'VE REMEMBERED HOW DELIGHTFUL THAT CAN BE.

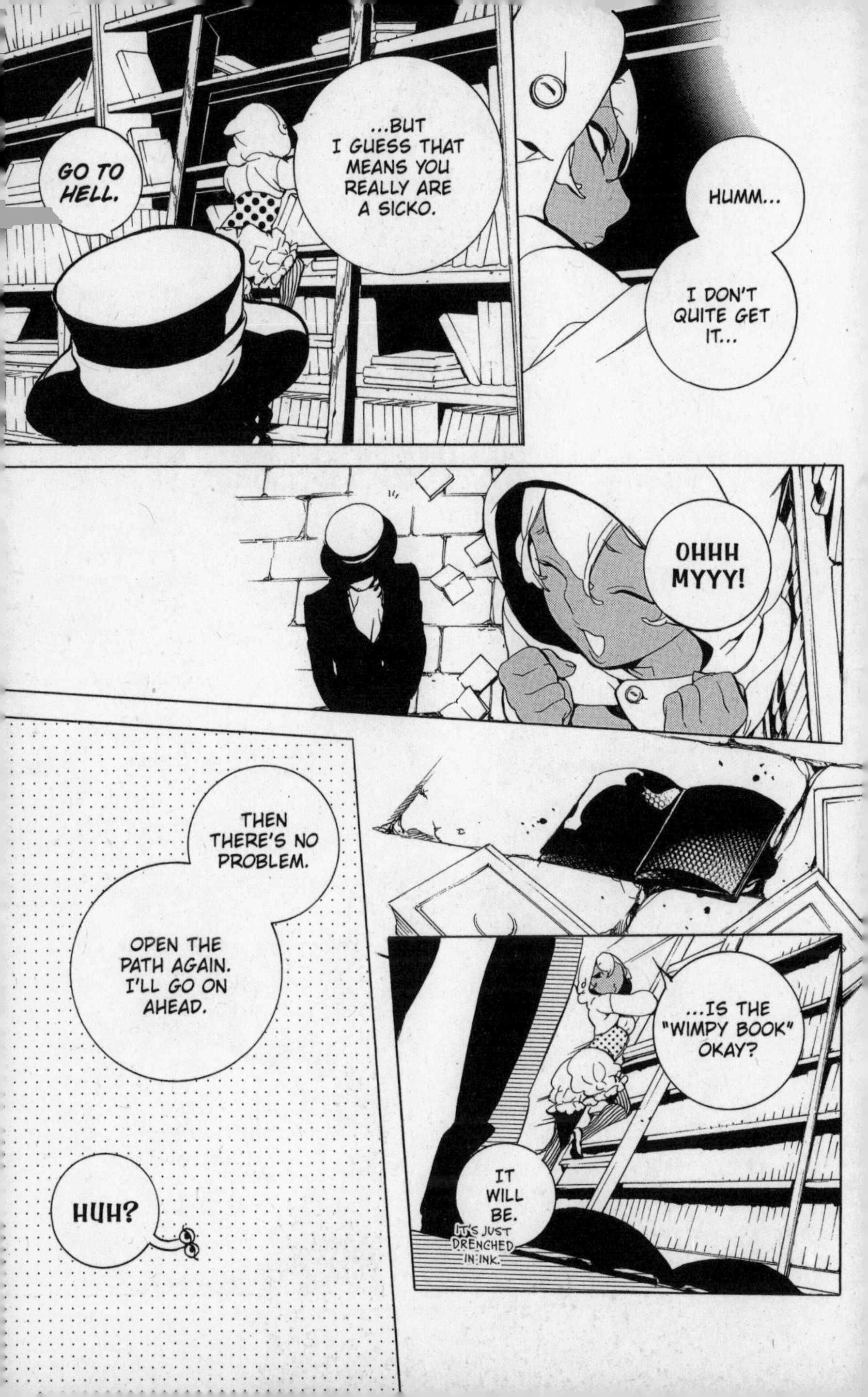
HUMM...
I DON'T QUITE GET IT...
...BUT I GUESS THAT MEANS YOU REALLY ARE A SICKO.
GO TO HELL.
OHHH MYYY!
...IS THE "WIMPY BOOK" OKAY?
IT WILL BE.
IT'S JUST DRENCHED IN INK.
THEN THERE'S NO PROBLEM.
OPEN THE PATH AGAIN. I'LL GO ON AHEAD.
HUH?

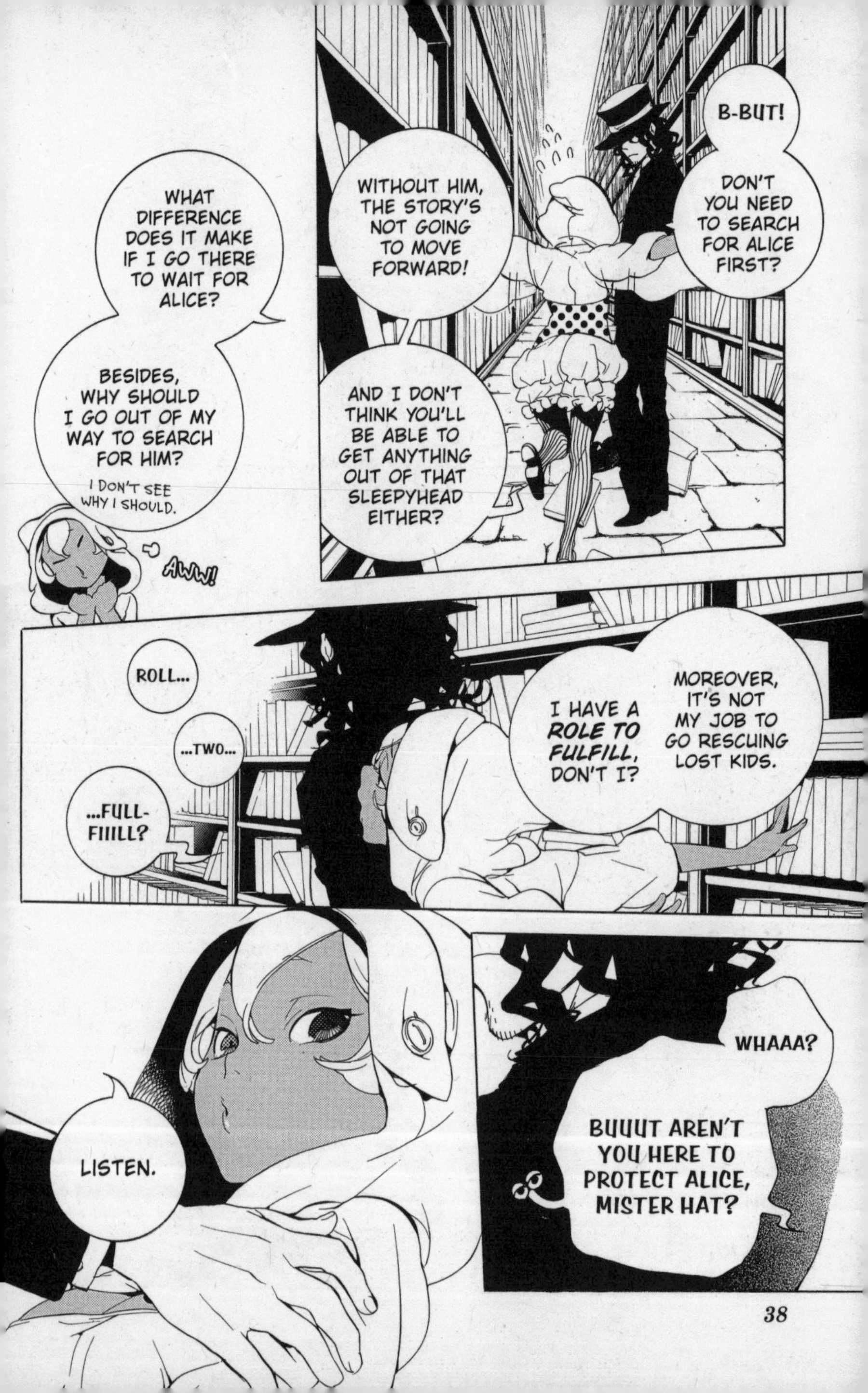
B-BUT!
DON'T YOU NEED TO SEARCH FOR ALICE FIRST?
WITHOUT HIM, THE STORY'S NOT GOING TO MOVE FORWARD!
AND I DON'T THINK YOU'LL BE ABLE TO GET ANYTHING OUT OF THAT SLEEPYHEAD EITHER?
WHAT DIFFERENCE DOES IT MAKE IF I GO THERE TO WAIT FOR ALICE?
BESIDES, WHY SHOULD I GO OUT OF MY WAY TO SEARCH FOR HIM?
I DON'T SEE WHY I SHOULD.
AWW!
MOREOVER, IT'S NOT MY JOB TO GO RESCUING LOST KIDS.
I HAVE A *ROLE TO FULFILL*, DON'T I?
ROLL...
...TWO...
...FULL-FIIILL?
WHAAA?
BUUUT AREN'T YOU HERE TO PROTECT ALICE, MISTER HAT?
LISTEN.

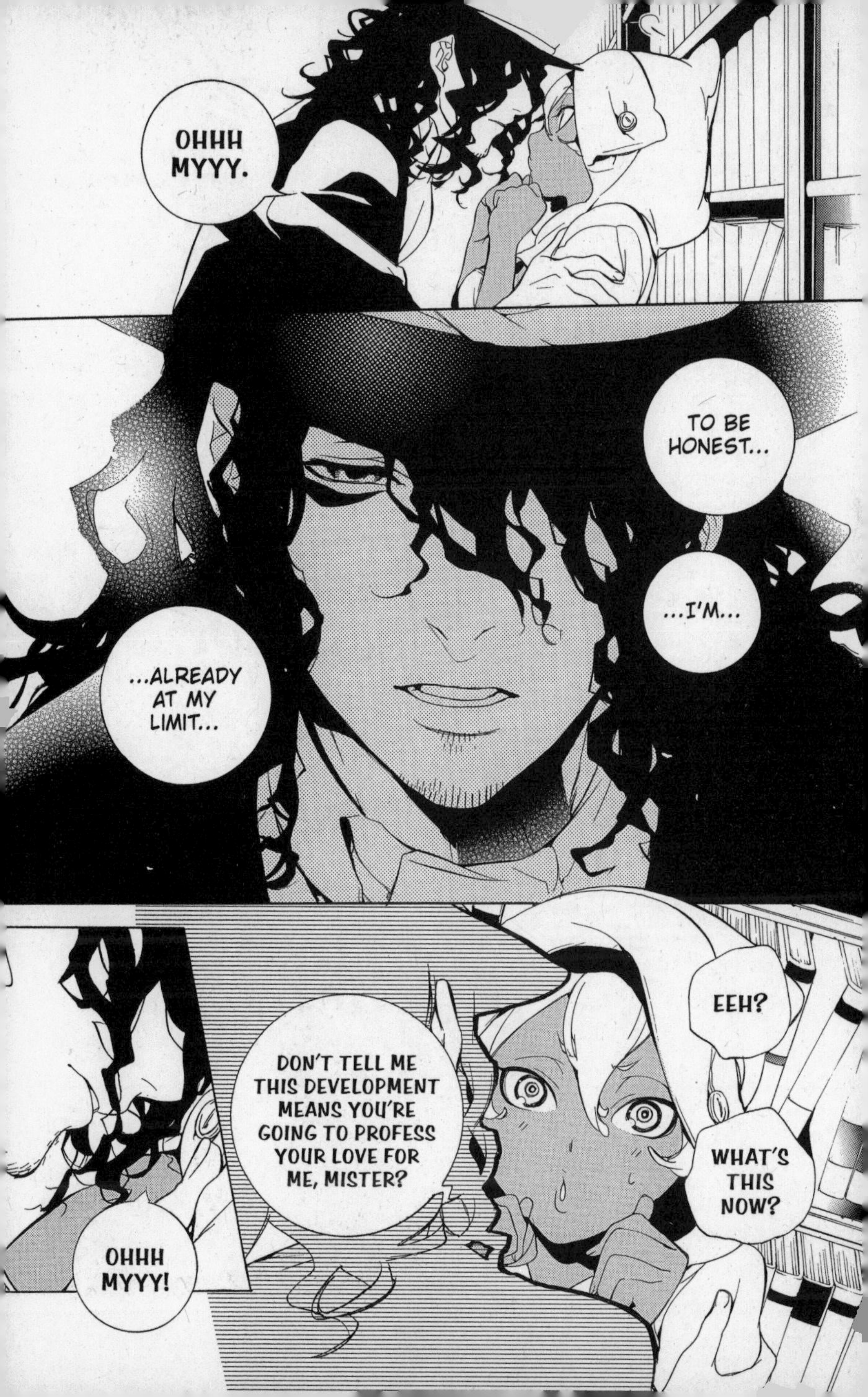
OHHH MYYY.
TO BE HONEST...
...I'M...
...ALREADY AT MY LIMIT...
EEH?
WHAT'S THIS NOW?
DON'T TELL ME THIS DEVELOPMENT MEANS YOU'RE GOING TO PROFESS YOUR LOVE FOR ME, MISTER?
OHHH MYYY!

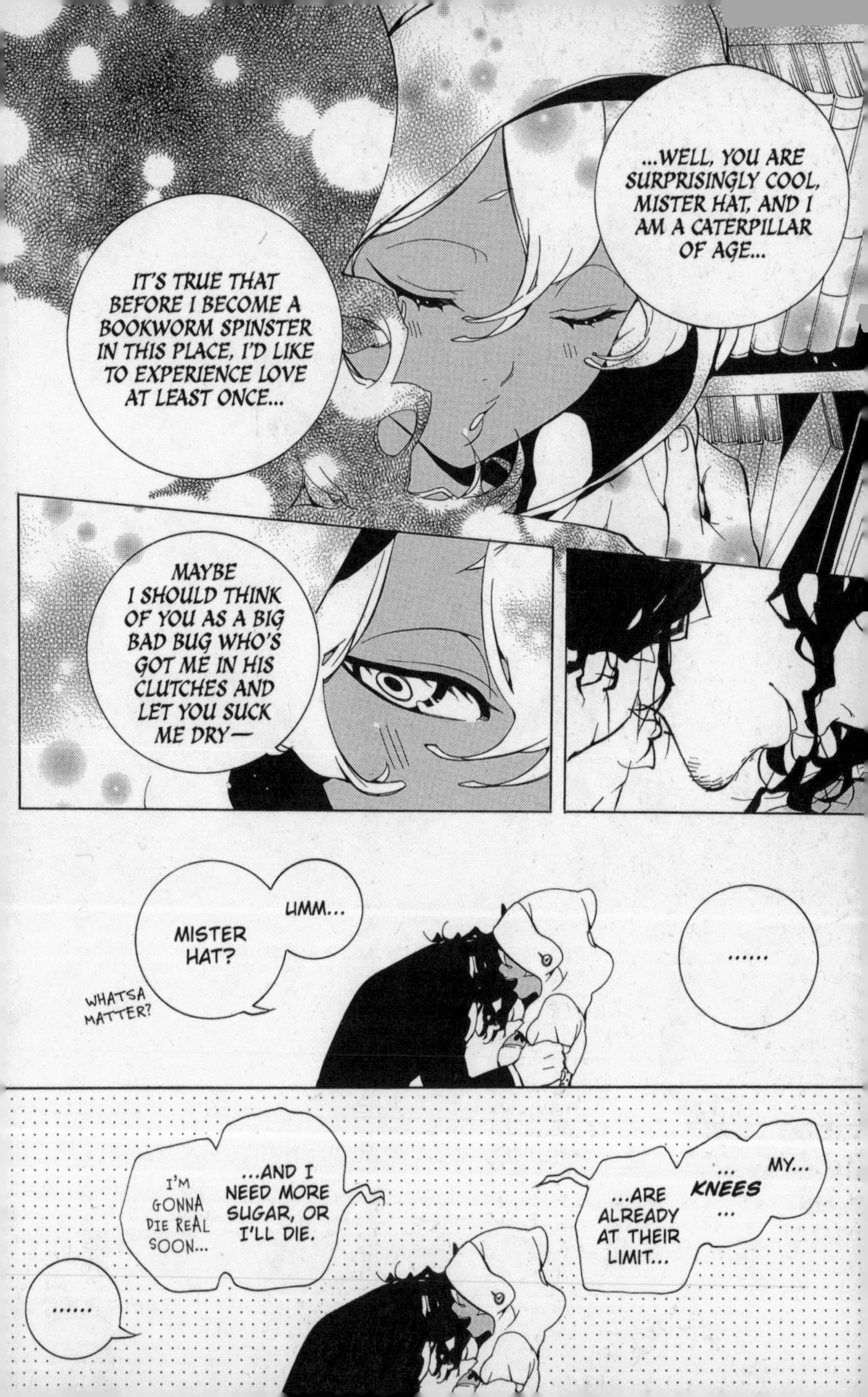
...WELL, YOU ARE SURPRISINGLY COOL, MISTER HAT, AND I AM A CATERPILLAR OF AGE...
IT'S TRUE THAT BEFORE I BECOME A BOOKWORM SPINSTER IN THIS PLACE, I'D LIKE TO EXPERIENCE LOVE AT LEAST ONCE...
MAYBE I SHOULD THINK OF YOU AS A BIG BAD BUG WHO'S GOT ME IN HIS CLUTCHES AND LET YOU SUCK ME DRY—
......
UMM... MISTER HAT?
WHATSA MATTER?
...MY... KNEES... ...ARE ALREADY AT THEIR LIMIT...
...AND I NEED MORE SUGAR, OR I'LL DIE.
I'M GONNA DIE REAL SOON...
......

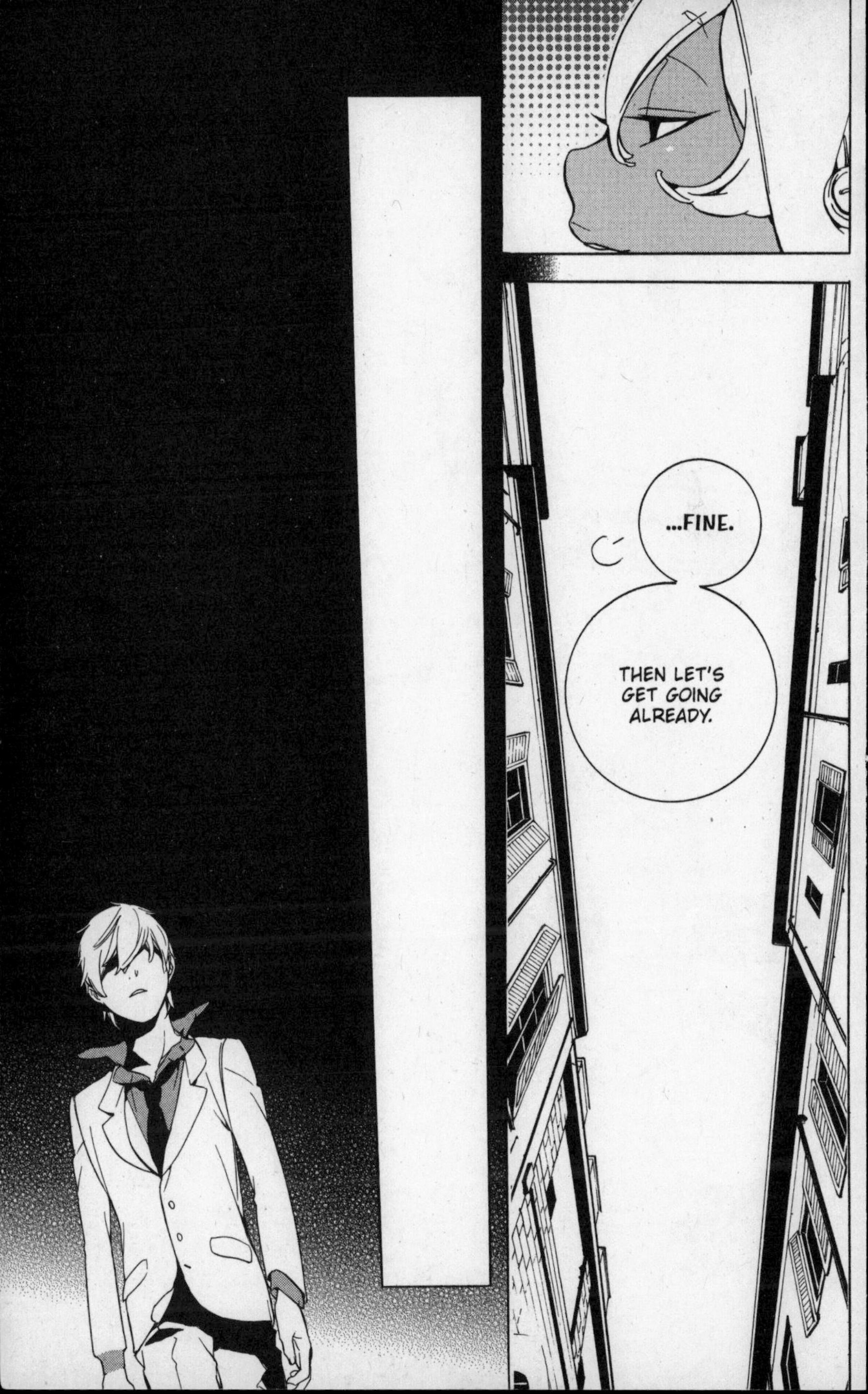
...FINE.
THEN LET'S GET GOING ALREADY.

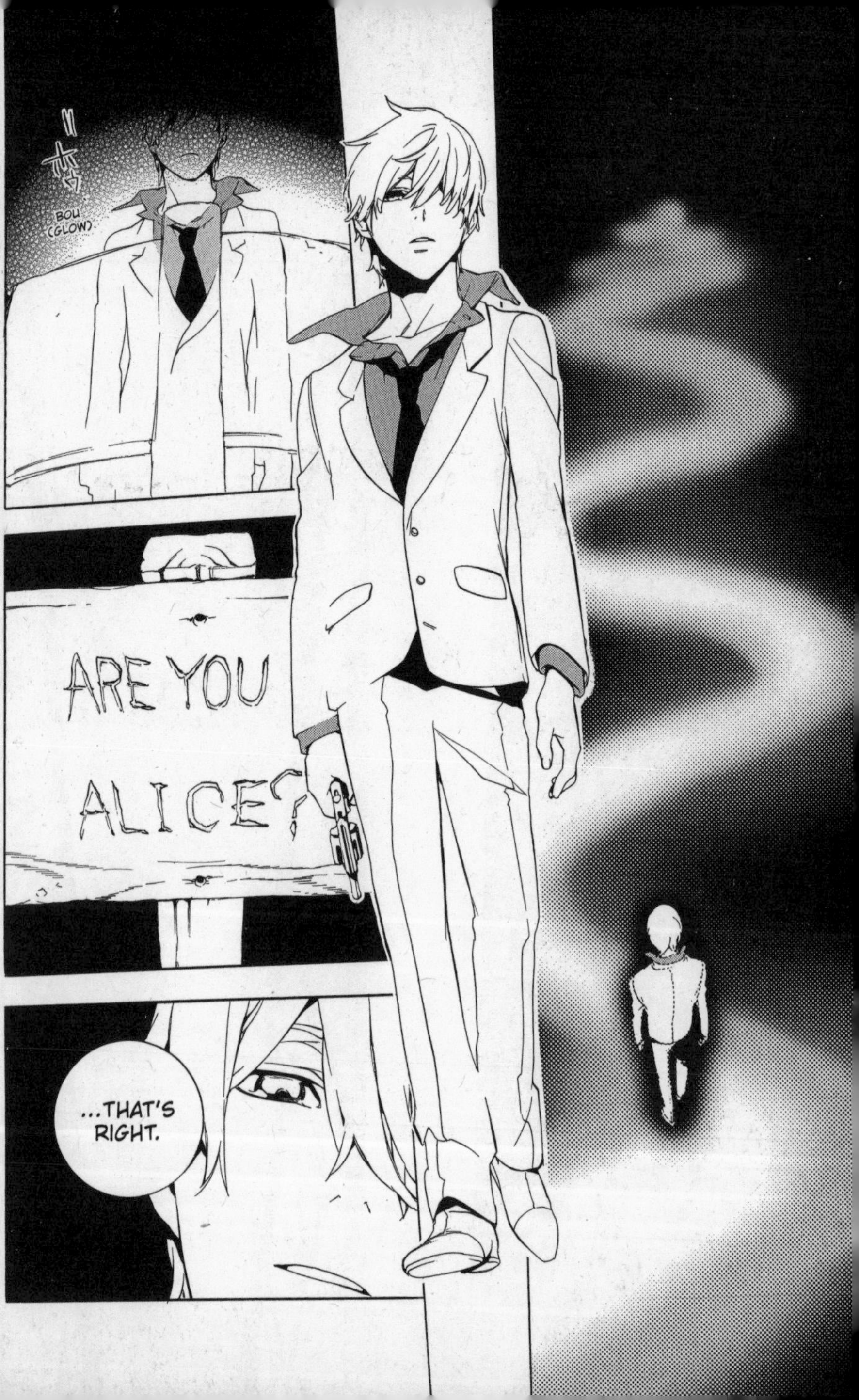
ぼ
BOU (GLOW)
ARE YOU ALICE?
...THAT'S RIGHT.

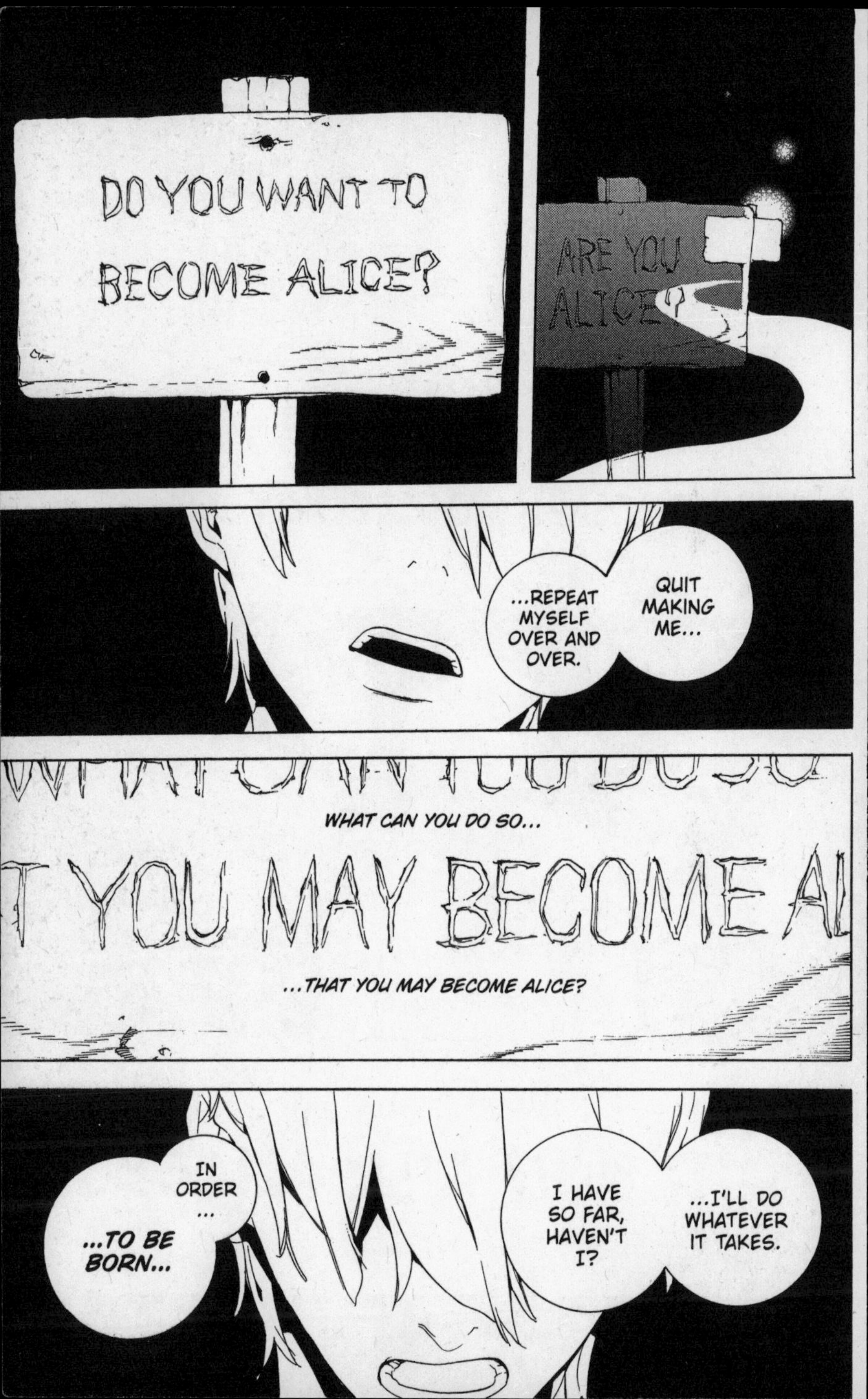
ARE YOU ALICE?
DO YOU WANT TO BECOME ALICE?
QUIT MAKING ME...
...REPEAT MYSELF OVER AND OVER.
WHAT CAN YOU DO SO...
YOU MAY BECOME
...THAT YOU MAY BECOME ALICE?
...I'LL DO WHATEVER IT TAKES.
I HAVE SO FAR, HAVEN'T I?
IN ORDER...
...TO BE BORN...

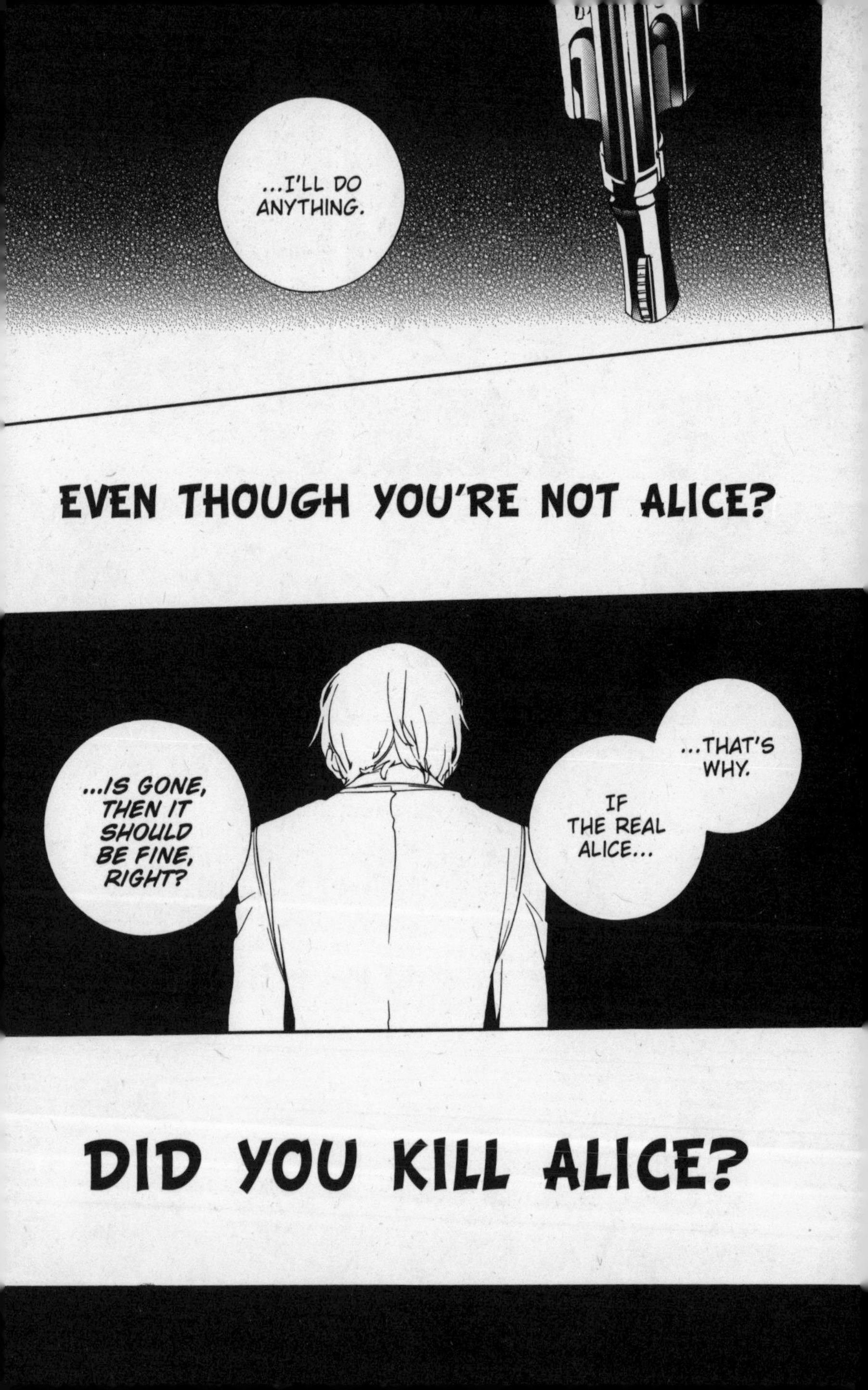
...I'LL DO ANYTHING.
EVEN THOUGH YOU'RE NOT ALICE?
...THAT'S WHY.
IF THE REAL ALICE...
...IS GONE, THEN IT SHOULD BE FINE, RIGHT?
DID YOU KILL ALICE?

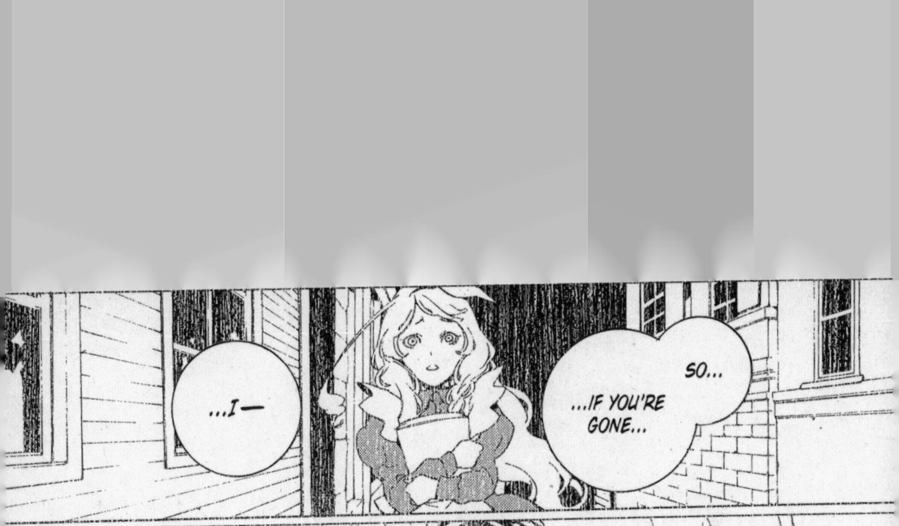
SO...
...IF YOU'RE GONE...
...I—

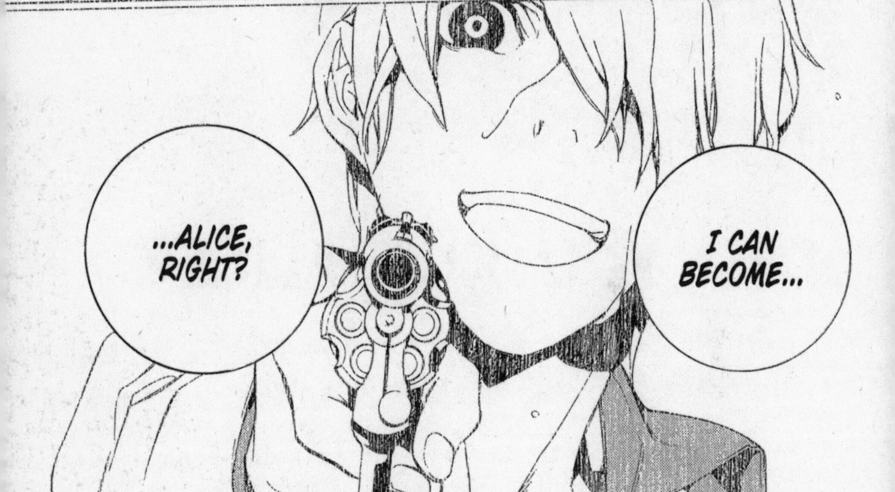
I CAN BECOME...
...ALICE, RIGHT?

DID YOU KILL ALICE?

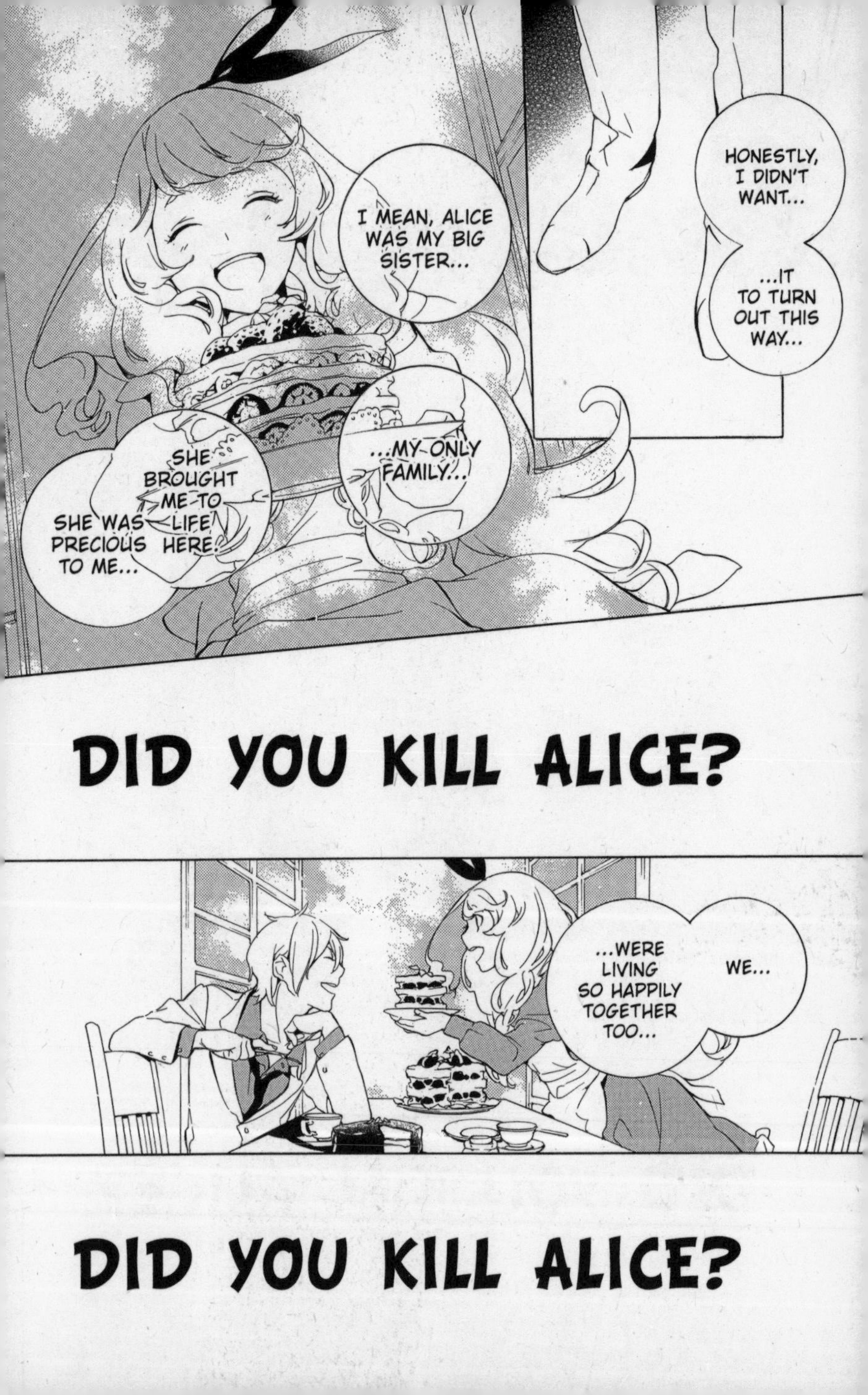
HONESTLY, I DIDN'T WANT...
...IT TO TURN OUT THIS WAY...
I MEAN, ALICE WAS MY BIG SISTER...
...MY ONLY FAMILY...
SHE BROUGHT ME TO LIFE HERE.
SHE WAS PRECIOUS TO ME...
DID YOU KILL ALICE?
WE...
...WERE LIVING SO HAPPILY TOGETHER TOO...
DID YOU KILL ALICE?

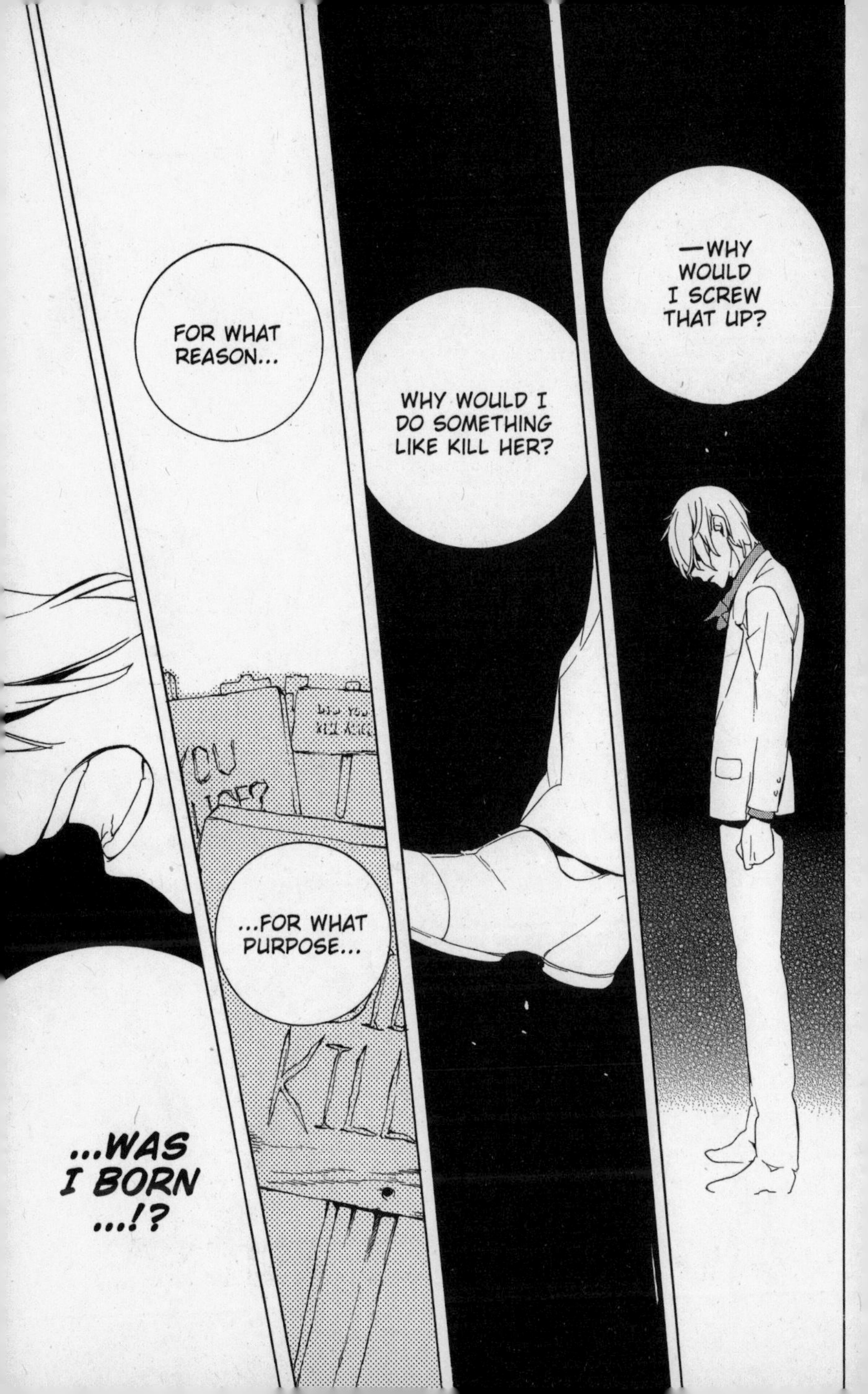
—WHY WOULD I SCREW THAT UP?
WHY WOULD I DO SOMETHING LIKE KILL HER?
FOR WHAT REASON...
...FOR WHAT PURPOSE...
...WAS I BORN ...!?

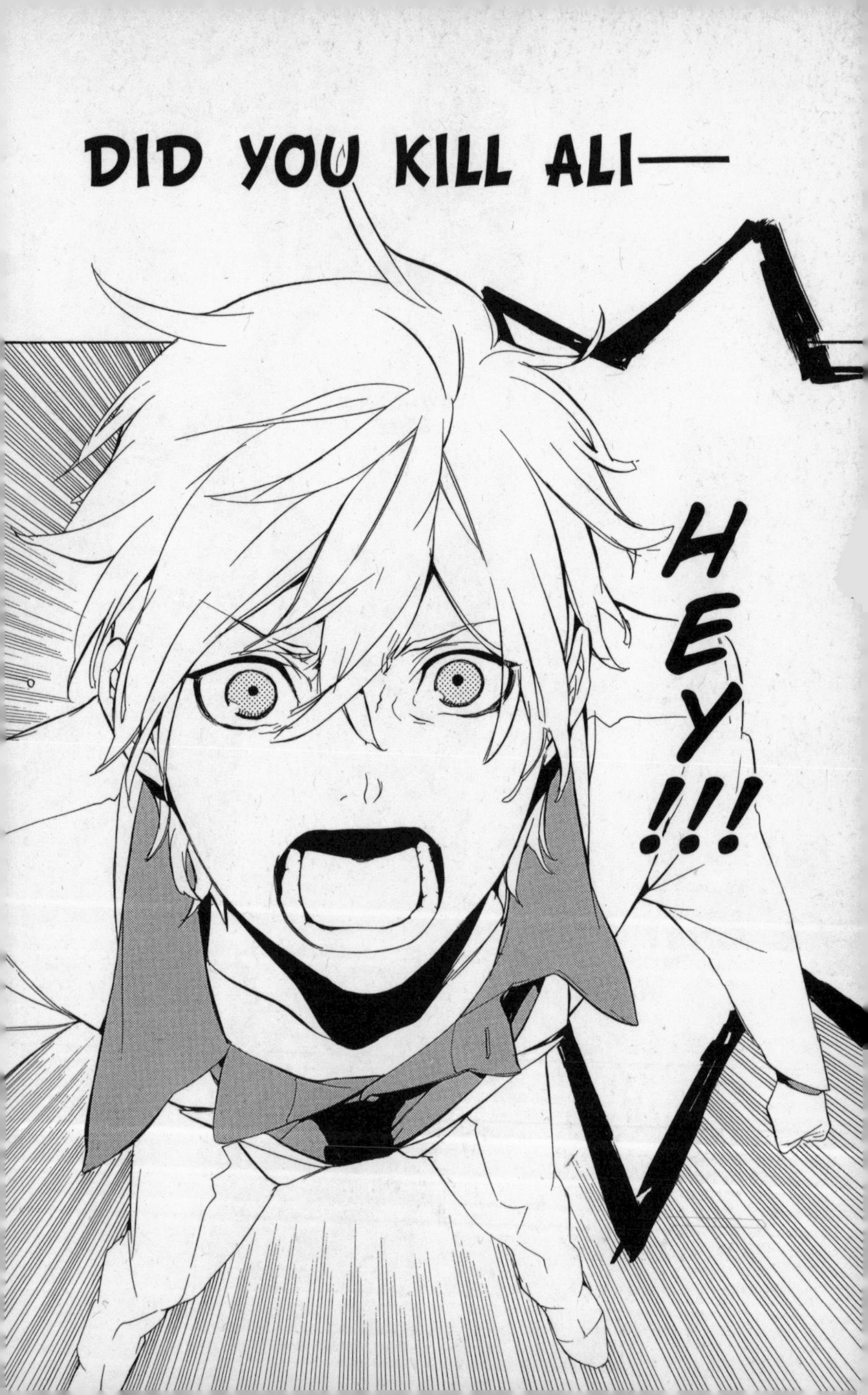
DID YOU KILL ALI—
HEY!!!

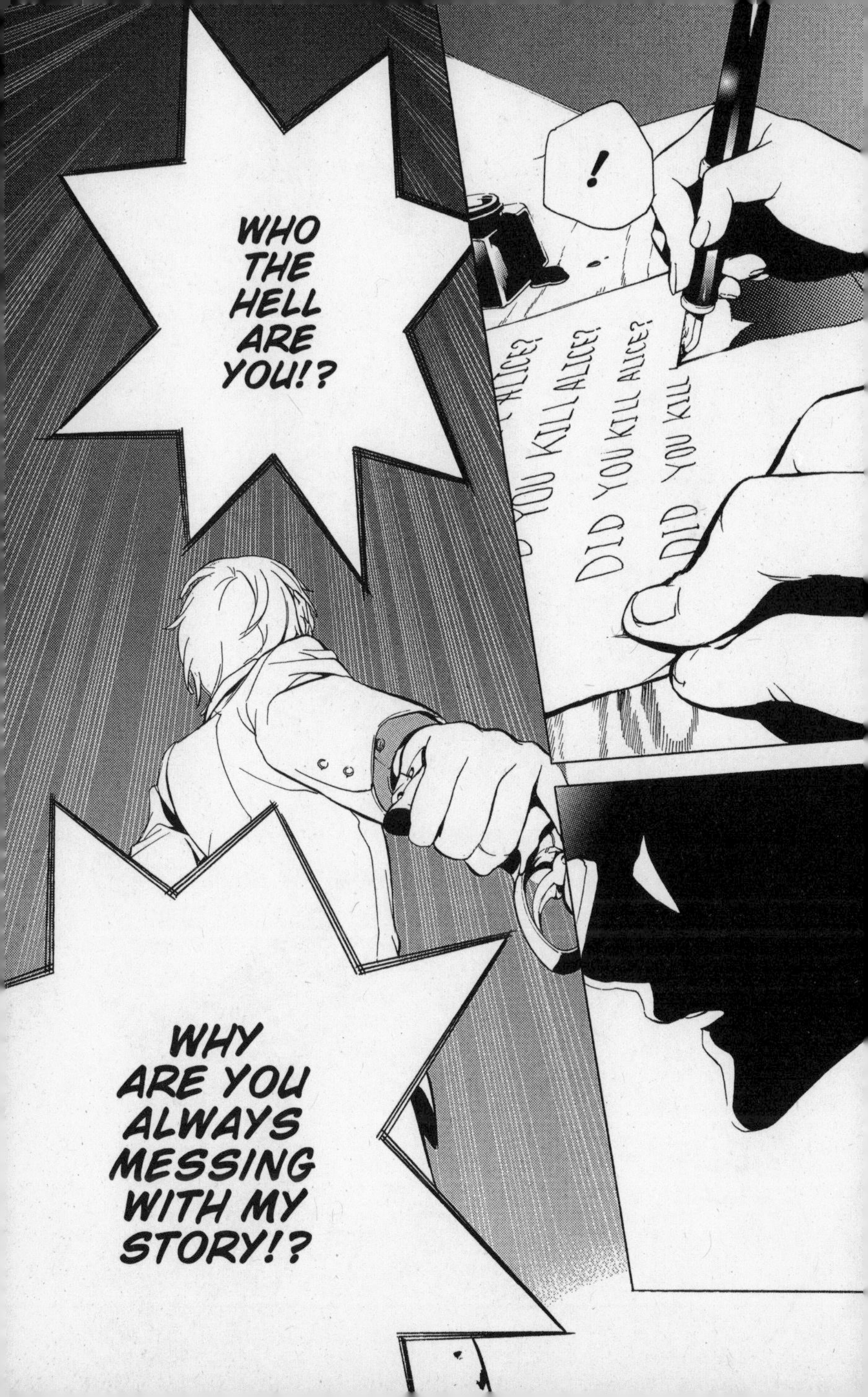
!
DID YOU KILL ALICE?
DID YOU KILL
WHO THE HELL ARE YOU!?
WHY ARE YOU ALWAYS MESSING WITH MY STORY!?

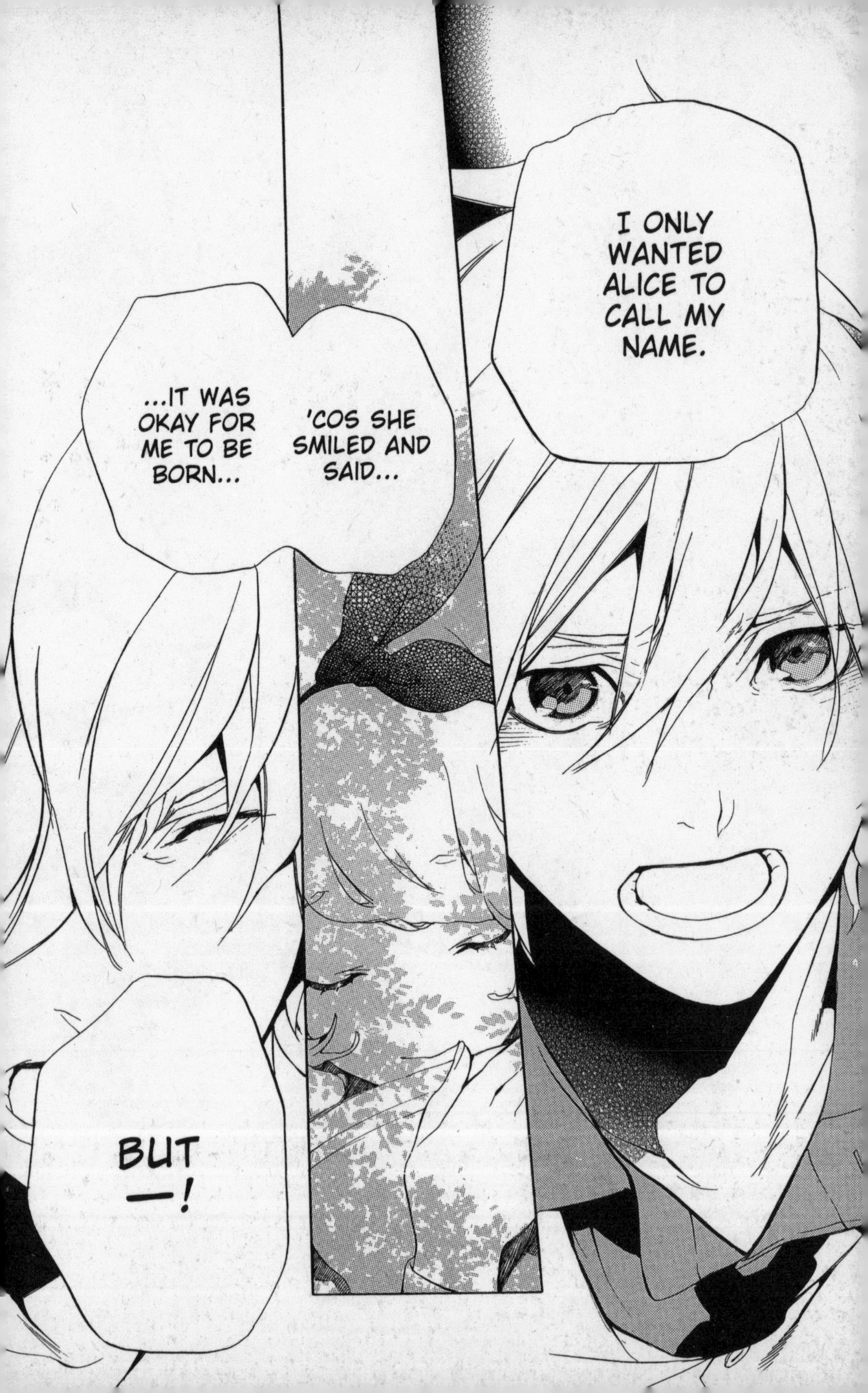
I ONLY WANTED ALICE TO CALL MY NAME.
'COS SHE SMILED AND SAID...
...IT WAS OKAY FOR ME TO BE BORN...
BUT—!

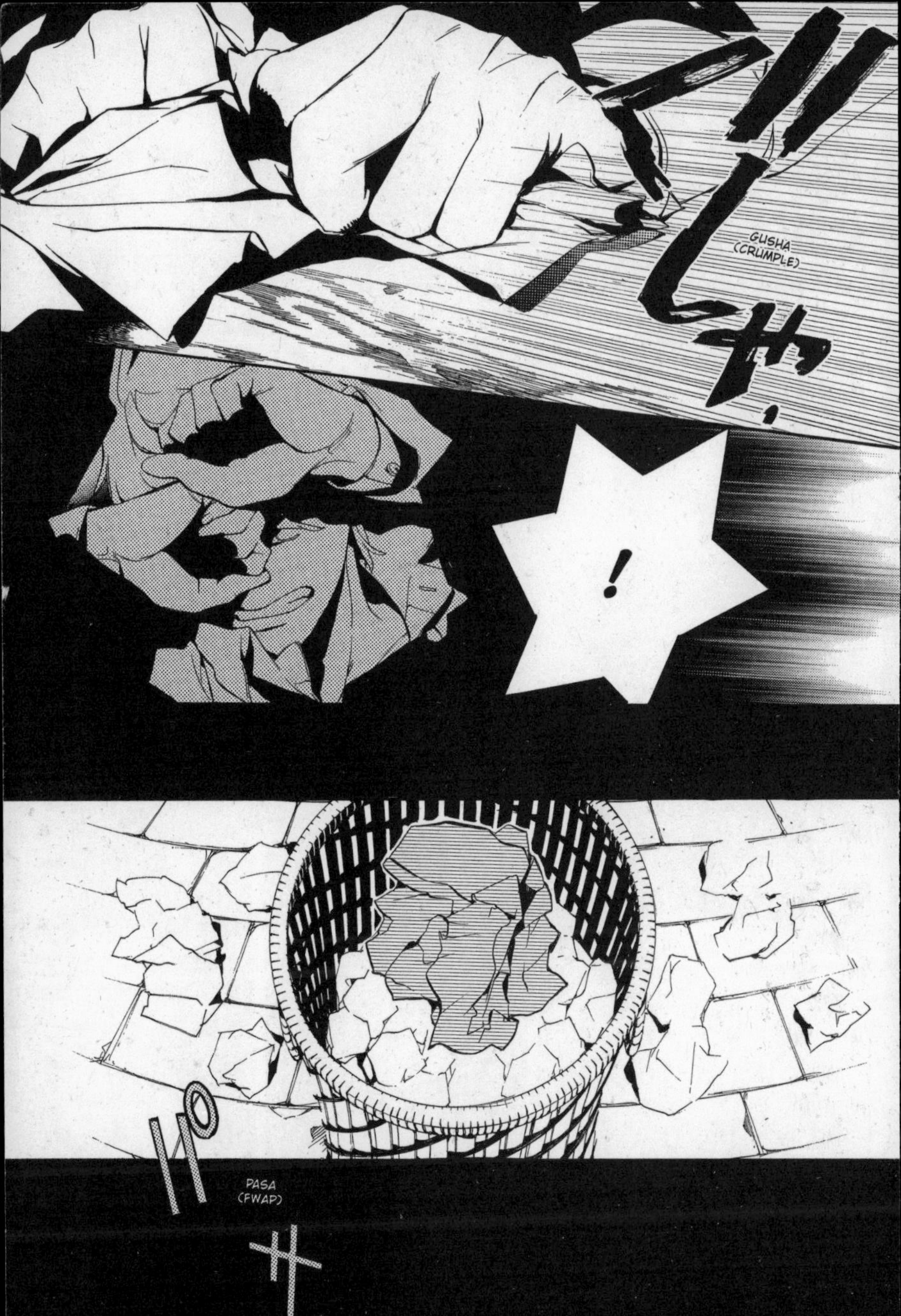
GUSHA
(CRUMPLE)
!
PASA
(FWAP)

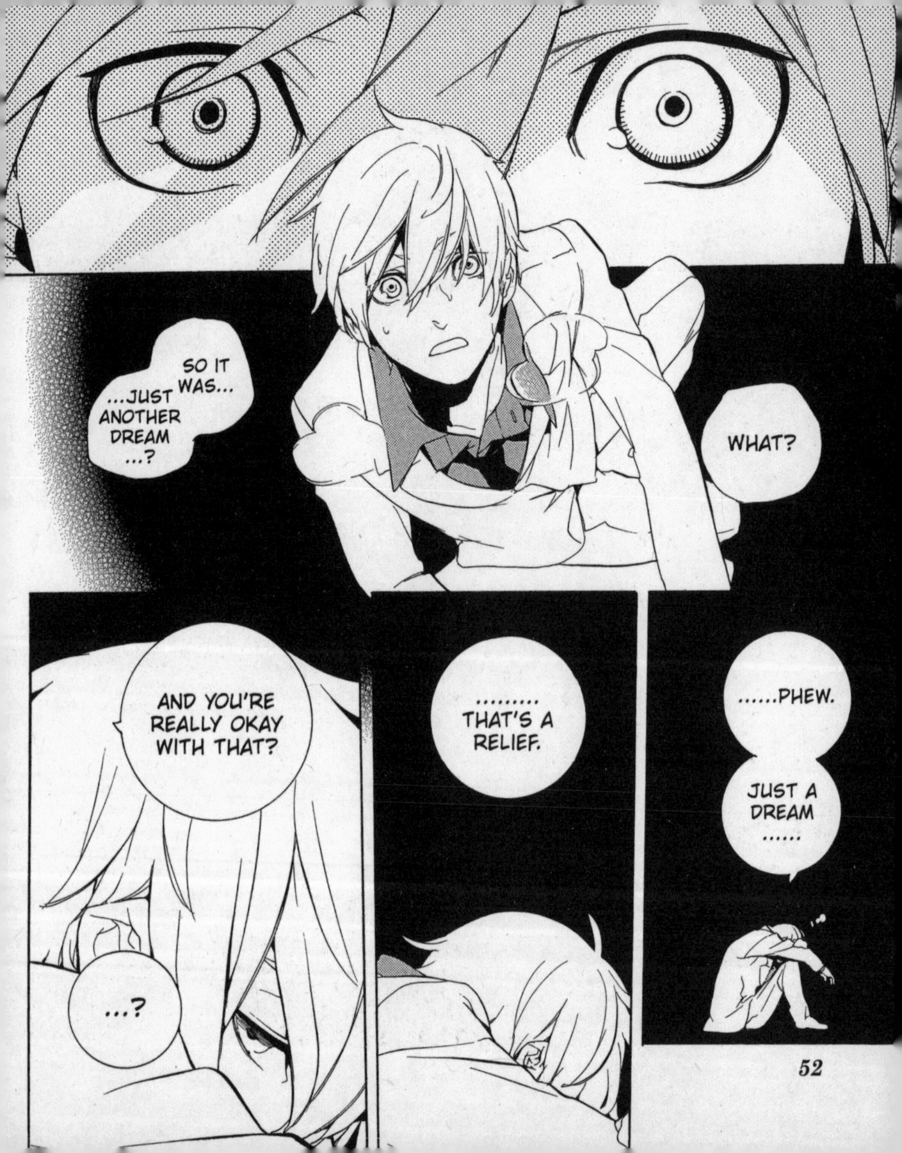
SO IT WAS... ...JUST ANOTHER DREAM ...?
WHAT?
......PHEW.
JUST A DREAM ......
.... THAT'S A RELIEF.
AND YOU'RE REALLY OKAY WITH THAT?
...?

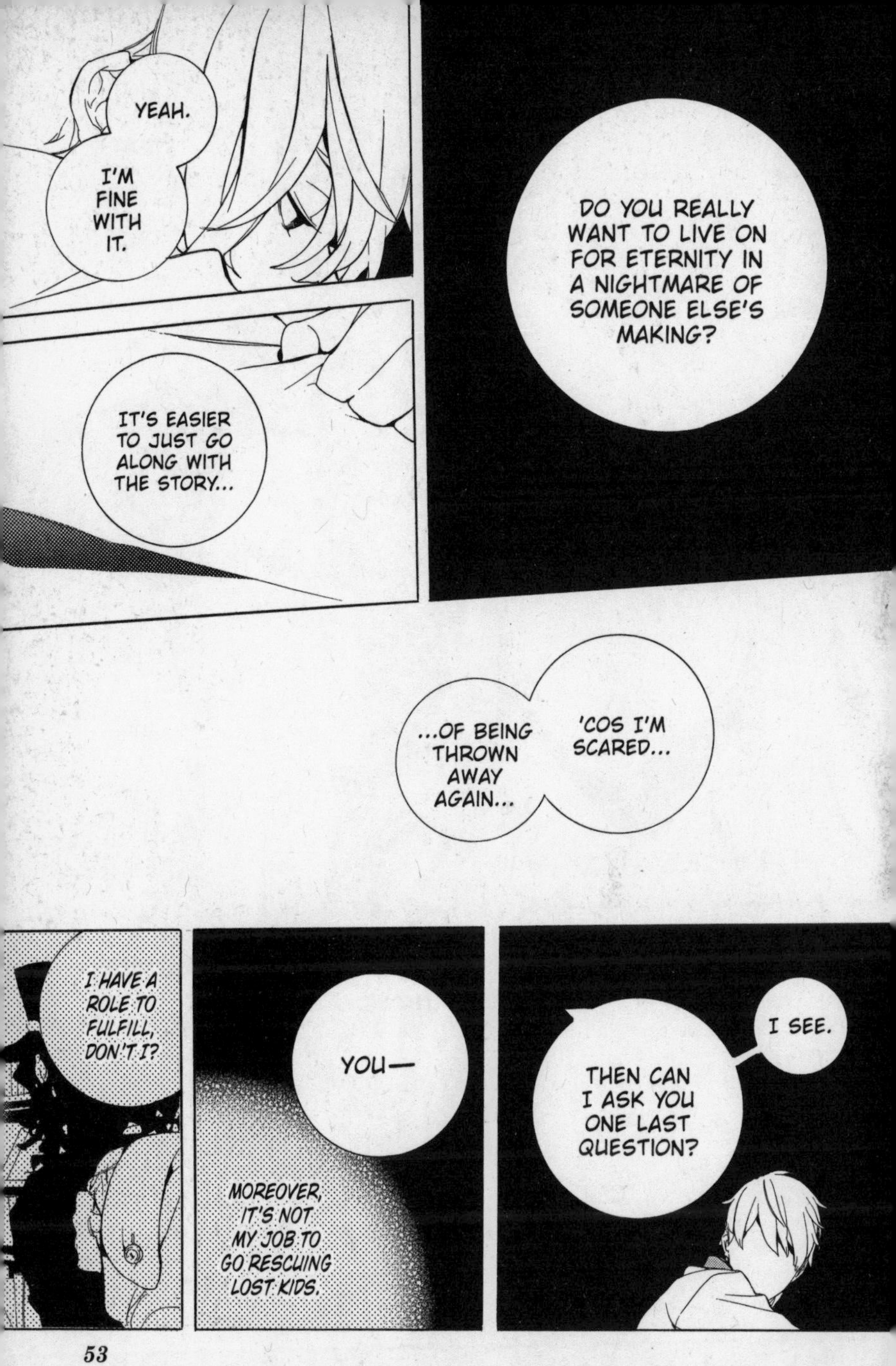
DO YOU REALLY WANT TO LIVE ON FOR ETERNITY IN A NIGHTMARE OF SOMEONE ELSE'S MAKING?
YEAH.
I'M FINE WITH IT.
IT'S EASIER TO JUST GO ALONG WITH THE STORY...
'COS I'M SCARED...
...OF BEING THROWN AWAY AGAIN...
I SEE.
THEN CAN I ASK YOU ONE LAST QUESTION?
YOU—
MOREOVER, IT'S NOT MY JOB TO GO RESCUING LOST KIDS.
I HAVE A ROLE TO FULFILL, DON'T I?

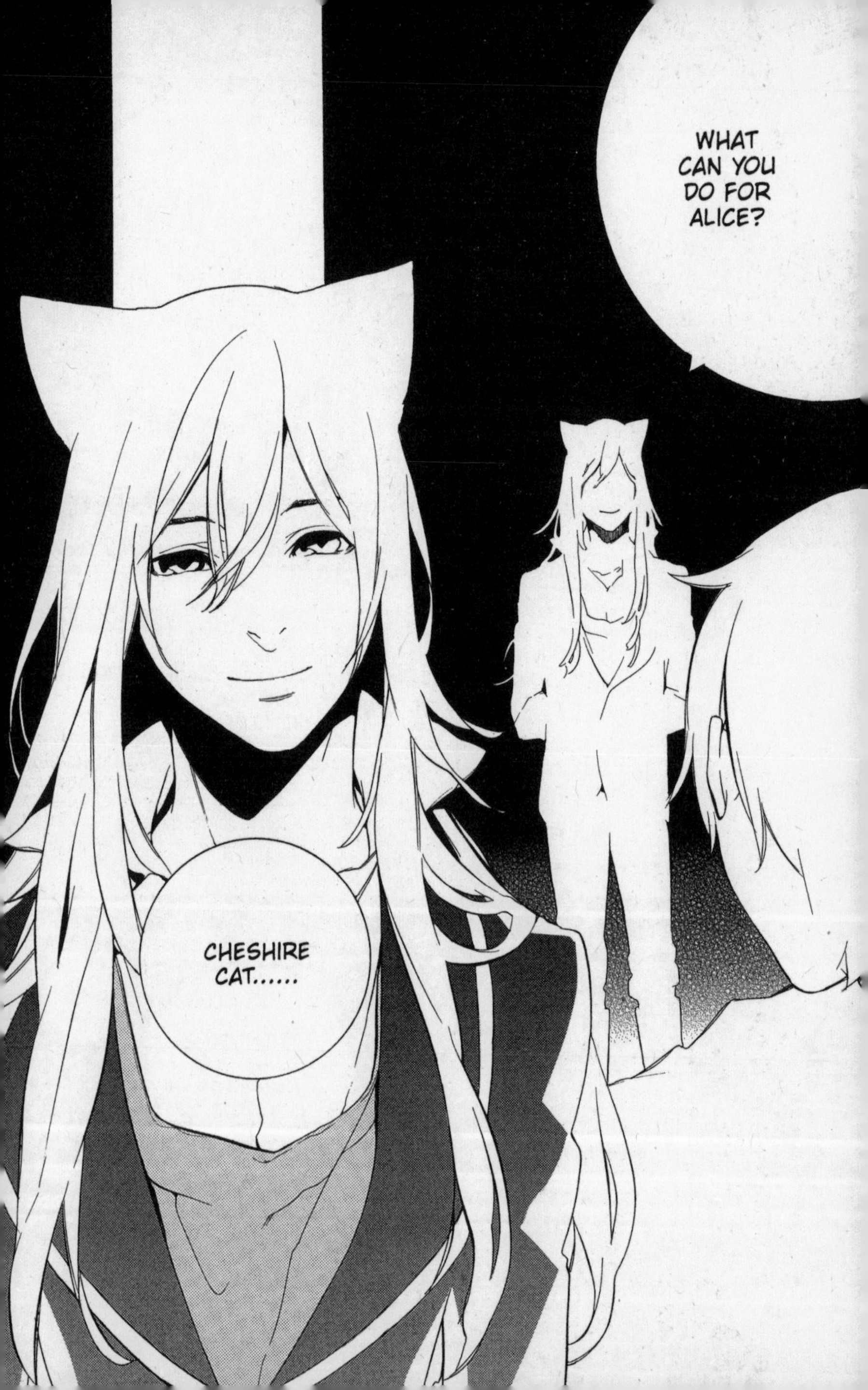
WHAT CAN YOU DO FOR ALICE?
CHESHIRE CAT......

Chapter 20

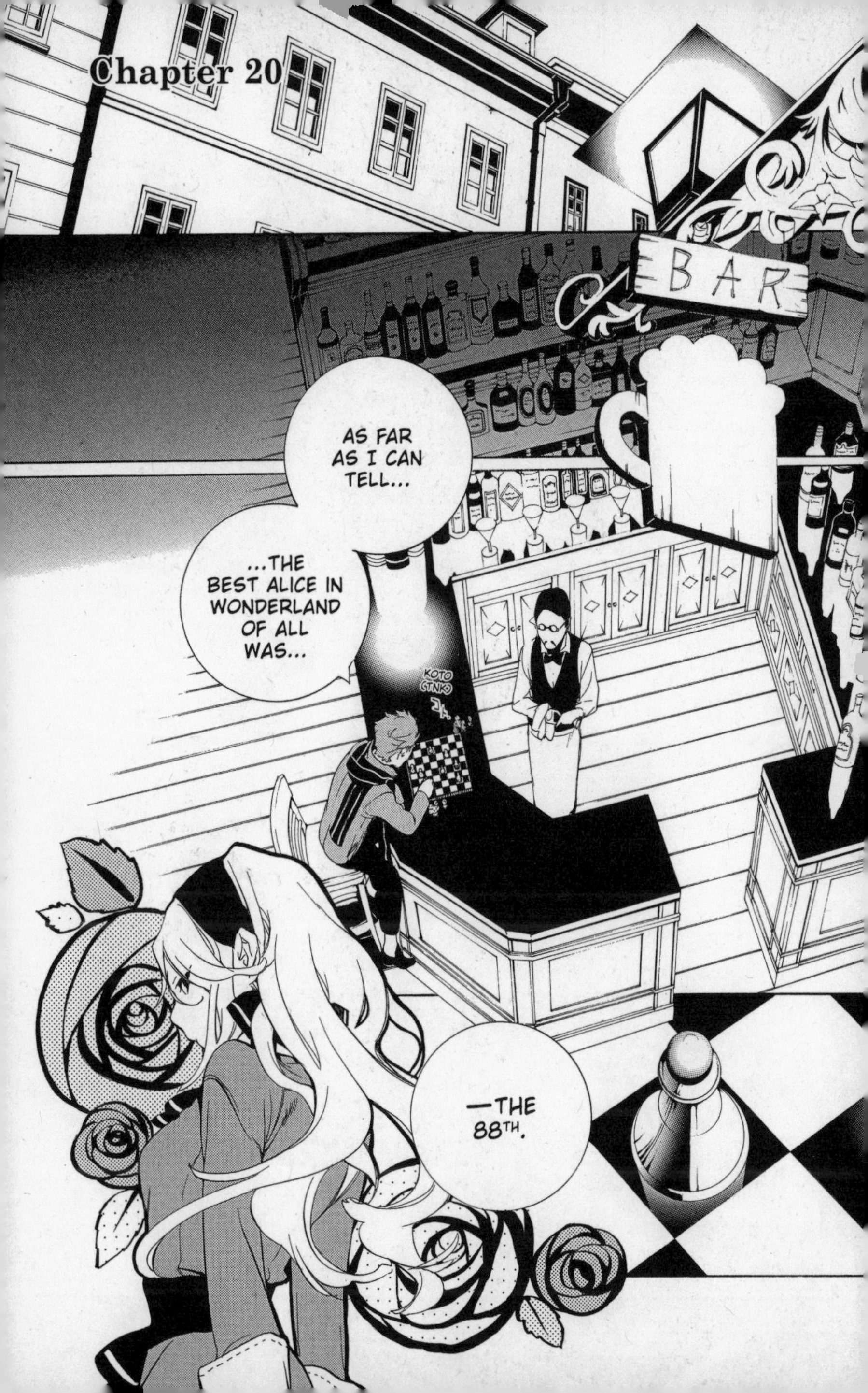
BAR
AS FAR AS I CAN TELL...
...THE BEST ALICE IN WONDERLAND OF ALL WAS...
KOTO (TNK)
—THE 88TH.

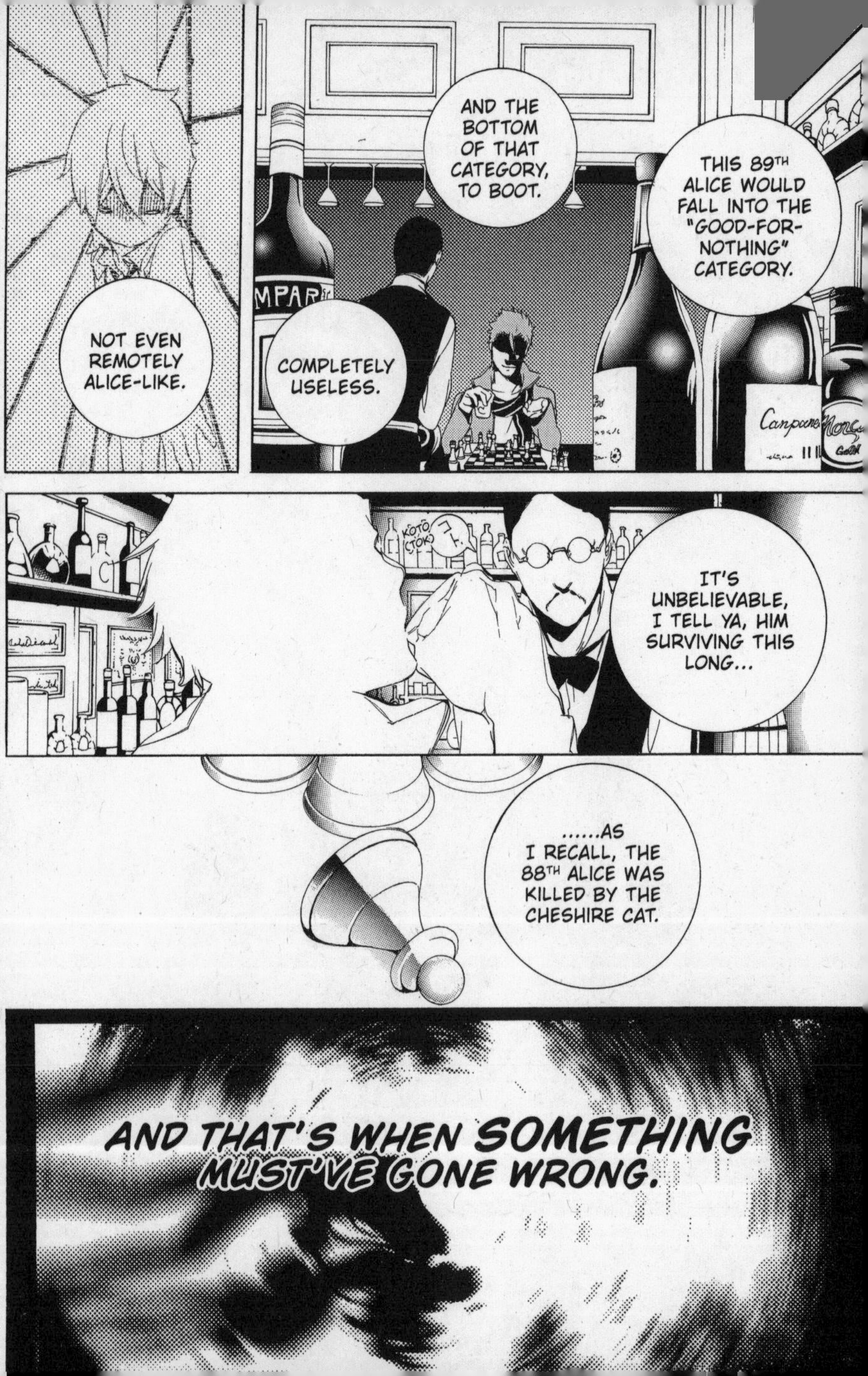
THIS 89TH ALICE WOULD FALL INTO THE "GOOD-FOR-NOTHING" CATEGORY.
AND THE BOTTOM OF THAT CATEGORY, TO BOOT.
COMPLETELY USELESS.
NOT EVEN REMOTELY ALICE-LIKE.
KOTO (TOK)
IT'S UNBELIEVABLE, I TELL YA, HIM SURVIVING THIS LONG...
......AS I RECALL, THE 88TH ALICE WAS KILLED BY THE CHESHIRE CAT.
AND THAT'S WHEN SOMETHING MUST'VE GONE WRONG.

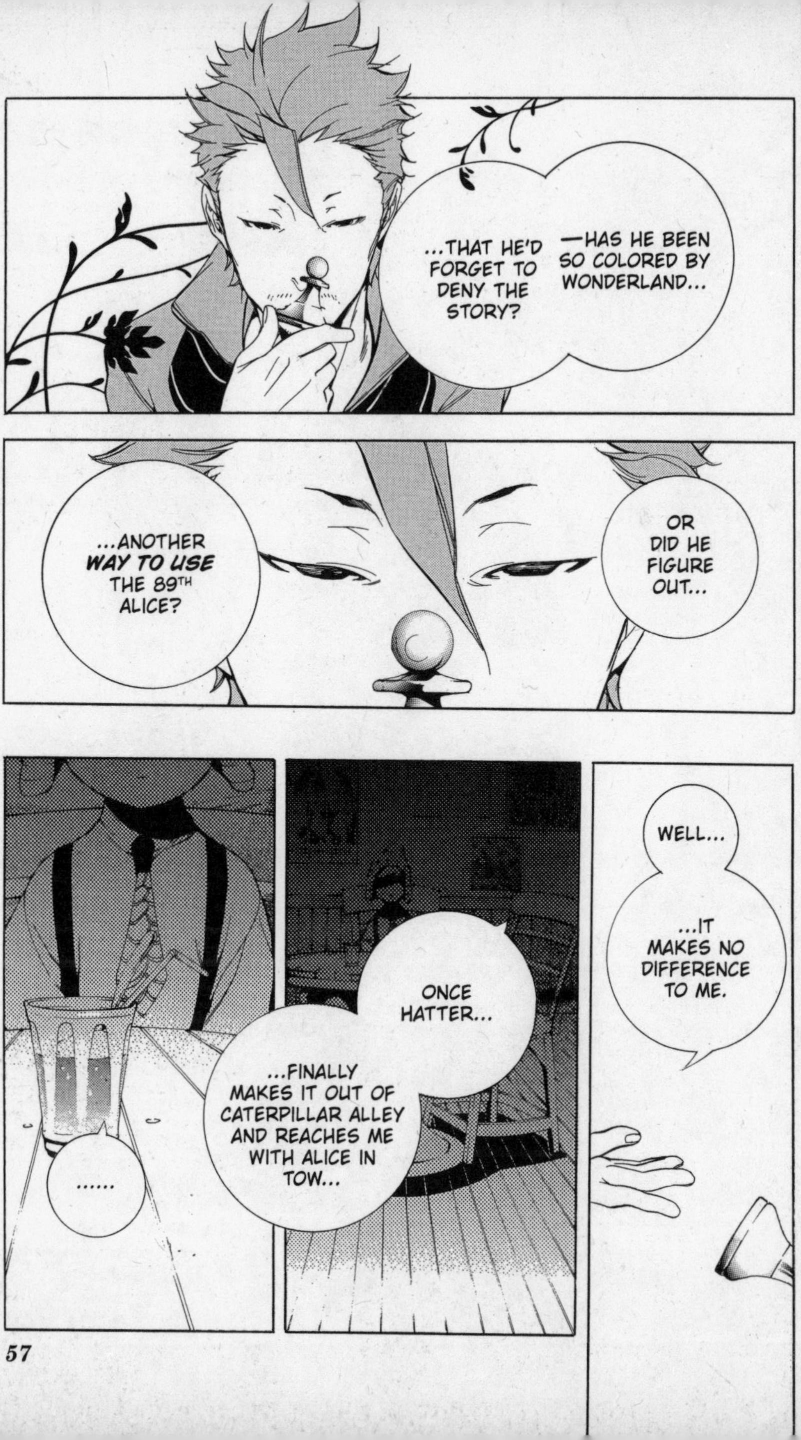
—HAS HE BEEN SO COLORED BY WONDERLAND...
...THAT HE'D FORGET TO DENY THE STORY?
OR DID HE FIGURE OUT...
...ANOTHER WAY TO USE THE 89TH ALICE?
WELL...
...IT MAKES NO DIFFERENCE TO ME.
ONCE HATTER...
...FINALLY MAKES IT OUT OF CATERPILLAR ALLEY AND REACHES ME WITH ALICE IN TOW...
......

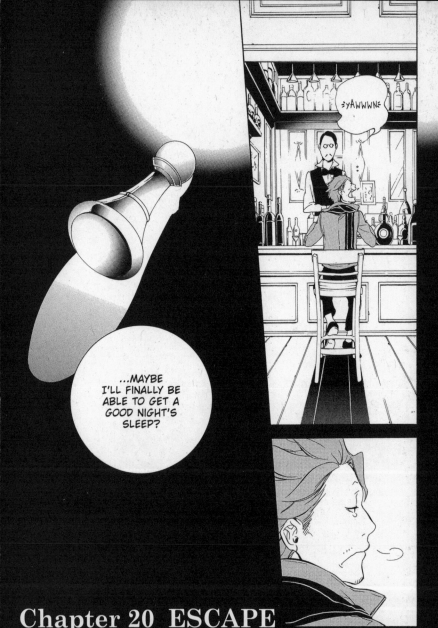

≥YAWWWN≤

...MAYBE I'LL FINALLY BE ABLE TO GET A GOOD NIGHT'S SLEEP?

Chapter 20 ESCAPE

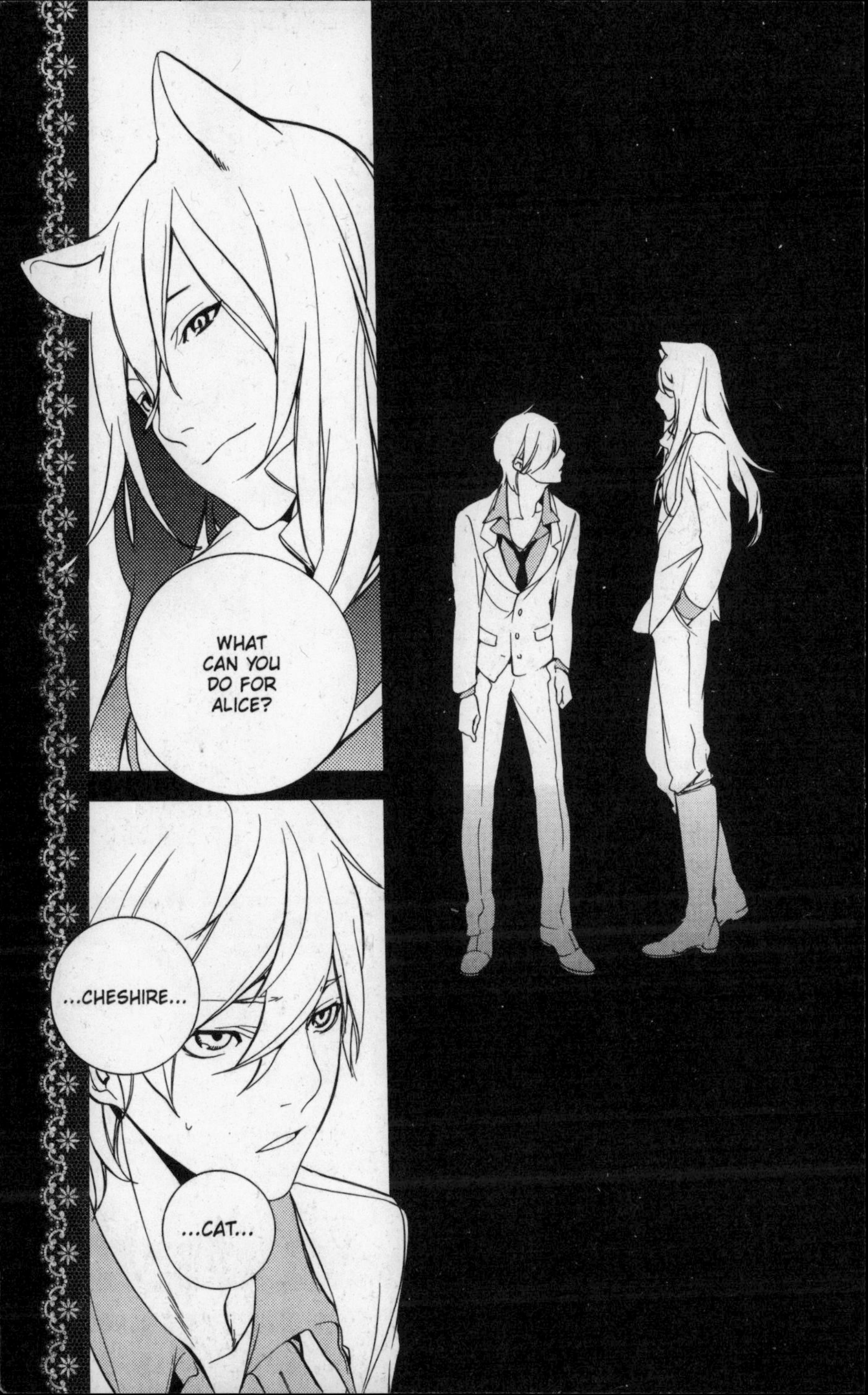
WHAT CAN YOU DO FOR ALICE?
...CHESHIRE...
...CAT...

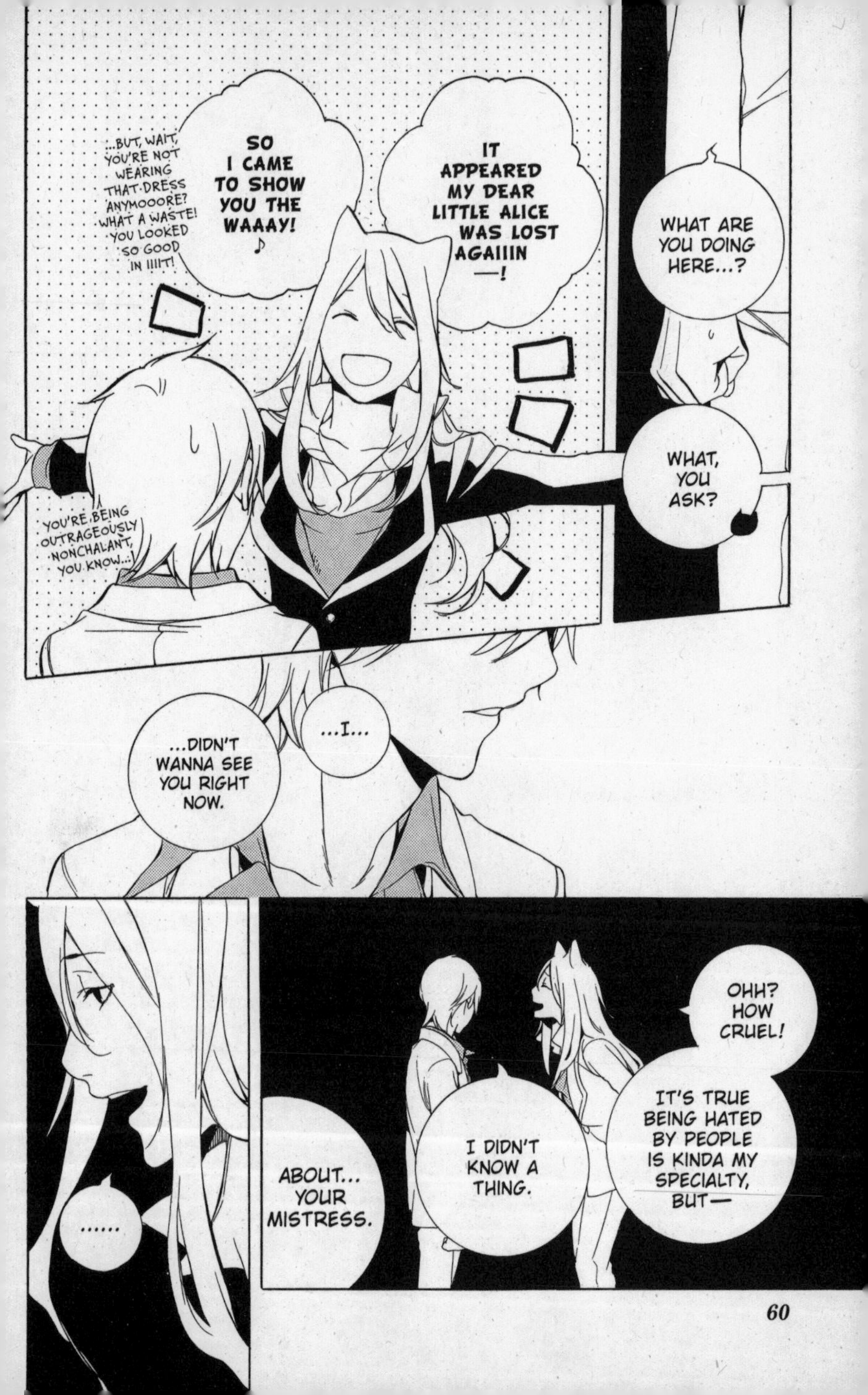
WHAT ARE YOU DOING HERE...?
WHAT, YOU ASK?
IT APPEARED MY DEAR LITTLE ALICE WAS LOST AGAIIIN—!
SO I CAME TO SHOW YOU THE WAAAY! ♪
...BUT, WAIT, YOU'RE NOT WEARING THAT DRESS ANYMOOORE? WHAT A WASTE! YOU LOOKED SO GOOD IN IIIIT!
YOU'RE BEING OUTRAGEOUSLY NONCHALANT, YOU KNOW...!
...I...
...DIDN'T WANNA SEE YOU RIGHT NOW.
OHH? HOW CRUEL!
IT'S TRUE BEING HATED BY PEOPLE IS KINDA MY SPECIALTY, BUT—
I DIDN'T KNOW A THING.
ABOUT... YOUR MISTRESS.
......

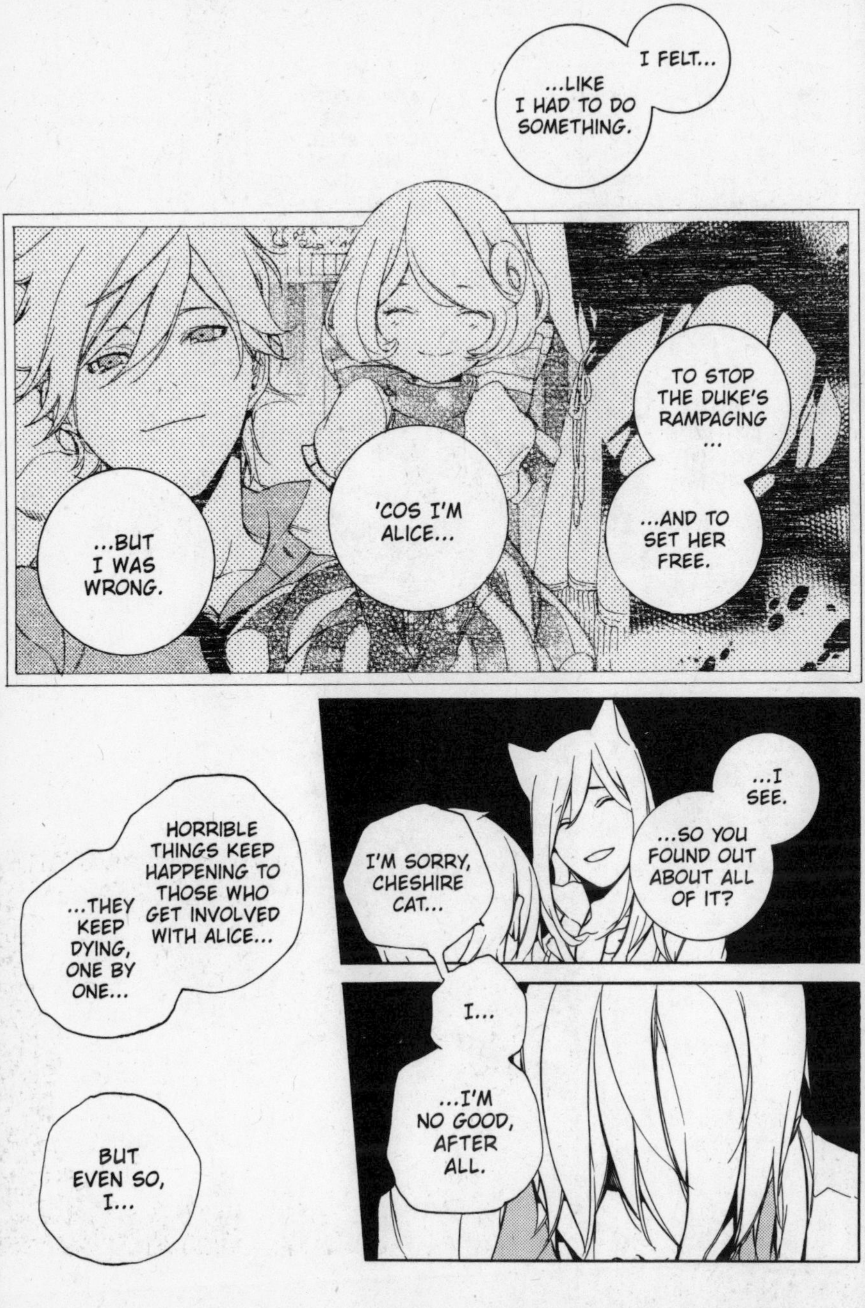
I FELT...
...LIKE I HAD TO DO SOMETHING.
TO STOP THE DUKE'S RAMPAGING ...
...AND TO SET HER FREE.
'COS I'M ALICE...
...BUT I WAS WRONG.
...I SEE.
...SO YOU FOUND OUT ABOUT ALL OF IT?
I'M SORRY, CHESHIRE CAT...
I...
...I'M NO GOOD, AFTER ALL.
HORRIBLE THINGS KEEP HAPPENING TO THOSE WHO GET INVOLVED WITH ALICE...
...THEY KEEP DYING, ONE BY ONE...
BUT EVEN SO, I...

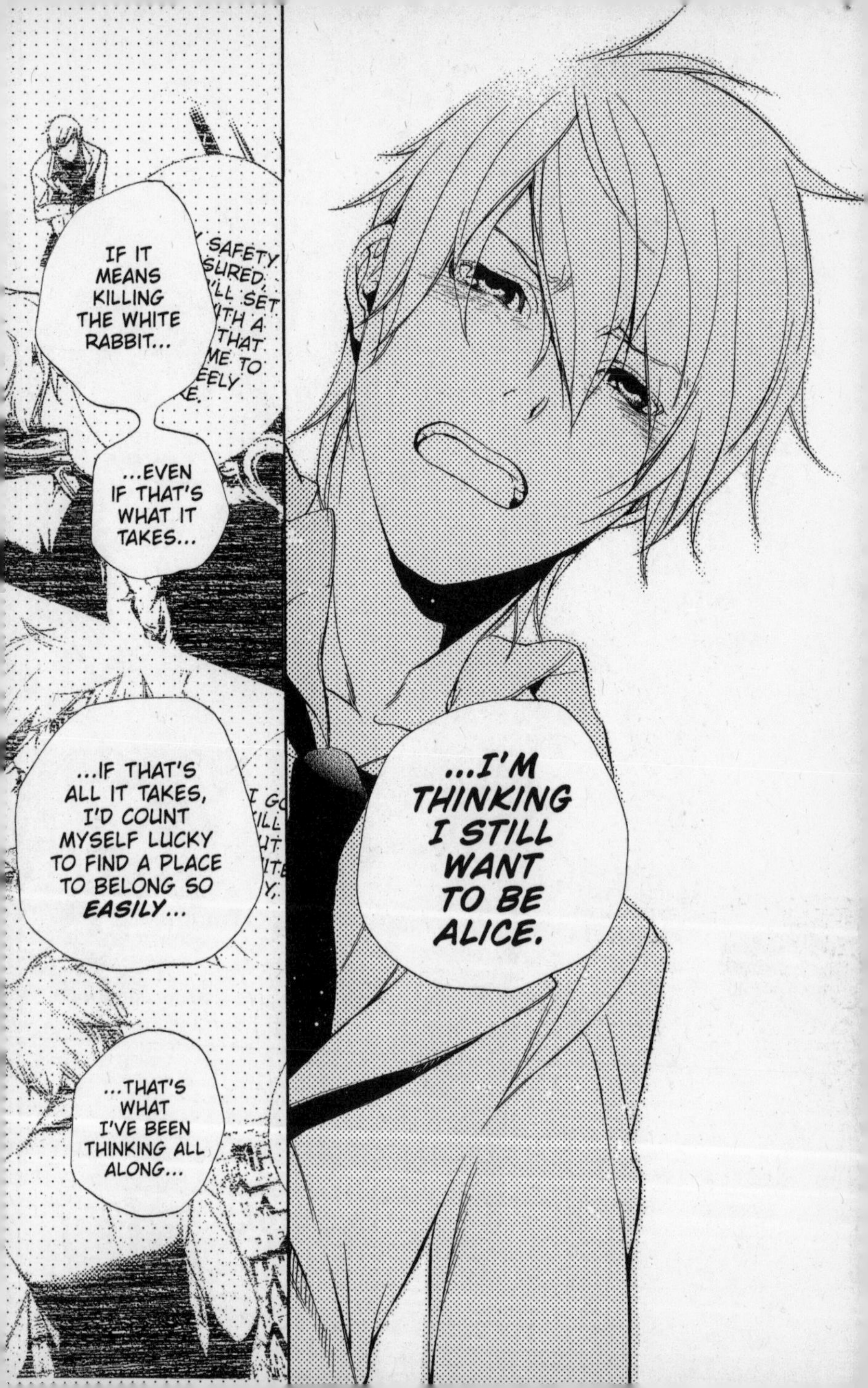
...I'M THINKING I STILL WANT TO BE ALICE.
IF IT MEANS KILLING THE WHITE RABBIT...
...EVEN IF THAT'S WHAT IT TAKES...
...IF THAT'S ALL IT TAKES, I'D COUNT MYSELF LUCKY TO FIND A PLACE TO BELONG SO *EASILY*...
...THAT'S WHAT I'VE BEEN THINKING ALL ALONG...

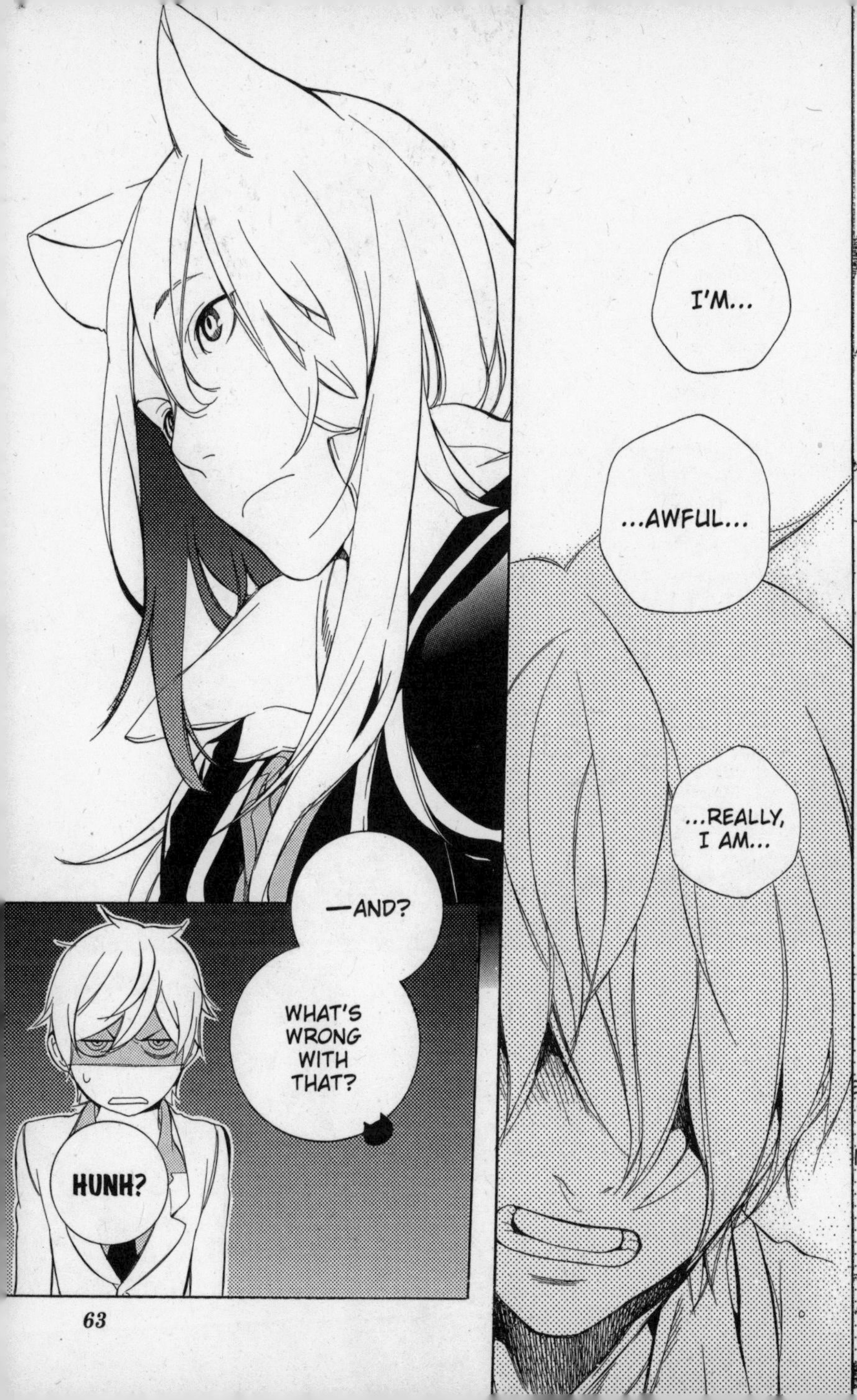
I'M...
...AWFUL...
...REALLY, I AM...
—AND?
WHAT'S WRONG WITH THAT?
HUNH?

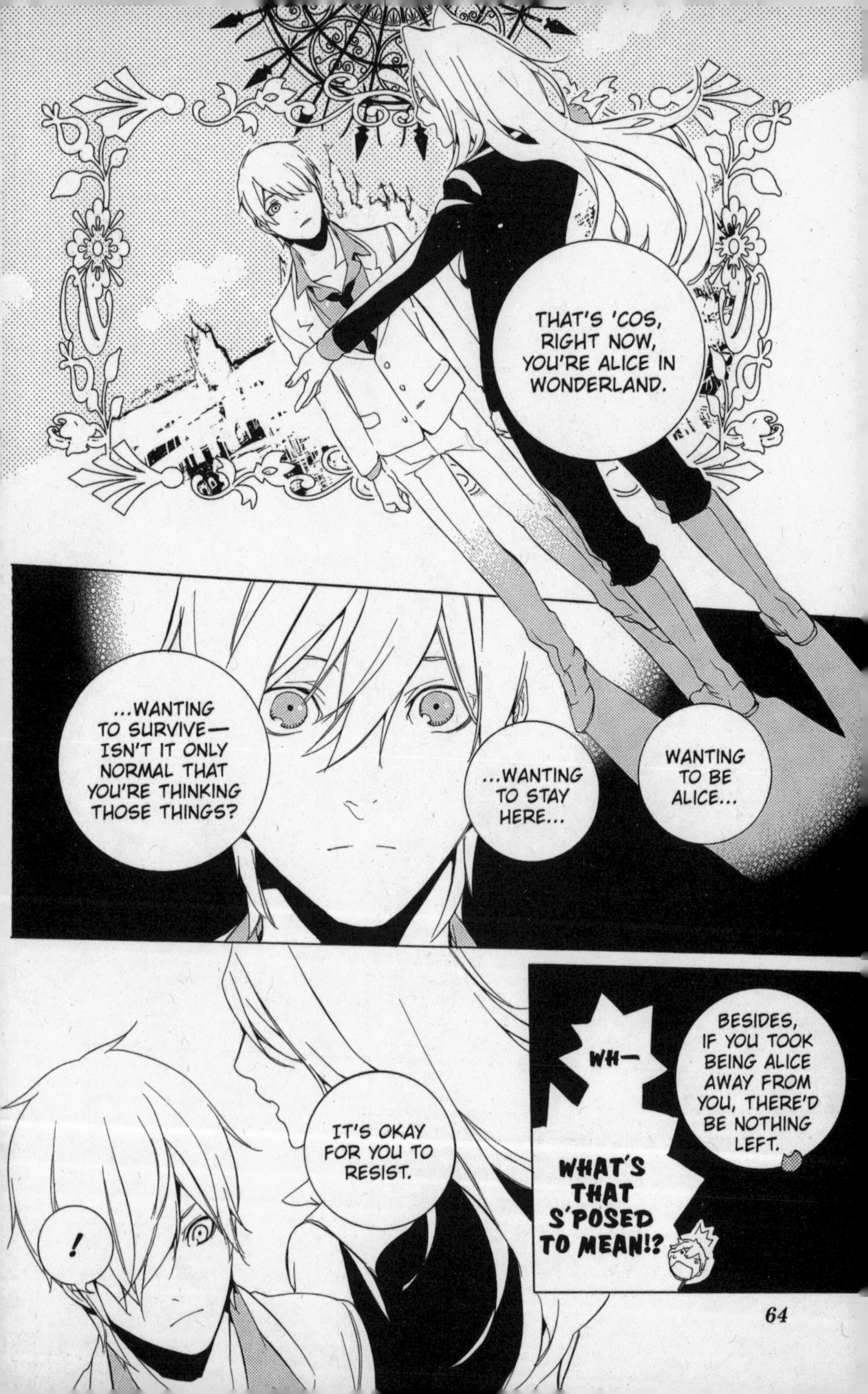
THAT'S 'COS, RIGHT NOW, YOU'RE ALICE IN WONDERLAND.
WANTING TO BE ALICE...
...WANTING TO STAY HERE...
...WANTING TO SURVIVE—ISN'T IT ONLY NORMAL THAT YOU'RE THINKING THOSE THINGS?
BESIDES, IF YOU TOOK BEING ALICE AWAY FROM YOU, THERE'D BE NOTHING LEFT.
WH—
WHAT'S THAT S'POSED TO MEAN!?
IT'S OKAY FOR YOU TO RESIST.
!

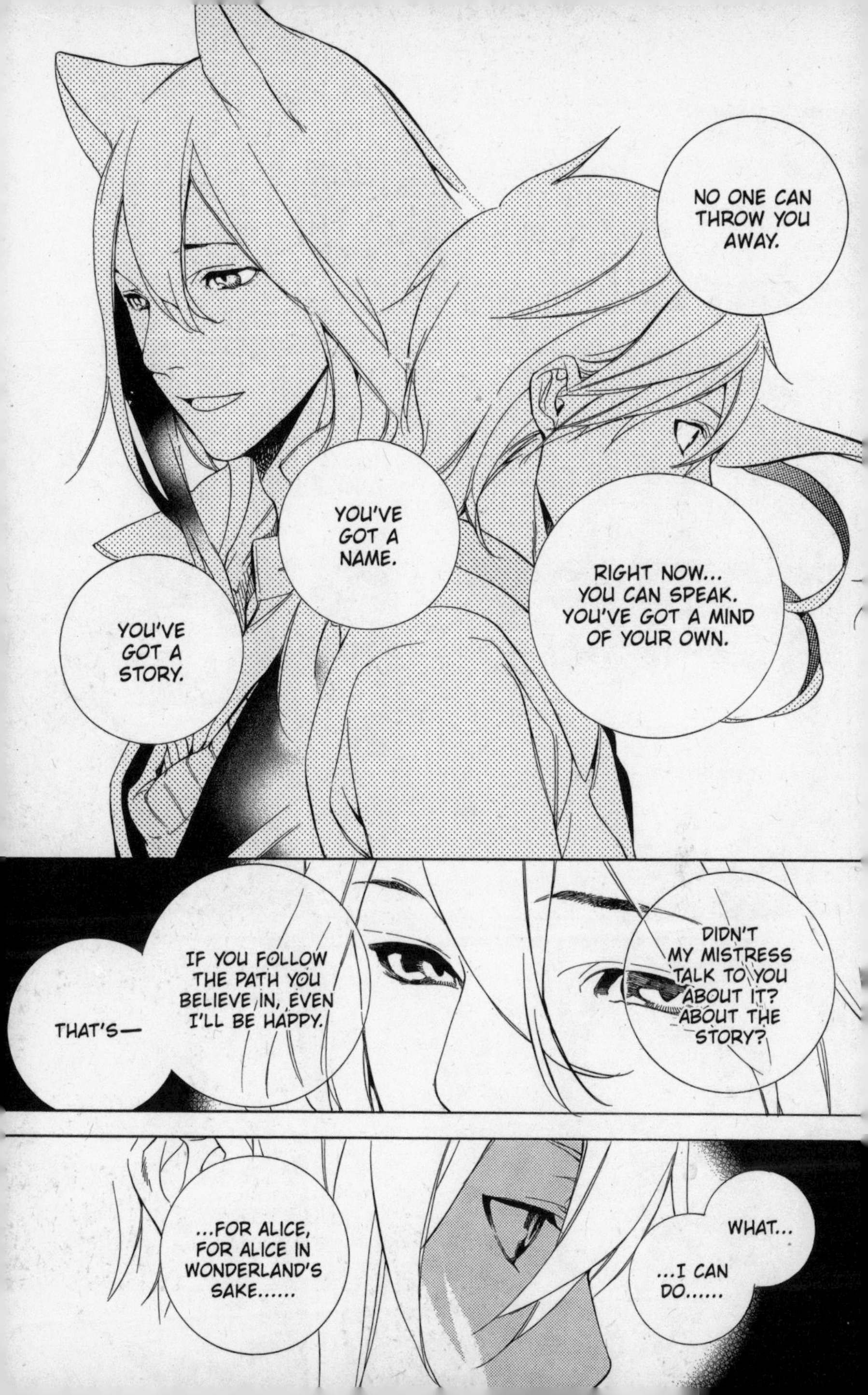
NO ONE CAN THROW YOU AWAY.
RIGHT NOW... YOU CAN SPEAK. YOU'VE GOT A MIND OF YOUR OWN.
YOU'VE GOT A NAME.
YOU'VE GOT A STORY.
DIDN'T MY MISTRESS TALK TO YOU ABOUT IT? ABOUT THE STORY?
IF YOU FOLLOW THE PATH YOU BELIEVE IN, EVEN I'LL BE HAPPY.
THAT'S—
WHAT...
...I CAN DO......
...FOR ALICE, FOR ALICE IN WONDERLAND'S SAKE......

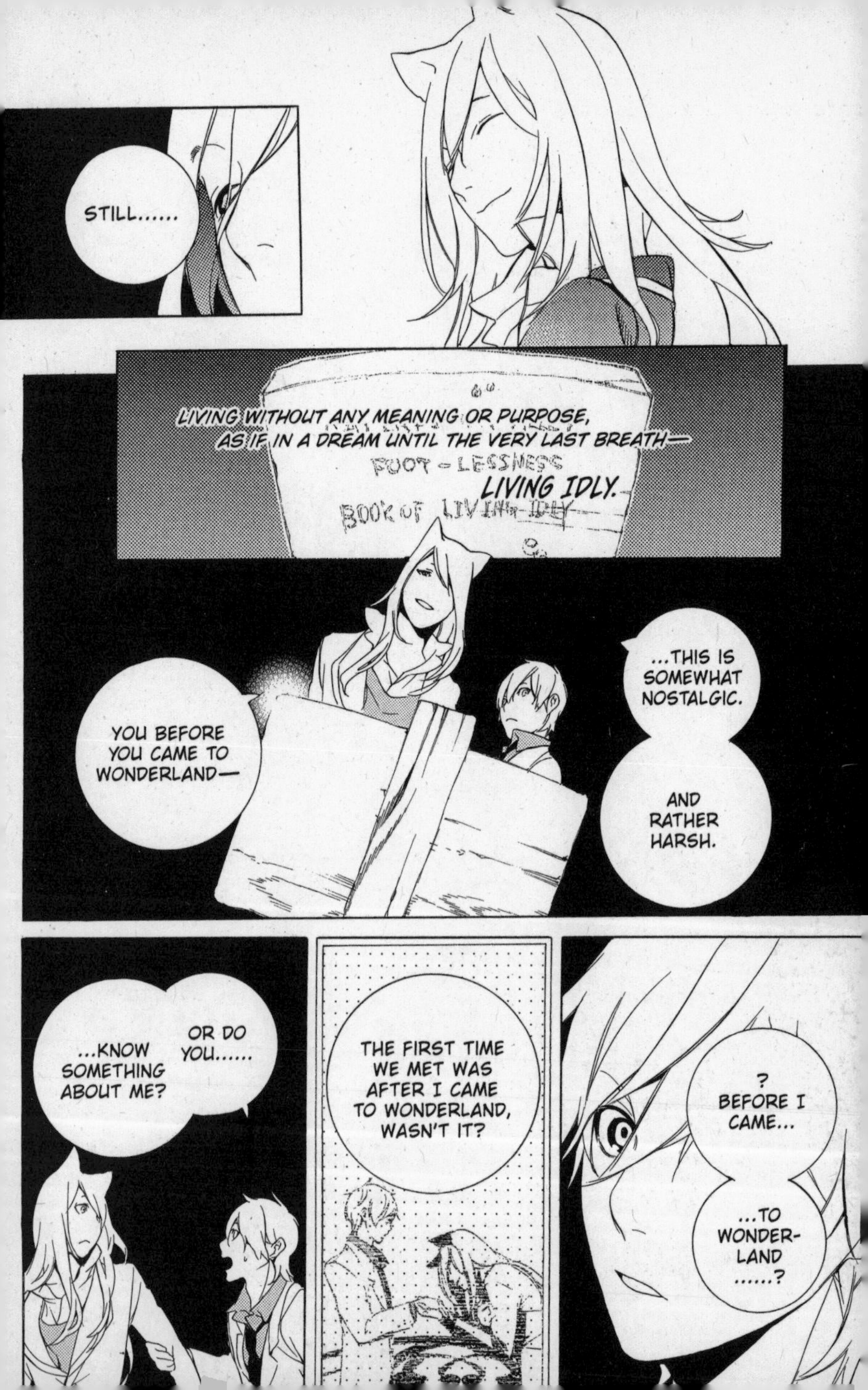
STILL......
LIVING WITHOUT ANY MEANING OR PURPOSE, AS IF IN A DREAM UNTIL THE VERY LAST BREATH—
FOOT-LESSNESS
LIVING IDLY.
BOOK OF LIVING IDLY
...THIS IS SOMEWHAT NOSTALGIC.
AND RATHER HARSH.
YOU BEFORE YOU CAME TO WONDERLAND—
? BEFORE I CAME...
...TO WONDER-LAND ......?
THE FIRST TIME WE MET WAS AFTER I CAME TO WONDERLAND, WASN'T IT?
OR DO YOU......
...KNOW SOMETHING ABOUT ME?

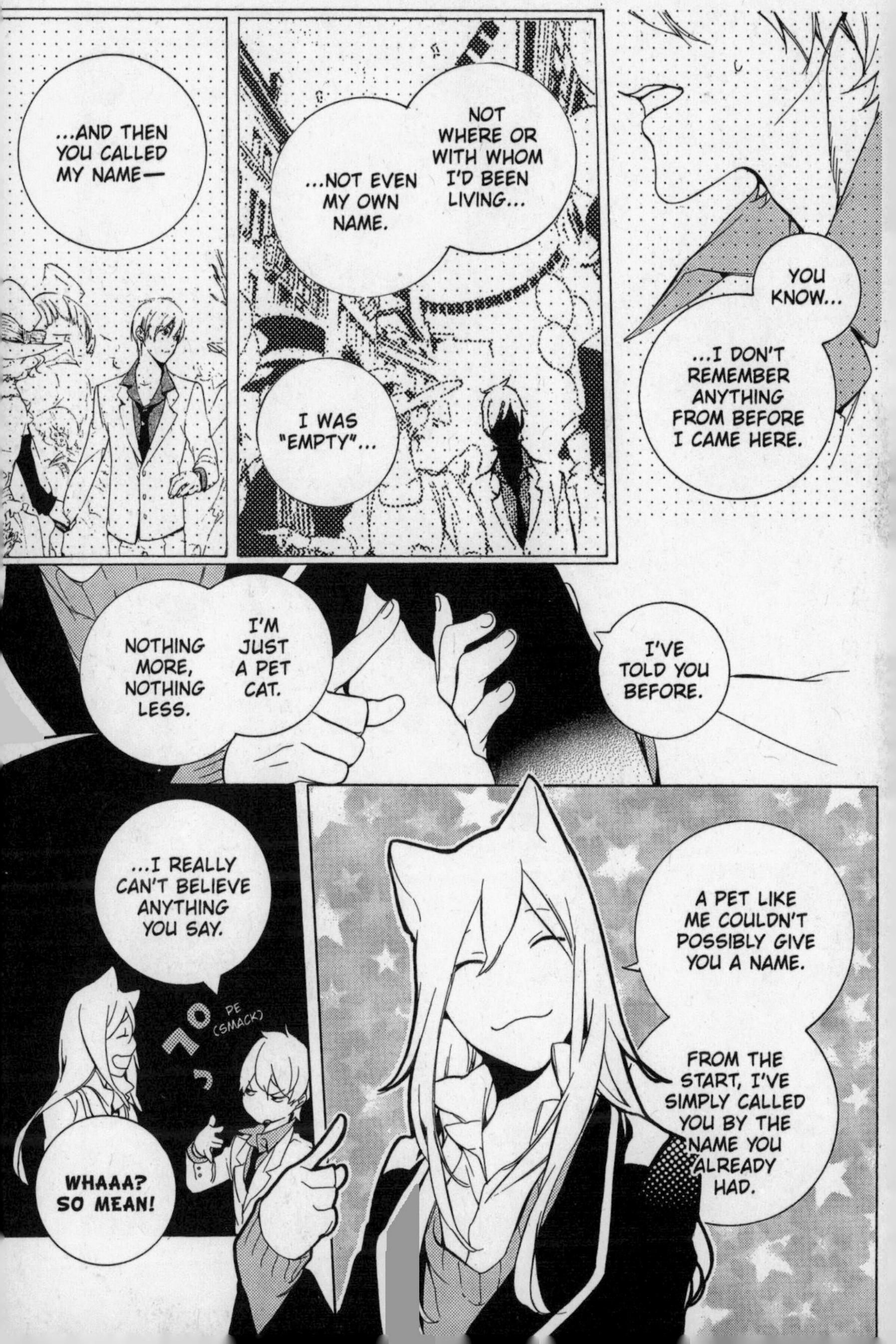
YOU KNOW...
...I DON'T REMEMBER ANYTHING FROM BEFORE I CAME HERE.
NOT WHERE OR WITH WHOM I'D BEEN LIVING...
...NOT EVEN MY OWN NAME.
I WAS "EMPTY"...
...AND THEN YOU CALLED MY NAME—
I'VE TOLD YOU BEFORE.
I'M JUST A PET CAT.
NOTHING MORE, NOTHING LESS.
A PET LIKE ME COULDN'T POSSIBLY GIVE YOU A NAME.
FROM THE START, I'VE SIMPLY CALLED YOU BY THE NAME YOU ALREADY HAD.
...I REALLY CAN'T BELIEVE ANYTHING YOU SAY.
PE
(SMACK)
WHAAA? SO MEAN!

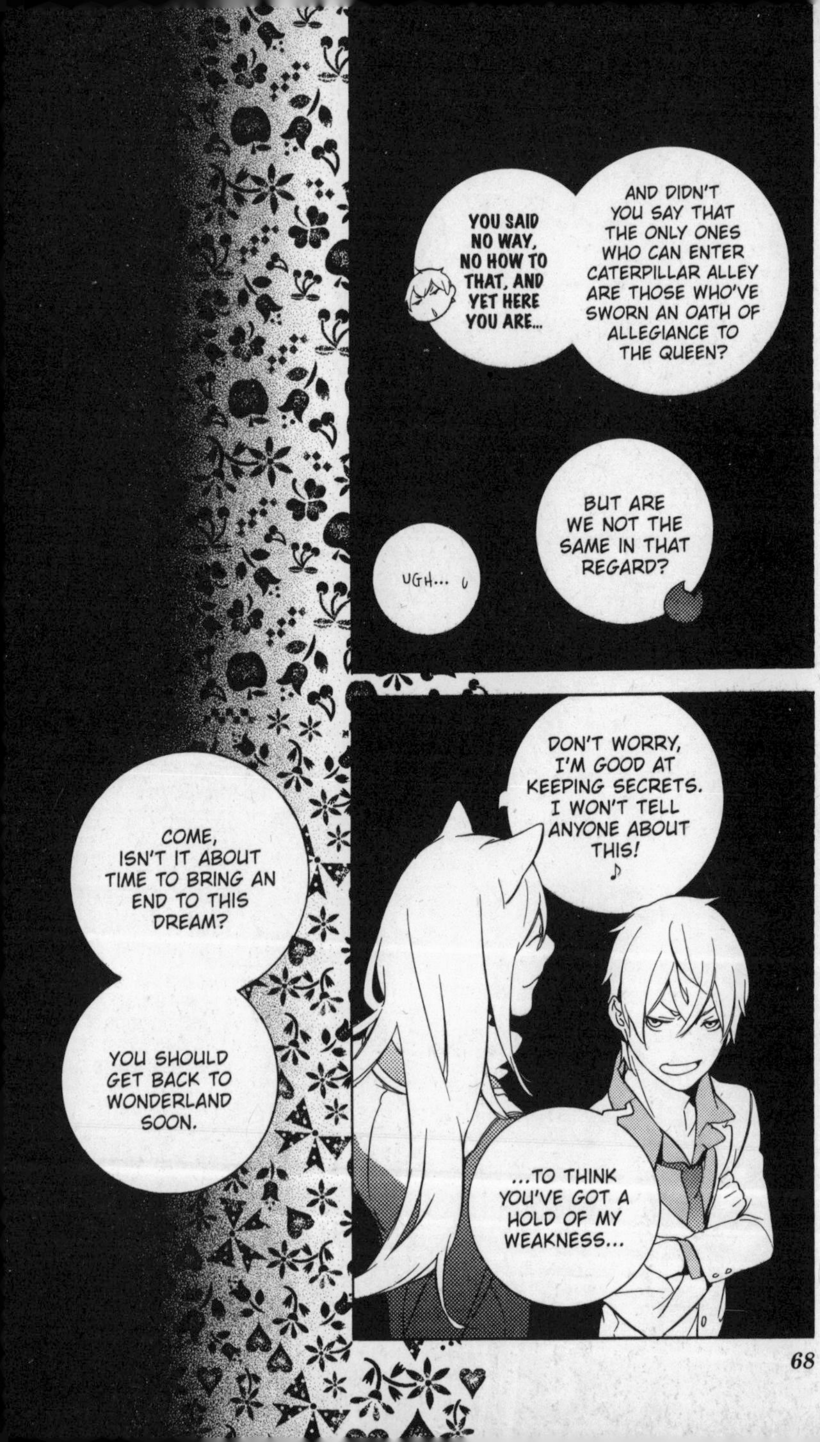
AND DIDN'T YOU SAY THAT THE ONLY ONES WHO CAN ENTER CATERPILLAR ALLEY ARE THOSE WHO'VE SWORN AN OATH OF ALLEGIANCE TO THE QUEEN?
YOU SAID NO WAY, NO HOW TO THAT, AND YET HERE YOU ARE...
BUT ARE WE NOT THE SAME IN THAT REGARD?
UGH...
DON'T WORRY, I'M GOOD AT KEEPING SECRETS. I WON'T TELL ANYONE ABOUT THIS! ♪
...TO THINK YOU'VE GOT A HOLD OF MY WEAKNESS...
COME, ISN'T IT ABOUT TIME TO BRING AN END TO THIS DREAM?
YOU SHOULD GET BACK TO WONDERLAND SOON.

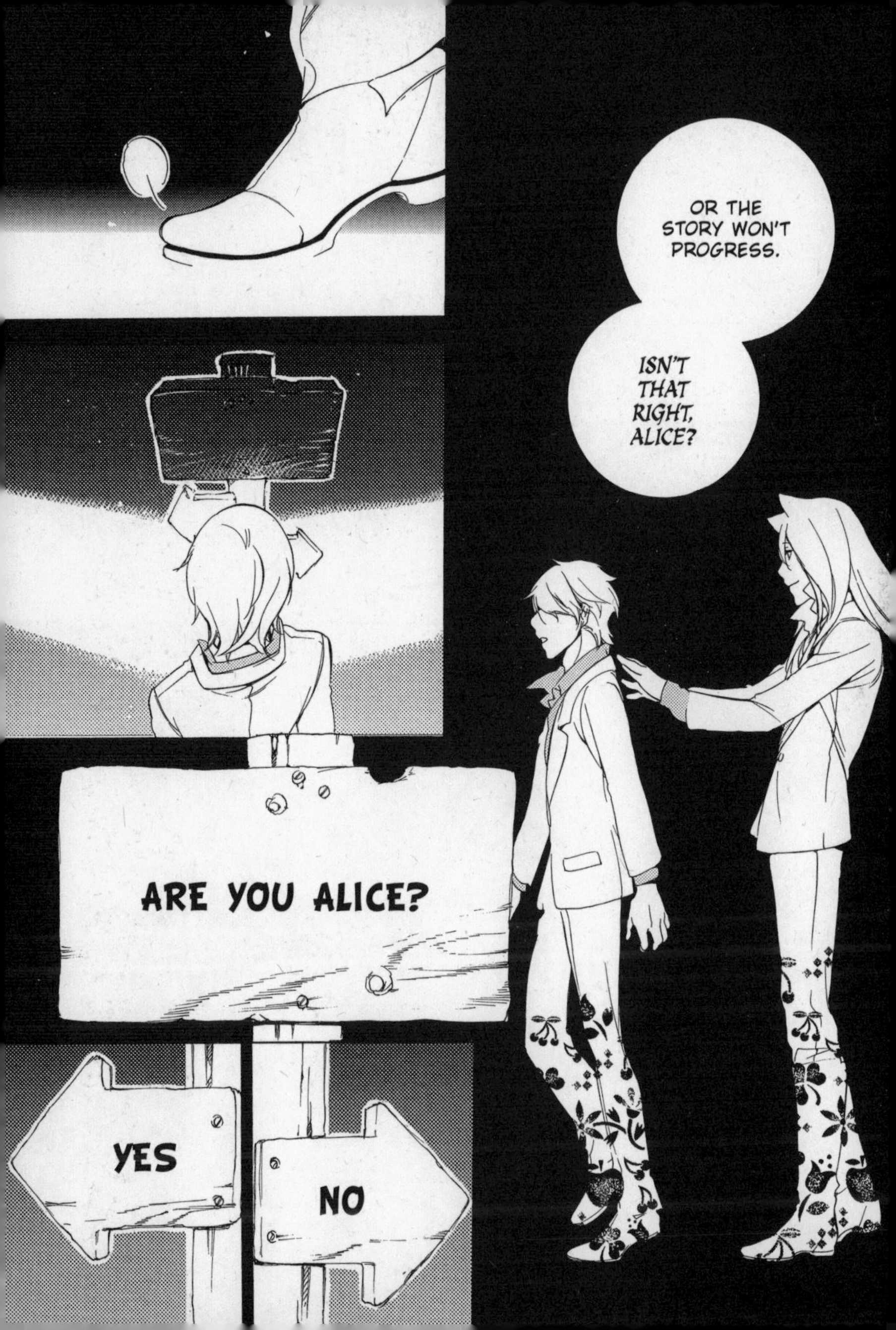
OR THE STORY WON'T PROGRESS.
ISN'T THAT RIGHT, ALICE?
ARE YOU ALICE?
YES
NO

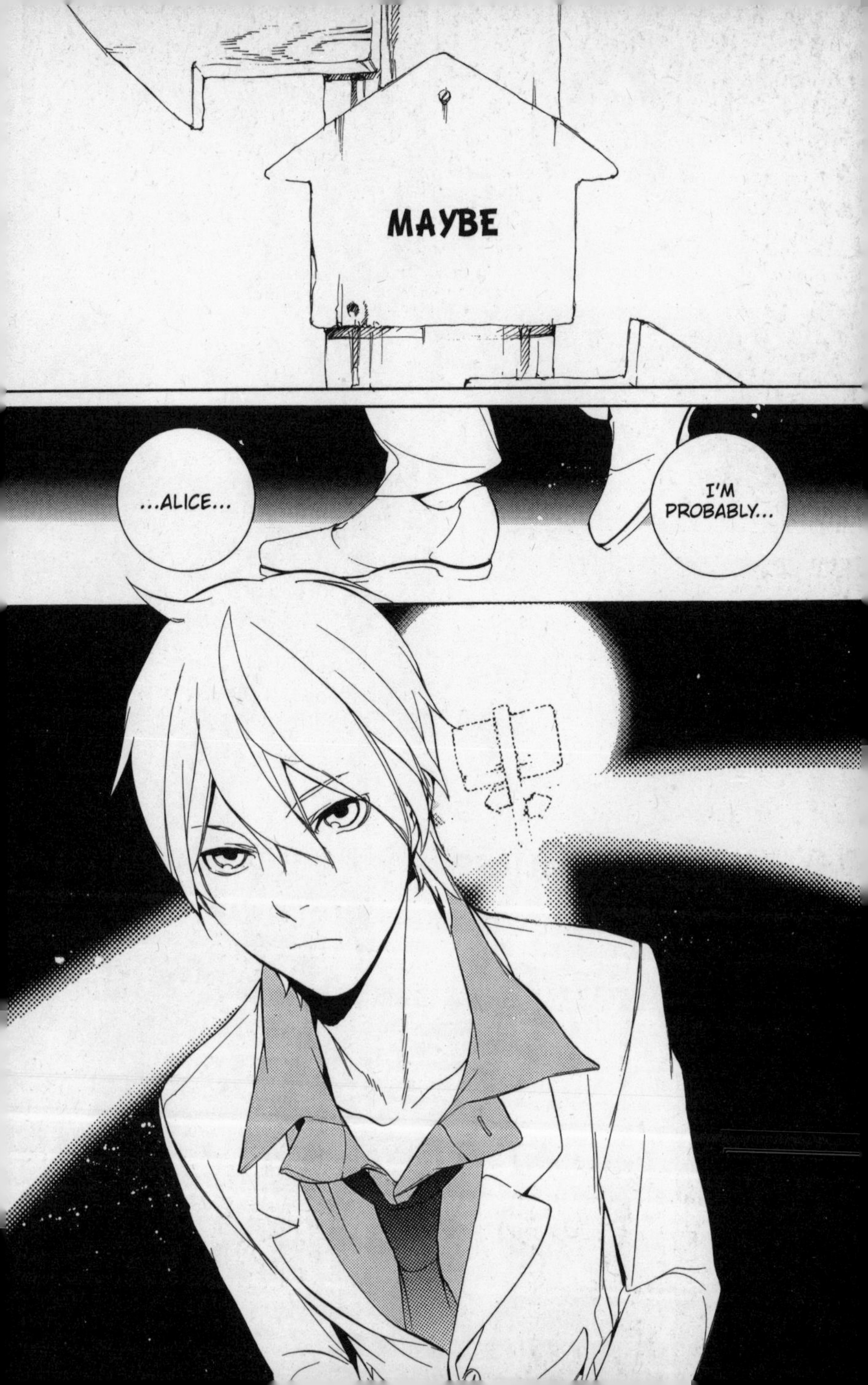
MAYBE
I'M PROBABLY...
...ALICE...

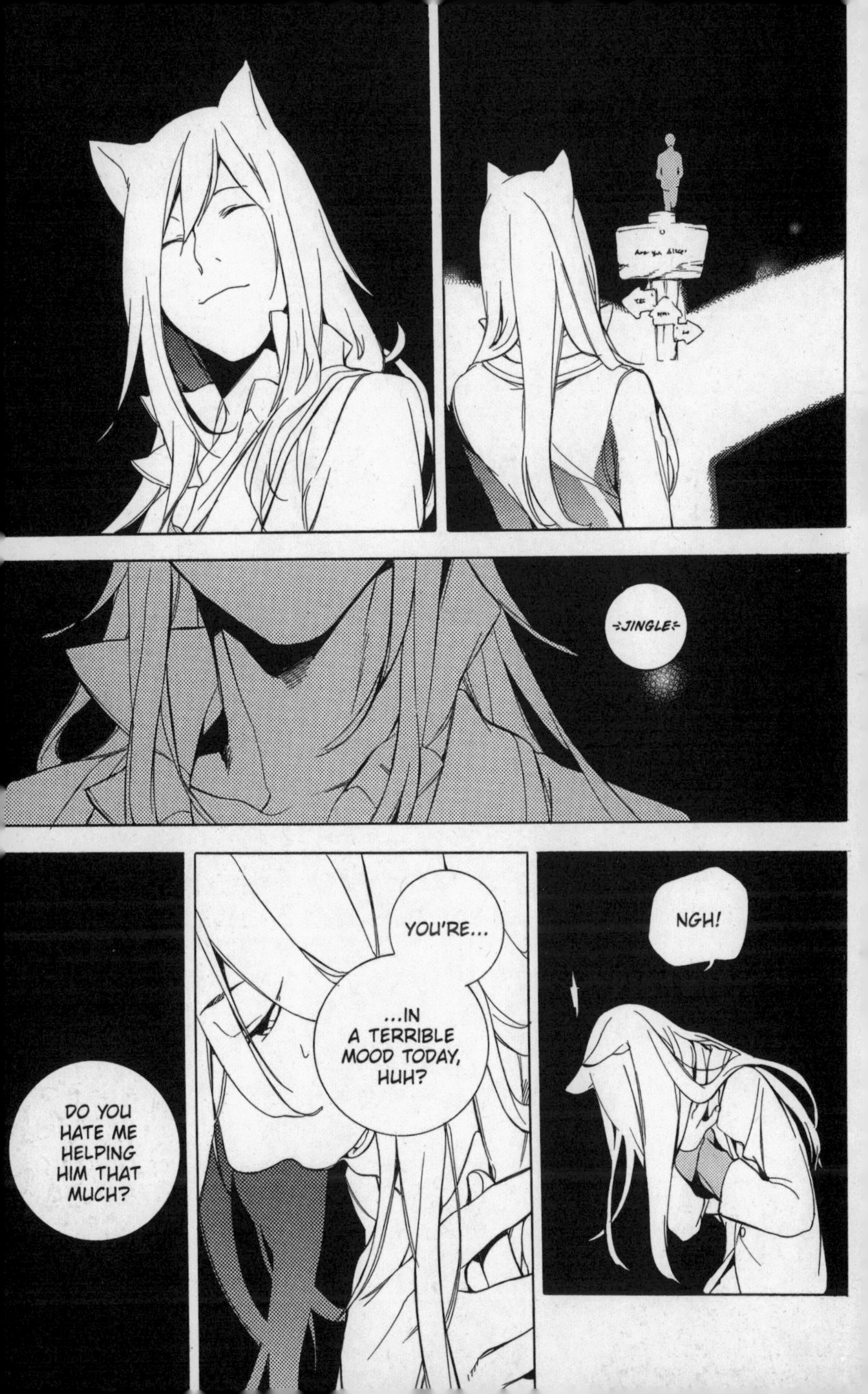
JINGLE
NGH!
YOU'RE...
...IN A TERRIBLE MOOD TODAY, HUH?
DO YOU HATE ME HELPING HIM THAT MUCH?

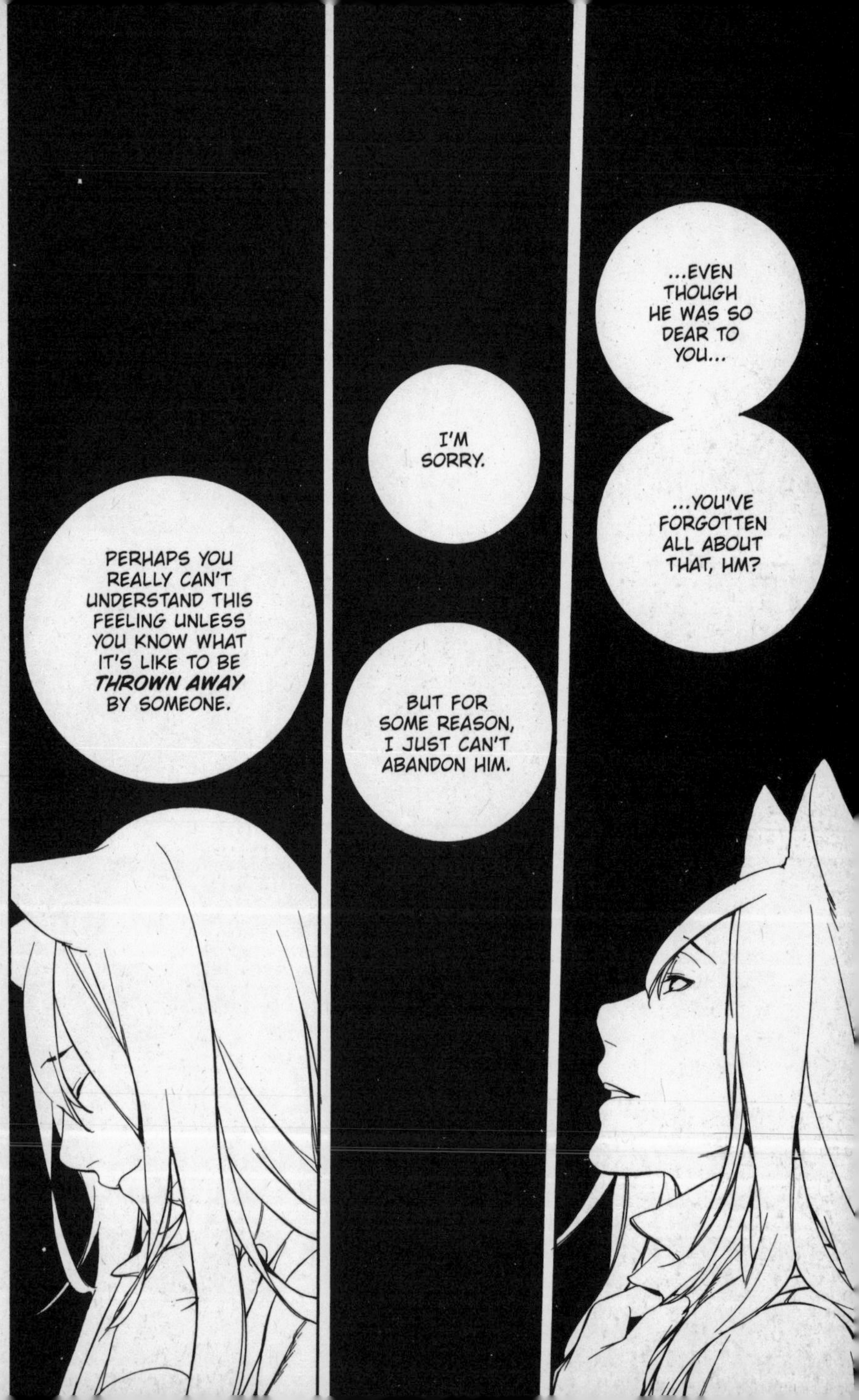
...EVEN THOUGH HE WAS SO DEAR TO YOU...
...YOU'VE FORGOTTEN ALL ABOUT THAT, HM?
I'M SORRY.
BUT FOR SOME REASON, I JUST CAN'T ABANDON HIM.
PERHAPS YOU REALLY CAN'T UNDERSTAND THIS FEELING UNLESS YOU KNOW WHAT IT'S LIKE TO BE ***THROWN AWAY*** BY SOMEONE.

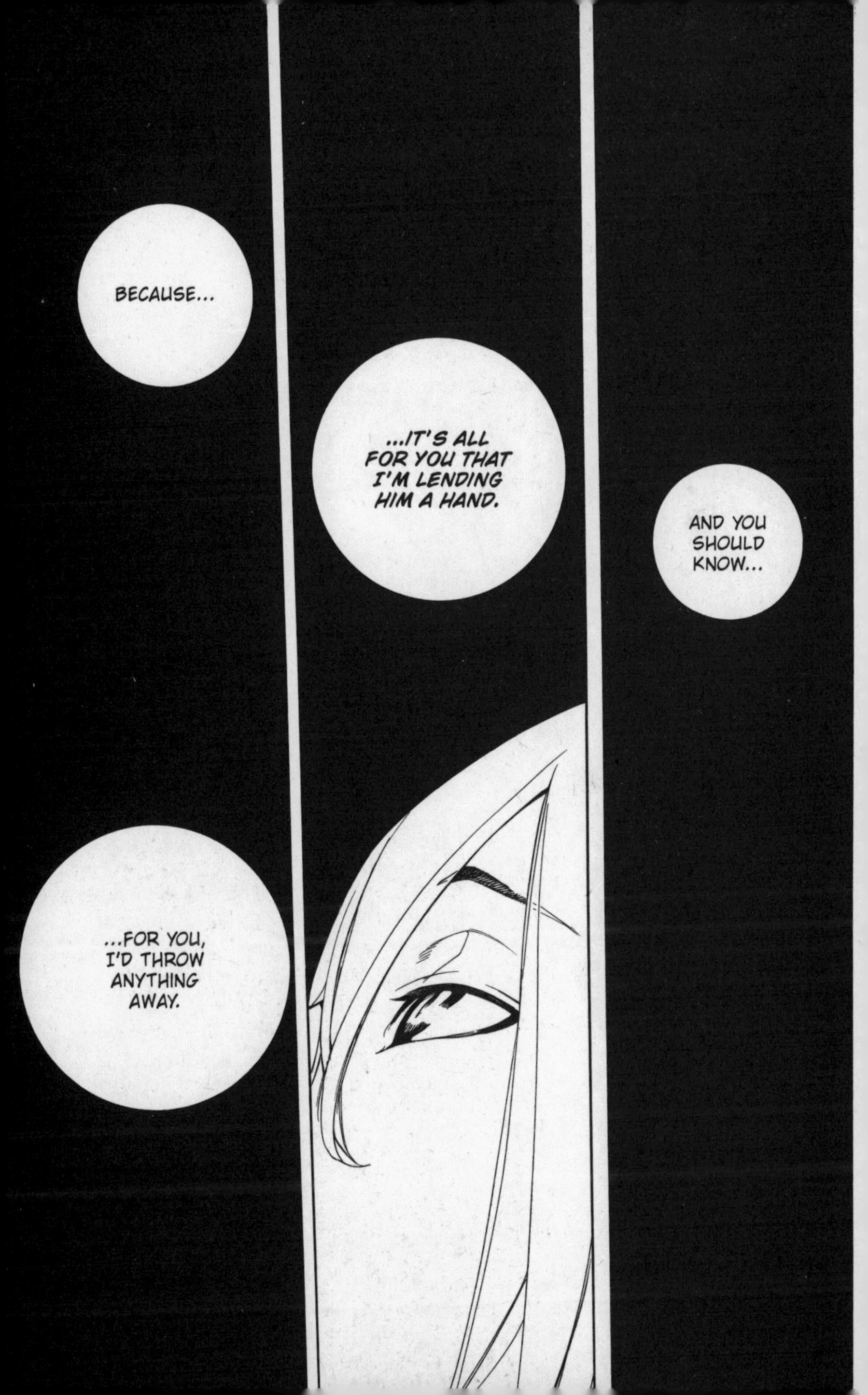
BECAUSE...
...IT'S ALL FOR YOU THAT I'M LENDING HIM A HAND.
AND YOU SHOULD KNOW...
...FOR YOU, I'D THROW ANYTHING AWAY.

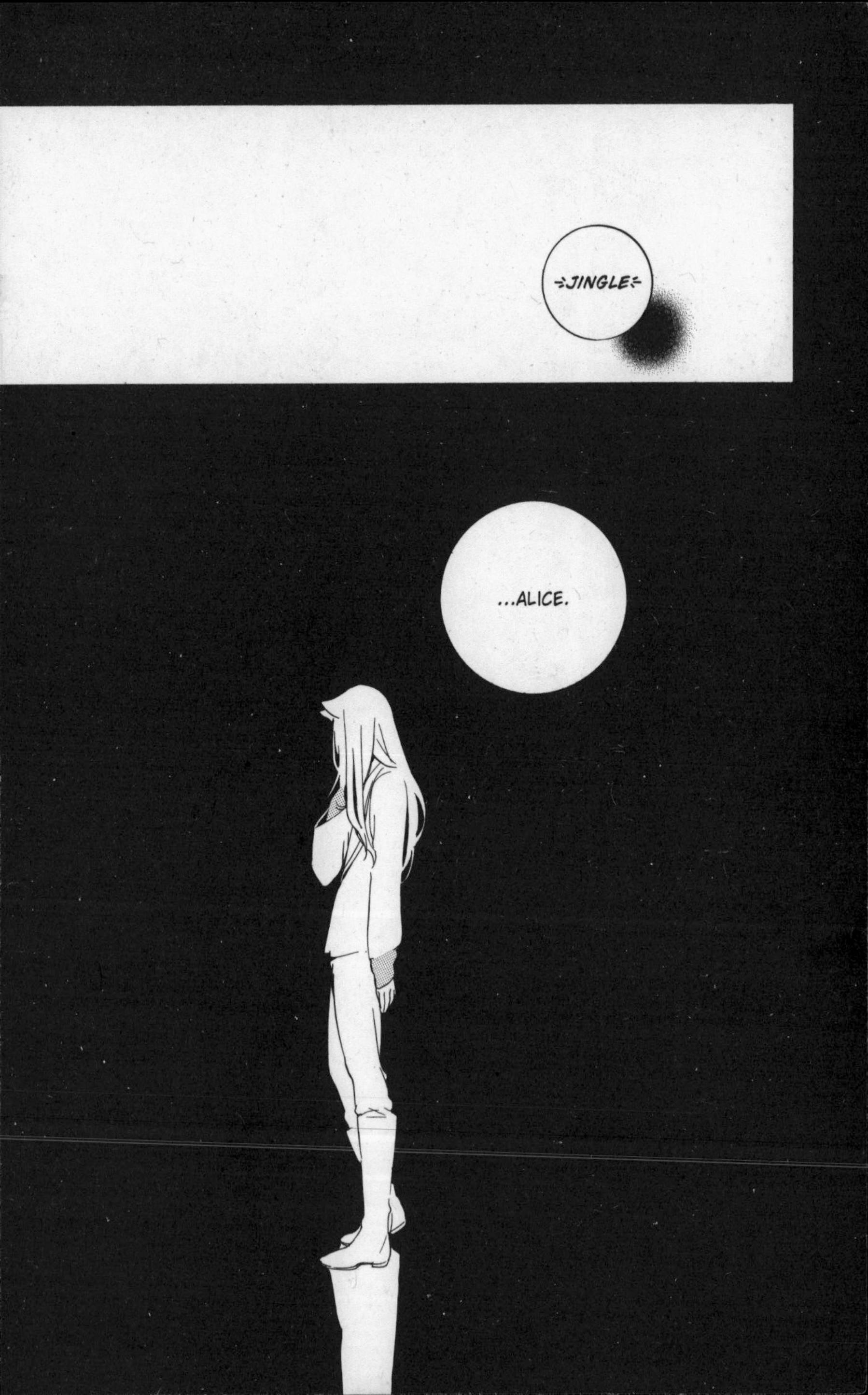
JINGLE
...ALICE.

Chapter 21

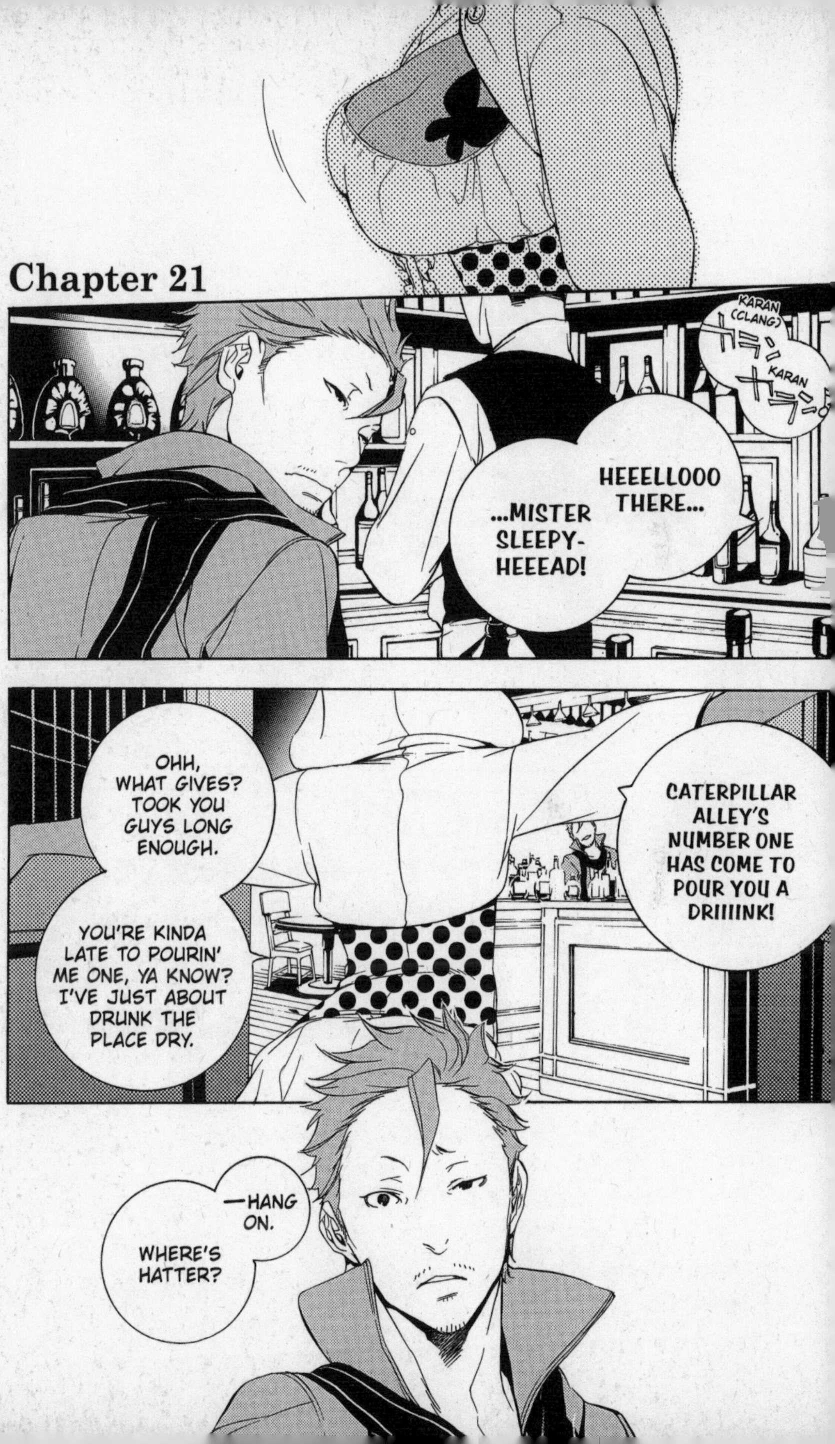
KARAN (CLANG)
KARAN
HEEELLOOO THERE...
...MISTER SLEEPY-HEEEAD!
CATERPILLAR ALLEY'S NUMBER ONE HAS COME TO POUR YOU A DRIIIINK!
OHH, WHAT GIVES? TOOK YOU GUYS LONG ENOUGH.
YOU'RE KINDA LATE TO POURIN' ME ONE, YA KNOW? I'VE JUST ABOUT DRUNK THE PLACE DRY.
—HANG ON.
WHERE'S HATTER?

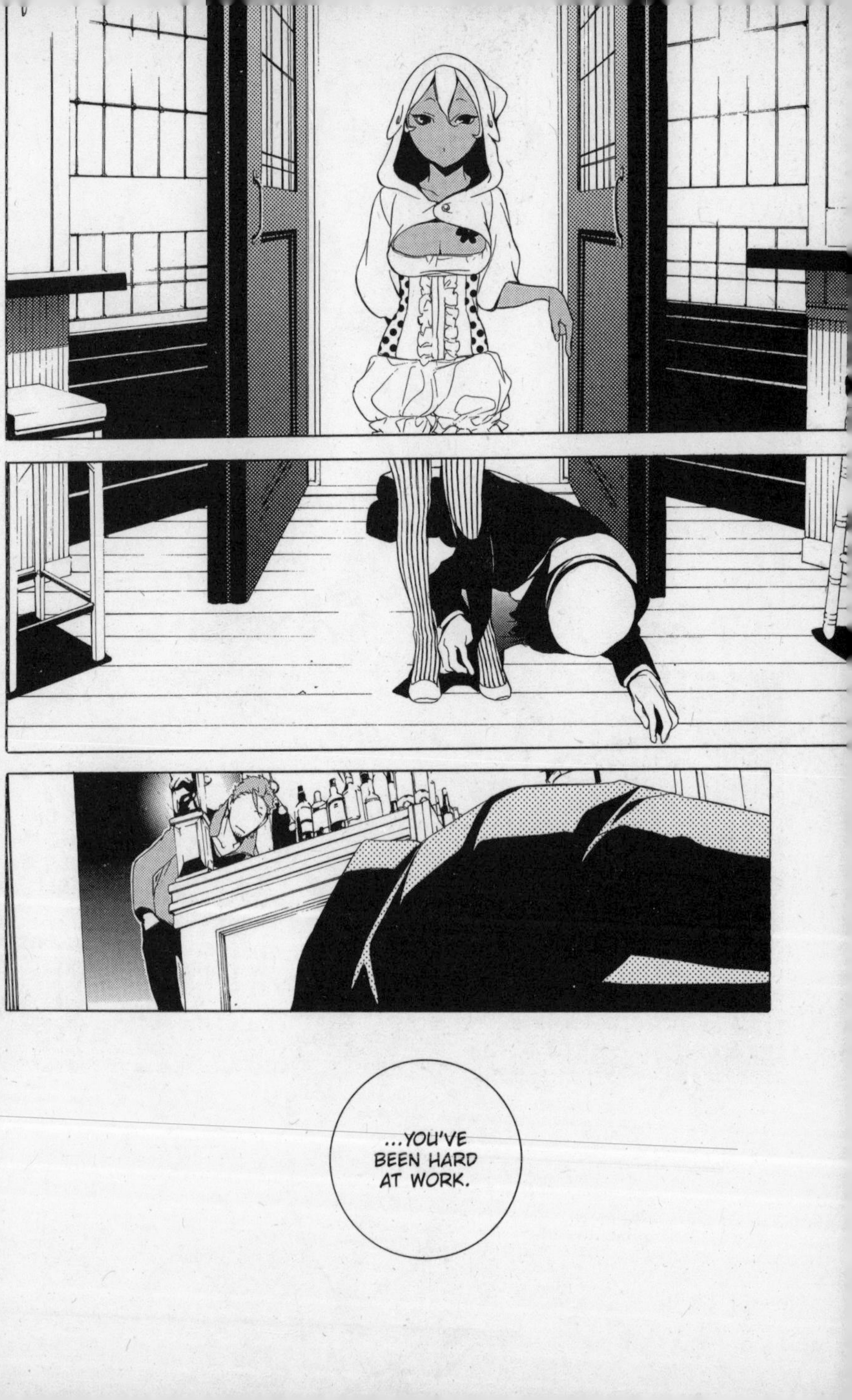

...YOU'VE BEEN HARD AT WORK.

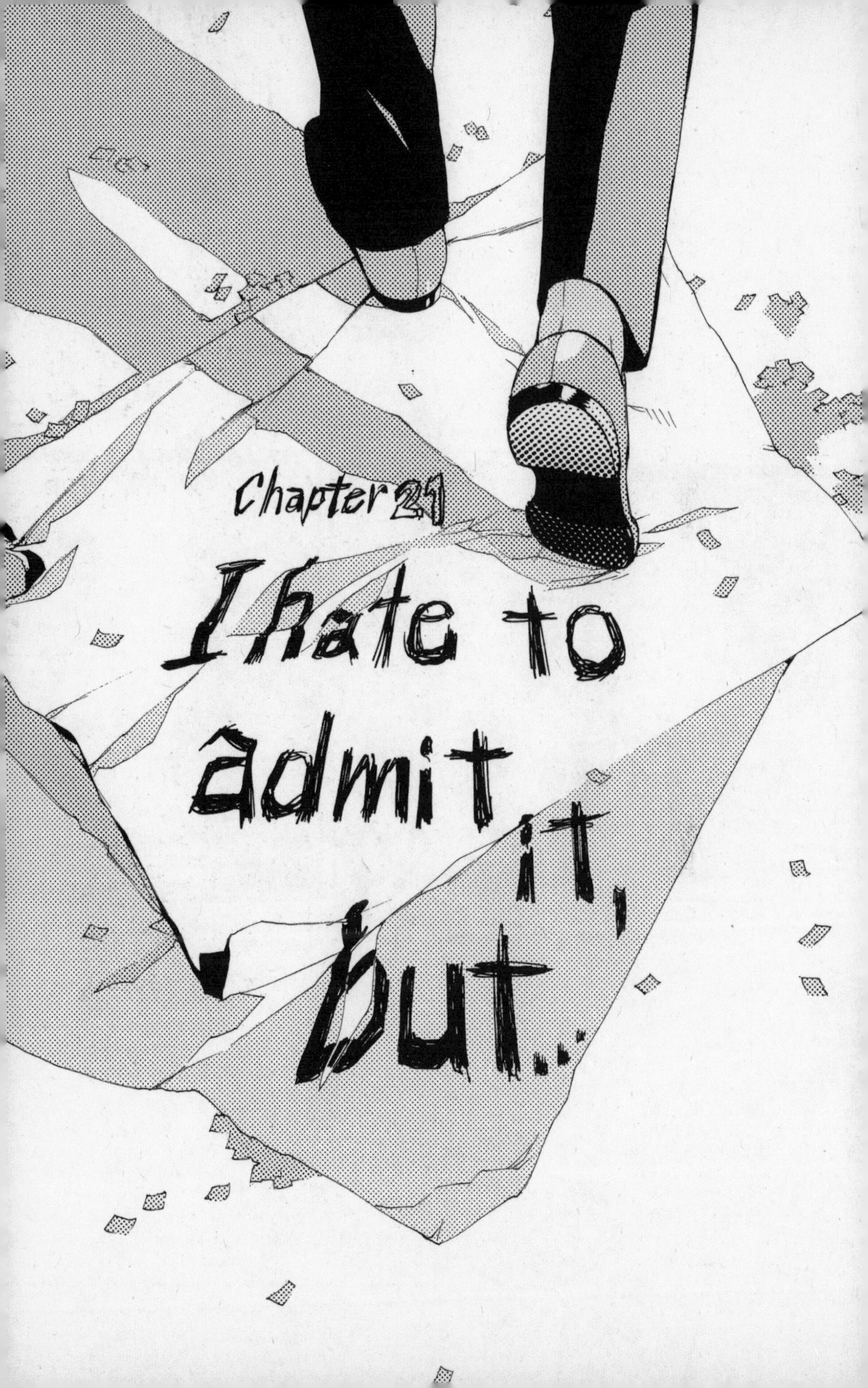
Chapter 21
I hate to admit it, but...

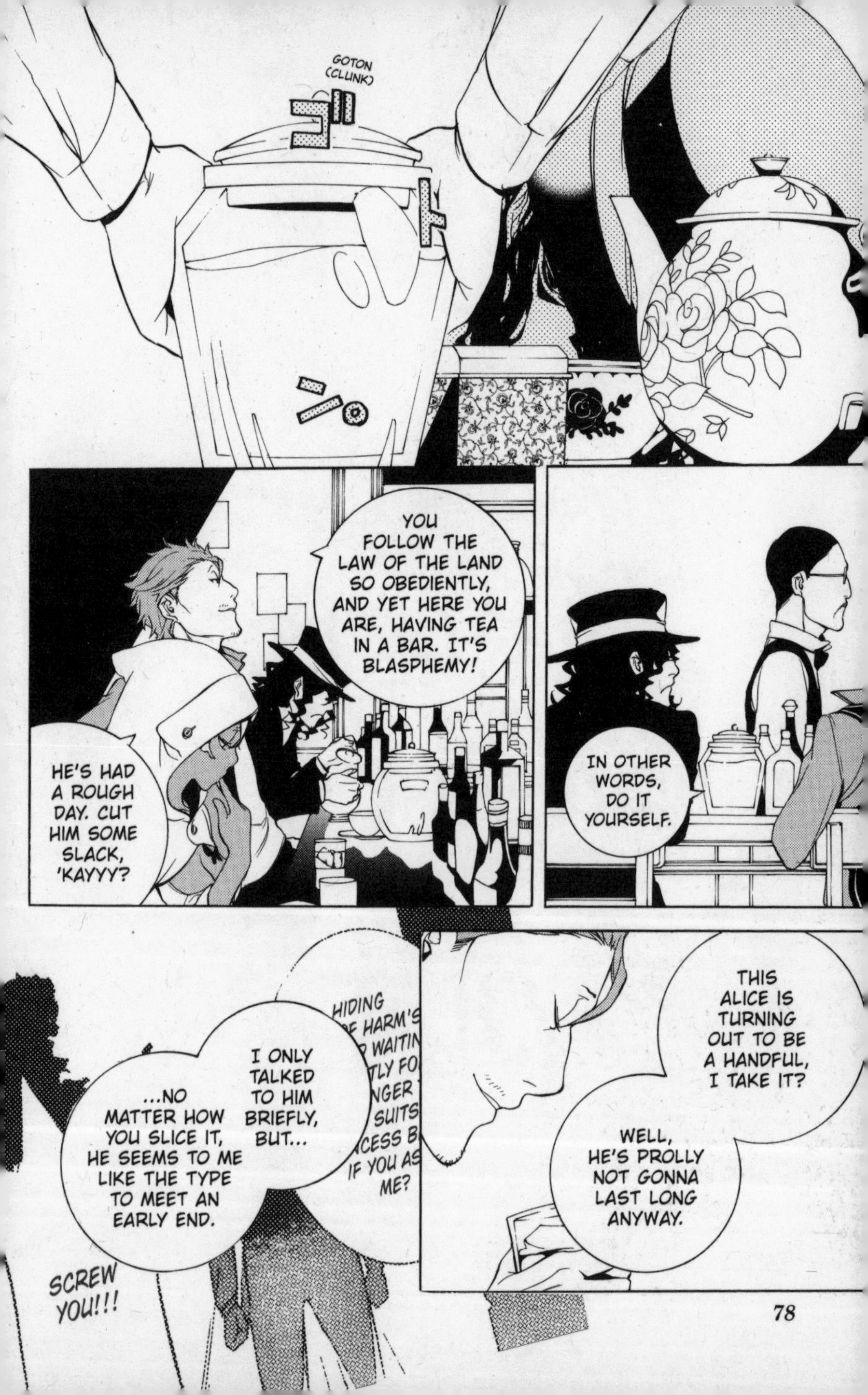
GOTON (CLUNK)
ゴト
IN OTHER WORDS, DO IT YOURSELF.
YOU FOLLOW THE LAW OF THE LAND SO OBEDIENTLY, AND YET HERE YOU ARE, HAVING TEA IN A BAR. IT'S BLASPHEMY!
HE'S HAD A ROUGH DAY. CUT HIM SOME SLACK, 'KAYYY?
THIS ALICE IS TURNING OUT TO BE A HANDFUL, I TAKE IT?
WELL, HE'S PROLLY NOT GONNA LAST LONG ANYWAY.
I ONLY TALKED TO HIM BRIEFLY, BUT...
...NO MATTER HOW YOU SLICE IT, HE SEEMS TO ME LIKE THE TYPE TO MEET AN EARLY END.
SCREW YOU!!!

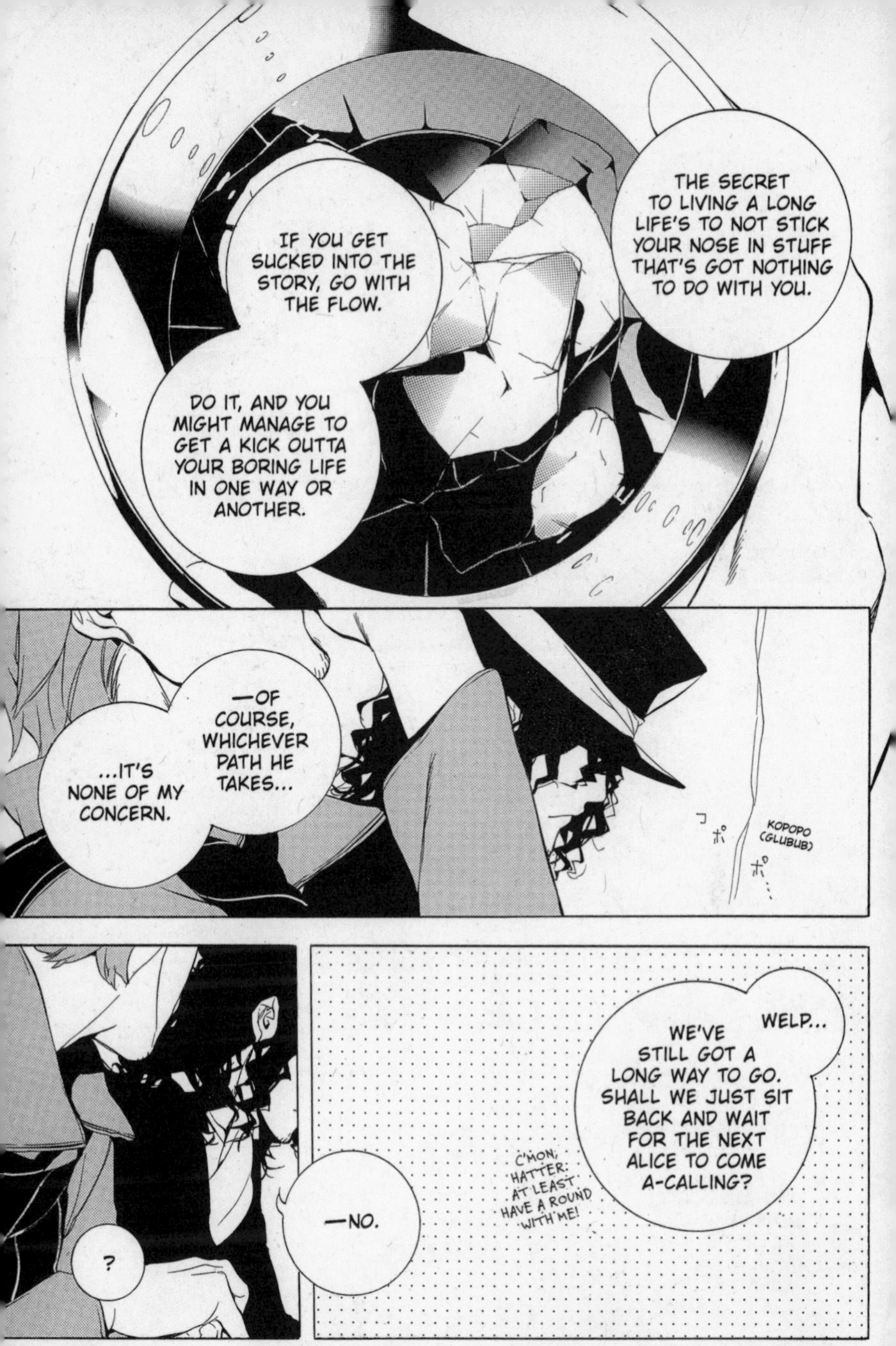
THE SECRET TO LIVING A LONG LIFE'S TO NOT STICK YOUR NOSE IN STUFF THAT'S GOT NOTHING TO DO WITH YOU.
IF YOU GET SUCKED INTO THE STORY, GO WITH THE FLOW.
DO IT, AND YOU MIGHT MANAGE TO GET A KICK OUTTA YOUR BORING LIFE IN ONE WAY OR ANOTHER.
—OF COURSE, WHICHEVER PATH HE TAKES...
...IT'S NONE OF MY CONCERN.
コポポ…
KOPOPO (GLUBUB)
WELP...
WE'VE STILL GOT A LONG WAY TO GO. SHALL WE JUST SIT BACK AND WAIT FOR THE NEXT ALICE TO COME A-CALLING?
C'MON, HATTER! AT LEAST HAVE A ROUND WITH ME!
—NO.
?

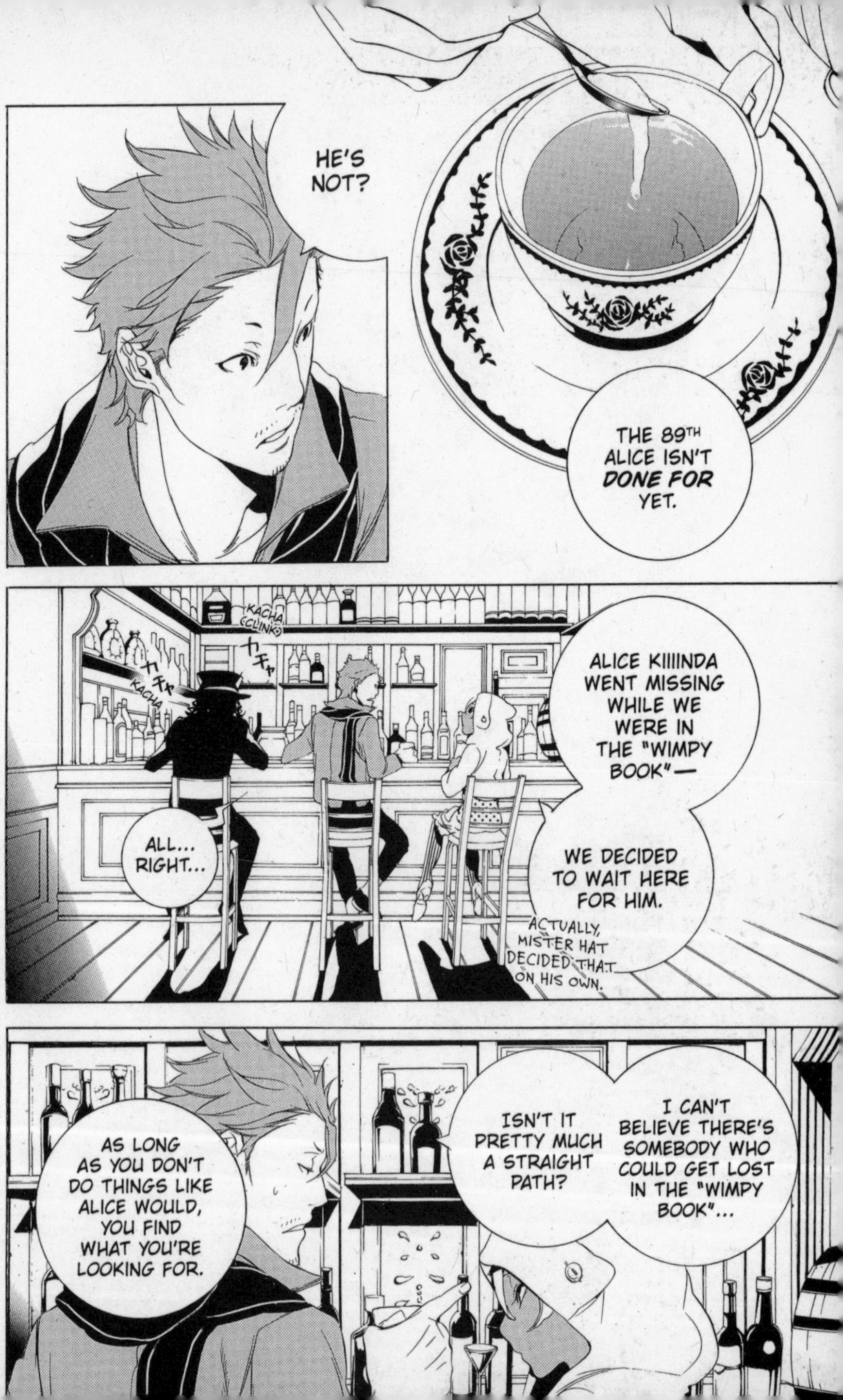
THE 89TH ALICE ISN'T DONE FOR YET.
HE'S NOT?
ALICE KIIIINDA WENT MISSING WHILE WE WERE IN THE "WIMPY BOOK"—
WE DECIDED TO WAIT HERE FOR HIM.
ACTUALLY, MISTER HAT DECIDED THAT ON HIS OWN.
KACHA (CLINK)
カチャ
カチャ
KACHA
ALL... RIGHT...
I CAN'T BELIEVE THERE'S SOMEBODY WHO COULD GET LOST IN THE "WIMPY BOOK"...
ISN'T IT PRETTY MUCH A STRAIGHT PATH?
AS LONG AS YOU DON'T DO THINGS LIKE ALICE WOULD, YOU FIND WHAT YOU'RE LOOKING FOR.

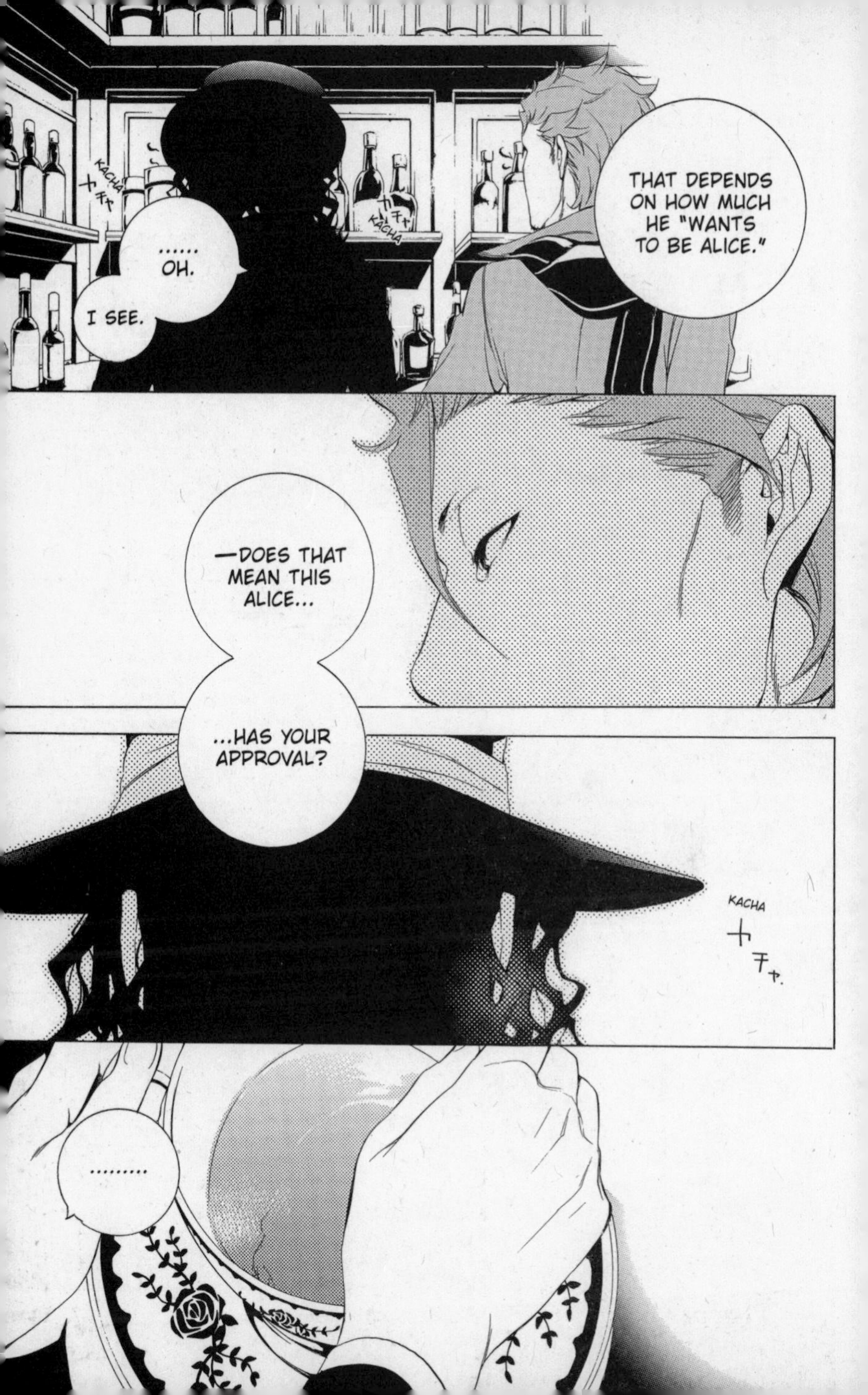
THAT DEPENDS ON HOW MUCH HE "WANTS TO BE ALICE."
KACHA
KACHA
...... OH.
I SEE.
—DOES THAT MEAN THIS ALICE...
...HAS YOUR APPROVAL?
KACHA
....

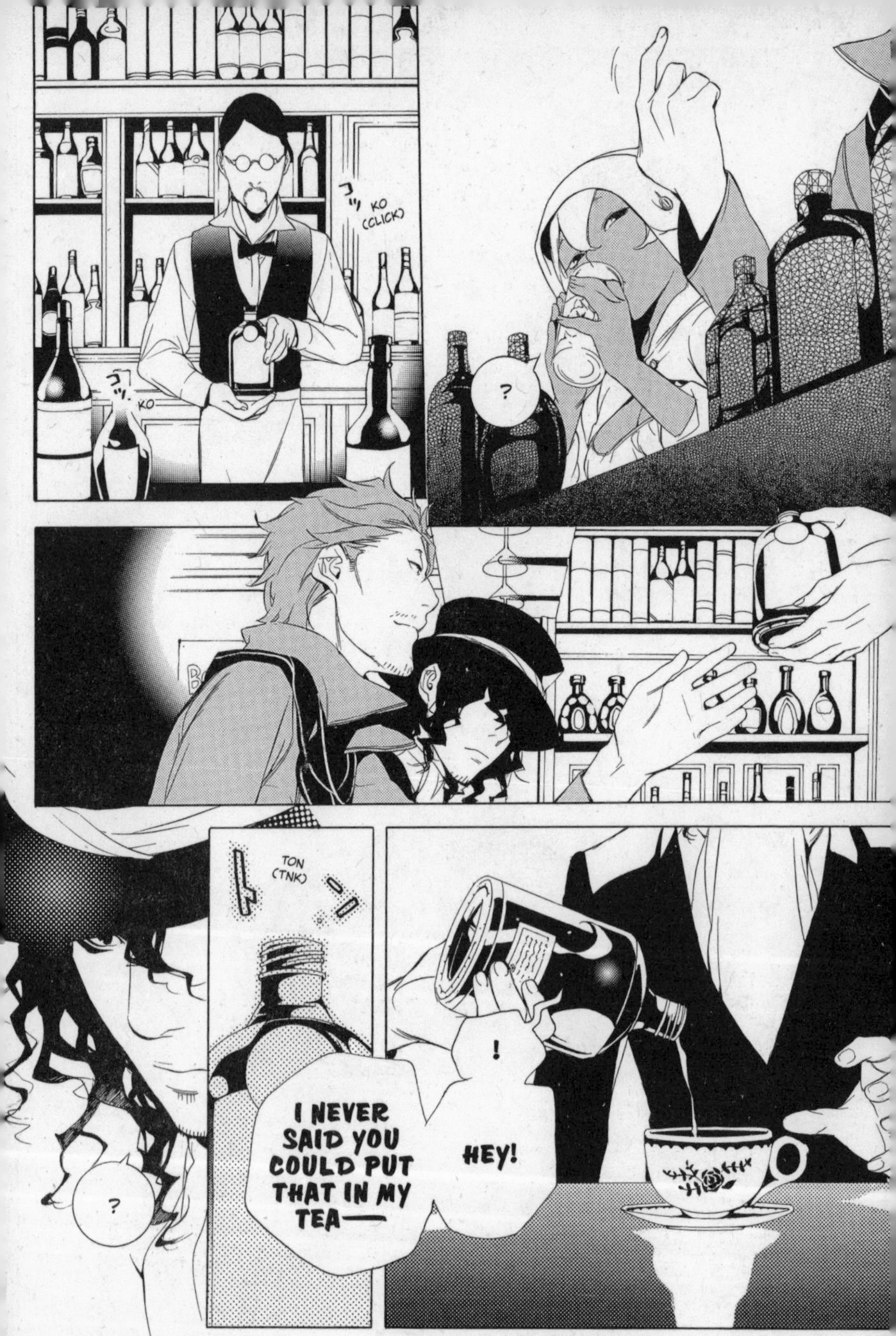
?
ゴッ
KO
(CLICK)
ゴッ
KO
!
HEY!
I NEVER SAID YOU COULD PUT THAT IN MY TEA—
TON
(TNK)
?

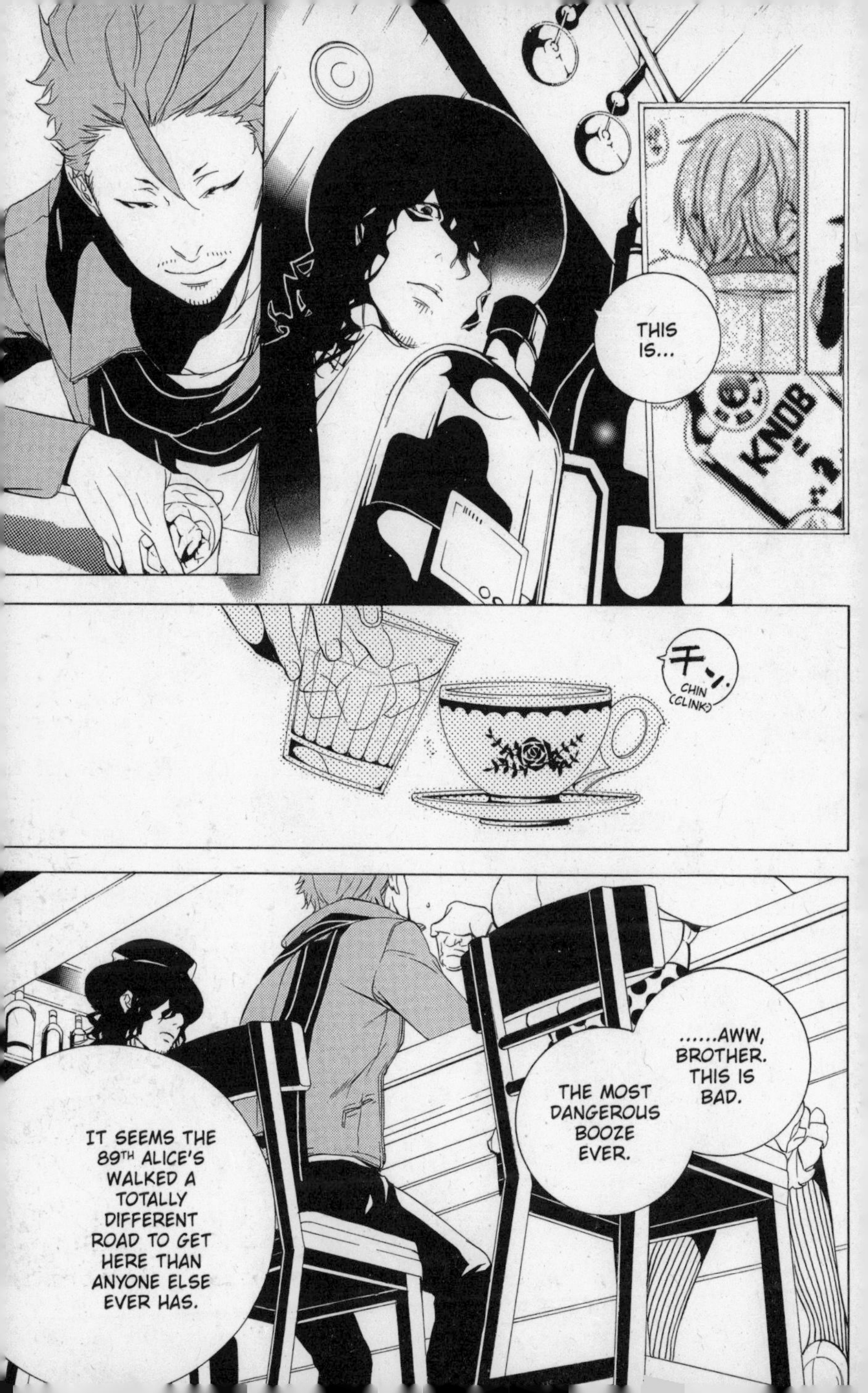
THIS IS...
KNOB
チン
CHIN (CLINK)
......AWW, BROTHER. THIS IS BAD.
THE MOST DANGEROUS BOOZE EVER.
IT SEEMS THE 89TH ALICE'S WALKED A TOTALLY DIFFERENT ROAD TO GET HERE THAN ANYONE ELSE EVER HAS.

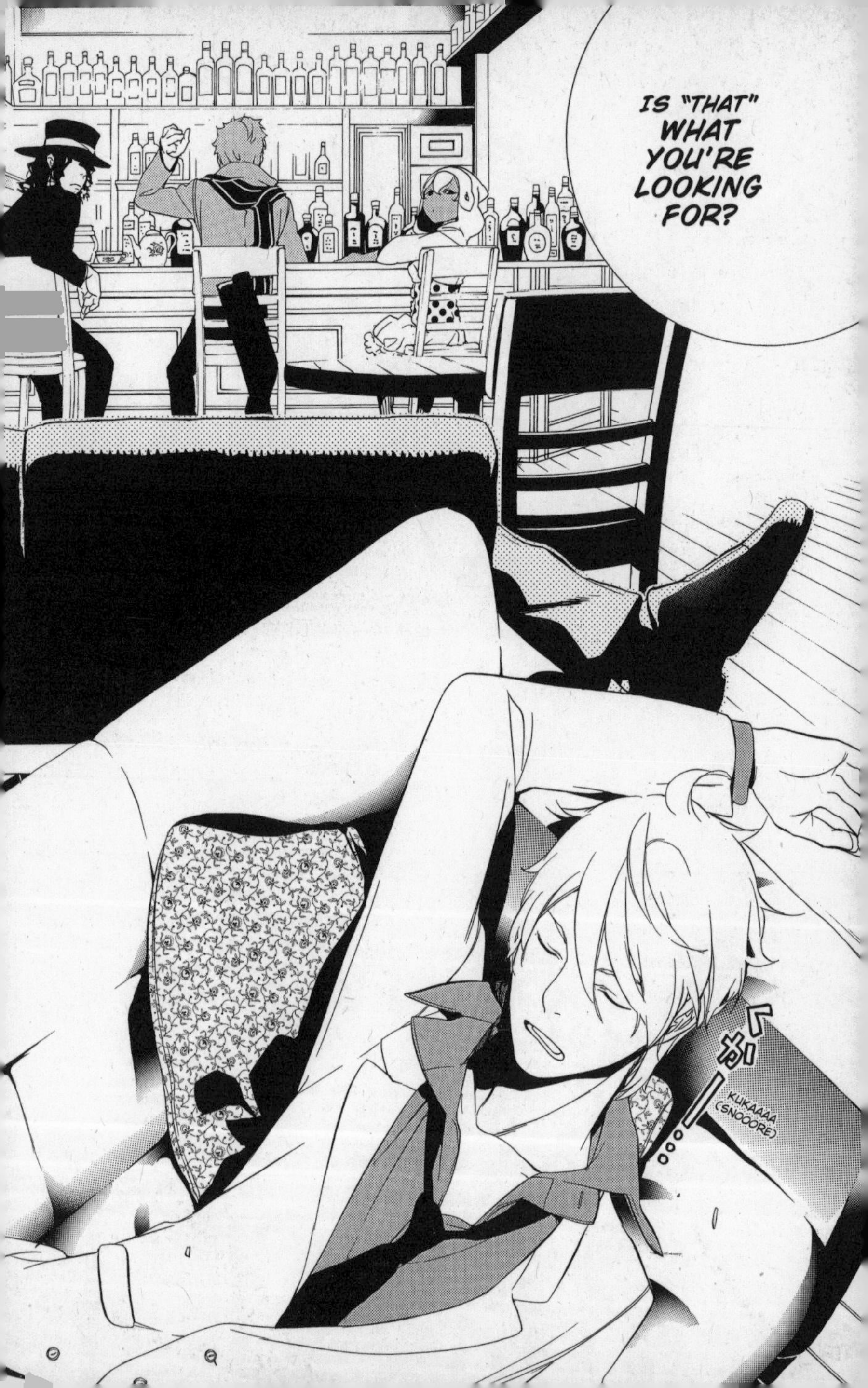
IS "THAT" WHAT YOU'RE LOOKING FOR?
くか～…
KUKAAAA (SNOOORE)

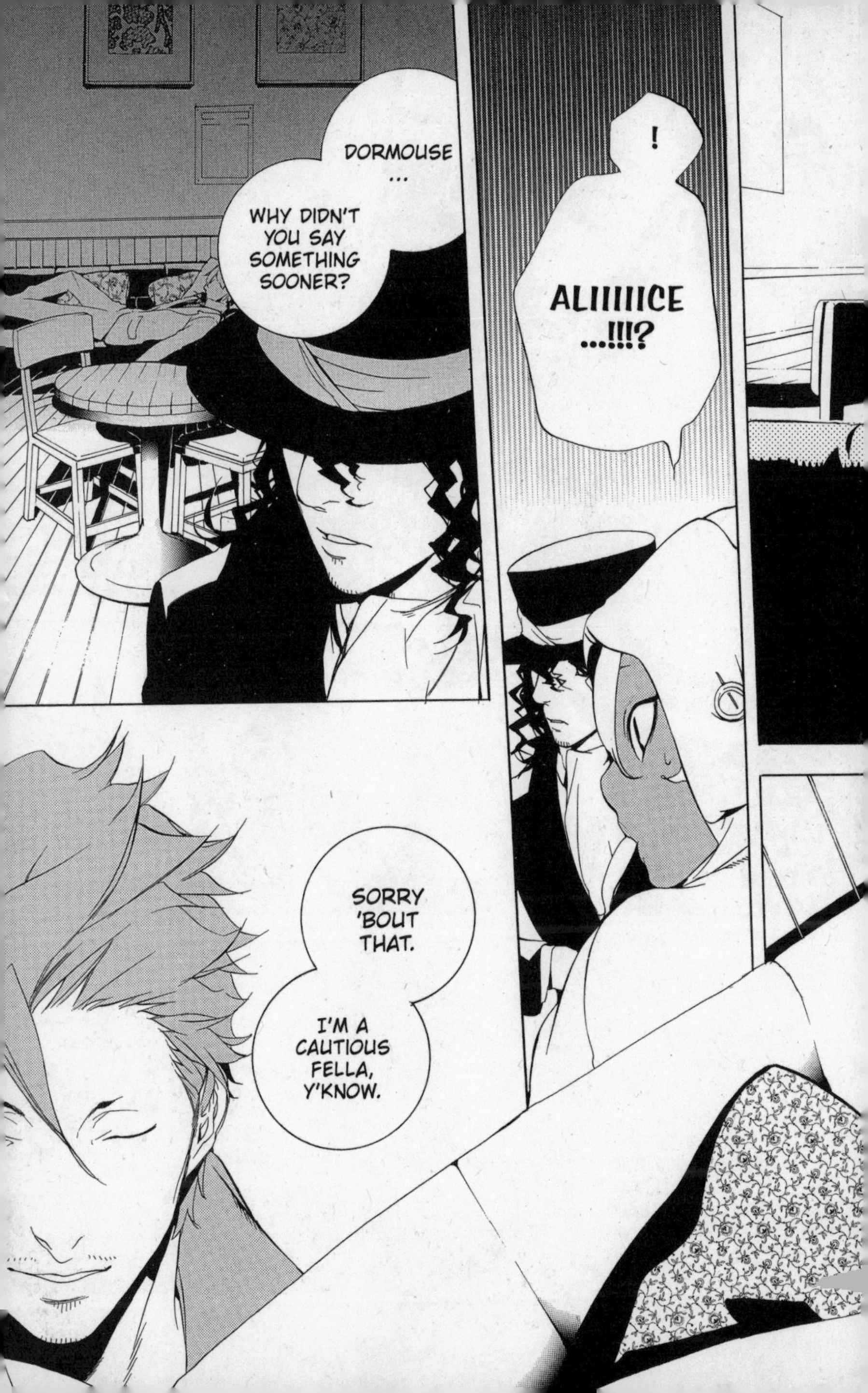
!
ALIIIIICE ...!!!?
DORMOUSE ...
WHY DIDN'T YOU SAY SOMETHING SOONER?
SORRY 'BOUT THAT.
I'M A CAUTIOUS FELLA, Y'KNOW.

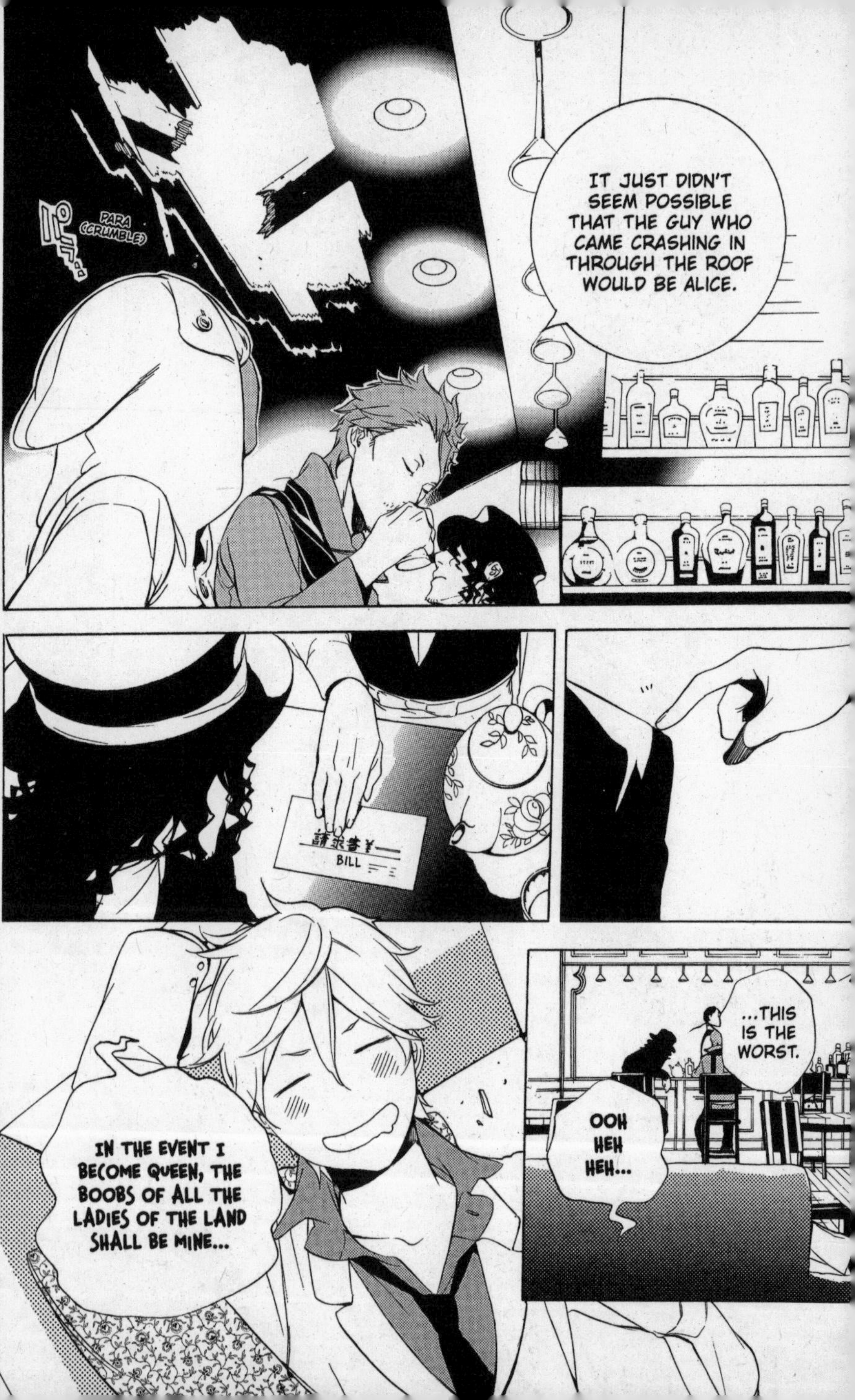
IT JUST DIDN'T SEEM POSSIBLE THAT THE GUY WHO CAME CRASHING IN THROUGH THE ROOF WOULD BE ALICE.
PARA (CRUMBLE)
請求書 ¥
BILL
...THIS IS THE WORST.
OOH HEH HEH...
IN THE EVENT I BECOME QUEEN, THE BOOBS OF ALL THE LADIES OF THE LAND SHALL BE MINE...

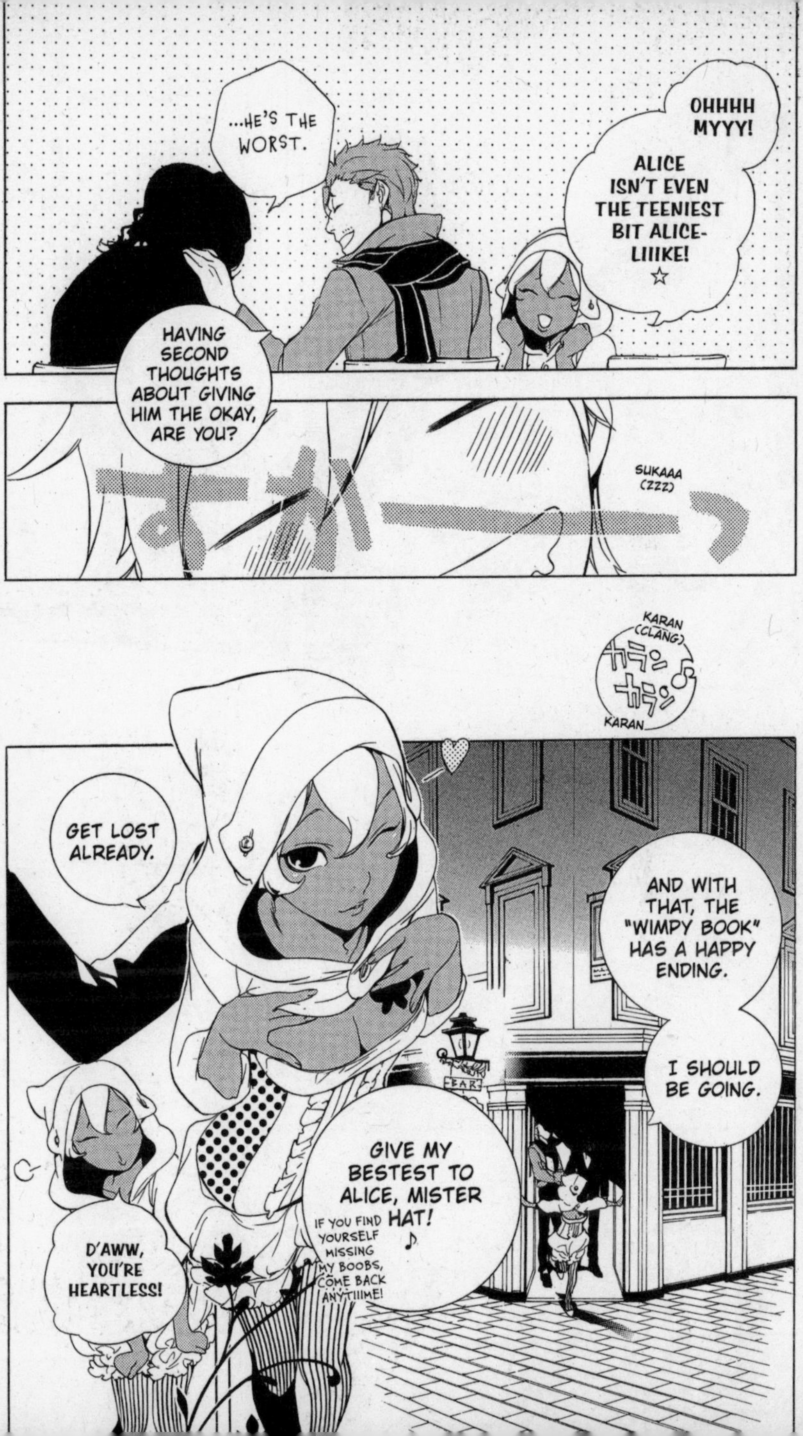
OHHHH MYYY!
ALICE ISN'T EVEN THE TEENIEST BIT ALICE-LIIIKE! ☆
...HE'S THE WORST.
HAVING SECOND THOUGHTS ABOUT GIVING HIM THE OKAY, ARE YOU?
SUKAAA (ZZZ)
KARAN (CLANG) KARAN
AND WITH THAT, THE "WIMPY BOOK" HAS A HAPPY ENDING.
I SHOULD BE GOING.
GET LOST ALREADY.
GIVE MY BESTEST TO ALICE, MISTER HAT! ♪
IF YOU FIND YOURSELF MISSING MY BOOBS, COME BACK ANYTIIIME!
D'AWW, YOU'RE HEARTLESS!

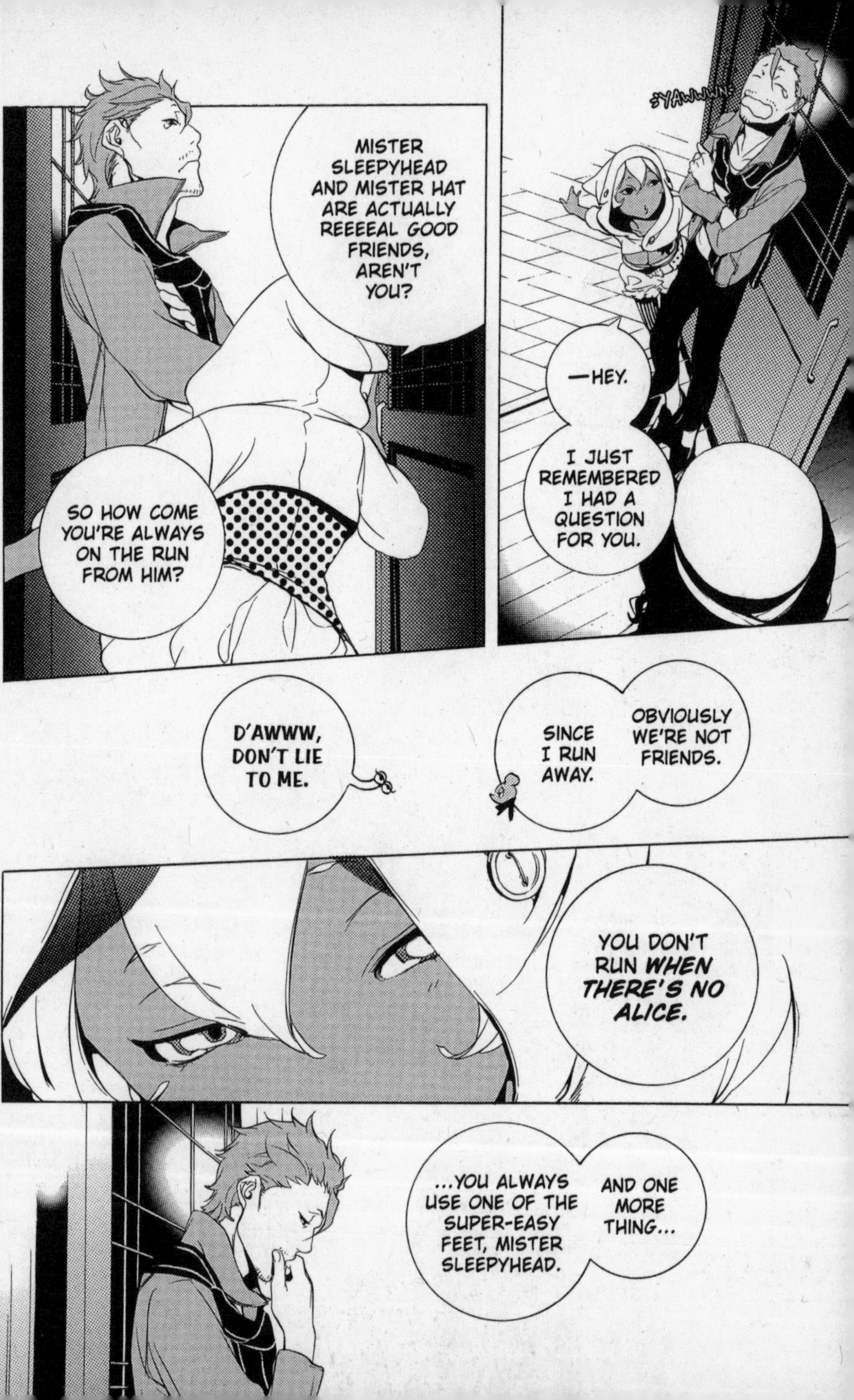
YAWWWN
—HEY.
I JUST REMEMBERED I HAD A QUESTION FOR YOU.
MISTER SLEEPYHEAD AND MISTER HAT ARE ACTUALLY REEEEAL GOOD FRIENDS, AREN'T YOU?
SO HOW COME YOU'RE ALWAYS ON THE RUN FROM HIM?
OBVIOUSLY WE'RE NOT FRIENDS.
SINCE I RUN AWAY.
D'AWWW, DON'T LIE TO ME.
YOU DON'T RUN *WHEN THERE'S NO ALICE.*
AND ONE MORE THING...
...YOU ALWAYS USE ONE OF THE SUPER-EASY FEET, MISTER SLEEPYHEAD.

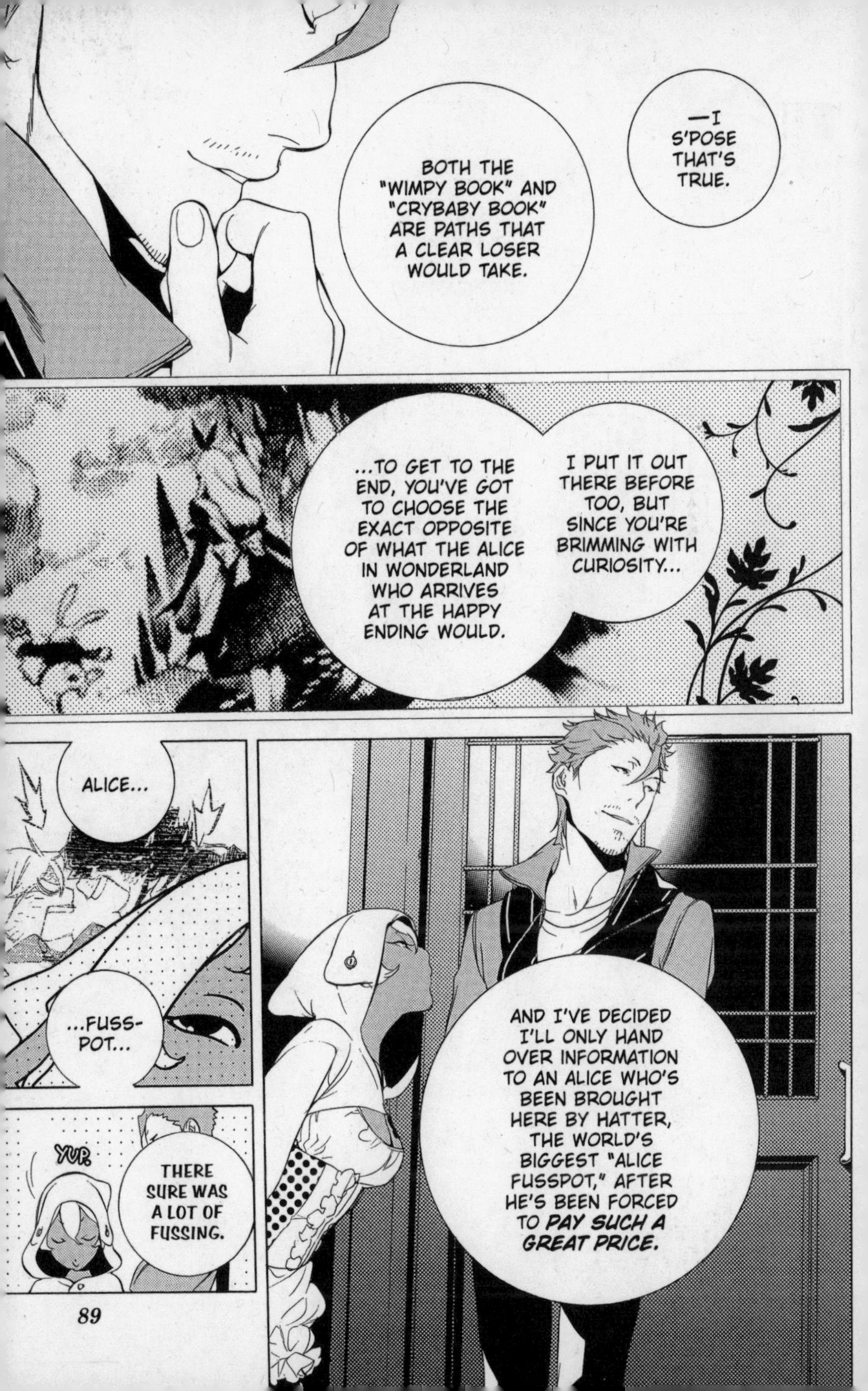
—I S'POSE THAT'S TRUE.
BOTH THE "WIMPY BOOK" AND "CRYBABY BOOK" ARE PATHS THAT A CLEAR LOSER WOULD TAKE.
I PUT IT OUT THERE BEFORE TOO, BUT SINCE YOU'RE BRIMMING WITH CURIOSITY...
...TO GET TO THE END, YOU'VE GOT TO CHOOSE THE EXACT OPPOSITE OF WHAT THE ALICE IN WONDERLAND WHO ARRIVES AT THE HAPPY ENDING WOULD.
AND I'VE DECIDED I'LL ONLY HAND OVER INFORMATION TO AN ALICE WHO'S BEEN BROUGHT HERE BY HATTER, THE WORLD'S BIGGEST "ALICE FUSSPOT," AFTER HE'S BEEN FORCED TO PAY SUCH A GREAT PRICE.
ALICE...
...FUSS-POT...
YUP.
THERE SURE WAS A LOT OF FUSSING.

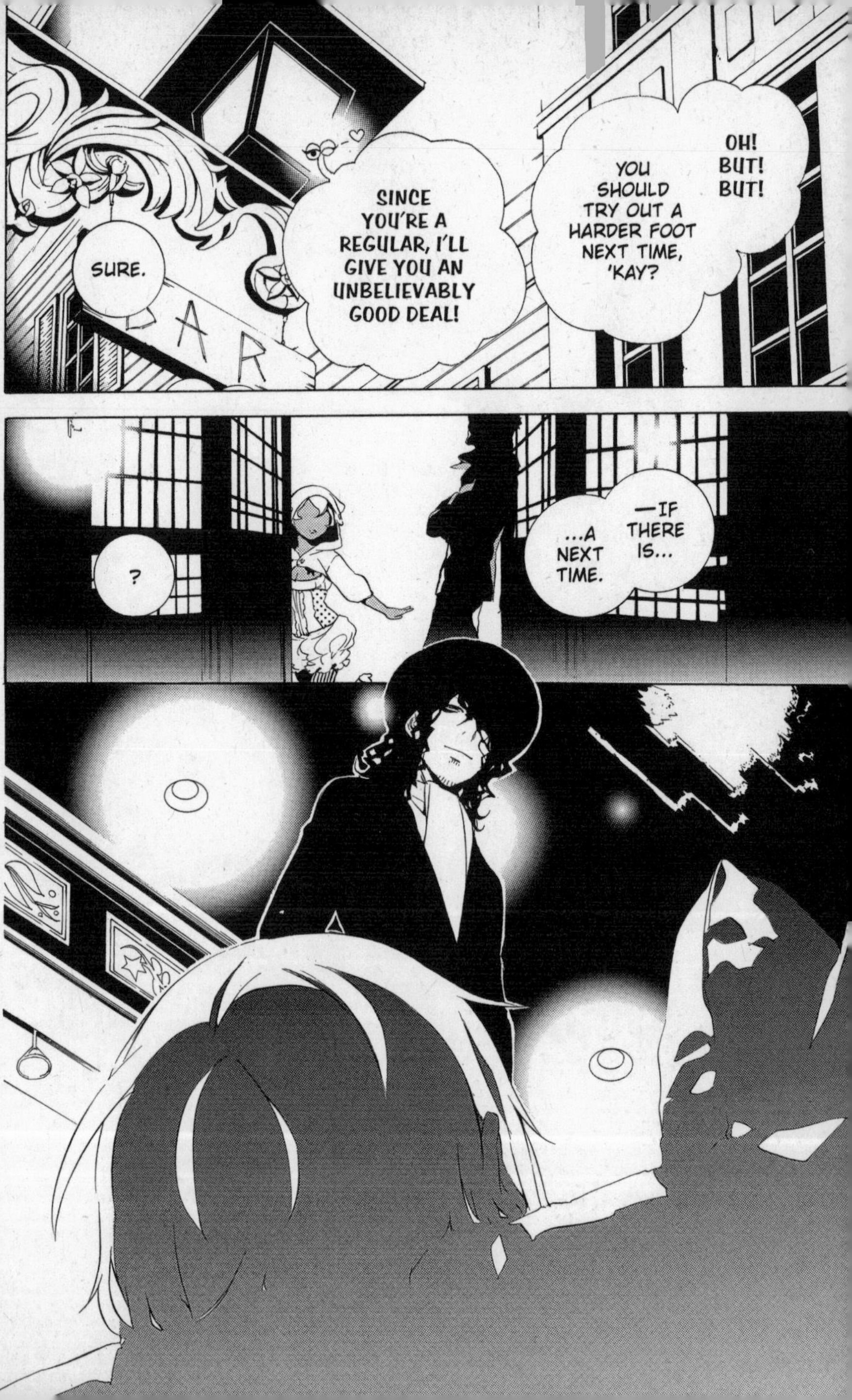
OH! BUT! BUT!
YOU SHOULD TRY OUT A HARDER FOOT NEXT TIME, 'KAY?
SINCE YOU'RE A REGULAR, I'LL GIVE YOU AN UNBELIEVABLY GOOD DEAL!
SURE.
—IF THERE IS...
...A NEXT TIME.
?

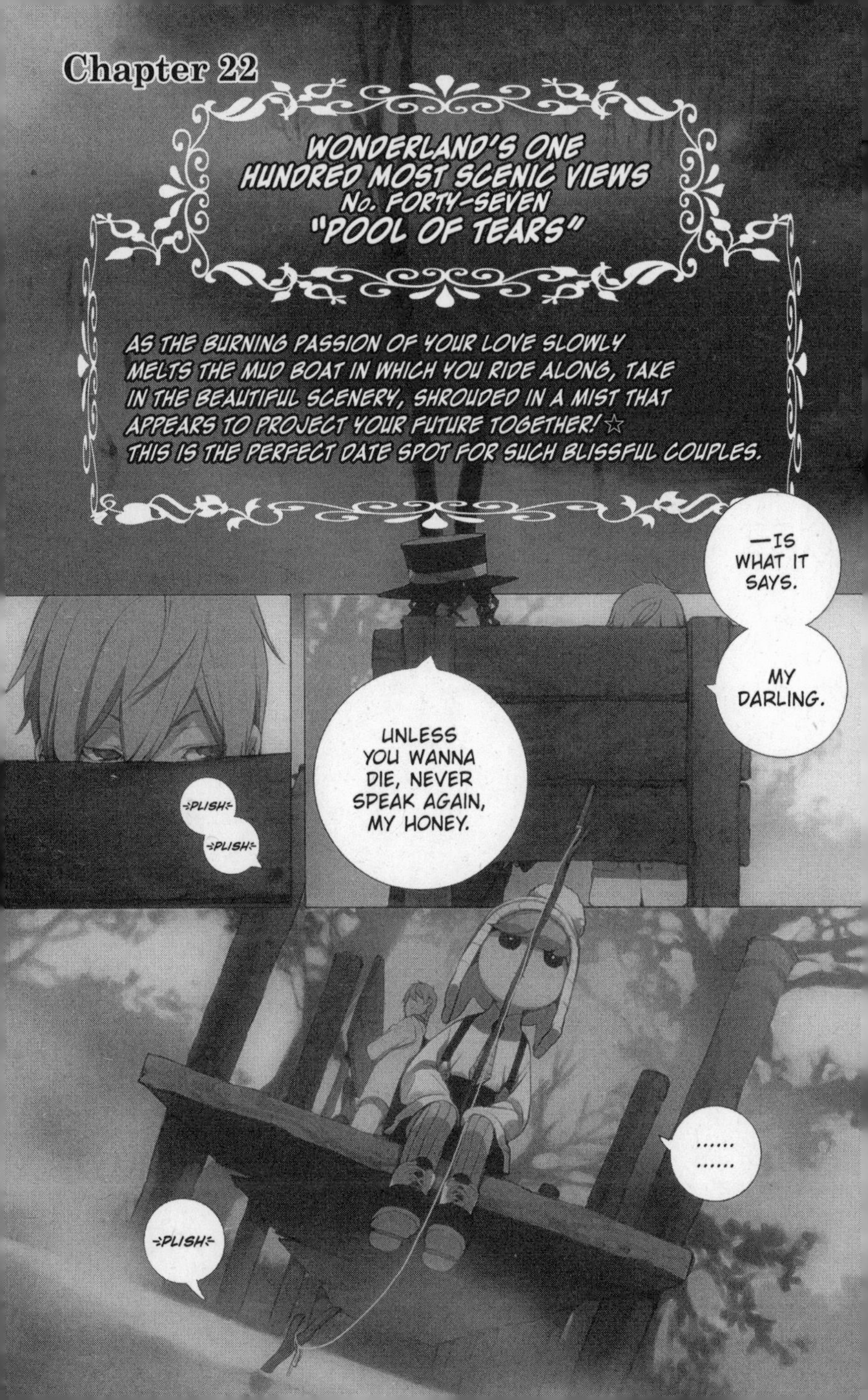
Chapter 22
WONDERLAND'S ONE HUNDRED MOST SCENIC VIEWS
No. FORTY-SEVEN
"POOL OF TEARS"
AS THE BURNING PASSION OF YOUR LOVE SLOWLY MELTS THE MUD BOAT IN WHICH YOU RIDE ALONG, TAKE IN THE BEAUTIFUL SCENERY, SHROUDED IN A MIST THAT APPEARS TO PROJECT YOUR FUTURE TOGETHER! ☆ THIS IS THE PERFECT DATE SPOT FOR SUCH BLISSFUL COUPLES.
—IS WHAT IT SAYS.
MY DARLING.
UNLESS YOU WANNA DIE, NEVER SPEAK AGAIN, MY HONEY.
PLISH
PLISH
......
......
PLISH

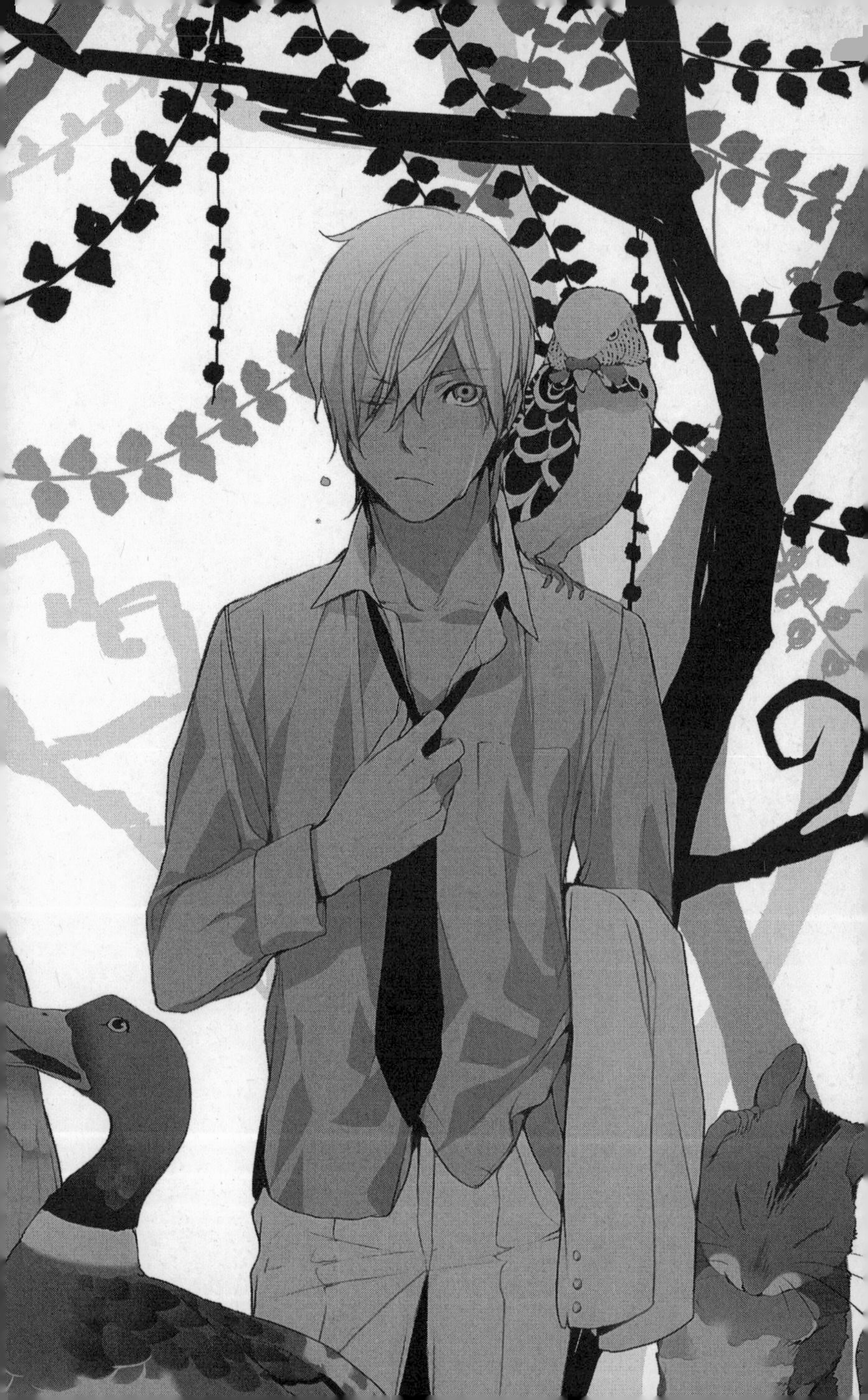

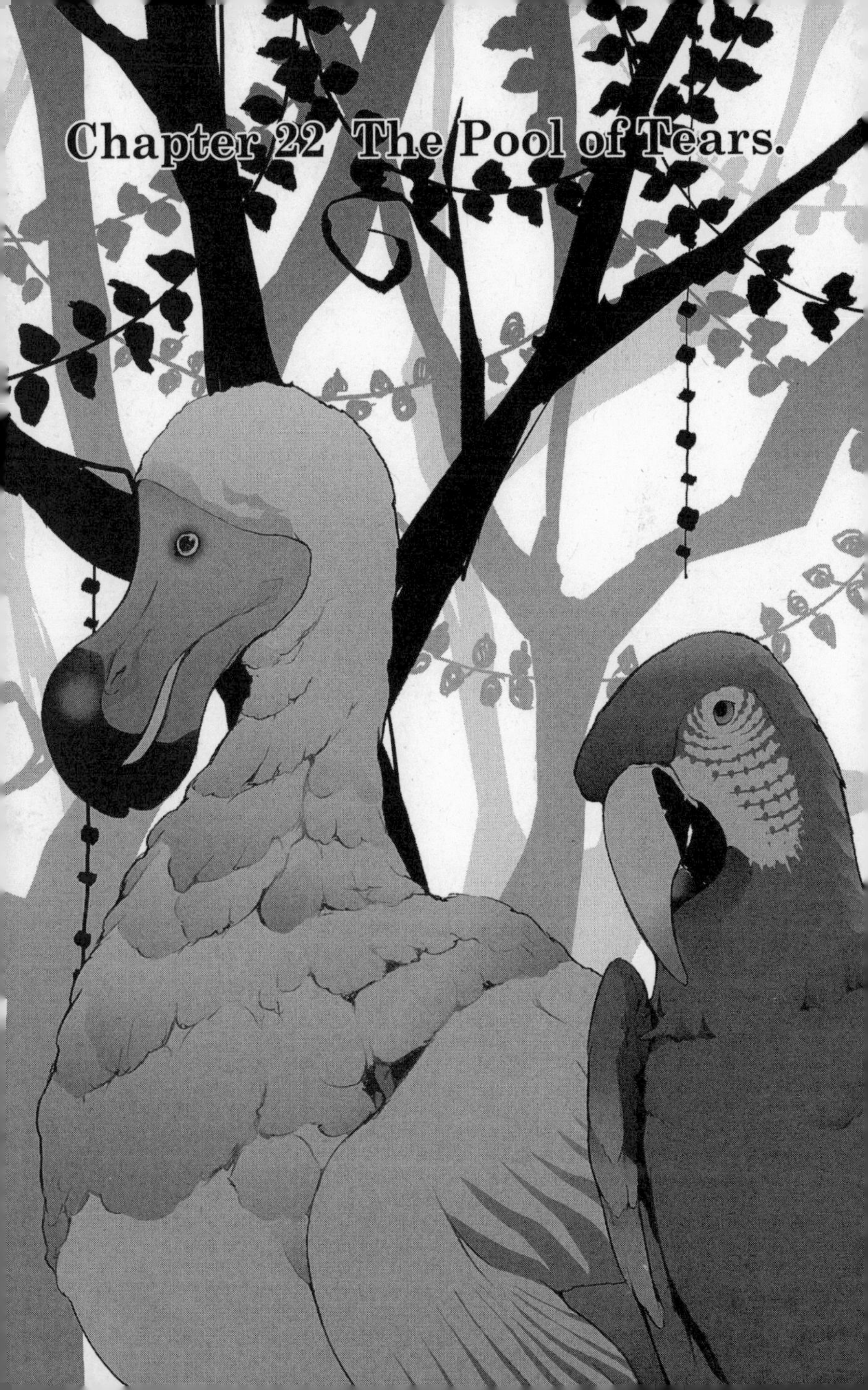
Chapter 22 The Pool of Tears.

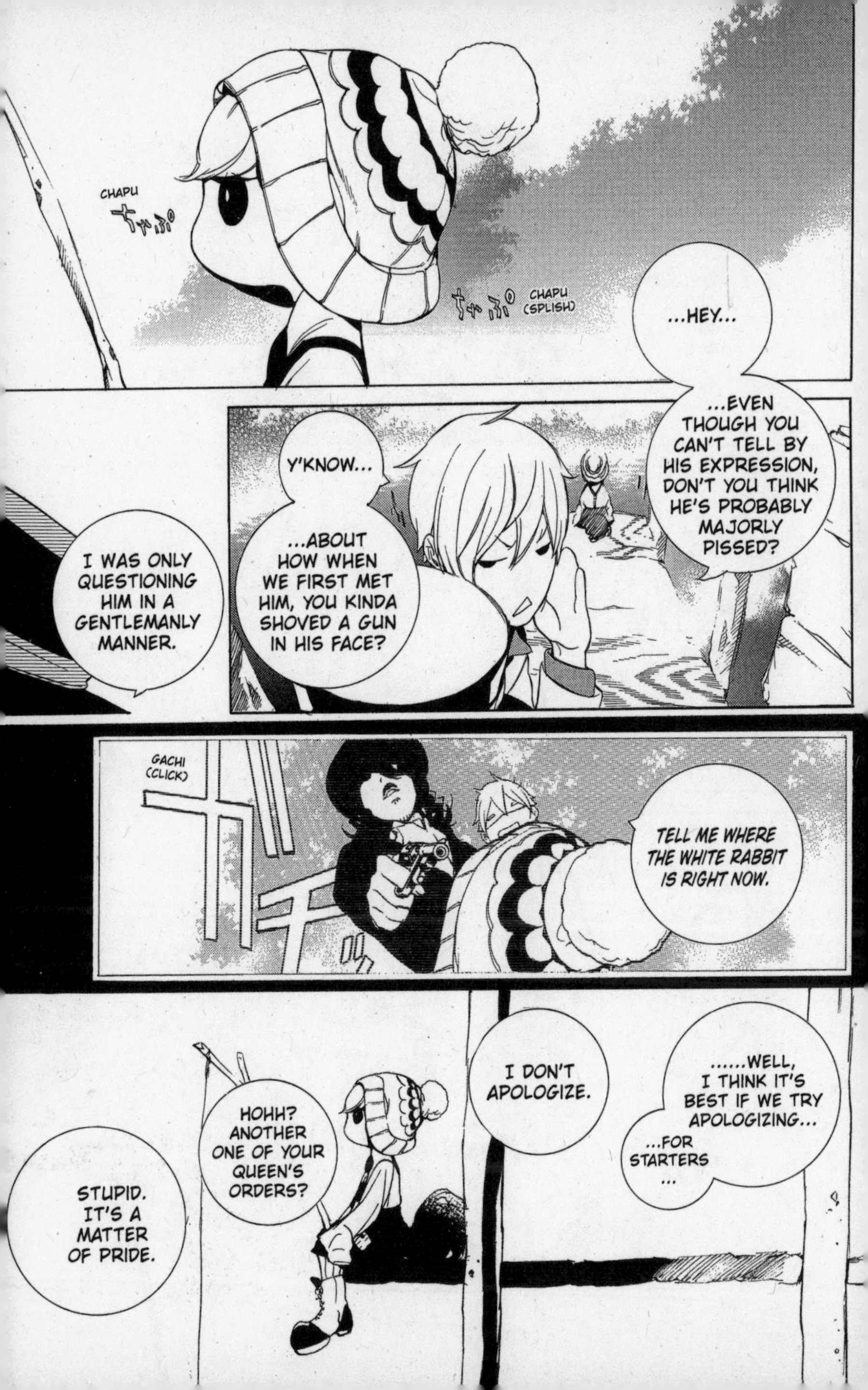
...HEY...
ちゃぷ CHAPU (SPLISH)
ちゃぷ CHAPU
...EVEN THOUGH YOU CAN'T TELL BY HIS EXPRESSION, DON'T YOU THINK HE'S PROBABLY MAJORLY PISSED?
Y'KNOW...
...ABOUT HOW WHEN WE FIRST MET HIM, YOU KINDA SHOVED A GUN IN HIS FACE?
I WAS ONLY QUESTIONING HIM IN A GENTLEMANLY MANNER.
TELL ME WHERE THE WHITE RABBIT IS RIGHT NOW.
GACHI (CLICK)
......WELL, I THINK IT'S BEST IF WE TRY APOLOGIZING...
...FOR STARTERS ...
I DON'T APOLOGIZE.
HOHH? ANOTHER ONE OF YOUR QUEEN'S ORDERS?
STUPID. IT'S A MATTER OF PRIDE.

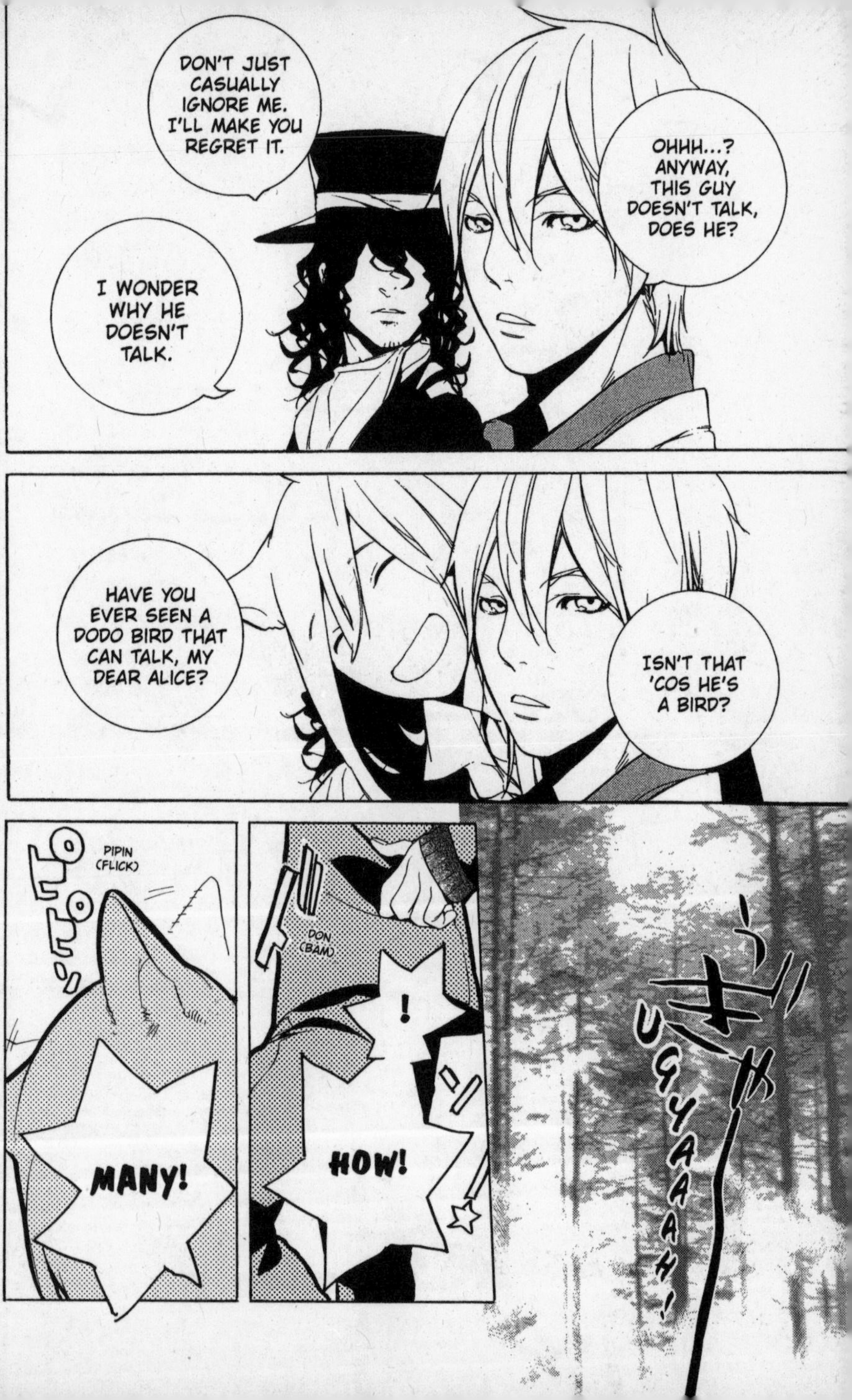
DON'T JUST CASUALLY IGNORE ME. I'LL MAKE YOU REGRET IT.
OHHH...? ANYWAY, THIS GUY DOESN'T TALK, DOES HE?
I WONDER WHY HE DOESN'T TALK.
ISN'T THAT 'COS HE'S A BIRD?
HAVE YOU EVER SEEN A DODO BIRD THAT CAN TALK, MY DEAR ALICE?
UGYAAAAH!
DON (BAM)
!
HOW!
PIPIN (FLICK)
MANY!

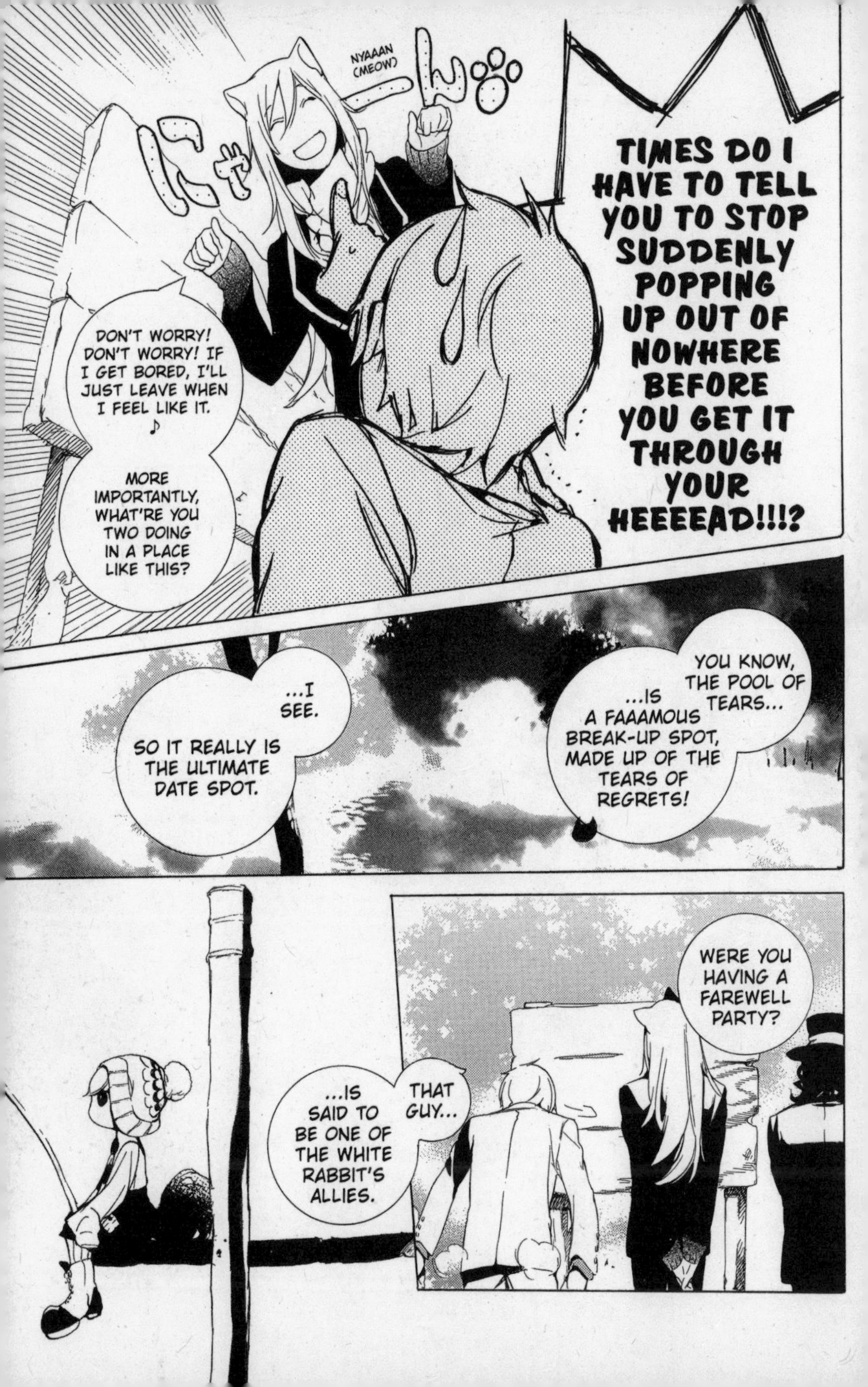
TIMES DO I HAVE TO TELL YOU TO STOP SUDDENLY POPPING UP OUT OF NOWHERE BEFORE YOU GET IT THROUGH YOUR HEEEEAD!!!?
NYAAAN (MEOW)
DON'T WORRY! DON'T WORRY! IF I GET BORED, I'LL JUST LEAVE WHEN I FEEL LIKE IT. ♪
MORE IMPORTANTLY, WHAT'RE YOU TWO DOING IN A PLACE LIKE THIS?
YOU KNOW, THE POOL OF TEARS...
...IS A FAAAMOUS BREAK-UP SPOT, MADE UP OF THE TEARS OF REGRETS!
...I SEE.
SO IT REALLY IS THE ULTIMATE DATE SPOT.
WERE YOU HAVING A FAREWELL PARTY?
THAT GUY...
...IS SAID TO BE ONE OF THE WHITE RABBIT'S ALLIES.

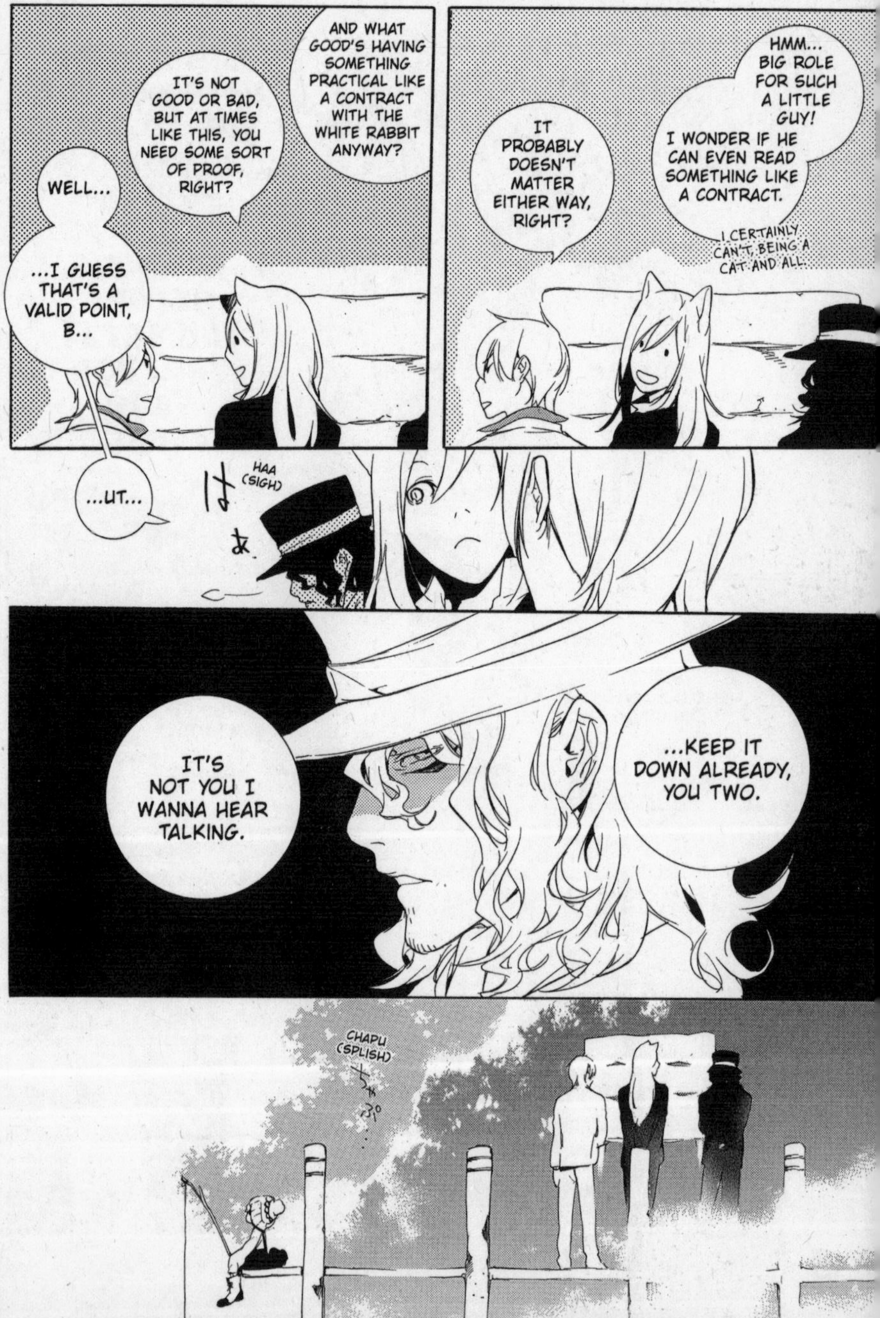
HMM... BIG ROLE FOR SUCH A LITTLE GUY!
I WONDER IF HE CAN EVEN READ SOMETHING LIKE A CONTRACT.
I CERTAINLY CAN'T, BEING A CAT AND ALL.
IT PROBABLY DOESN'T MATTER EITHER WAY, RIGHT?
AND WHAT GOOD'S HAVING SOMETHING PRACTICAL LIKE A CONTRACT WITH THE WHITE RABBIT ANYWAY?
IT'S NOT GOOD OR BAD, BUT AT TIMES LIKE THIS, YOU NEED SOME SORT OF PROOF, RIGHT?
WELL...
...I GUESS THAT'S A VALID POINT, B...
HAA (SIGH)
...UT...
...KEEP IT DOWN ALREADY, YOU TWO.
IT'S NOT YOU I WANNA HEAR TALKING.
CHAPU (SPLISH)

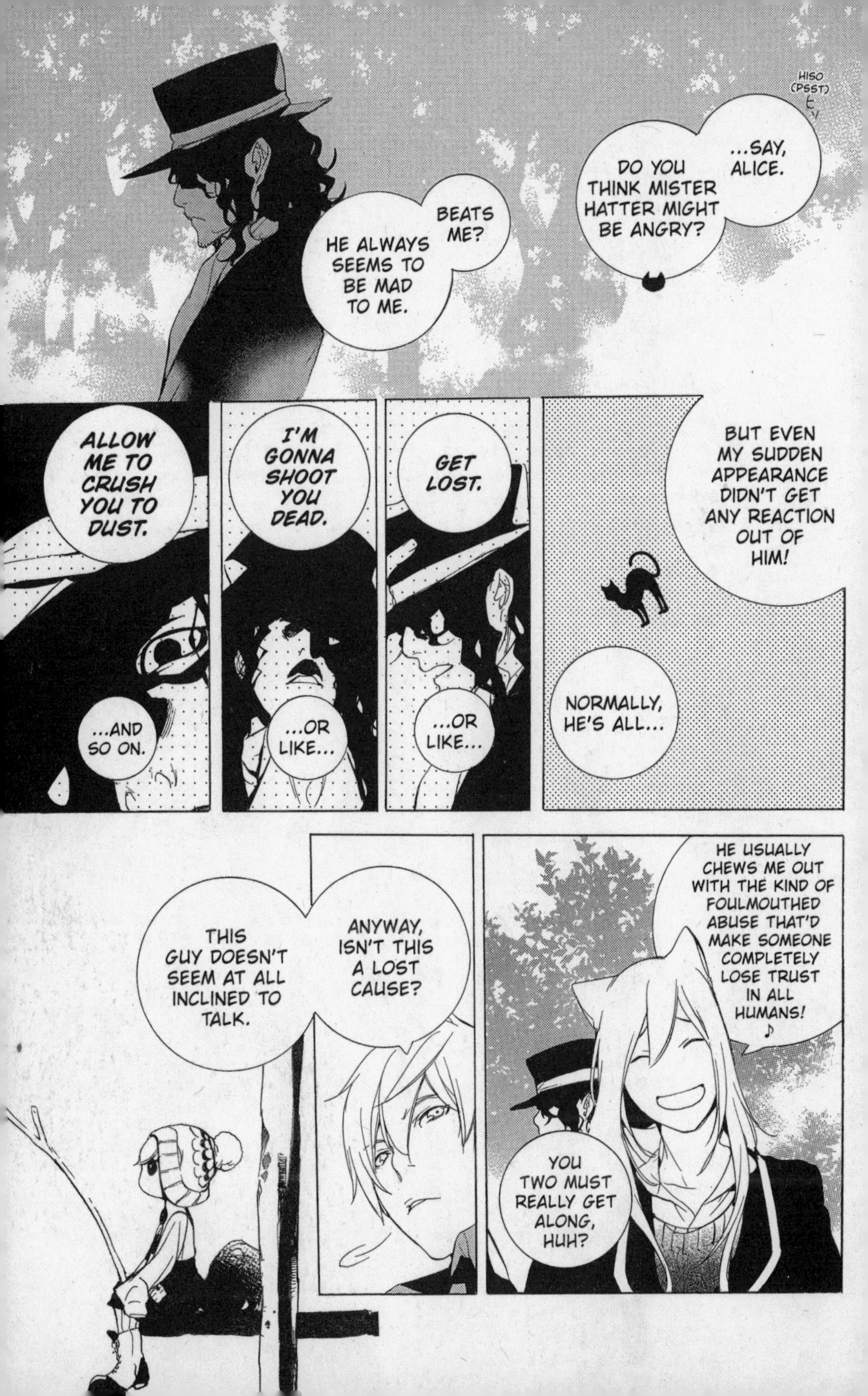
HISO (PSST)
...SAY, ALICE.
DO YOU THINK MISTER HATTER MIGHT BE ANGRY?
BEATS ME?
HE ALWAYS SEEMS TO BE MAD TO ME.
BUT EVEN MY SUDDEN APPEARANCE DIDN'T GET ANY REACTION OUT OF HIM!
NORMALLY, HE'S ALL...
GET LOST.
...OR LIKE...
I'M GONNA SHOOT YOU DEAD.
...OR LIKE...
ALLOW ME TO CRUSH YOU TO DUST.
...AND SO ON.
HE USUALLY CHEWS ME OUT WITH THE KIND OF FOULMOUTHED ABUSE THAT'D MAKE SOMEONE COMPLETELY LOSE TRUST IN ALL HUMANS! ♪
YOU TWO MUST REALLY GET ALONG, HUH?
ANYWAY, ISN'T THIS A LOST CAUSE?
THIS GUY DOESN'T SEEM AT ALL INCLINED TO TALK.

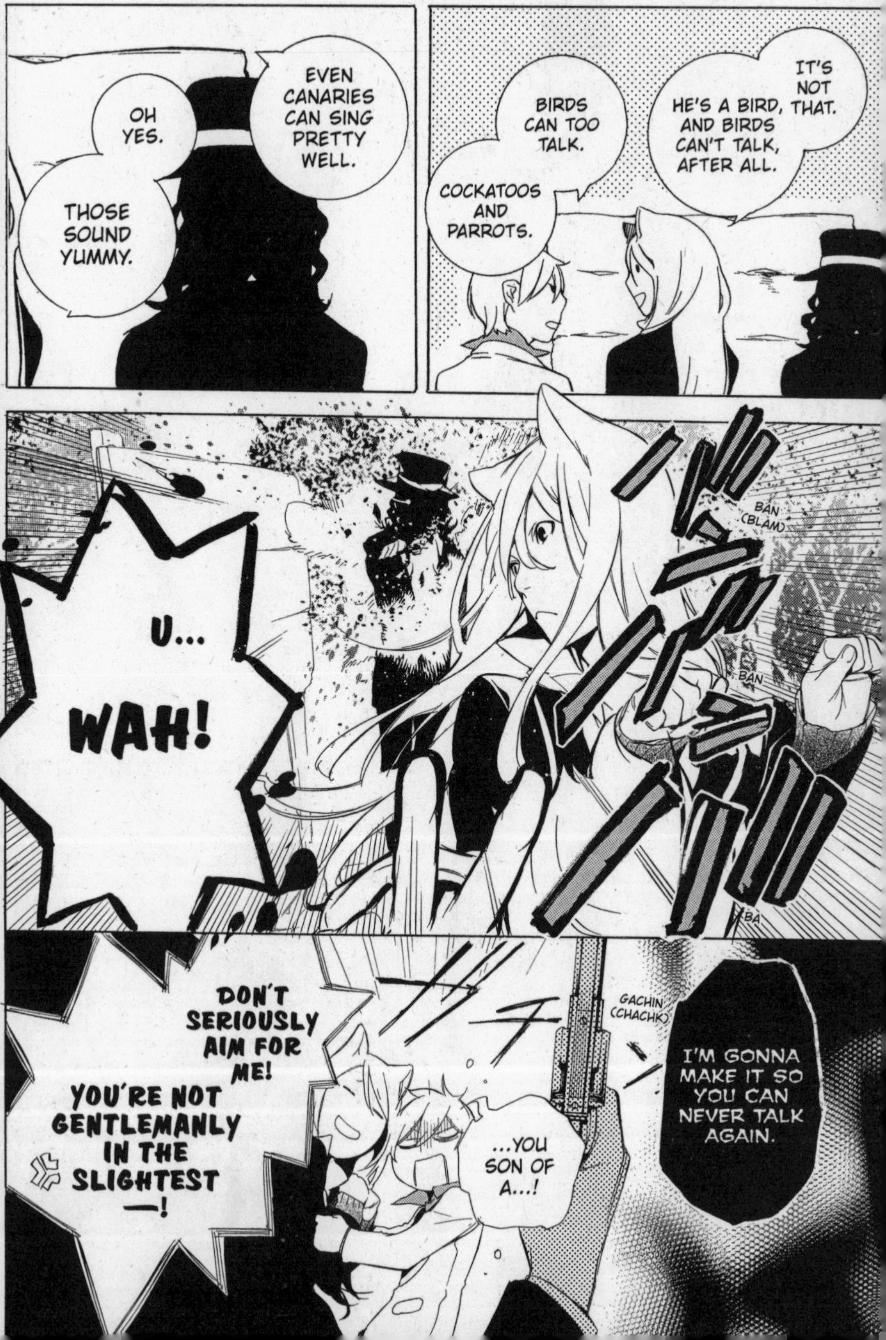
IT'S NOT THAT.
HE'S A BIRD, AND BIRDS CAN'T TALK, AFTER ALL.
BIRDS CAN TOO TALK.
COCKATOOS AND PARROTS.
EVEN CANARIES CAN SING PRETTY WELL.
OH YES.
THOSE SOUND YUMMY.
BAN (BLAM)
BAN
BA
U...
WAH!
GACHIN (CHACHK)
I'M GONNA MAKE IT SO YOU CAN NEVER TALK AGAIN.
...YOU SON OF A...!
DON'T SERIOUSLY AIM FOR ME!
YOU'RE NOT GENTLEMANLY IN THE SLIGHTEST—!

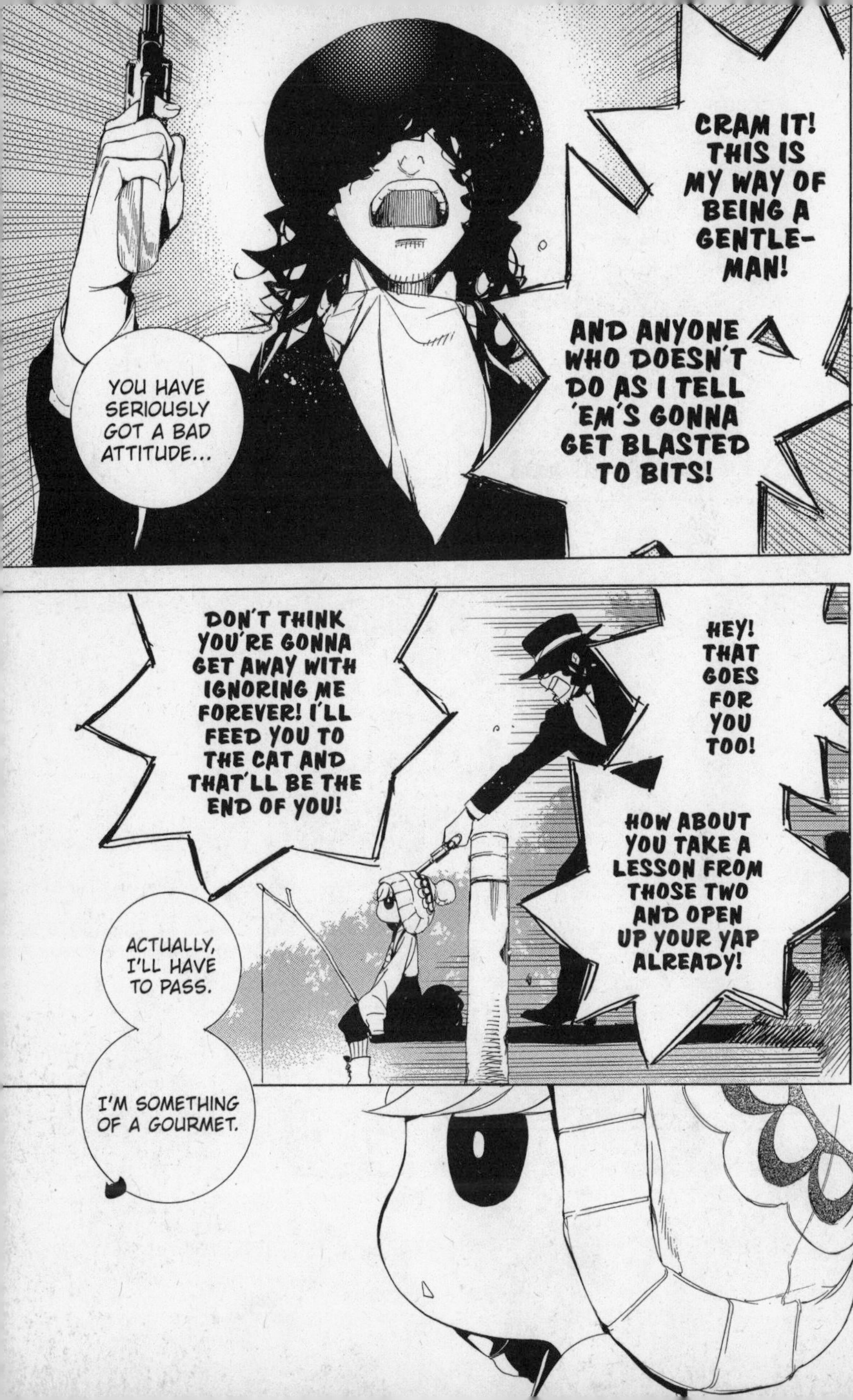
CRAM IT! THIS IS MY WAY OF BEING A GENTLE-MAN!
AND ANYONE WHO DOESN'T DO AS I TELL 'EM'S GONNA GET BLASTED TO BITS!
YOU HAVE SERIOUSLY GOT A BAD ATTITUDE...
HEY! THAT GOES FOR YOU TOO!
HOW ABOUT YOU TAKE A LESSON FROM THOSE TWO AND OPEN UP YOUR YAP ALREADY!
DON'T THINK YOU'RE GONNA GET AWAY WITH IGNORING ME FOREVER! I'LL FEED YOU TO THE CAT AND THAT'LL BE THE END OF YOU!
ACTUALLY, I'LL HAVE TO PASS.
I'M SOMETHING OF A GOURMET.

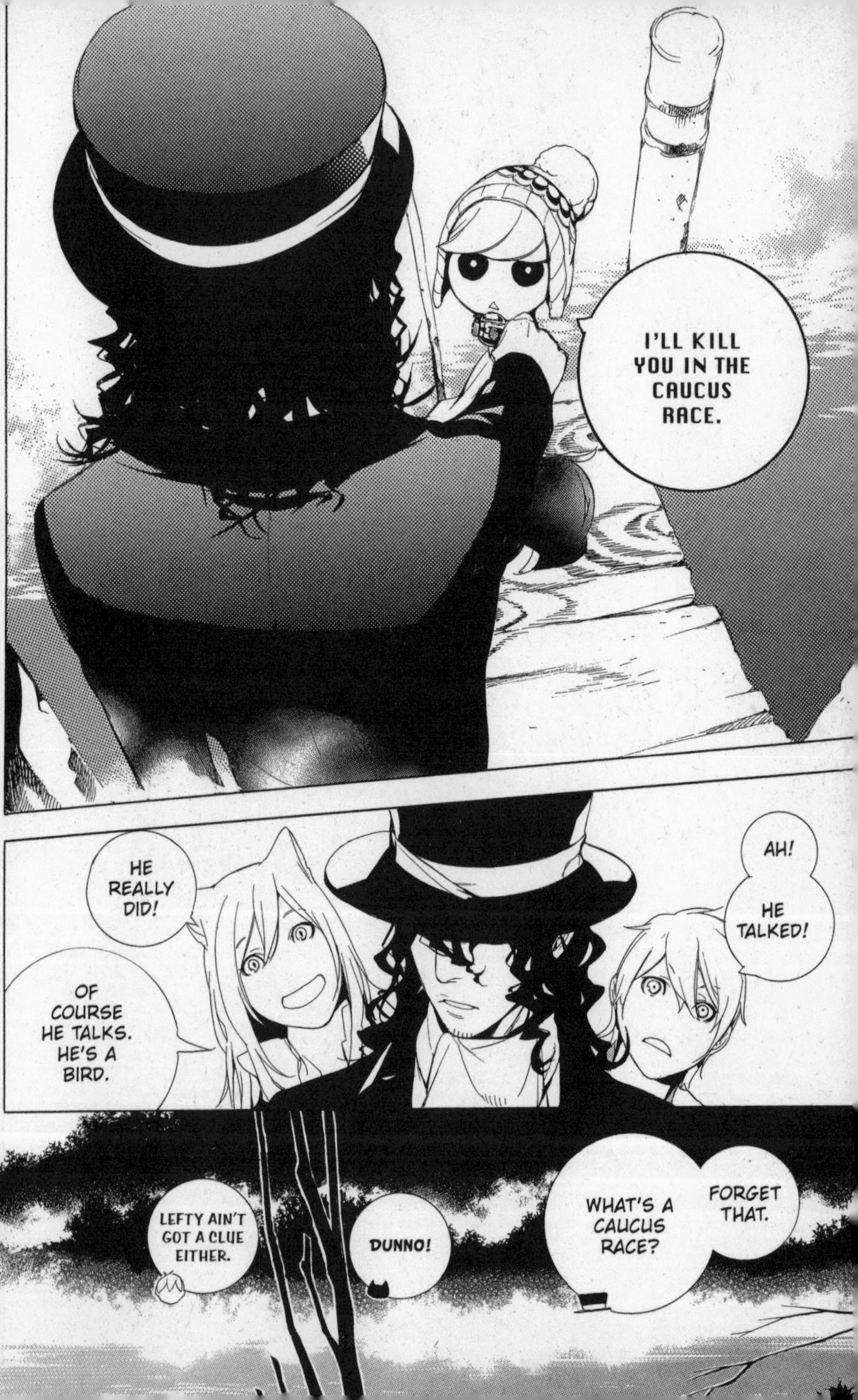
I'LL KILL YOU IN THE CAUCUS RACE.
AH!
HE TALKED!
HE REALLY DID!
OF COURSE HE TALKS. HE'S A BIRD.
FORGET THAT.
WHAT'S A CAUCUS RACE?
DUNNO!
LEFTY AIN'T GOT A CLUE EITHER.

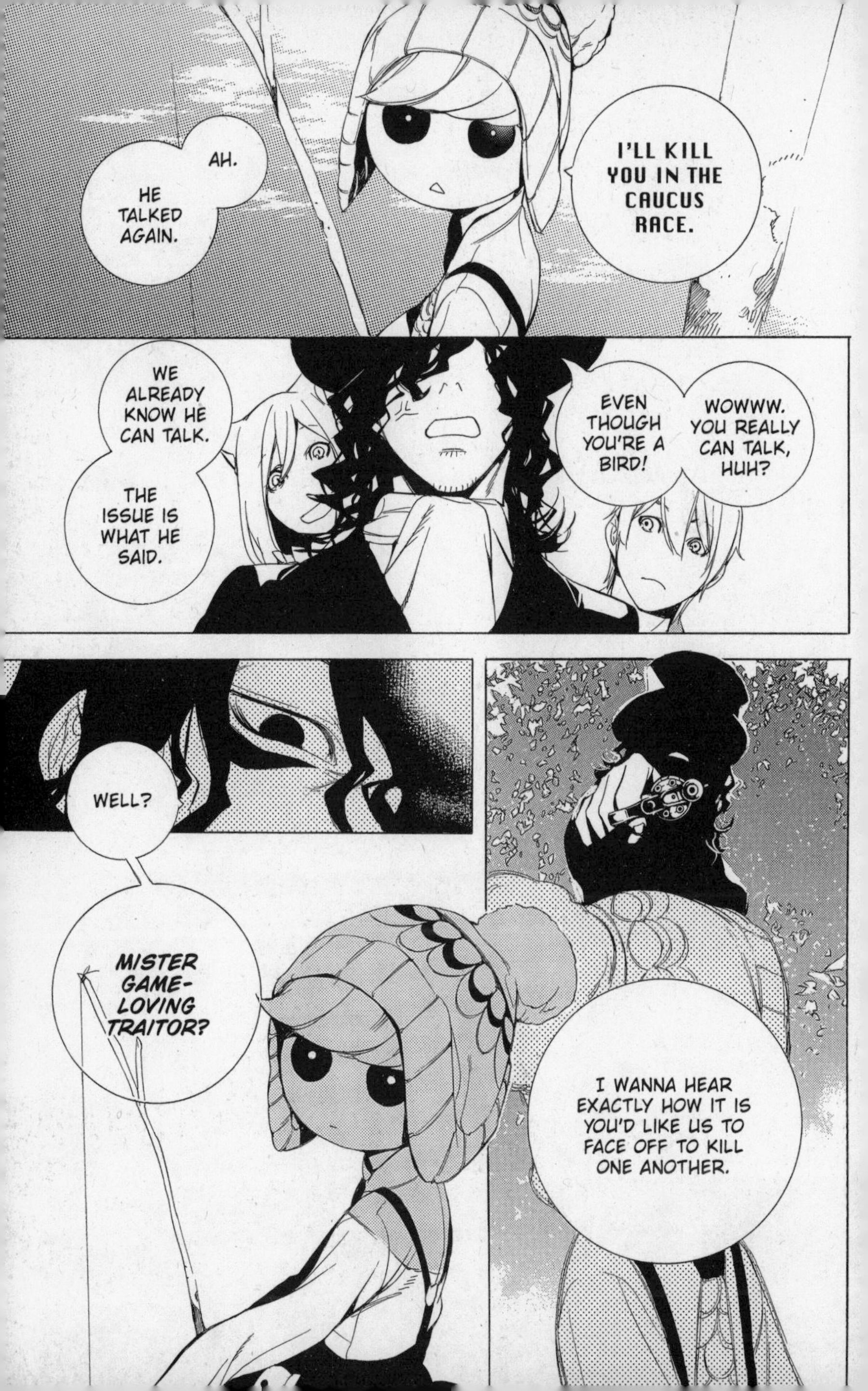
I'LL KILL YOU IN THE CAUCUS RACE.
AH.
HE TALKED AGAIN.
WOWWW. YOU REALLY CAN TALK, HUH?
EVEN THOUGH YOU'RE A BIRD!
WE ALREADY KNOW HE CAN TALK.
THE ISSUE IS WHAT HE SAID.
WELL?
MISTER GAME-LOVING TRAITOR?
I WANNA HEAR EXACTLY HOW IT IS YOU'D LIKE US TO FACE OFF TO KILL ONE ANOTHER.

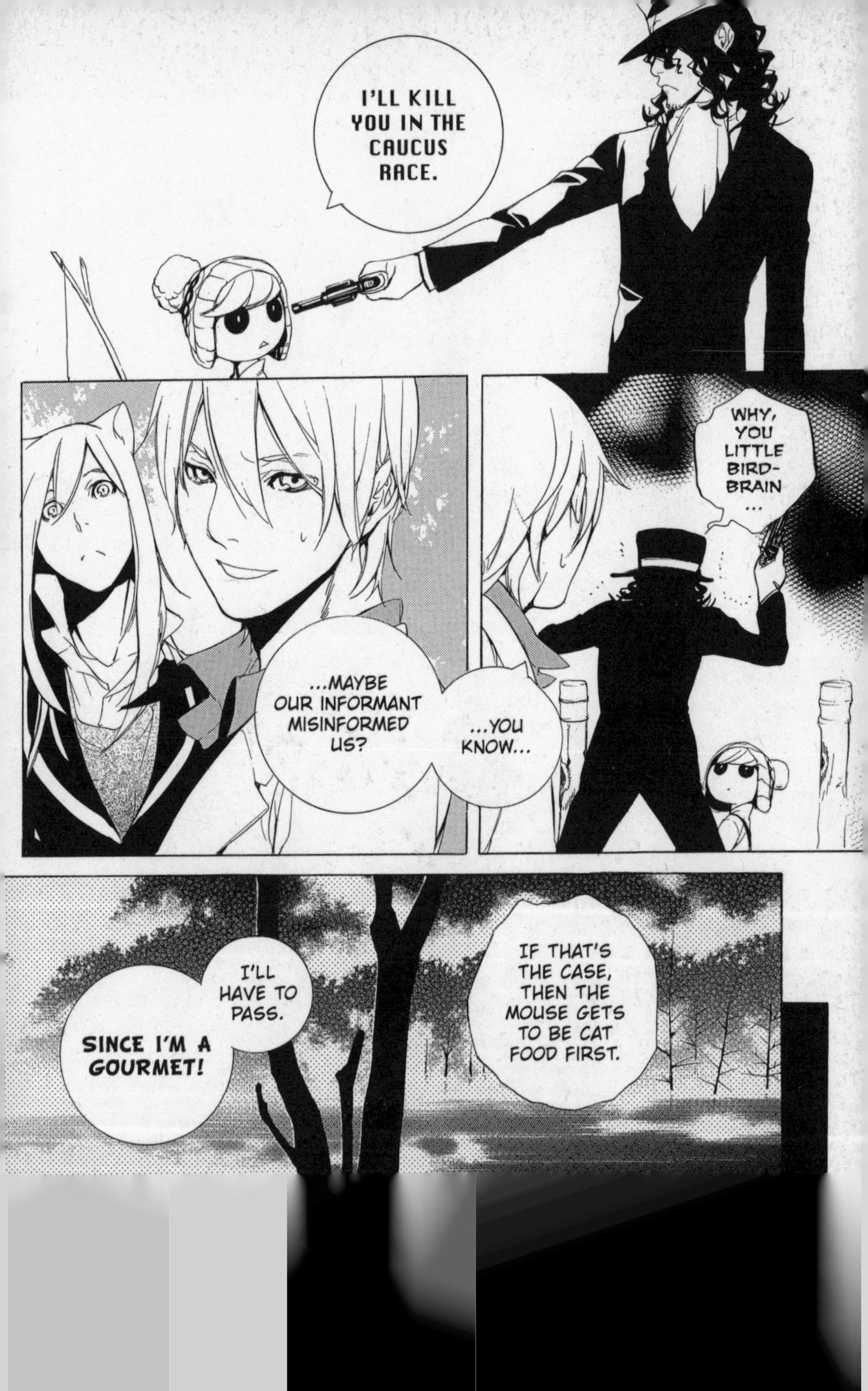

I'LL KILL YOU IN THE CAUCUS RACE.
WHY, YOU LITTLE BIRD-BRAIN ...
...YOU KNOW...
...MAYBE OUR INFORMANT MISINFORMED US?
IF THAT'S THE CASE, THEN THE MOUSE GETS TO BE CAT FOOD FIRST.
I'LL HAVE TO PASS.
SINCE I'M A GOURMET!

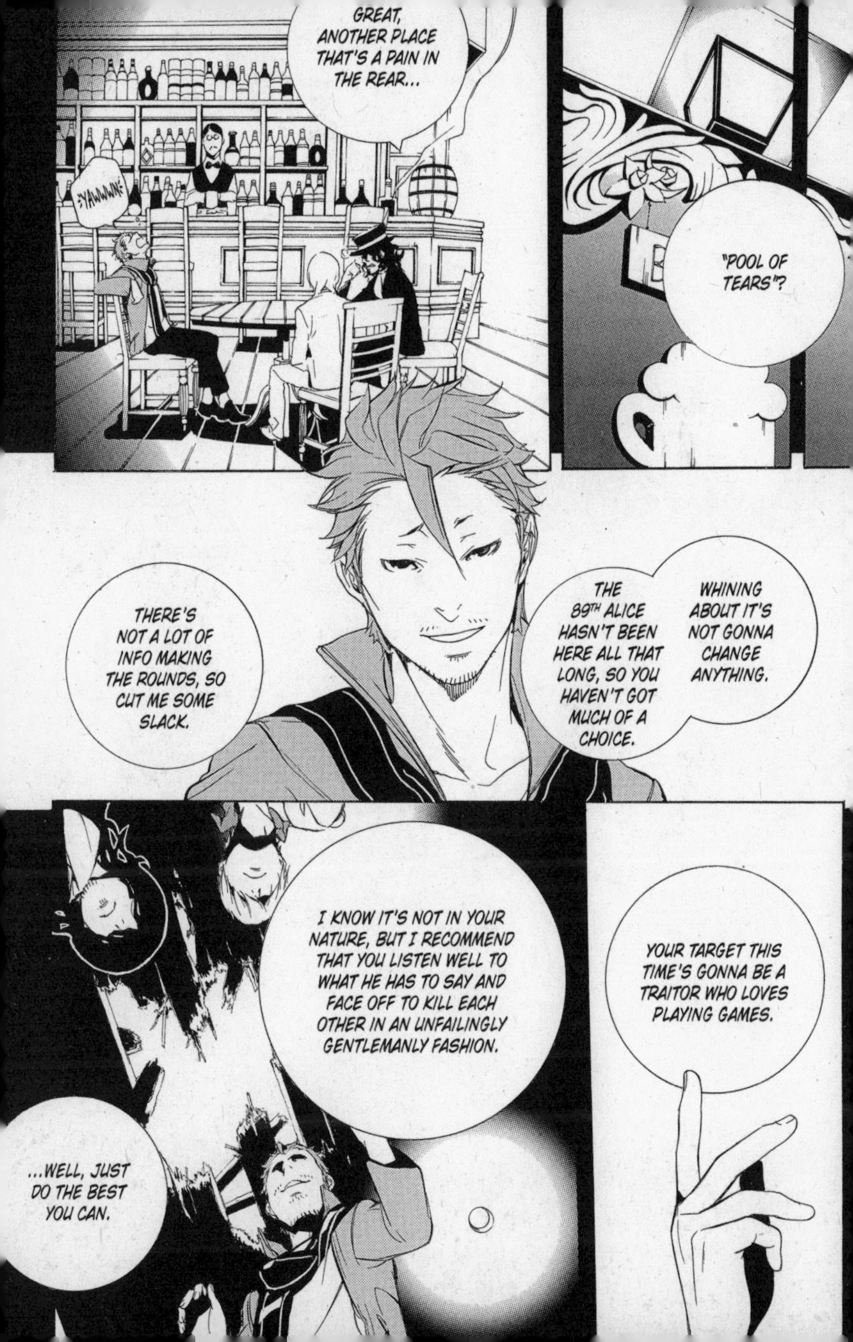
"POOL OF TEARS"?
GREAT, ANOTHER PLACE THAT'S A PAIN IN THE REAR...
YAWWWN
THE 89TH ALICE HASN'T BEEN HERE ALL THAT LONG, SO YOU HAVEN'T GOT MUCH OF A CHOICE.
WHINING ABOUT IT'S NOT GONNA CHANGE ANYTHING.
THERE'S NOT A LOT OF INFO MAKING THE ROUNDS, SO CUT ME SOME SLACK.
YOUR TARGET THIS TIME'S GONNA BE A TRAITOR WHO LOVES PLAYING GAMES.
I KNOW IT'S NOT IN YOUR NATURE, BUT I RECOMMEND THAT YOU LISTEN WELL TO WHAT HE HAS TO SAY AND FACE OFF TO KILL EACH OTHER IN AN UNFAILINGLY GENTLEMANLY FASHION.
...WELL, JUST DO THE BEST YOU CAN.

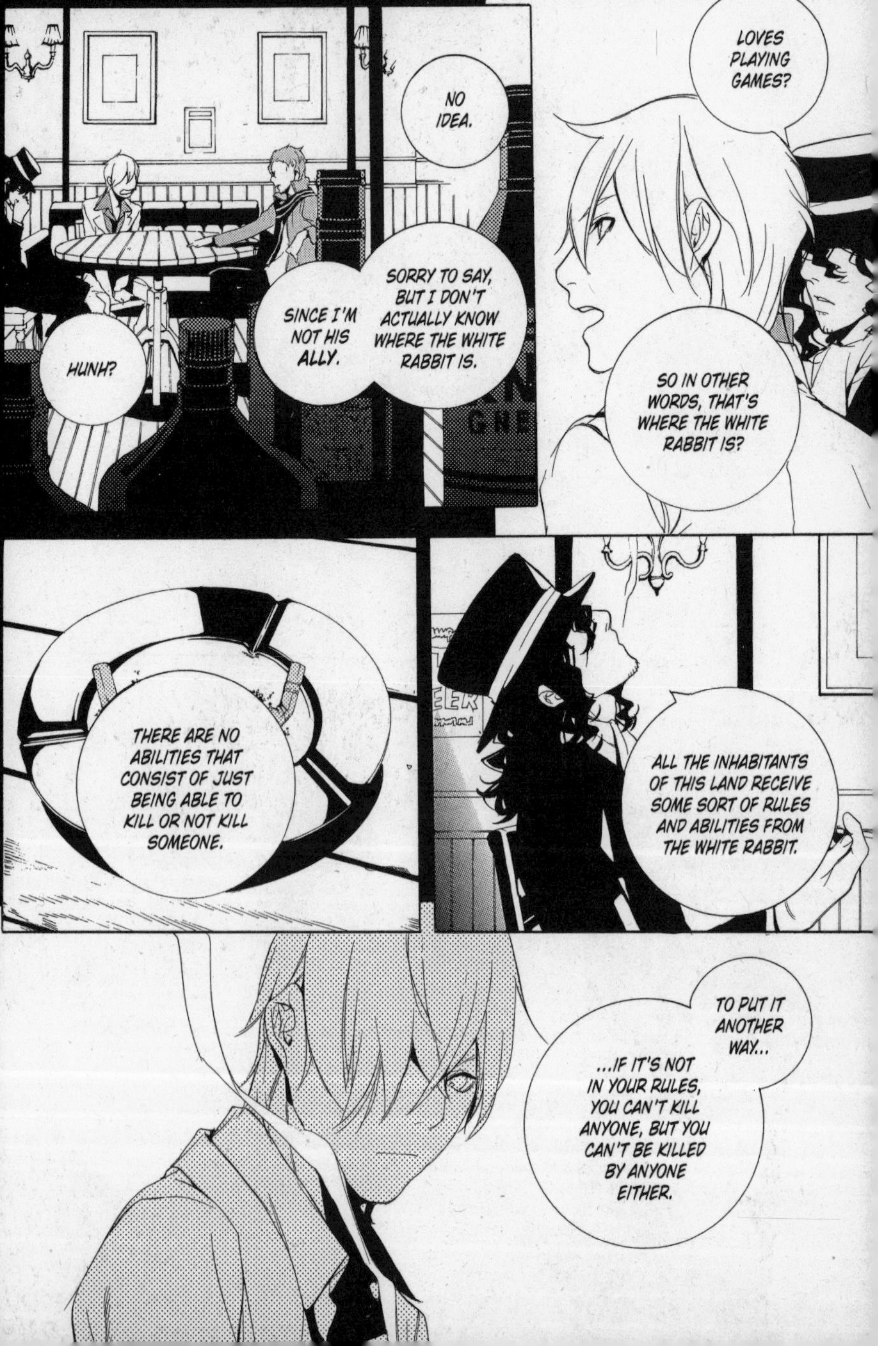
LOVES PLAYING GAMES?
SO IN OTHER WORDS, THAT'S WHERE THE WHITE RABBIT IS?
NO IDEA.
SORRY TO SAY, BUT I DON'T ACTUALLY KNOW WHERE THE WHITE RABBIT IS.
SINCE I'M NOT HIS ALLY.
HUNH?
ALL THE INHABITANTS OF THIS LAND RECEIVE SOME SORT OF RULES AND ABILITIES FROM THE WHITE RABBIT.
THERE ARE NO ABILITIES THAT CONSIST OF JUST BEING ABLE TO KILL OR NOT KILL SOMEONE.
TO PUT IT ANOTHER WAY...
...IF IT'S NOT IN YOUR RULES, YOU CAN'T KILL ANYONE, BUT YOU CAN'T BE KILLED BY ANYONE EITHER.

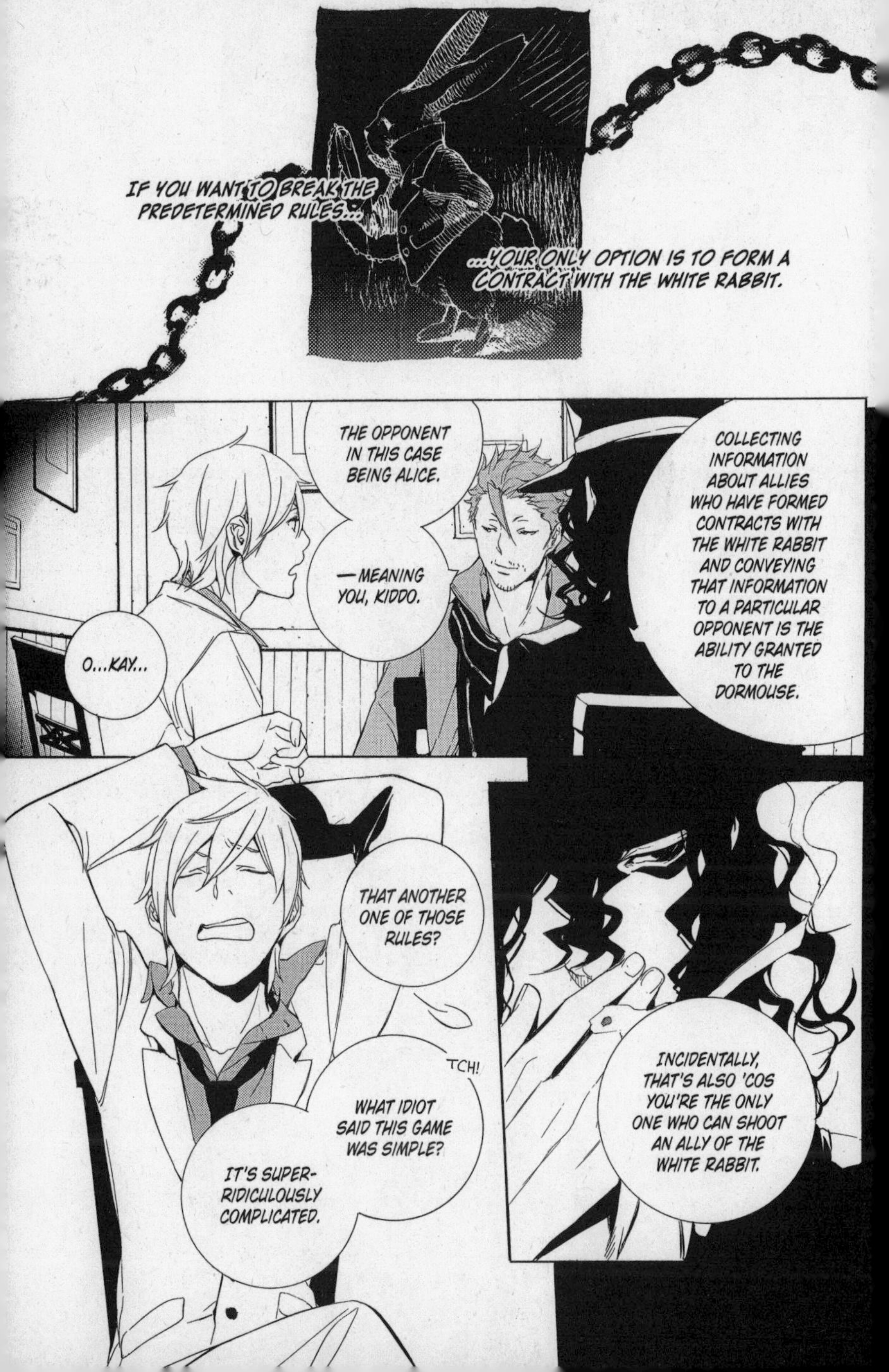
IF YOU WANT TO BREAK THE PREDETERMINED RULES...
...YOUR ONLY OPTION IS TO FORM A CONTRACT WITH THE WHITE RABBIT.
COLLECTING INFORMATION ABOUT ALLIES WHO HAVE FORMED CONTRACTS WITH THE WHITE RABBIT AND CONVEYING THAT INFORMATION TO A PARTICULAR OPPONENT IS THE ABILITY GRANTED TO THE DORMOUSE.
THE OPPONENT IN THIS CASE BEING ALICE.
—MEANING YOU, KIDDO.
O...KAY...
INCIDENTALLY, THAT'S ALSO 'COS YOU'RE THE ONLY ONE WHO CAN SHOOT AN ALLY OF THE WHITE RABBIT.
THAT ANOTHER ONE OF THOSE RULES?
TCH!
WHAT IDIOT SAID THIS GAME WAS SIMPLE?
IT'S SUPER-RIDICULOUSLY COMPLICATED.

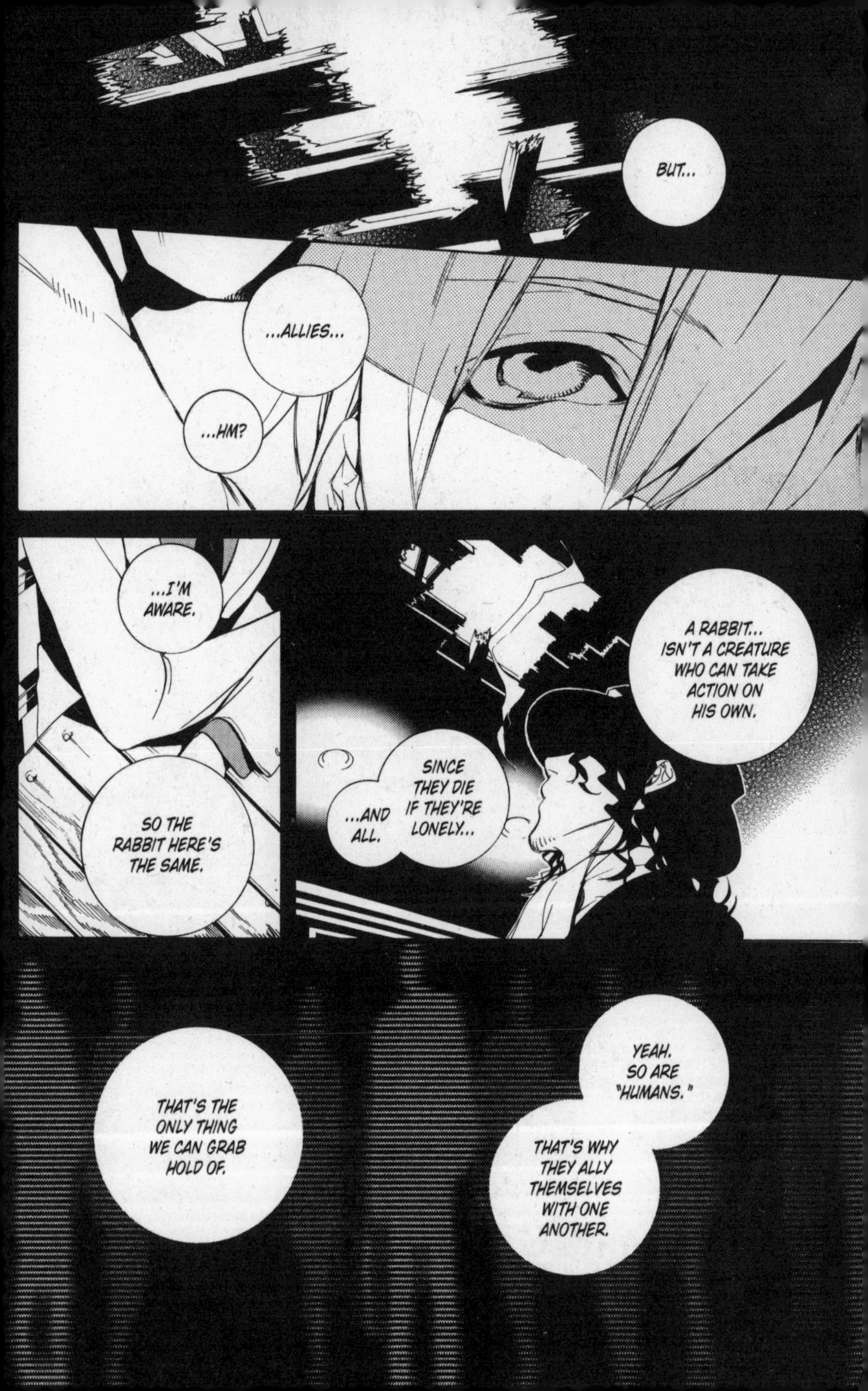
BUT...
...ALLIES...
...HM?
A RABBIT... ISN'T A CREATURE WHO CAN TAKE ACTION ON HIS OWN.
SINCE THEY DIE IF THEY'RE LONELY...
...AND ALL.
...I'M AWARE.
SO THE RABBIT HERE'S THE SAME.
YEAH. SO ARE "HUMANS."
THAT'S WHY THEY ALLY THEMSELVES WITH ONE ANOTHER.
THAT'S THE ONLY THING WE CAN GRAB HOLD OF.

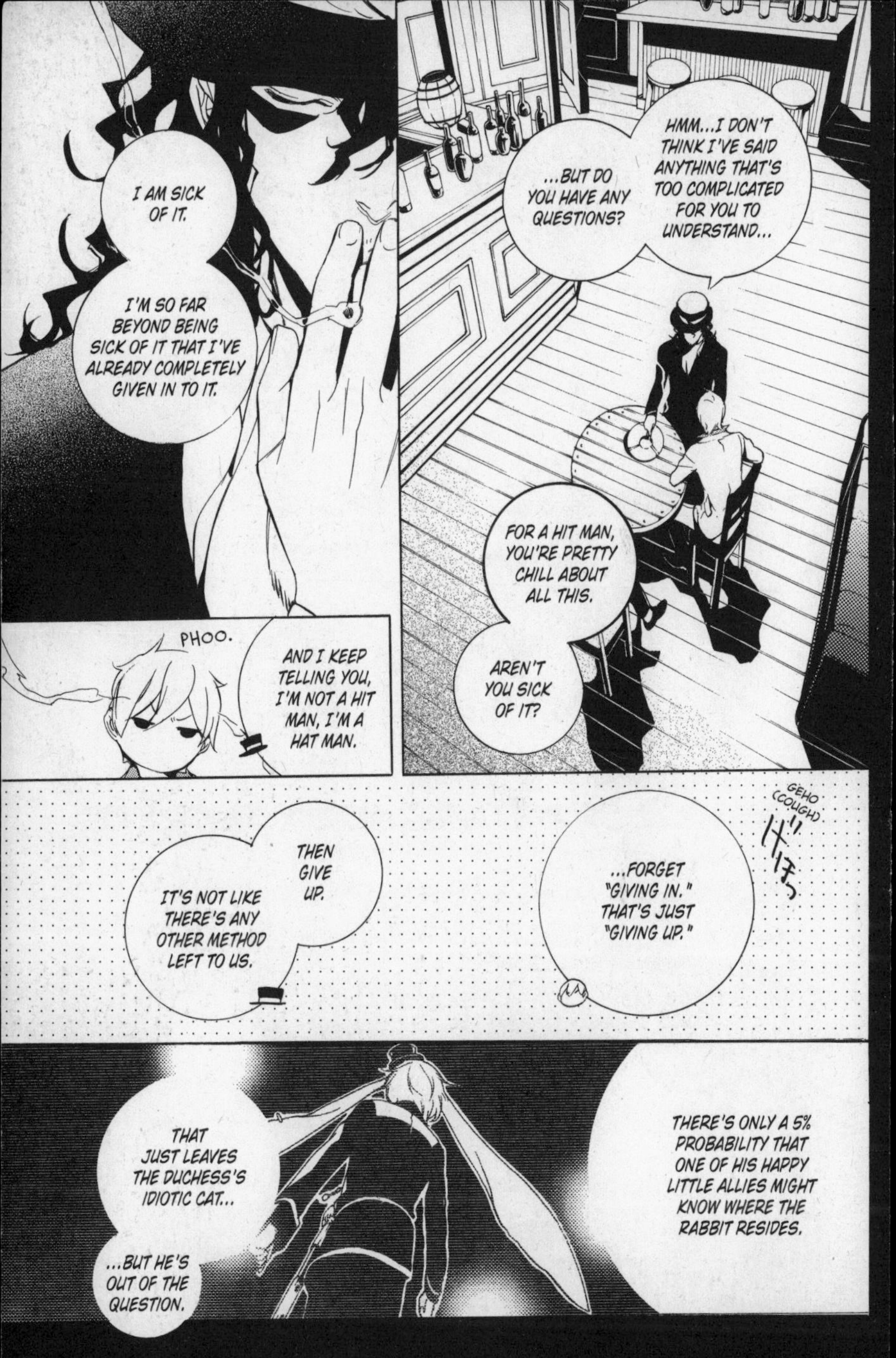
HMM...I DON'T THINK I'VE SAID ANYTHING THAT'S TOO COMPLICATED FOR YOU TO UNDERSTAND...
...BUT DO YOU HAVE ANY QUESTIONS?
FOR A HIT MAN, YOU'RE PRETTY CHILL ABOUT ALL THIS.
AREN'T YOU SICK OF IT?
I AM SICK OF IT.
I'M SO FAR BEYOND BEING SICK OF IT THAT I'VE ALREADY COMPLETELY GIVEN IN TO IT.
PHOO.
AND I KEEP TELLING YOU, I'M NOT A HIT MAN, I'M A HAT MAN.
GEHO (COUGH)
...FORGET "GIVING IN." THAT'S JUST "GIVING UP."
THEN GIVE UP.
IT'S NOT LIKE THERE'S ANY OTHER METHOD LEFT TO US.
THERE'S ONLY A 5% PROBABILITY THAT ONE OF HIS HAPPY LITTLE ALLIES MIGHT KNOW WHERE THE RABBIT RESIDES.
THAT JUST LEAVES THE DUCHESS'S IDIOTIC CAT...
...BUT HE'S OUT OF THE QUESTION.

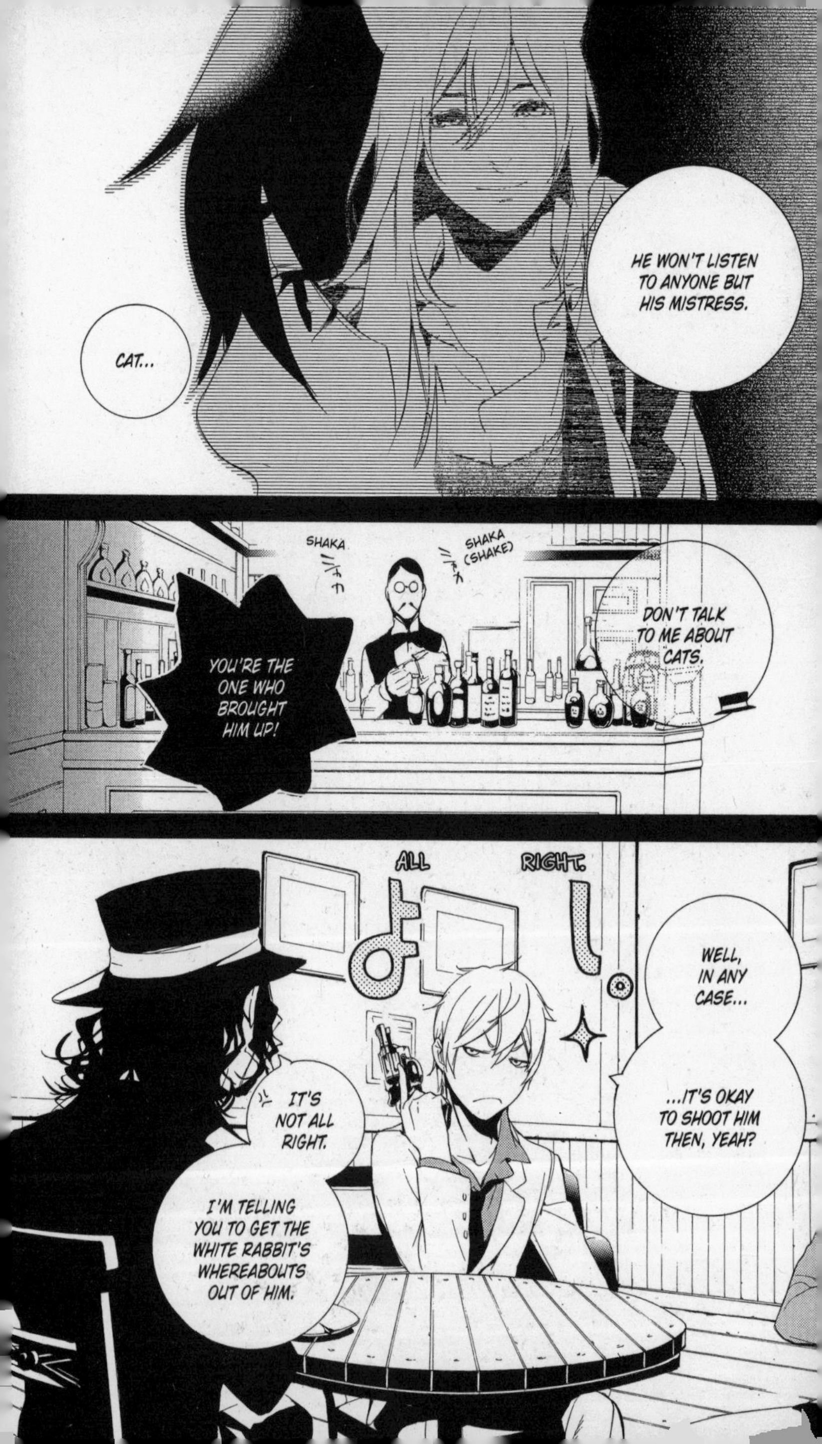
HE WON'T LISTEN TO ANYONE BUT HIS MISTRESS.
CAT...
SHAKA (SHAKE)
SHAKA
DON'T TALK TO ME ABOUT CATS.
YOU'RE THE ONE WHO BROUGHT HIM UP!
RIGHT.
ALL
WELL, IN ANY CASE...
...IT'S OKAY TO SHOOT HIM THEN, YEAH?
IT'S NOT ALL RIGHT.
I'M TELLING YOU TO GET THE WHITE RABBIT'S WHEREABOUTS OUT OF HIM.

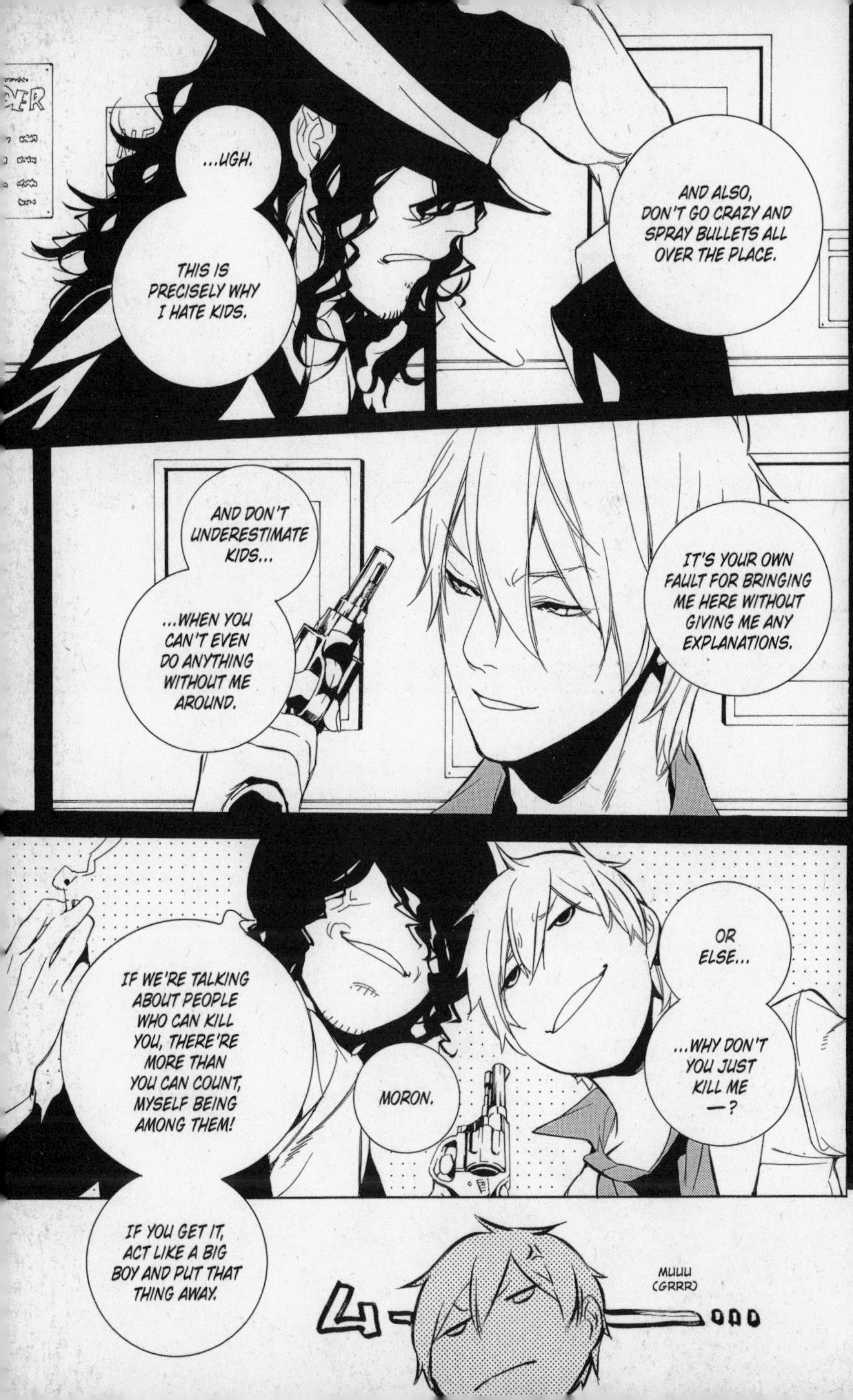
AND ALSO, DON'T GO CRAZY AND SPRAY BULLETS ALL OVER THE PLACE.
...UGH.
THIS IS PRECISELY WHY I HATE KIDS.
IT'S YOUR OWN FAULT FOR BRINGING ME HERE WITHOUT GIVING ME ANY EXPLANATIONS.
AND DON'T UNDERESTIMATE KIDS...
...WHEN YOU CAN'T EVEN DO ANYTHING WITHOUT ME AROUND.
OR ELSE...
...WHY DON'T YOU JUST KILL ME —?
IF WE'RE TALKING ABOUT PEOPLE WHO CAN KILL YOU, THERE'RE MORE THAN YOU CAN COUNT, MYSELF BEING AMONG THEM!
MORON.
IF YOU GET IT, ACT LIKE A BIG BOY AND PUT THAT THING AWAY.
MUUU (GRRR)

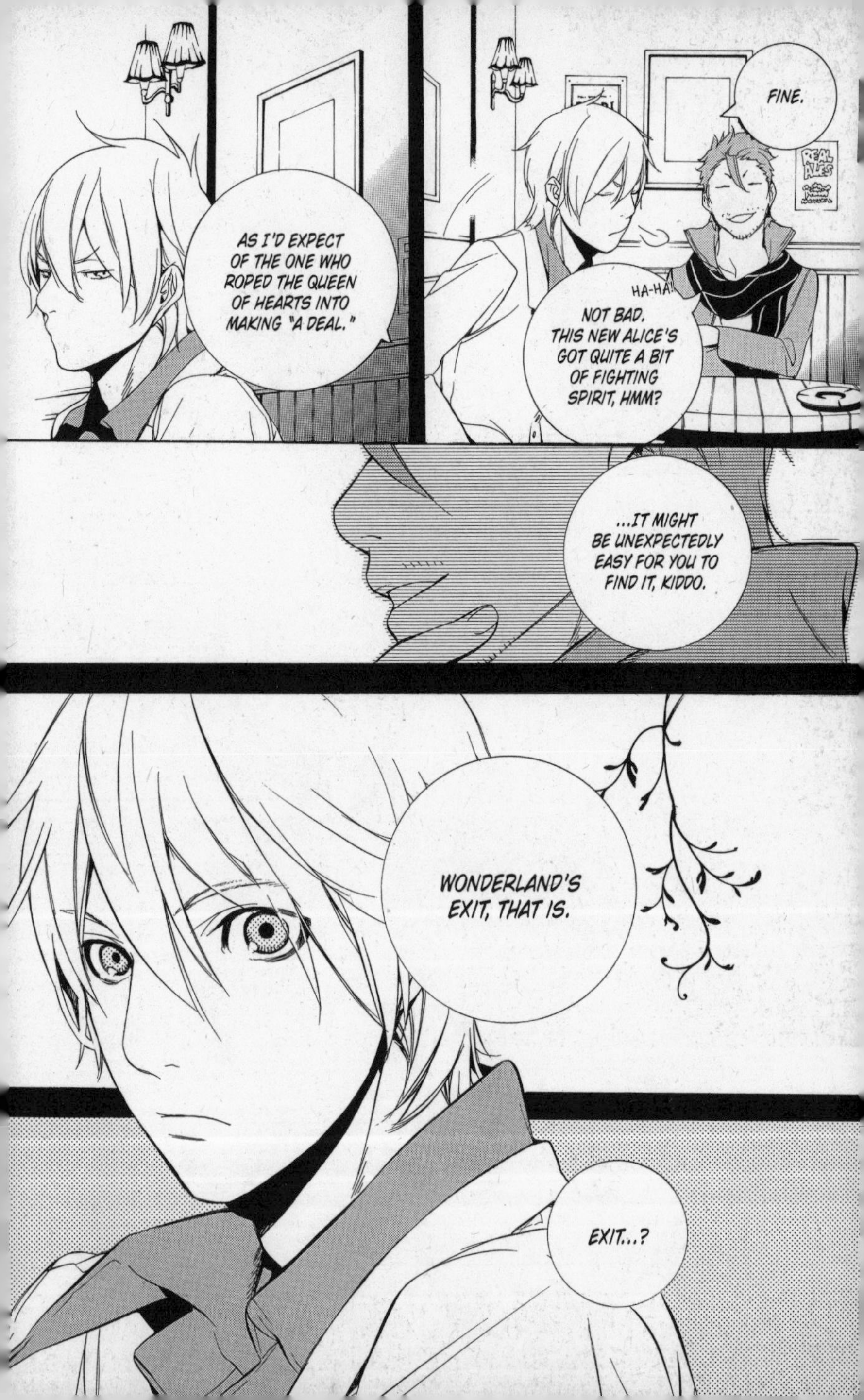
FINE.
REAL ALES
HA-HA!
NOT BAD. THIS NEW ALICE'S GOT QUITE A BIT OF FIGHTING SPIRIT, HMM?
AS I'D EXPECT OF THE ONE WHO ROPED THE QUEEN OF HEARTS INTO MAKING "A DEAL."
...IT MIGHT BE UNEXPECTEDLY EASY FOR YOU TO FIND IT, KIDDO.
WONDERLAND'S EXIT, THAT IS.
EXIT...?

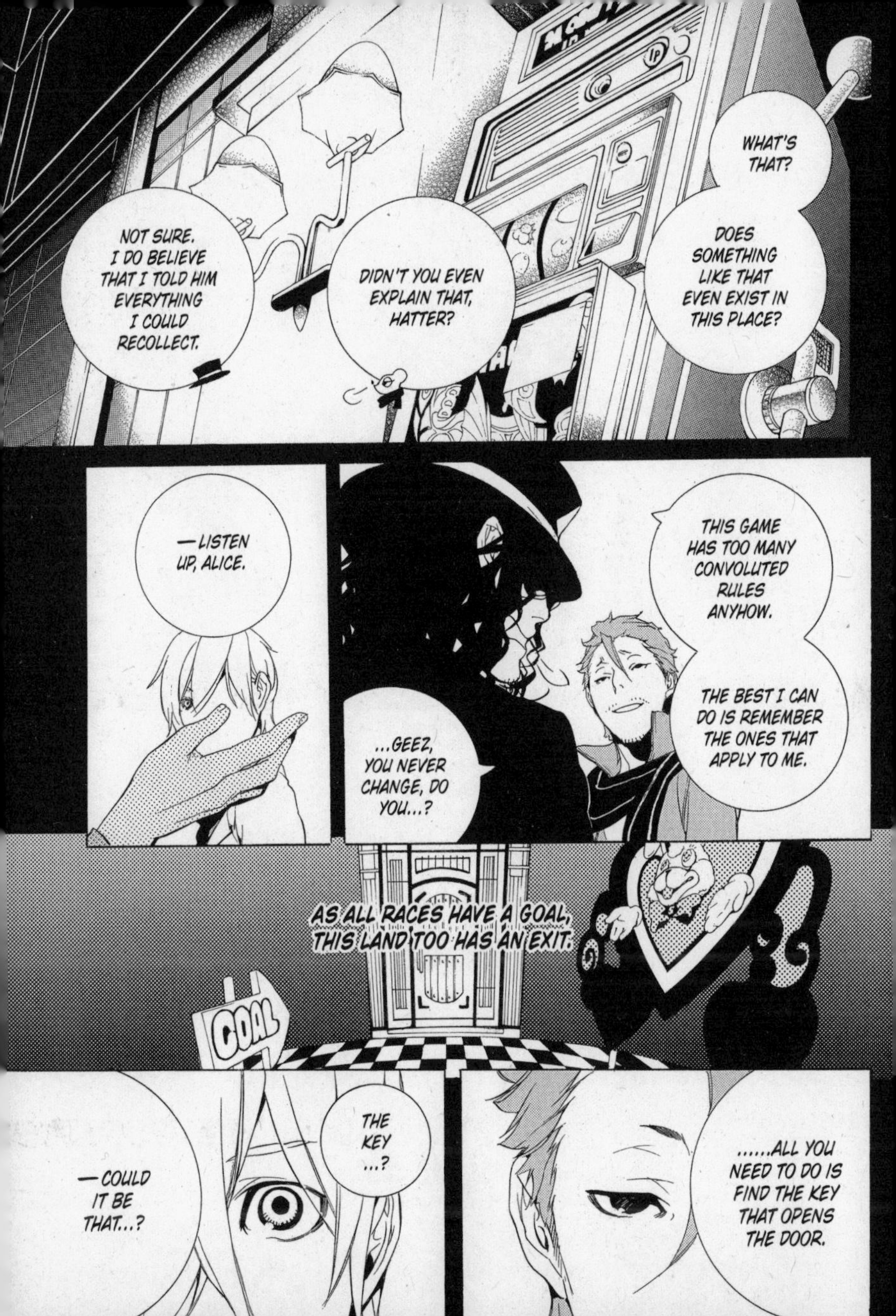
WHAT'S THAT?
DOES SOMETHING LIKE THAT EVEN EXIST IN THIS PLACE?
DIDN'T YOU EVEN EXPLAIN THAT, HATTER?
NOT SURE. I DO BELIEVE THAT I TOLD HIM EVERYTHING I COULD RECOLLECT.
THIS GAME HAS TOO MANY CONVOLUTED RULES ANYHOW.
THE BEST I CAN DO IS REMEMBER THE ONES THAT APPLY TO ME.
...GEEZ, YOU NEVER CHANGE, DO YOU...?
—LISTEN UP, ALICE.
AS ALL RACES HAVE A GOAL, THIS LAND TOO HAS AN EXIT.
GOAL
......ALL YOU NEED TO DO IS FIND THE KEY THAT OPENS THE DOOR.
THE KEY ...?
—COULD IT BE THAT...?

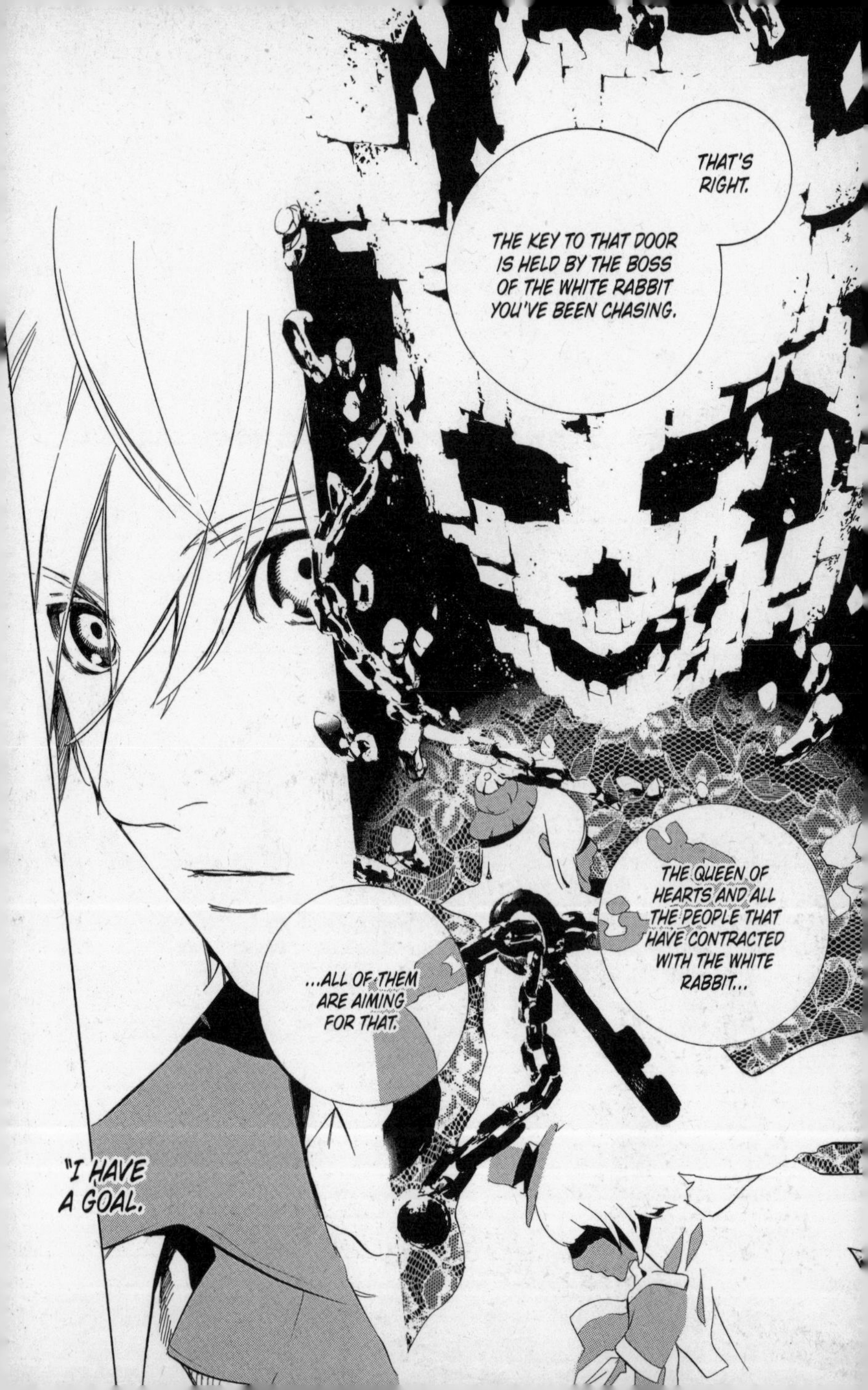
THAT'S RIGHT.
THE KEY TO THAT DOOR IS HELD BY THE BOSS OF THE WHITE RABBIT YOU'VE BEEN CHASING.
THE QUEEN OF HEARTS AND ALL THE PEOPLE THAT HAVE CONTRACTED WITH THE WHITE RABBIT...
...ALL OF THEM ARE AIMING FOR THAT.
"I HAVE A GOAL.

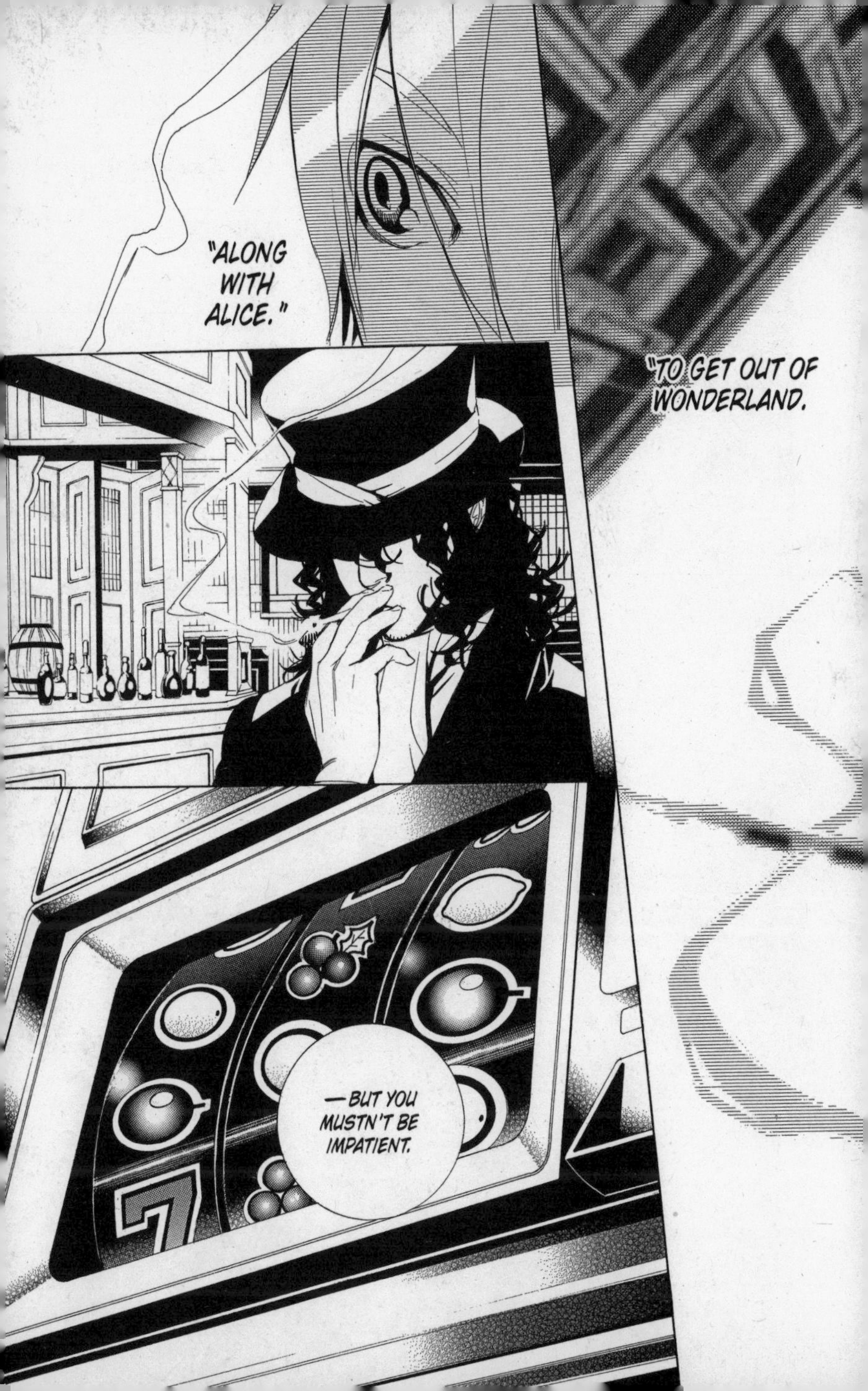
"TO GET OUT OF WONDERLAND.
"ALONG WITH ALICE."
—BUT YOU MUSTN'T BE IMPATIENT.

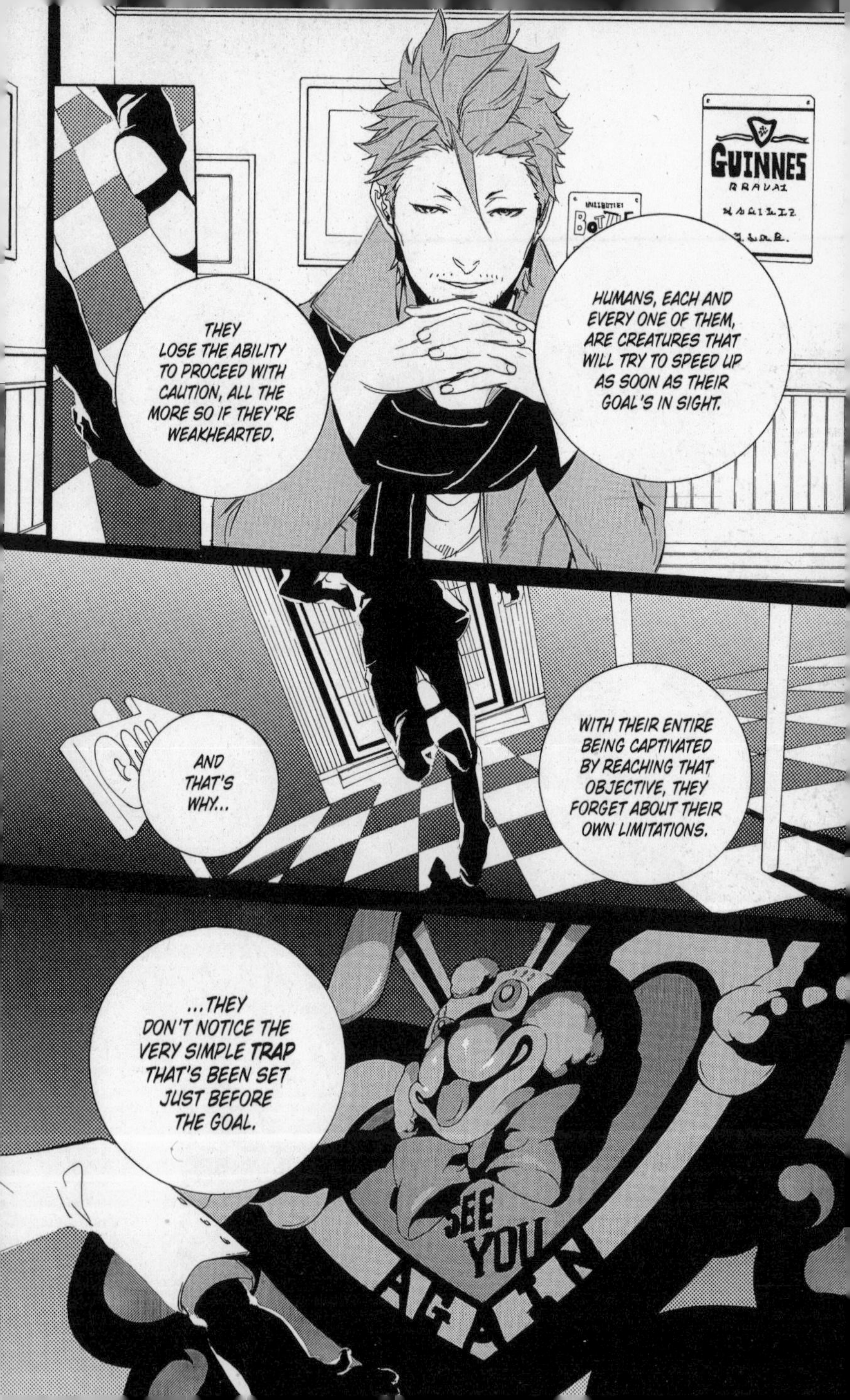
GUINNES
HUMANS, EACH AND EVERY ONE OF THEM, ARE CREATURES THAT WILL TRY TO SPEED UP AS SOON AS THEIR GOAL'S IN SIGHT.
THEY LOSE THE ABILITY TO PROCEED WITH CAUTION, ALL THE MORE SO IF THEY'RE WEAKHEARTED.
WITH THEIR ENTIRE BEING CAPTIVATED BY REACHING THAT OBJECTIVE, THEY FORGET ABOUT THEIR OWN LIMITATIONS.
AND THAT'S WHY...
...THEY DON'T NOTICE THE VERY SIMPLE TRAP THAT'S BEEN SET JUST BEFORE THE GOAL.
SEE YOU AGAIN

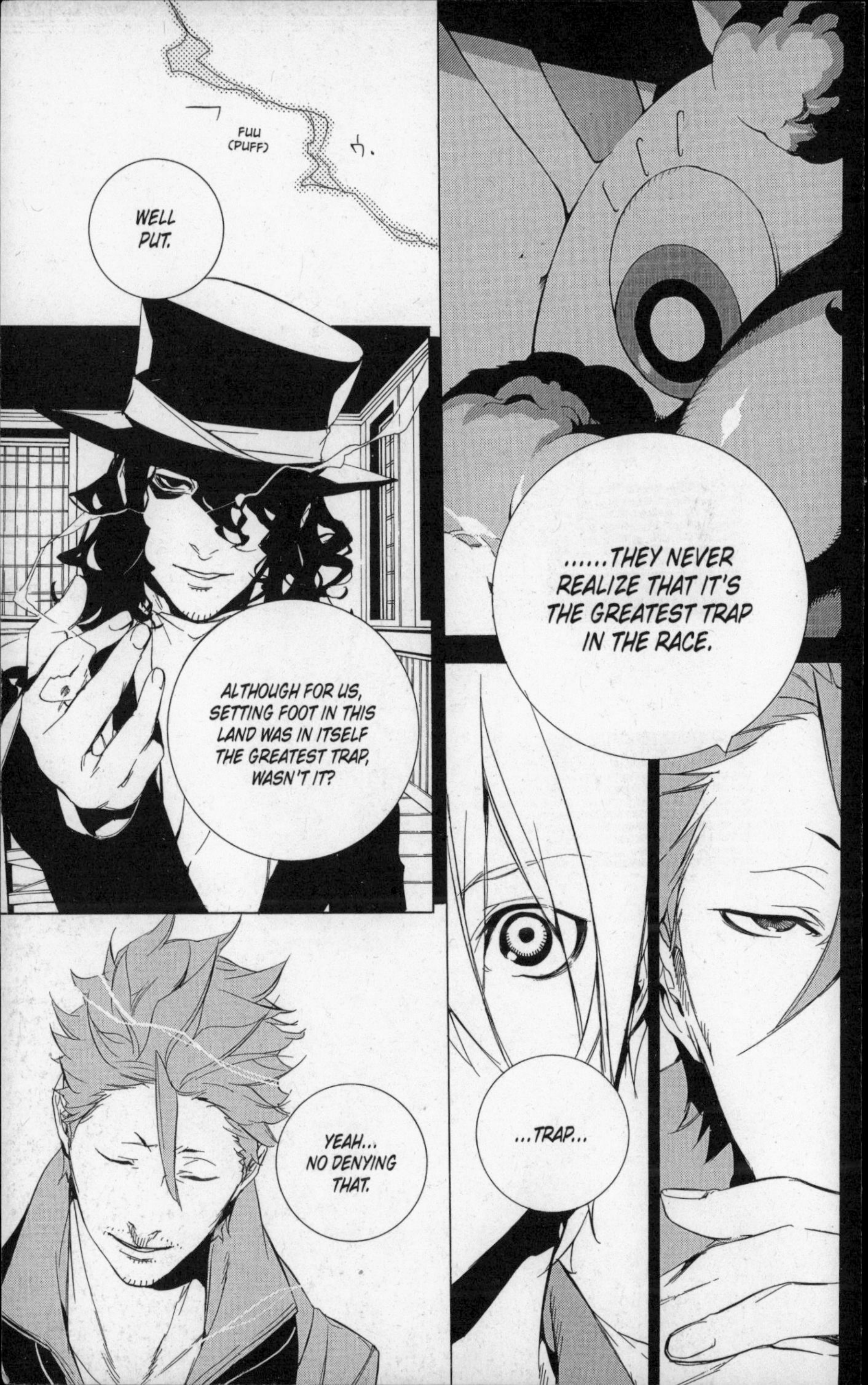
......THEY NEVER REALIZE THAT IT'S THE GREATEST TRAP IN THE RACE.
FUU (PUFF)
WELL PUT.
ALTHOUGH FOR US, SETTING FOOT IN THIS LAND WAS IN ITSELF THE GREATEST TRAP, WASN'T IT?
YEAH... NO DENYING THAT.
...TRAP...

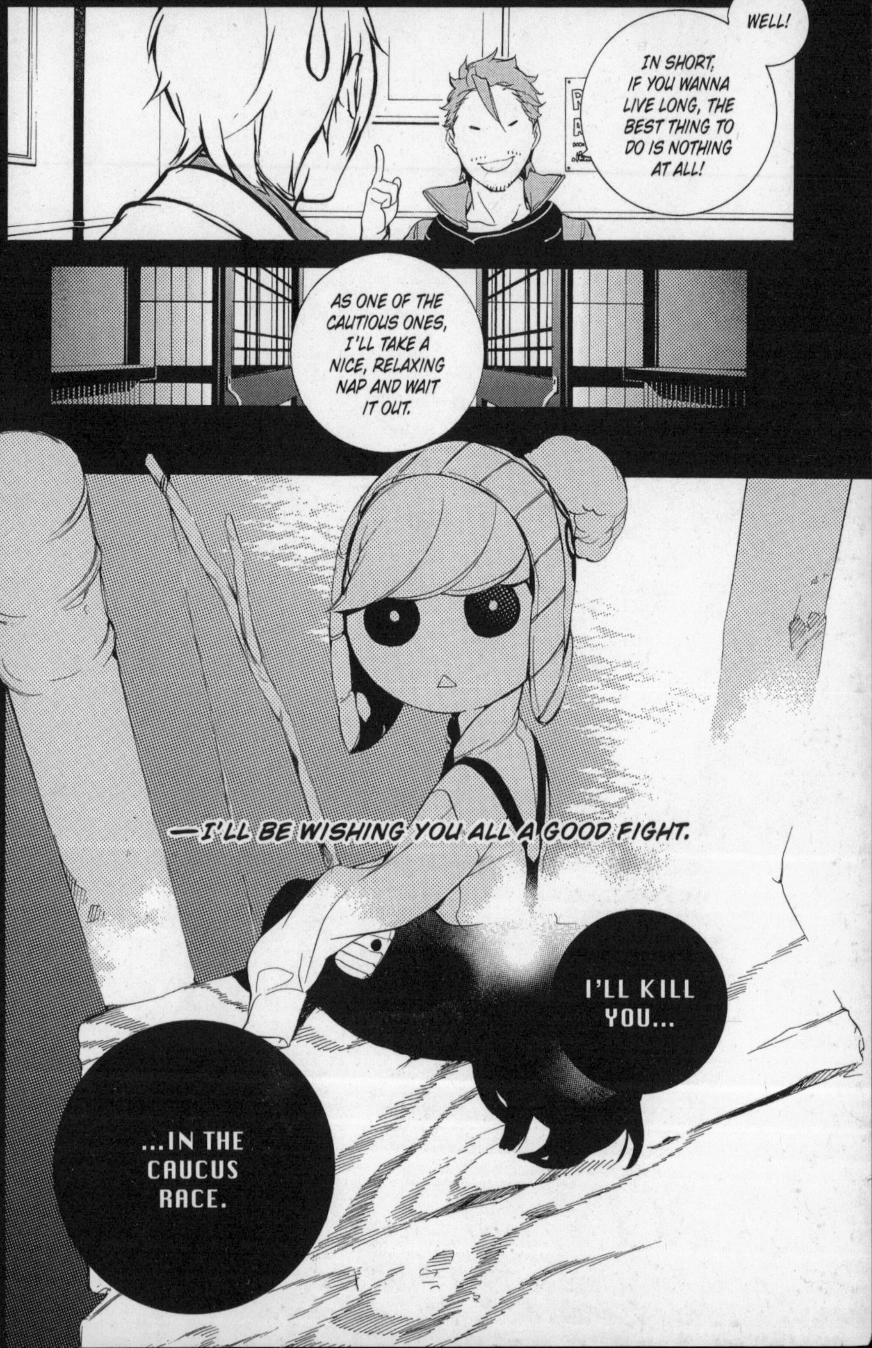
WELL!
IN SHORT, IF YOU WANNA LIVE LONG, THE BEST THING TO DO IS NOTHING AT ALL!
AS ONE OF THE CAUTIOUS ONES, I'LL TAKE A NICE, RELAXING NAP AND WAIT IT OUT.
—I'LL BE WISHING YOU ALL A GOOD FIGHT.
I'LL KILL YOU...
...IN THE CAUCUS RACE.

Chapter 23

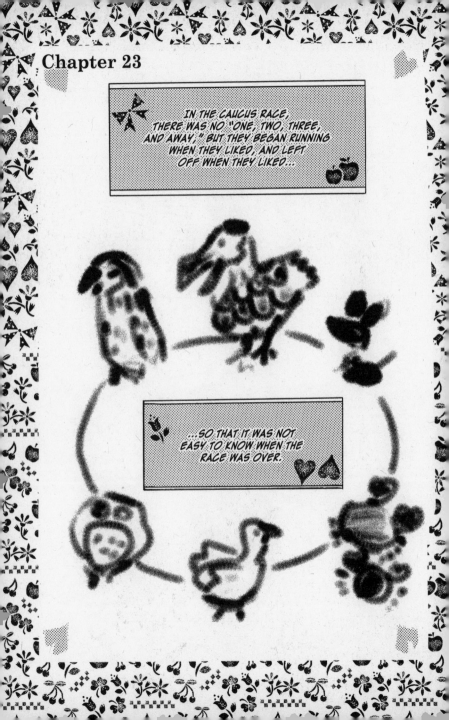

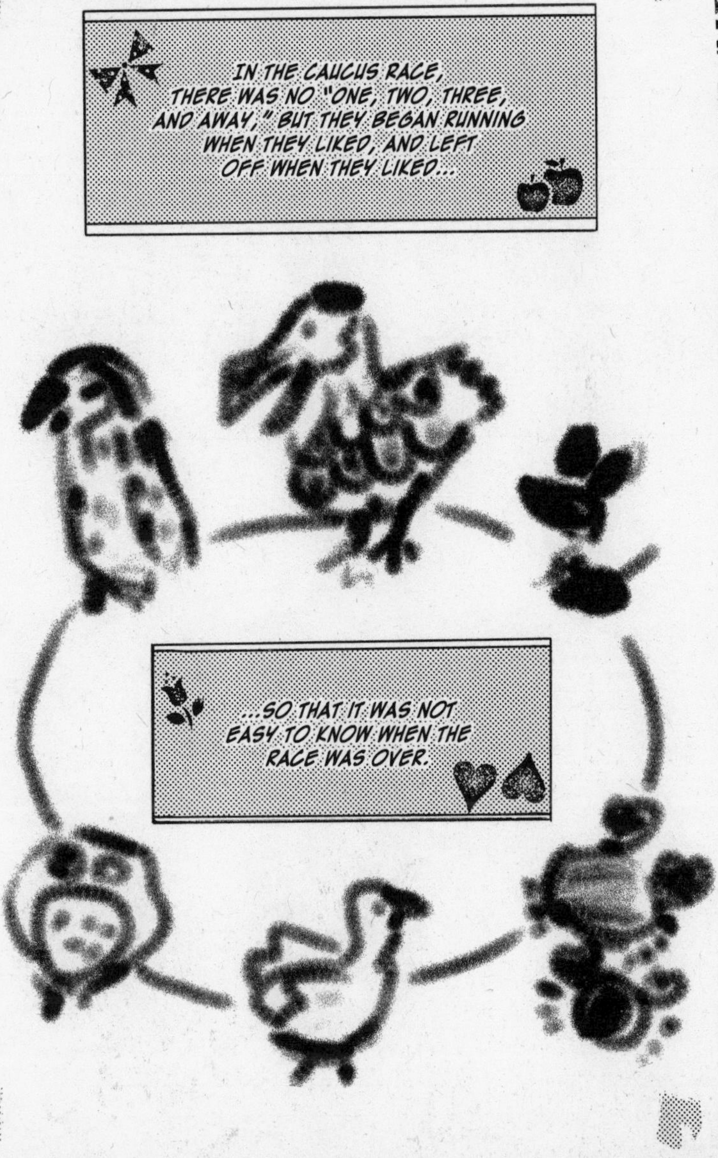
IN THE CAUCUS RACE, THERE WAS NO "ONE, TWO, THREE, AND AWAY," BUT THEY BEGAN RUNNING WHEN THEY LIKED, AND LEFT OFF WHEN THEY LIKED...
...SO THAT IT WAS NOT EASY TO KNOW WHEN THE RACE WAS OVER.

HOWEVER, WHEN THEY HAD BEEN RUNNING HALF AN HOUR OR SO, THE DODO SUDDENLY CALLED OUT...

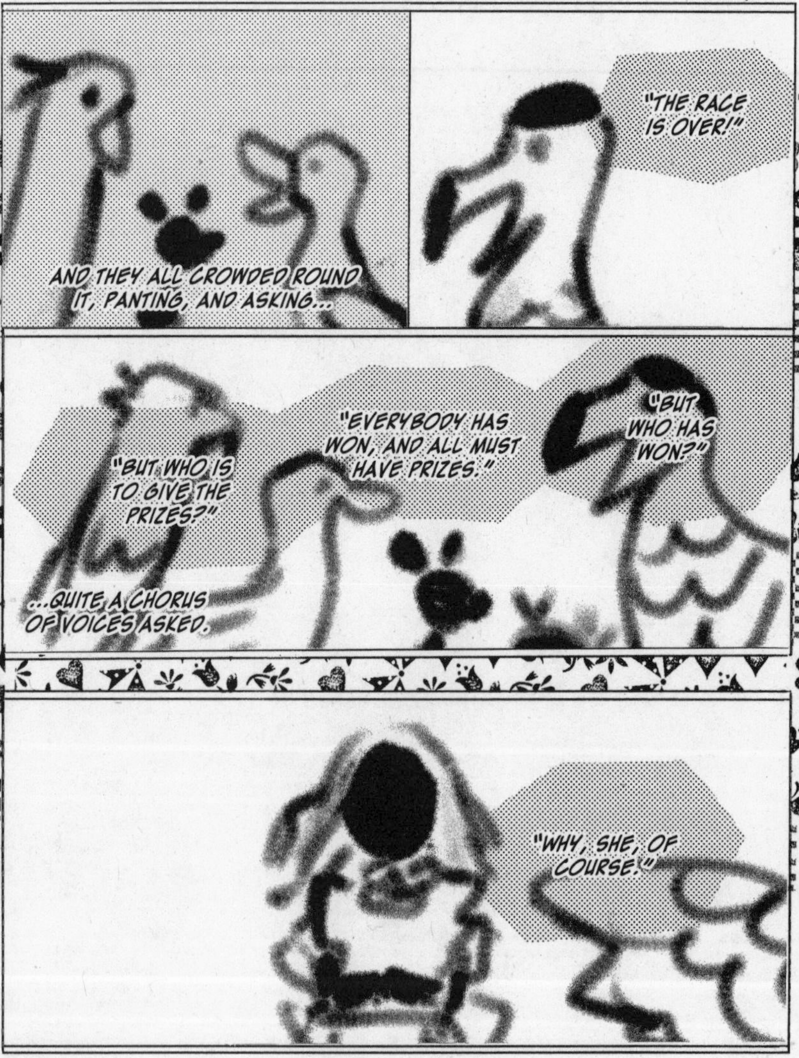
"THE RACE IS OVER!"
AND THEY ALL CROWDED ROUND IT, PANTING, AND ASKING...
"BUT WHO HAS WON?"
"EVERYBODY HAS WON, AND ALL MUST HAVE PRIZES."
"BUT WHO IS TO GIVE THE PRIZES?"
...QUITE A CHORUS OF VOICES ASKED.
"WHY, SHE, OF COURSE."

...SAID THE DODO, POINTING TO ALICE.

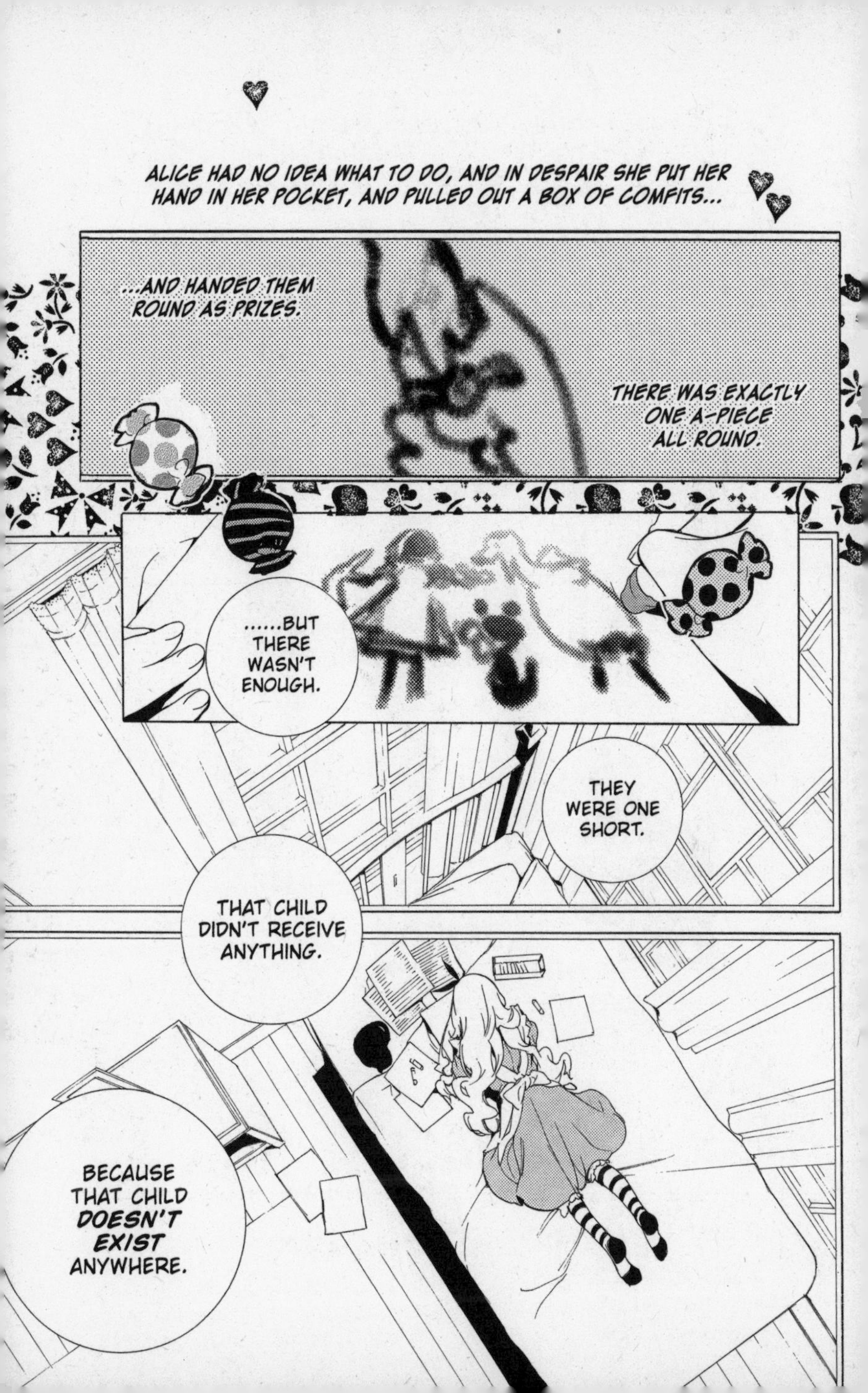
ALICE HAD NO IDEA WHAT TO DO, AND IN DESPAIR SHE PUT HER HAND IN HER POCKET, AND PULLED OUT A BOX OF COMFITS...
...AND HANDED THEM ROUND AS PRIZES.
THERE WAS EXACTLY ONE A-PIECE ALL ROUND.
......BUT THERE WASN'T ENOUGH.
THEY WERE ONE SHORT.
THAT CHILD DIDN'T RECEIVE ANYTHING.
BECAUSE THAT CHILD *DOESN'T EXIST* ANYWHERE.

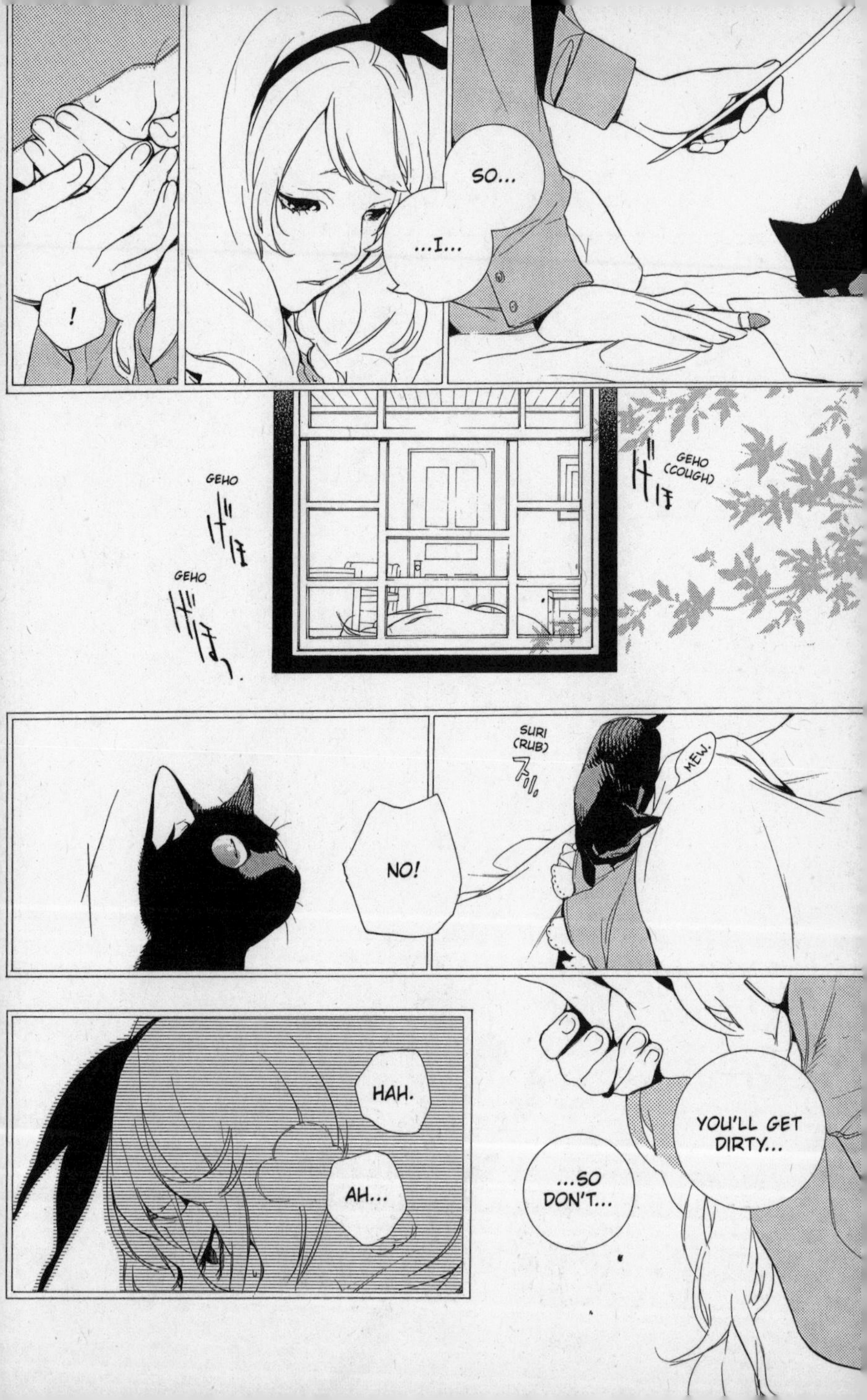
SO...
...I...
!
GEHO (COUGH)
げほ
GEHO
げほ
GEHO
げほっ
MEW.
SURI (RUB)
スリ
NO!
YOU'LL GET DIRTY...
...SO DON'T...
HAH.
AH...

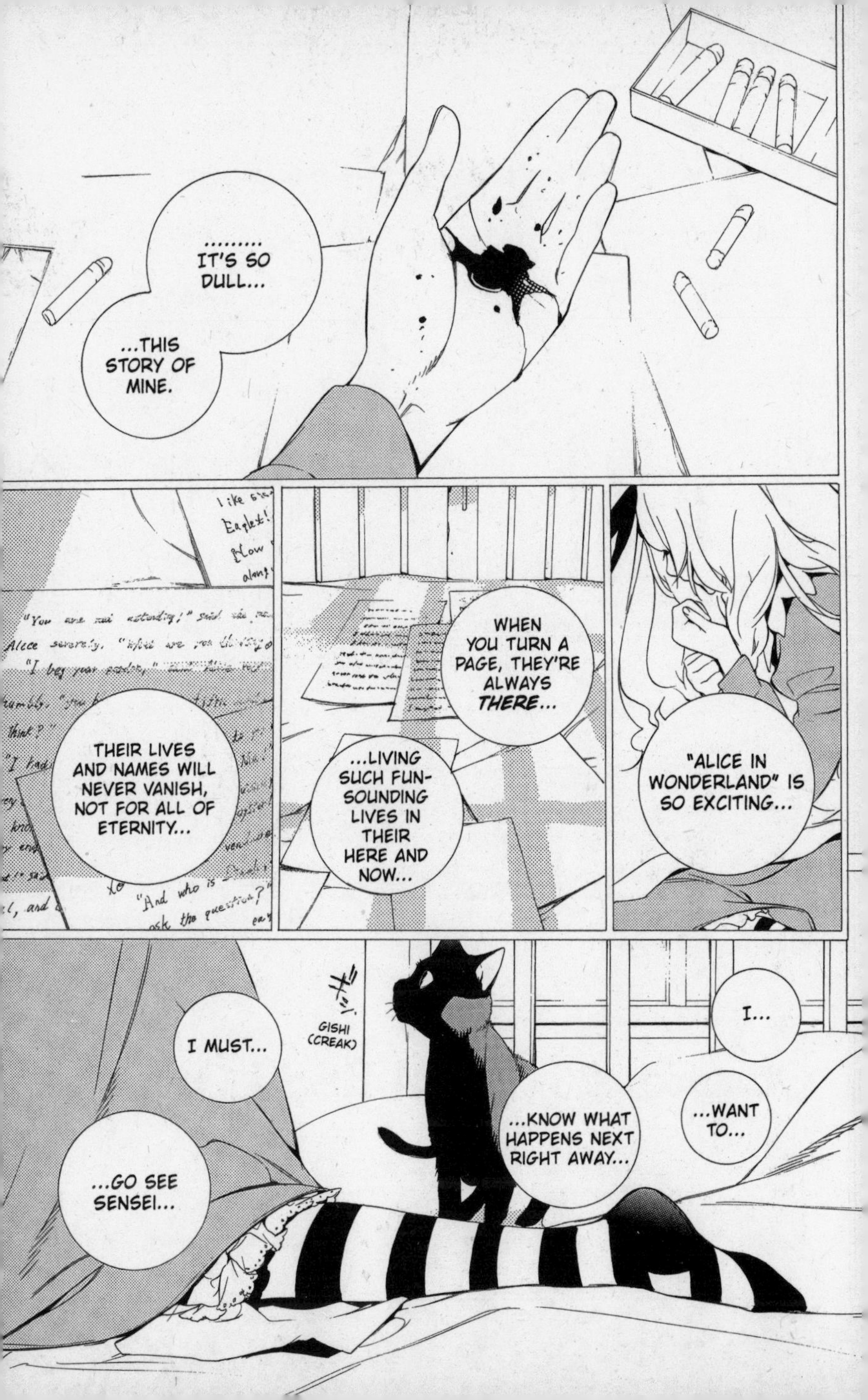
.... IT'S SO DULL...
...THIS STORY OF MINE.
"ALICE IN WONDERLAND" IS SO EXCITING...
WHEN YOU TURN A PAGE, THEY'RE ALWAYS *THERE*...
...LIVING SUCH FUN-SOUNDING LIVES IN THEIR HERE AND NOW...
THEIR LIVES AND NAMES WILL NEVER VANISH, NOT FOR ALL OF ETERNITY...
I...
...WANT TO...
...KNOW WHAT HAPPENS NEXT RIGHT AWAY...
GISHI (CREAK)
I MUST...
...GO SEE SENSEI...

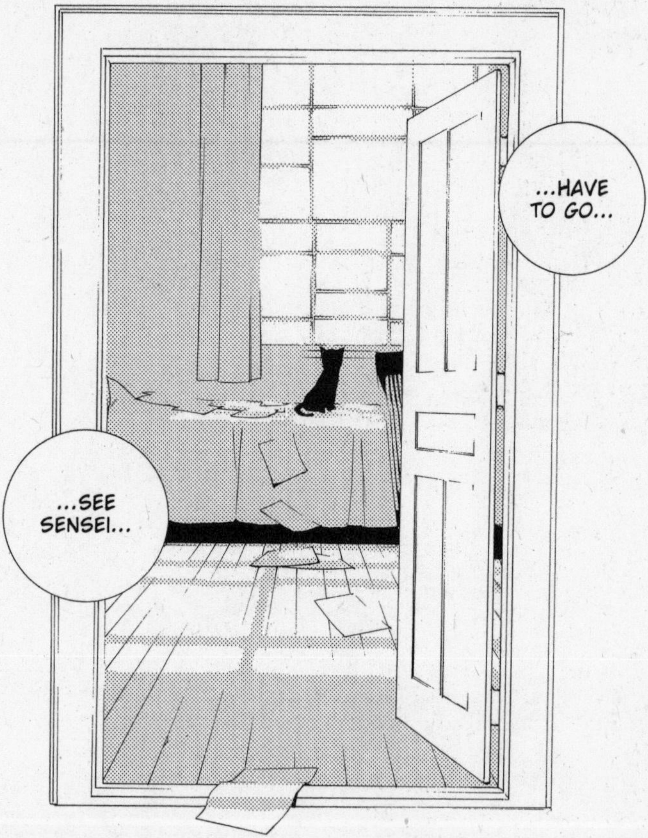
...HAVE TO GO...
...SEE SENSEI...

Chapter 23 ENDLESS LOOP.

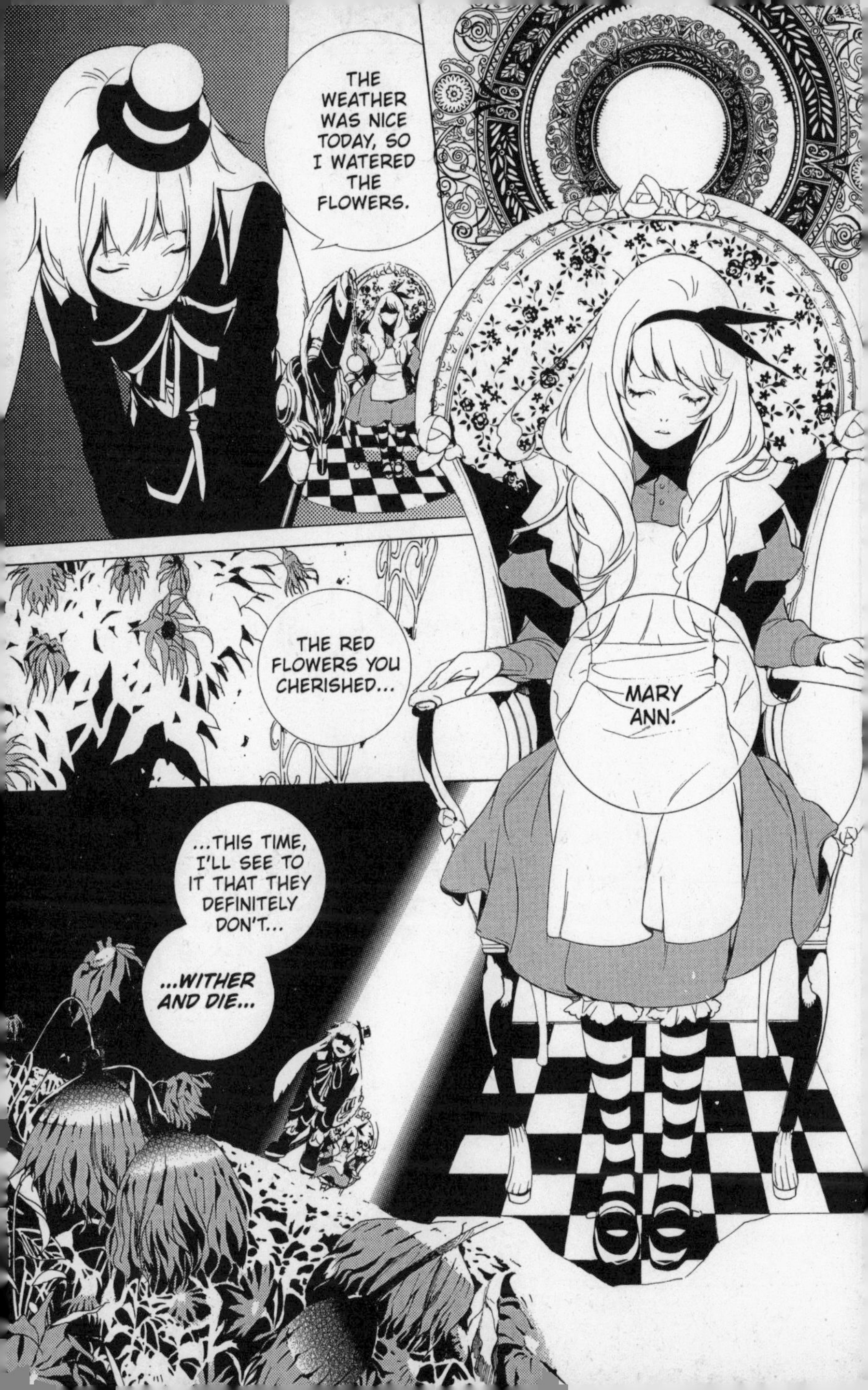
MARY ANN.
THE WEATHER WAS NICE TODAY, SO I WATERED THE FLOWERS.
THE RED FLOWERS YOU CHERISHED...
...THIS TIME, I'LL SEE TO IT THAT THEY DEFINITELY DON'T...
...WITHER AND DIE...

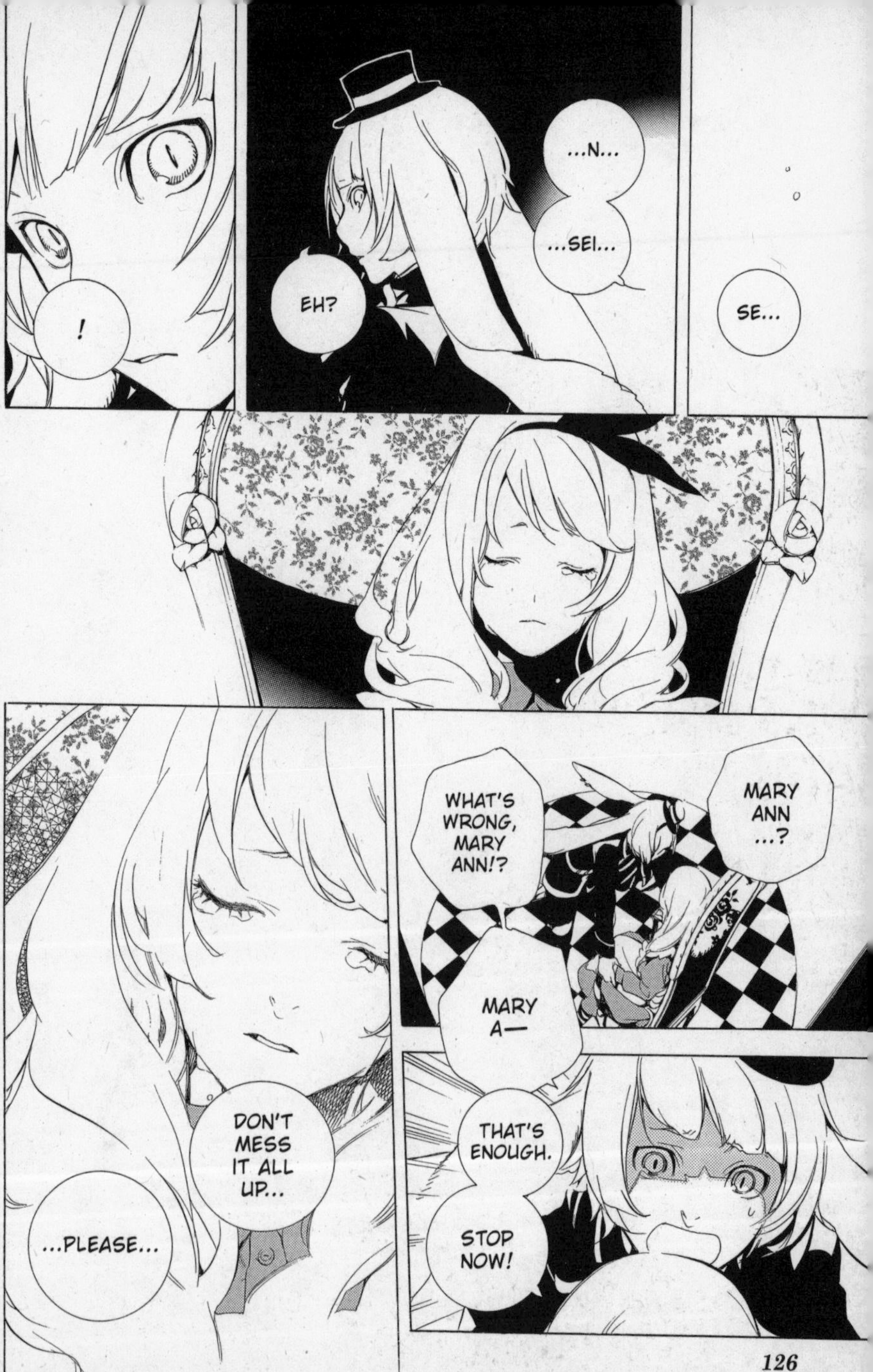
SE...
...N...
...SEI...
EH?
!
MARY ANN ...?
WHAT'S WRONG, MARY ANN!?
MARY A—
THAT'S ENOUGH.
STOP NOW!
DON'T MESS IT ALL UP...
...PLEASE...

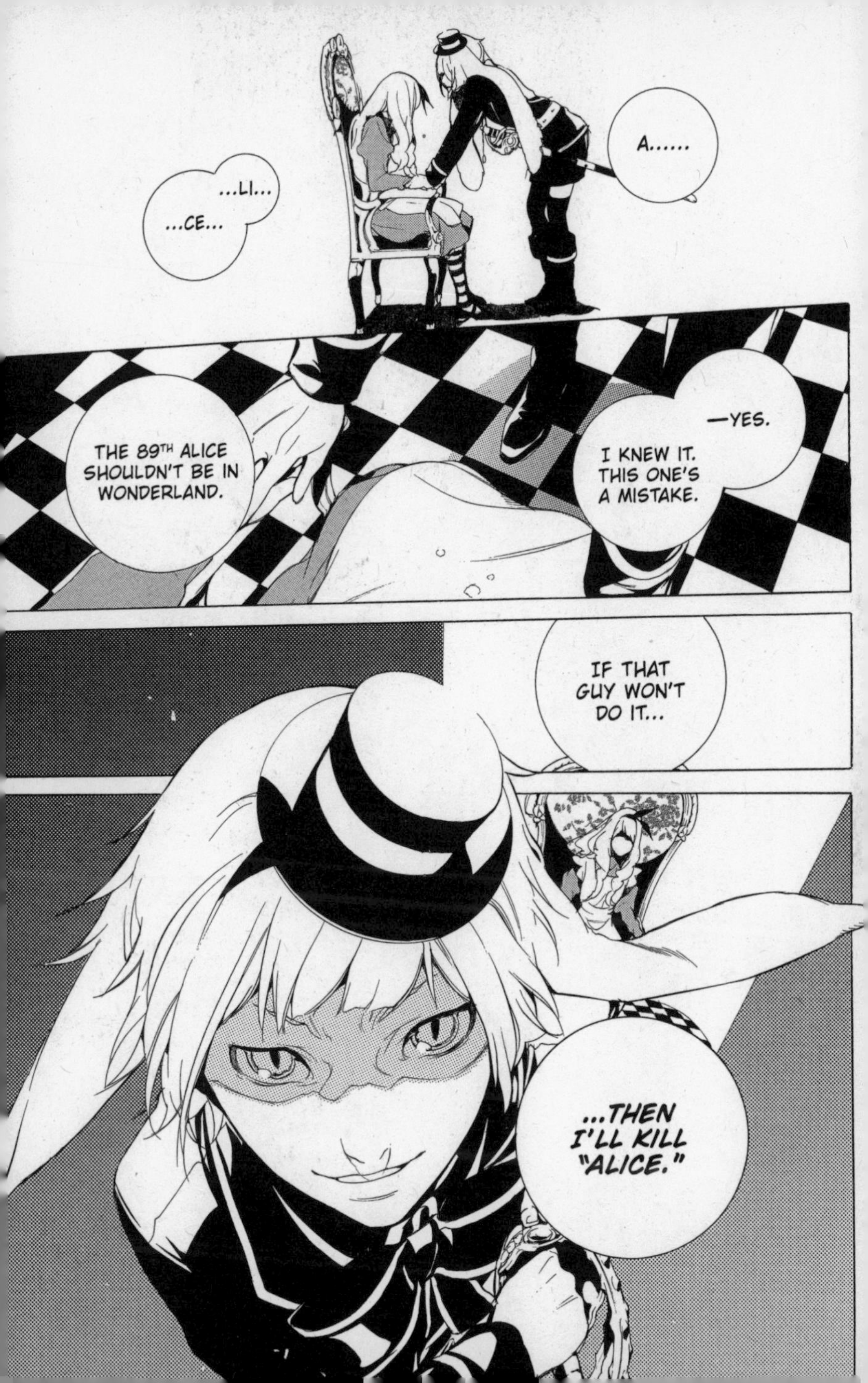
A......
...LI...
...CE...
—YES.
I KNEW IT. THIS ONE'S A MISTAKE.
THE 89TH ALICE SHOULDN'T BE IN WONDERLAND.
IF THAT GUY WON'T DO IT...
...THEN I'LL KILL "ALICE."

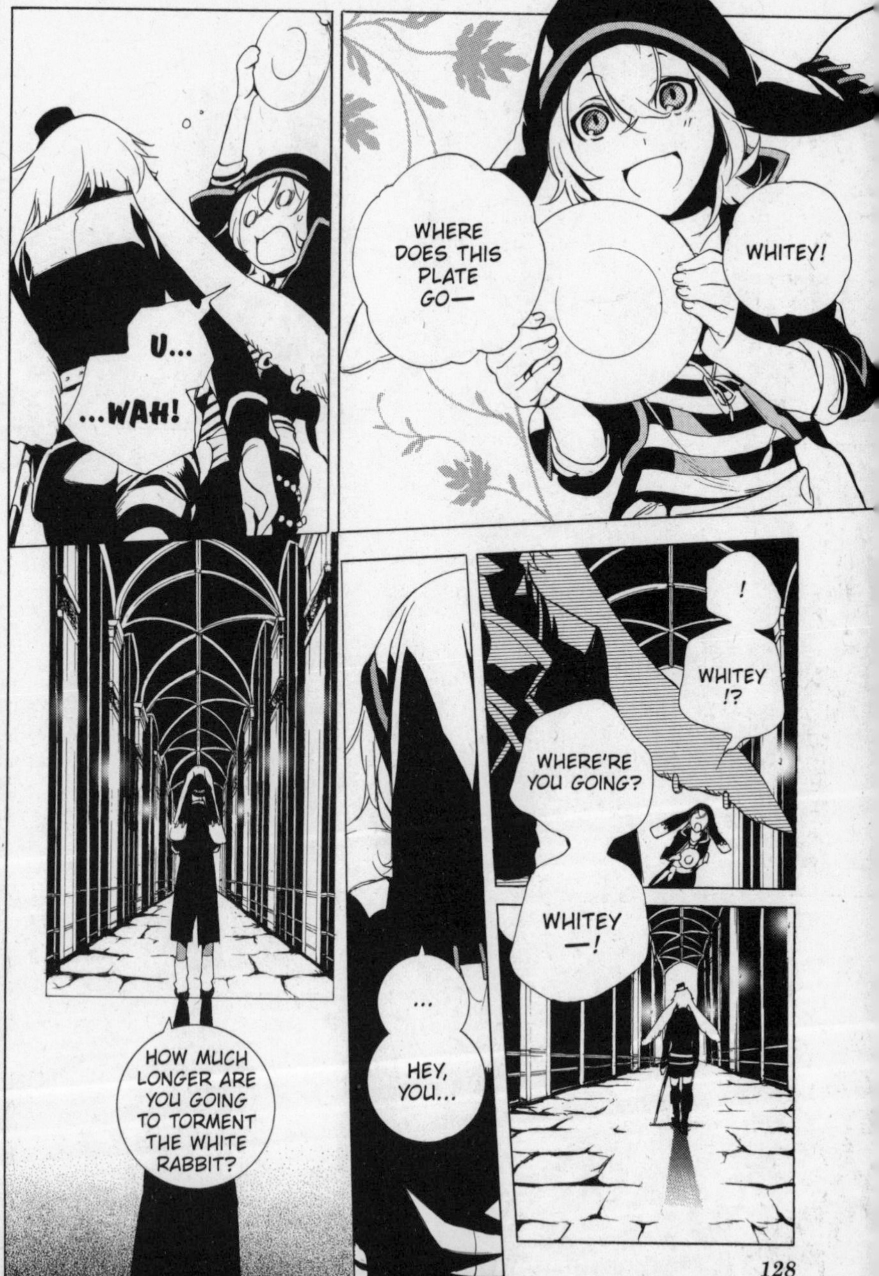
WHITEY!
WHERE DOES THIS PLATE GO—
U...
...WAH!
!
WHITEY !?
WHERE'RE YOU GOING?
WHITEY —!
...
HEY, YOU...
HOW MUCH LONGER ARE YOU GOING TO TORMENT THE WHITE RABBIT?

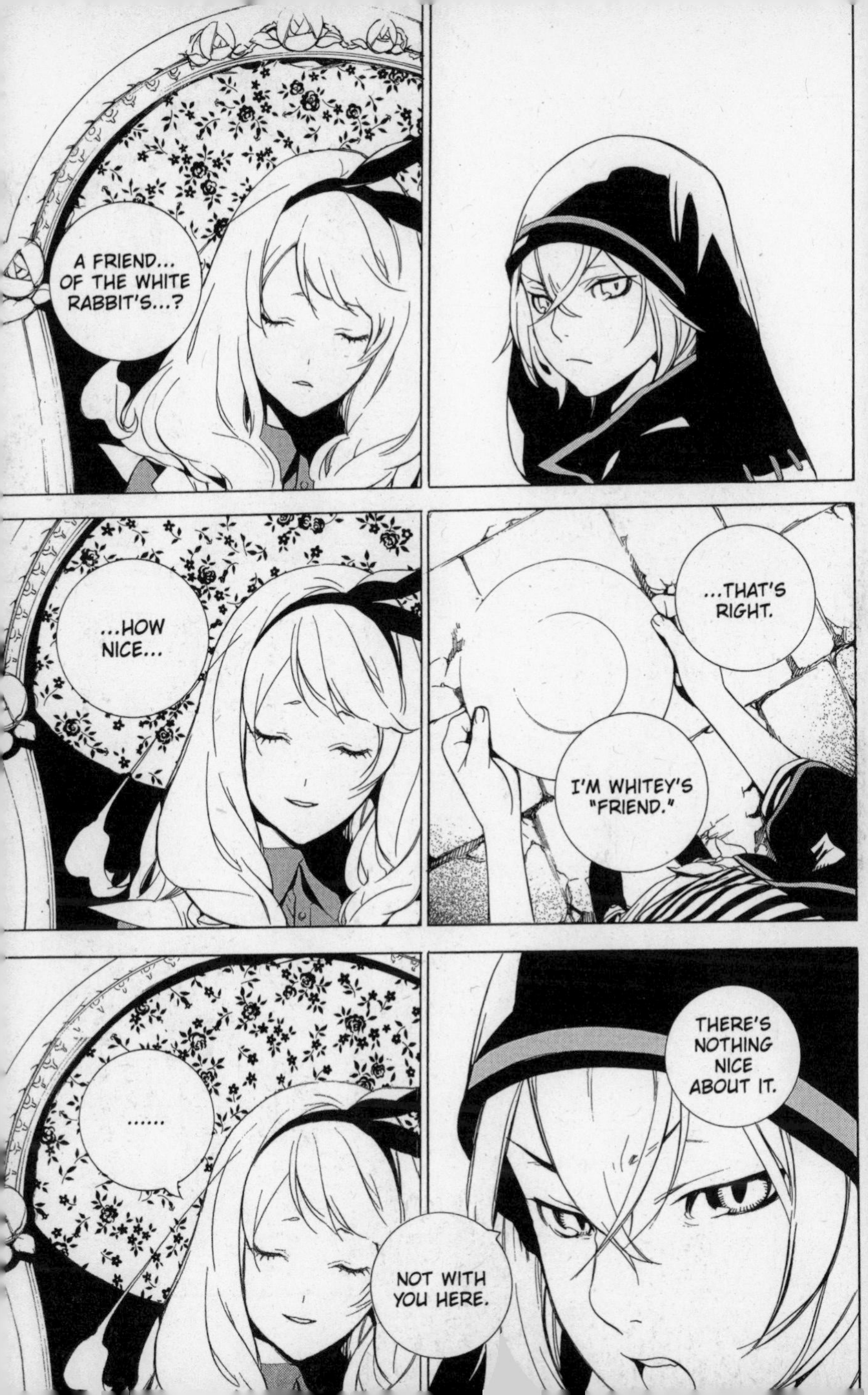
A FRIEND... OF THE WHITE RABBIT'S...?
...THAT'S RIGHT.
I'M WHITEY'S "FRIEND."
...HOW NICE...
THERE'S NOTHING NICE ABOUT IT.
......
NOT WITH YOU HERE.

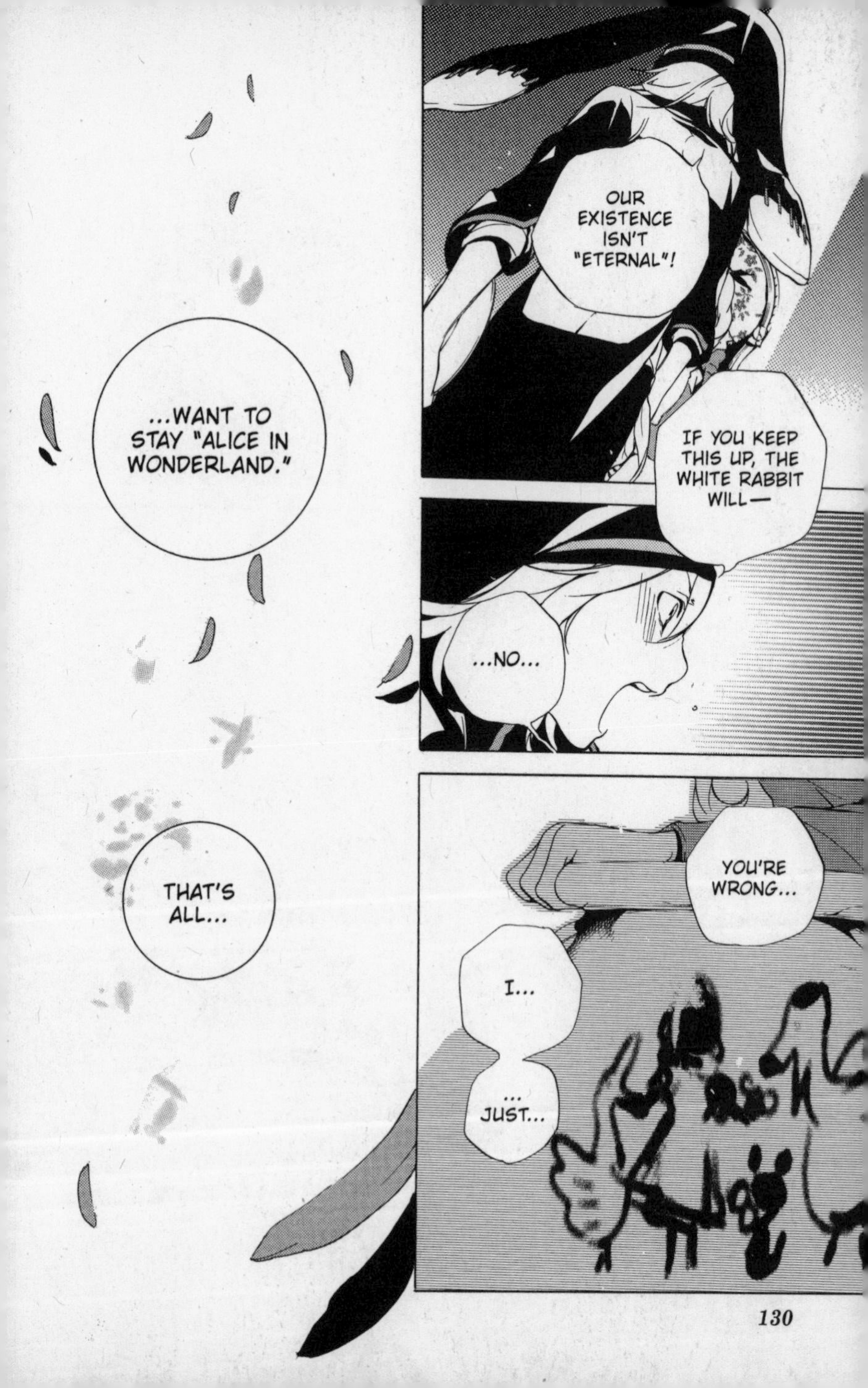
OUR EXISTENCE ISN'T "ETERNAL"!
IF YOU KEEP THIS UP, THE WHITE RABBIT WILL—
...NO...
YOU'RE WRONG...
I...
...JUST...
...WANT TO STAY "ALICE IN WONDERLAND."
THAT'S ALL...

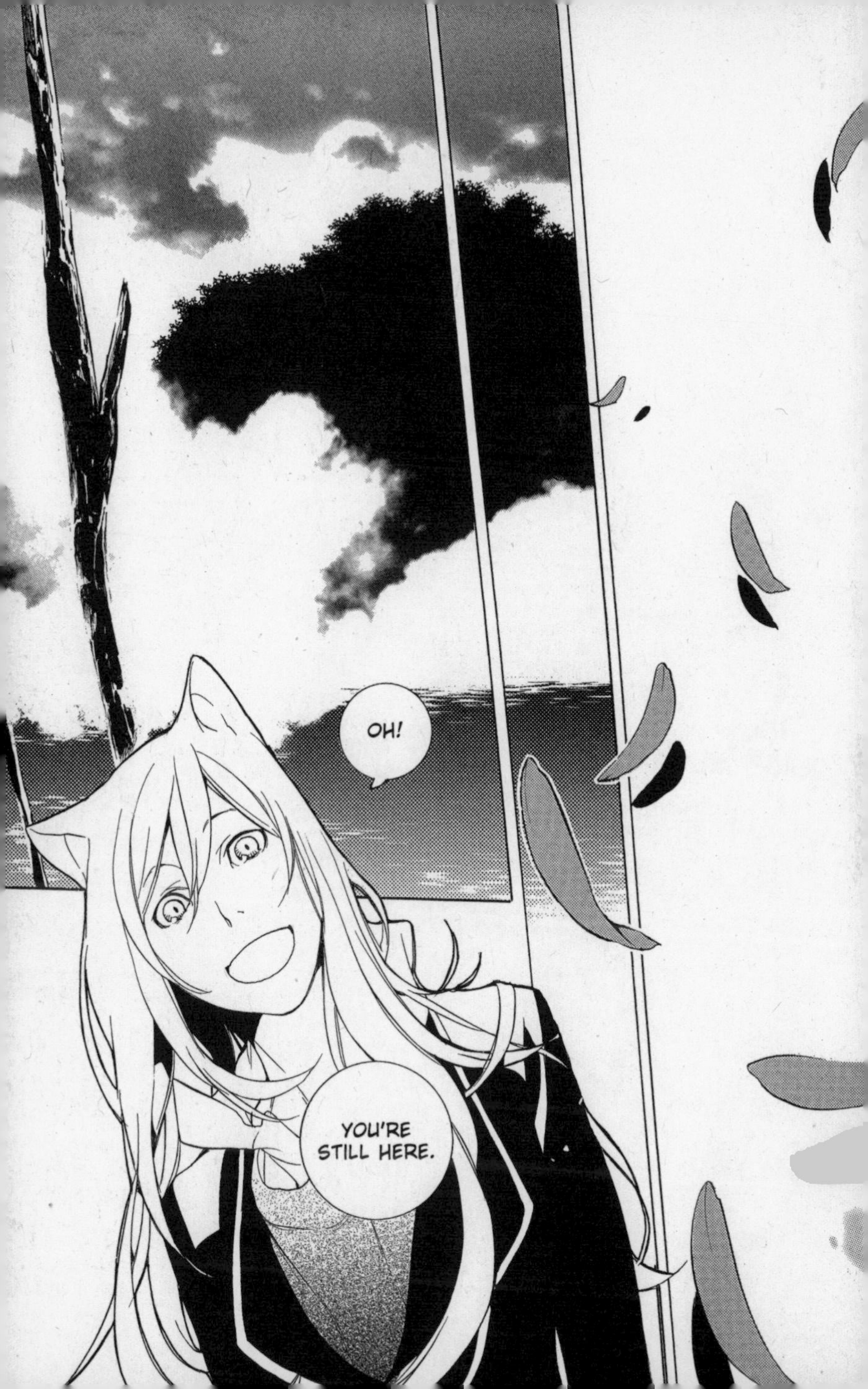
OH!
YOU'RE STILL HERE.

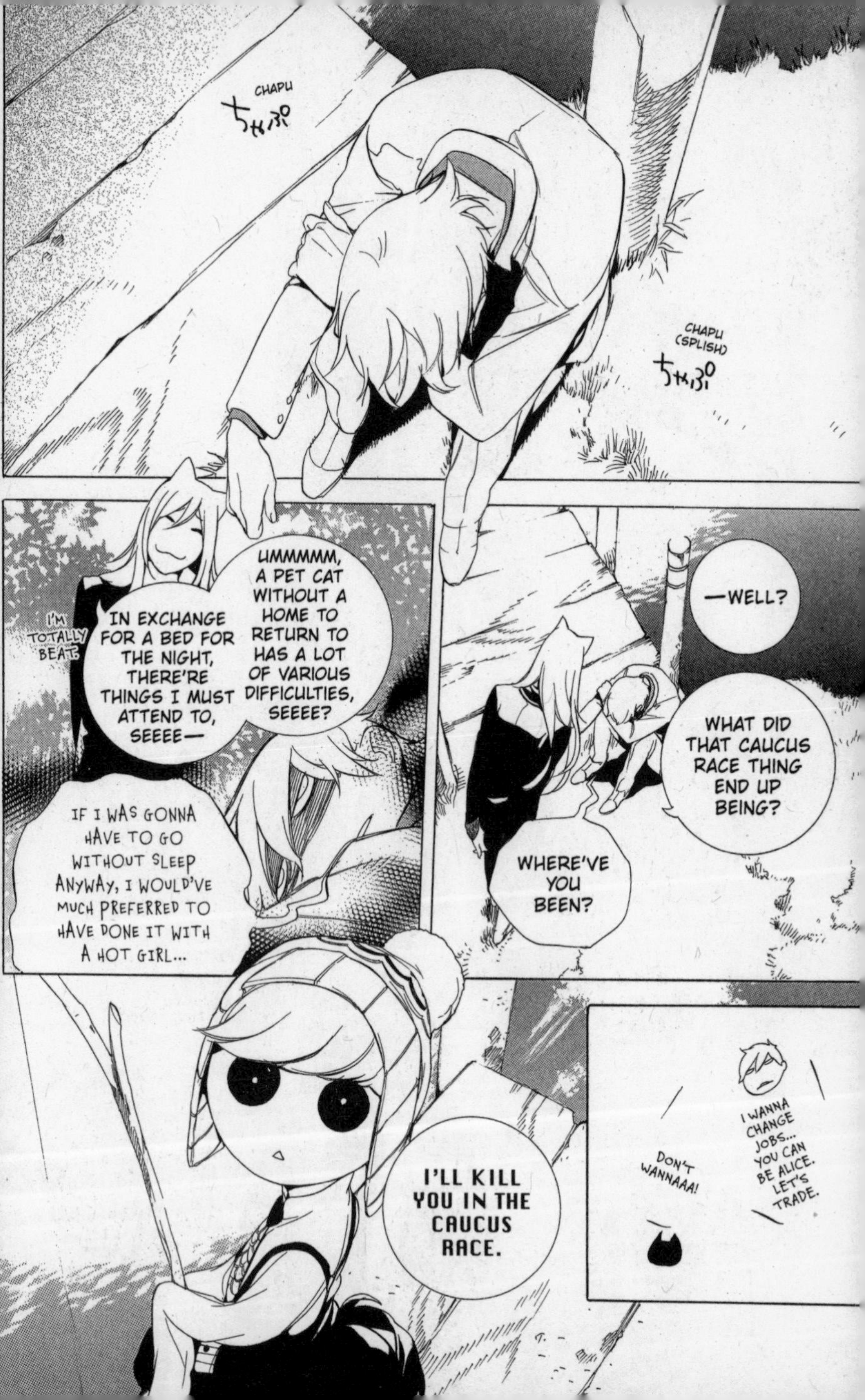
CHAPU (SPLISH)
ちゃぷ
CHAPU
ちゃぷ
—WELL?
WHAT DID THAT CAUCUS RACE THING END UP BEING?
WHERE'VE YOU BEEN?
UMMMMM, A PET CAT WITHOUT A HOME TO RETURN TO HAS A LOT OF VARIOUS DIFFICULTIES, SEEEE?
IN EXCHANGE FOR A BED FOR THE NIGHT, THERE'RE THINGS I MUST ATTEND TO, SEEEE—
I'M TOTALLY BEAT.
IF I WAS GONNA HAVE TO GO WITHOUT SLEEP ANYWAY, I WOULD'VE MUCH PREFERRED TO HAVE DONE IT WITH A HOT GIRL...
I WANNA CHANGE JOBS... YOU CAN BE ALICE. LET'S TRADE.
DON'T WANNAAA!
I'LL KILL YOU IN THE CAUCUS RACE.

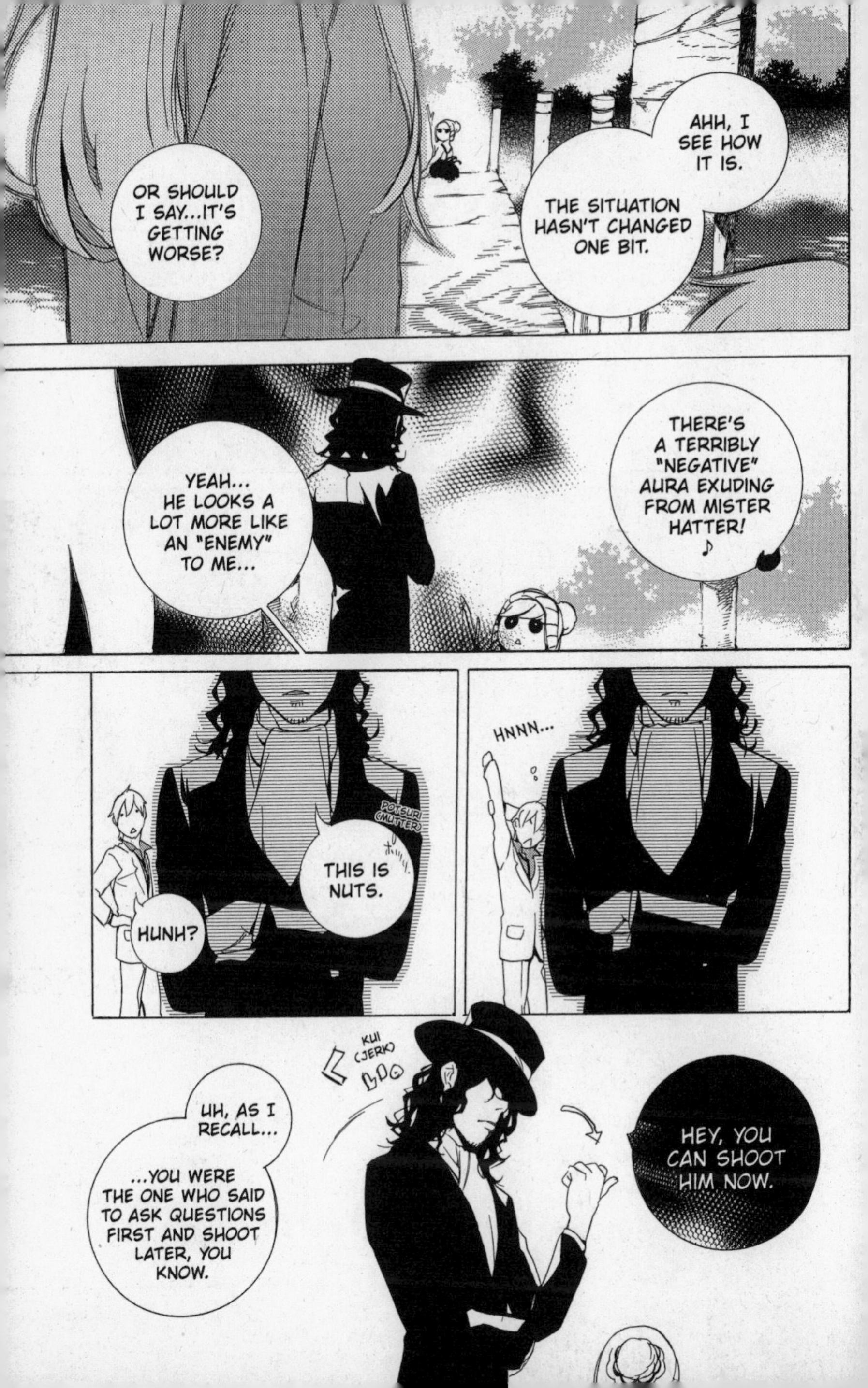
AHH, I SEE HOW IT IS.
THE SITUATION HASN'T CHANGED ONE BIT.
OR SHOULD I SAY...IT'S GETTING WORSE?
THERE'S A TERRIBLY "NEGATIVE" AURA EXUDING FROM MISTER HATTER! ♪
YEAH... HE LOOKS A LOT MORE LIKE AN "ENEMY" TO ME...
HNNN...
POTSURI (MUTTER)
THIS IS NUTS.
HUNH?
KUI (JERK)
HEY, YOU CAN SHOOT HIM NOW.
UH, AS I RECALL...
...YOU WERE THE ONE WHO SAID TO ASK QUESTIONS FIRST AND SHOOT LATER, YOU KNOW.

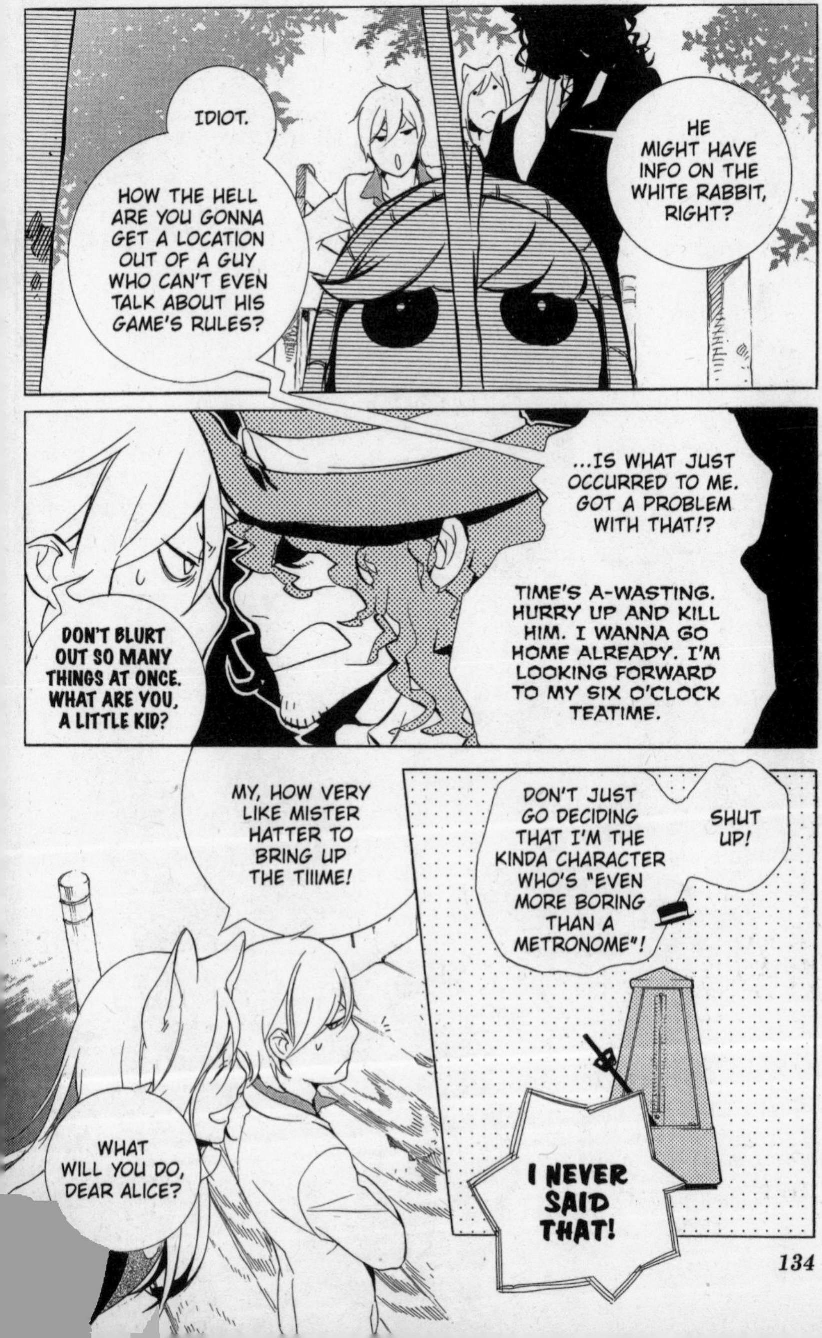
HE MIGHT HAVE INFO ON THE WHITE RABBIT, RIGHT?
IDIOT.
HOW THE HELL ARE YOU GONNA GET A LOCATION OUT OF A GUY WHO CAN'T EVEN TALK ABOUT HIS GAME'S RULES?
...IS WHAT JUST OCCURRED TO ME. GOT A PROBLEM WITH THAT!?
TIME'S A-WASTING. HURRY UP AND KILL HIM. I WANNA GO HOME ALREADY. I'M LOOKING FORWARD TO MY SIX O'CLOCK TEATIME.
DON'T BLURT OUT SO MANY THINGS AT ONCE. WHAT ARE YOU, A LITTLE KID?
SHUT UP!
DON'T JUST GO DECIDING THAT I'M THE KINDA CHARACTER WHO'S "EVEN MORE BORING THAN A METRONOME"!
I NEVER SAID THAT!
MY, HOW VERY LIKE MISTER HATTER TO BRING UP THE TIIIME!
WHAT WILL YOU DO, DEAR ALICE?

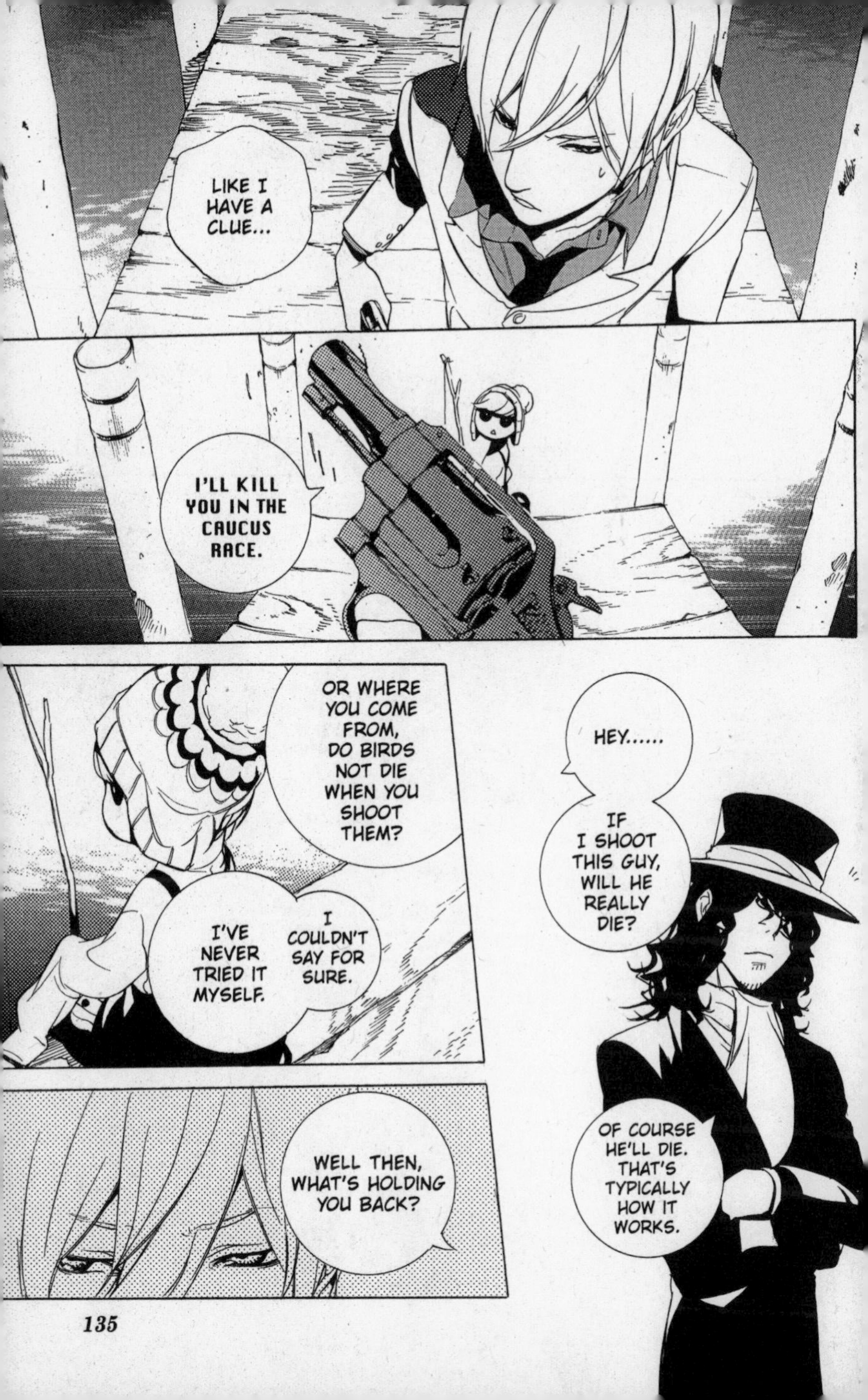
LIKE I HAVE A CLUE...
I'LL KILL YOU IN THE CAUCUS RACE.
HEY......
IF I SHOOT THIS GUY, WILL HE REALLY DIE?
OF COURSE HE'LL DIE. THAT'S TYPICALLY HOW IT WORKS.
OR WHERE YOU COME FROM, DO BIRDS NOT DIE WHEN YOU SHOOT THEM?
I COULDN'T SAY FOR SURE.
I'VE NEVER TRIED IT MYSELF.
WELL THEN, WHAT'S HOLDING YOU BACK?

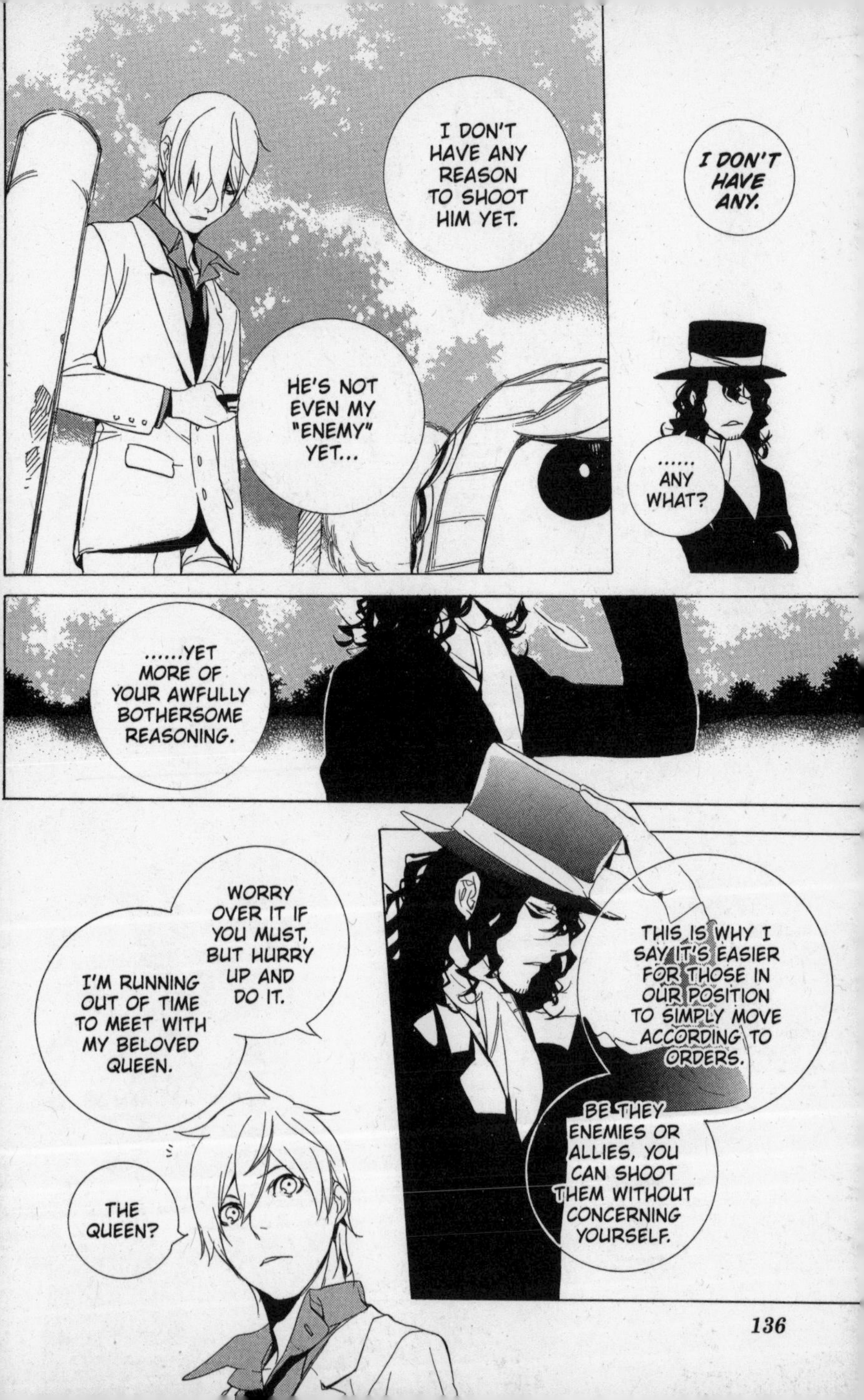

I DON'T HAVE ANY.
......ANY WHAT?
I DON'T HAVE ANY REASON TO SHOOT HIM YET.
HE'S NOT EVEN MY "ENEMY" YET...
......YET MORE OF YOUR AWFULLY BOTHERSOME REASONING.
THIS IS WHY I SAY IT'S EASIER FOR THOSE IN OUR POSITION TO SIMPLY MOVE ACCORDING TO ORDERS.
BE THEY ENEMIES OR ALLIES, YOU CAN SHOOT THEM WITHOUT CONCERNING YOURSELF.
WORRY OVER IT IF YOU MUST, BUT HURRY UP AND DO IT.
I'M RUNNING OUT OF TIME TO MEET WITH MY BELOVED QUEEN.
THE QUEEN?

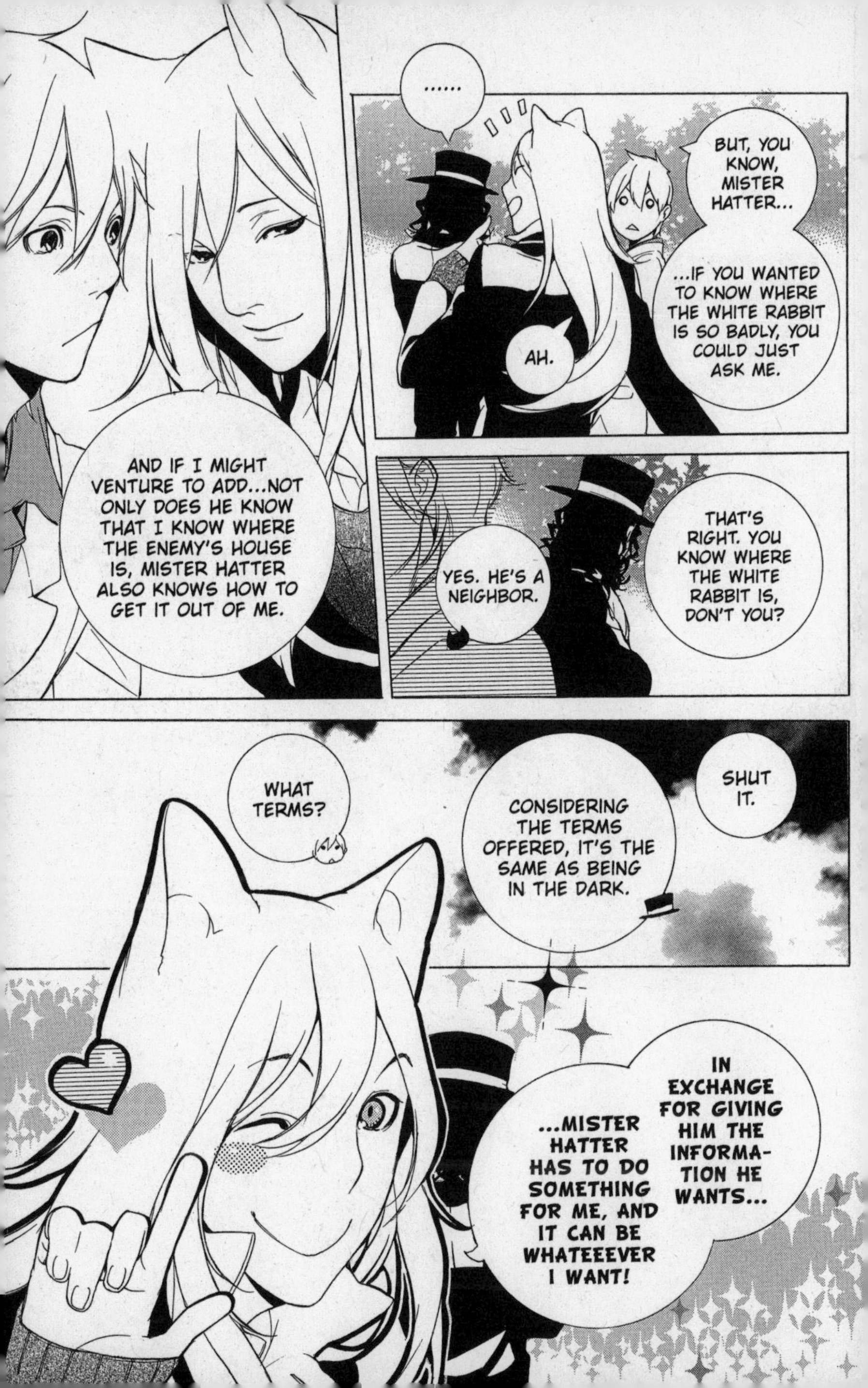
......
BUT, YOU KNOW, MISTER HATTER...
...IF YOU WANTED TO KNOW WHERE THE WHITE RABBIT IS SO BADLY, YOU COULD JUST ASK ME.
AH.
THAT'S RIGHT. YOU KNOW WHERE THE WHITE RABBIT IS, DON'T YOU?
YES. HE'S A NEIGHBOR.
AND IF I MIGHT VENTURE TO ADD...NOT ONLY DOES HE KNOW THAT I KNOW WHERE THE ENEMY'S HOUSE IS, MISTER HATTER ALSO KNOWS HOW TO GET IT OUT OF ME.
SHUT IT.
CONSIDERING THE TERMS OFFERED, IT'S THE SAME AS BEING IN THE DARK.
WHAT TERMS?
IN EXCHANGE FOR GIVING HIM THE INFORMATION HE WANTS...
...MISTER HATTER HAS TO DO SOMETHING FOR ME, AND IT CAN BE WHATEEEVER I WANT!

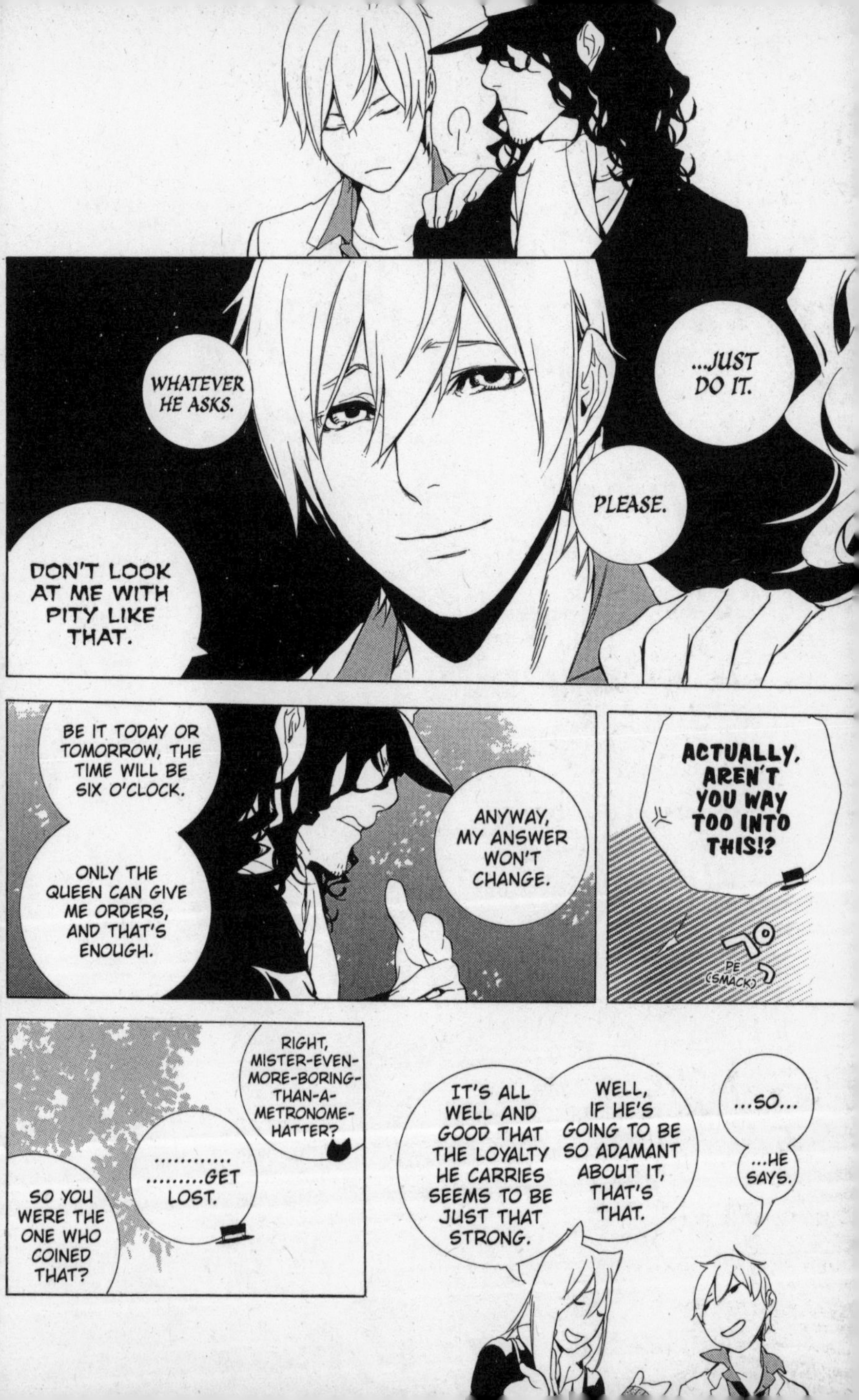
...JUST DO IT.
PLEASE.
WHATEVER HE ASKS.
DON'T LOOK AT ME WITH PITY LIKE THAT.
ACTUALLY, AREN'T YOU WAY TOO INTO THIS!?
PE (SMACK)
BE IT TODAY OR TOMORROW, THE TIME WILL BE SIX O'CLOCK.
ONLY THE QUEEN CAN GIVE ME ORDERS, AND THAT'S ENOUGH.
ANYWAY, MY ANSWER WON'T CHANGE.
...SO...
...HE SAYS.
WELL, IF HE'S GOING TO BE SO ADAMANT ABOUT IT, THAT'S THAT.
IT'S ALL WELL AND GOOD THAT THE LOYALTY HE CARRIES SEEMS TO BE JUST THAT STRONG.
RIGHT, MISTER-EVEN-MORE-BORING-THAN-A-METRONOME-HATTER?
....GET LOST.
SO YOU WERE THE ONE WHO COINED THAT?

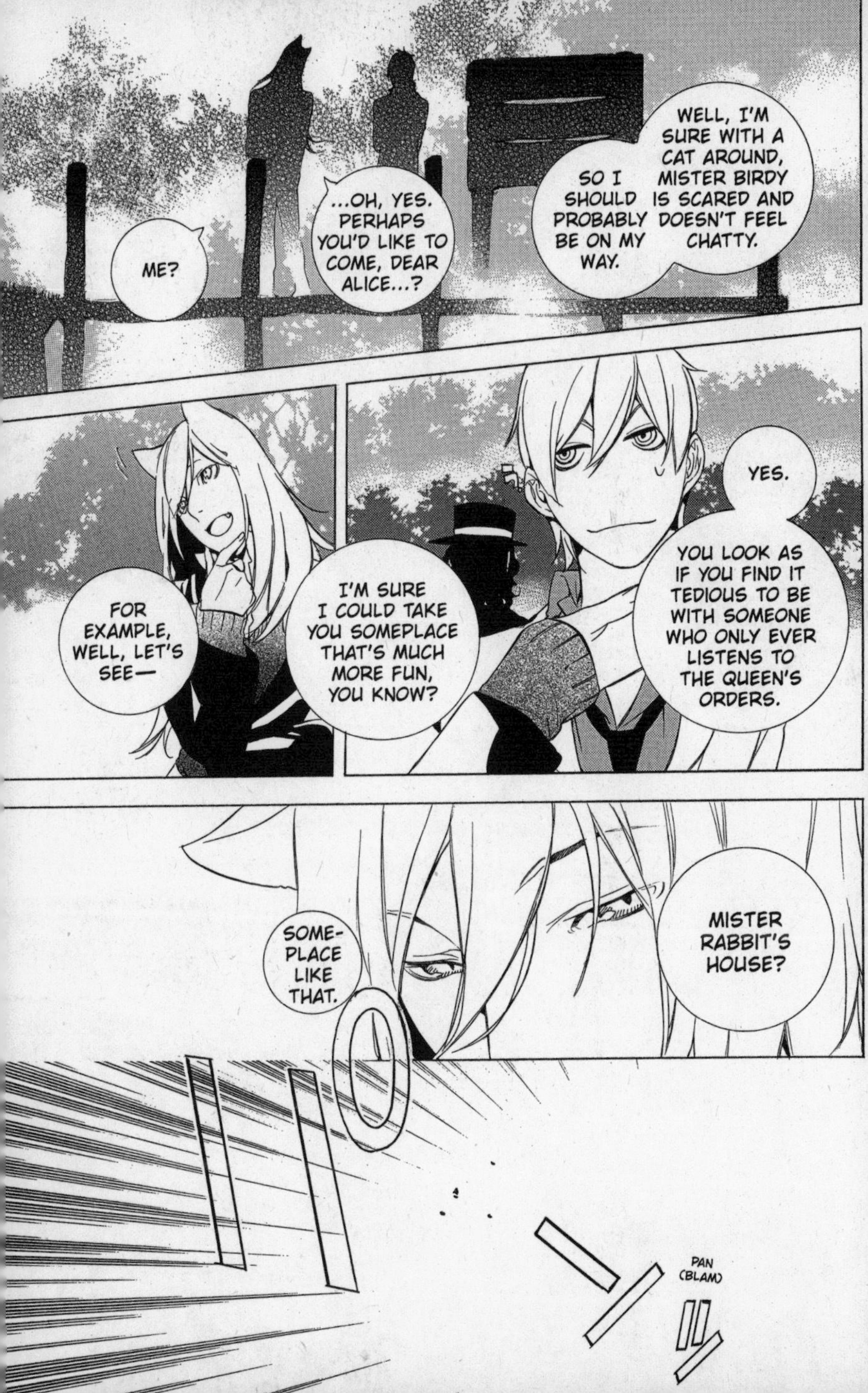
WELL, I'M SURE WITH A CAT AROUND, MISTER BIRDY IS SCARED AND DOESN'T FEEL CHATTY.
SO I SHOULD PROBABLY BE ON MY WAY.
...OH, YES. PERHAPS YOU'D LIKE TO COME, DEAR ALICE...?
ME?
YES.
YOU LOOK AS IF YOU FIND IT TEDIOUS TO BE WITH SOMEONE WHO ONLY EVER LISTENS TO THE QUEEN'S ORDERS.
I'M SURE I COULD TAKE YOU SOMEPLACE THAT'S MUCH MORE FUN, YOU KNOW?
FOR EXAMPLE, WELL, LET'S SEE—
MISTER RABBIT'S HOUSE?
SOME-PLACE LIKE THAT.
PAN (BLAM)

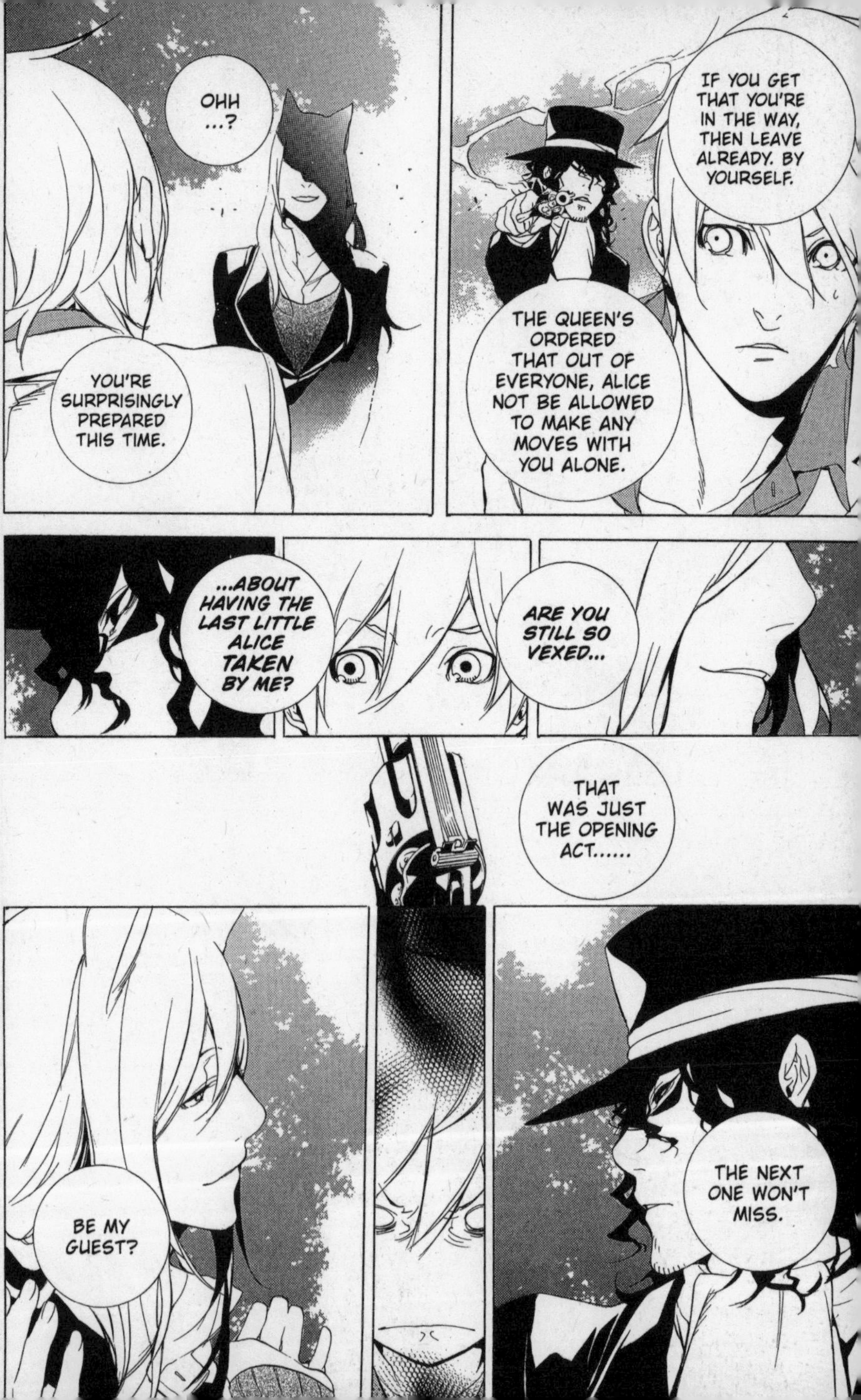

IF YOU GET THAT YOU'RE IN THE WAY, THEN LEAVE ALREADY. BY YOURSELF.
THE QUEEN'S ORDERED THAT OUT OF EVERYONE, ALICE NOT BE ALLOWED TO MAKE ANY MOVES WITH YOU ALONE.
OHH ...?
YOU'RE SURPRISINGLY PREPARED THIS TIME.
ARE YOU STILL SO VEXED...
...ABOUT HAVING THE LAST LITTLE ALICE TAKEN BY ME?
THAT WAS JUST THE OPENING ACT......
THE NEXT ONE WON'T MISS.
BE MY GUEST?

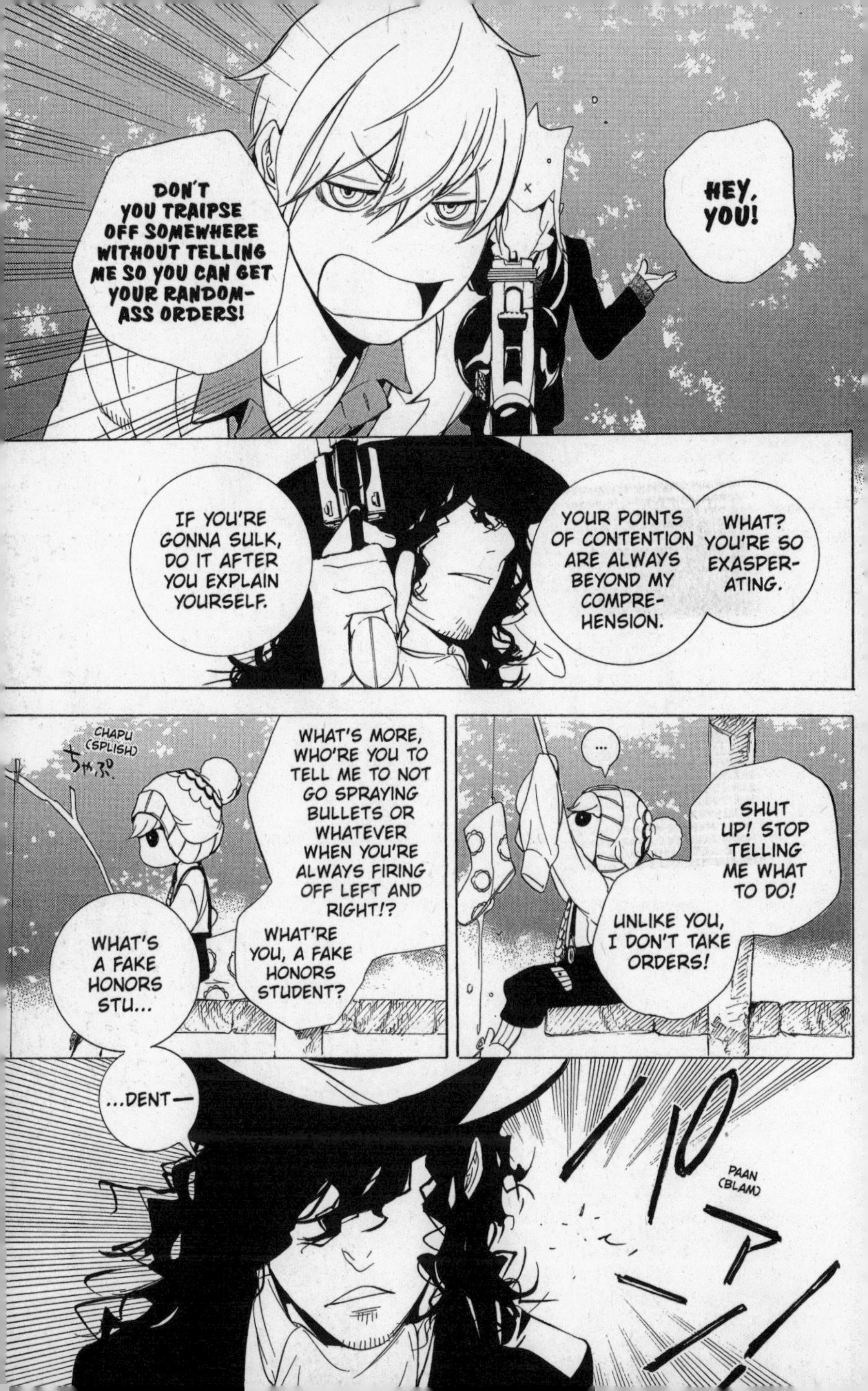
HEY, YOU!
DON'T YOU TRAIPSE OFF SOMEWHERE WITHOUT TELLING ME SO YOU CAN GET YOUR RANDOM-ASS ORDERS!
WHAT? YOU'RE SO EXASPER-ATING.
YOUR POINTS OF CONTENTION ARE ALWAYS BEYOND MY COMPRE-HENSION.
IF YOU'RE GONNA SULK, DO IT AFTER YOU EXPLAIN YOURSELF.
...
SHUT UP! STOP TELLING ME WHAT TO DO!
UNLIKE YOU, I DON'T TAKE ORDERS!
WHAT'S MORE, WHO'RE YOU TO TELL ME TO NOT GO SPRAYING BULLETS OR WHATEVER WHEN YOU'RE ALWAYS FIRING OFF LEFT AND RIGHT!?
WHAT'RE YOU, A FAKE HONORS STUDENT?
CHAPU (SPLISH)
ちゃぷ
WHAT'S A FAKE HONORS STU...
...DENT—
PAAN (BLAM)

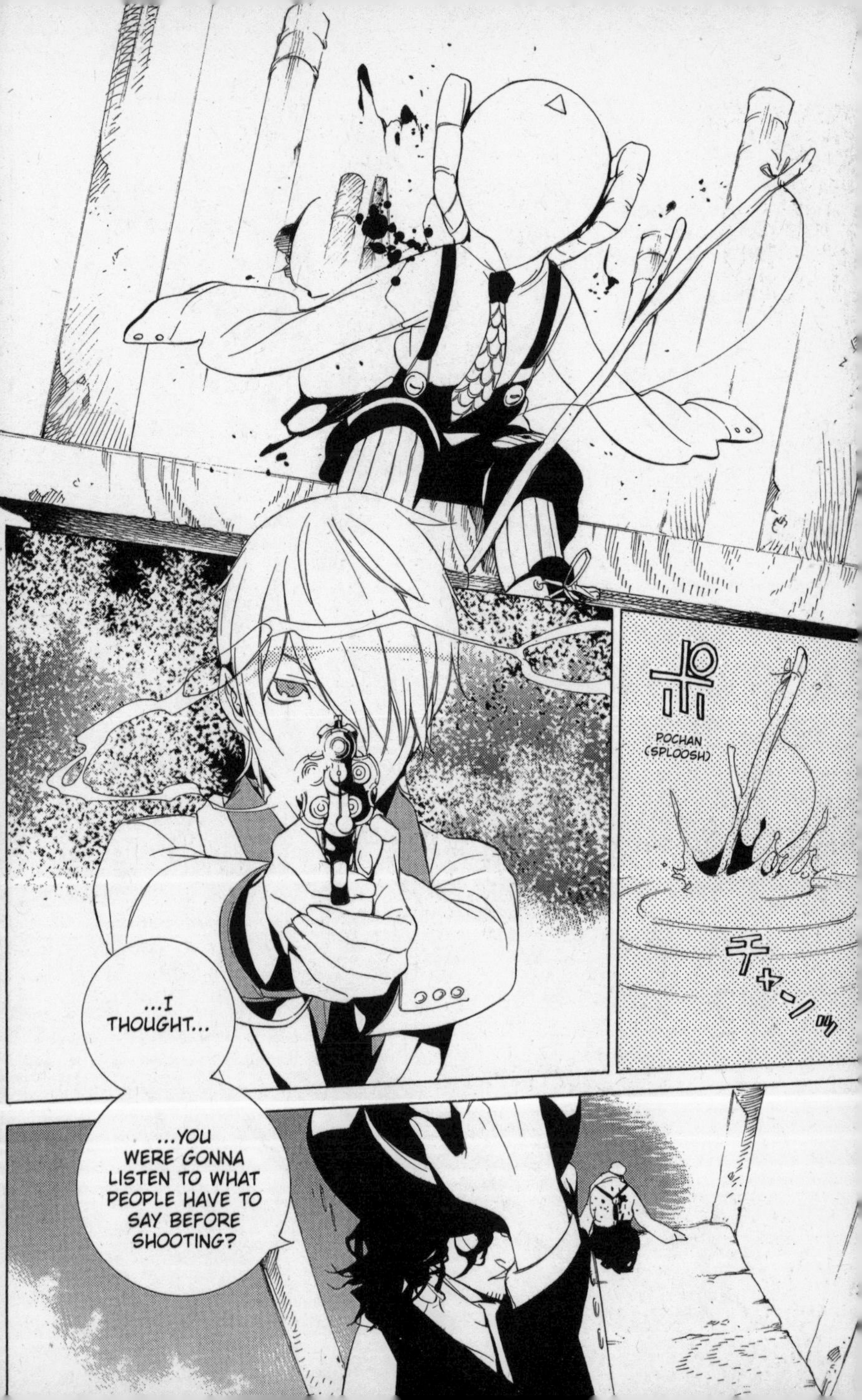
ポチャ
POCHAN (SPLOOSH)
チャーノ
...I THOUGHT...
...YOU WERE GONNA LISTEN TO WHAT PEOPLE HAVE TO SAY BEFORE SHOOTING?

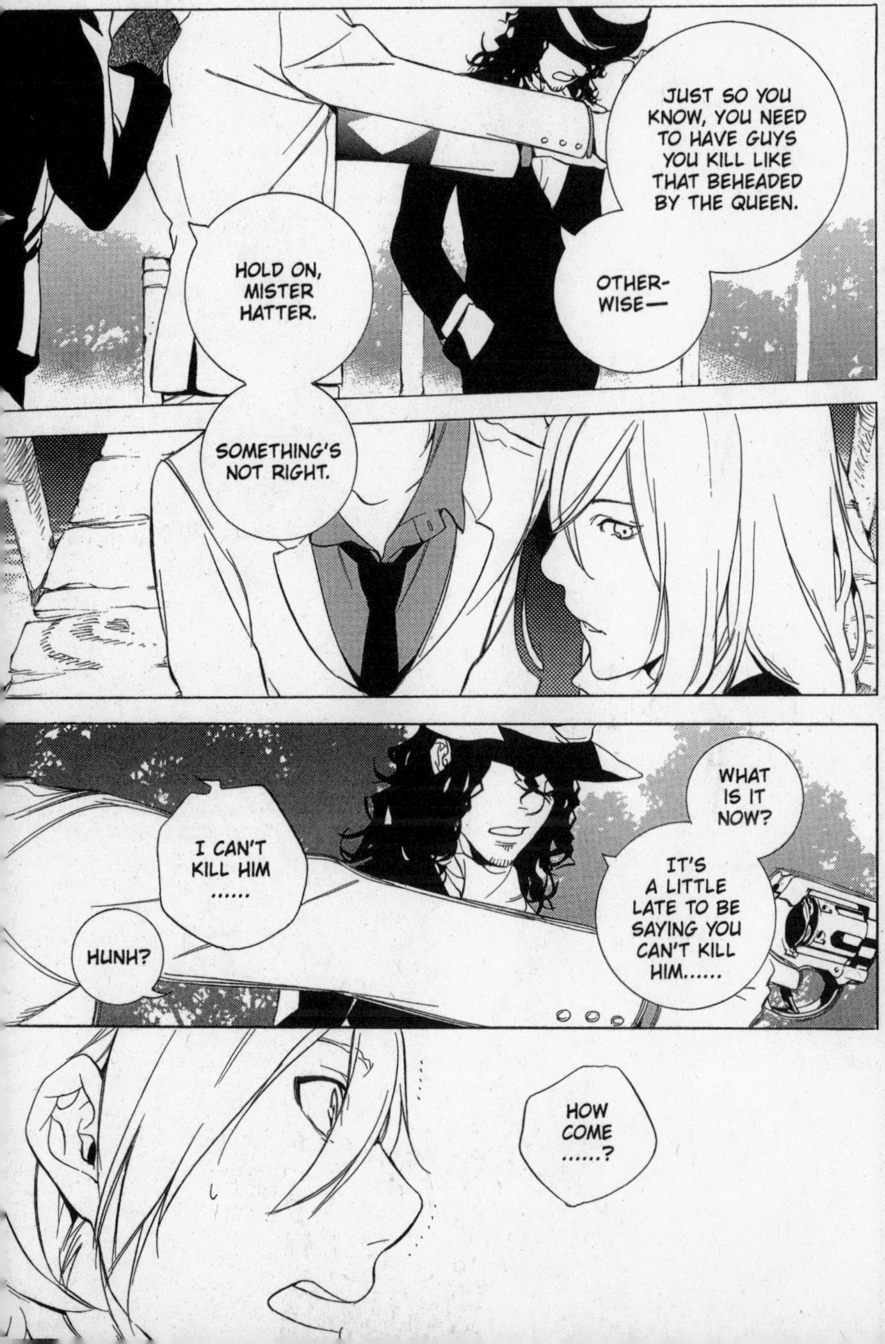
JUST SO YOU KNOW, YOU NEED TO HAVE GUYS YOU KILL LIKE THAT BEHEADED BY THE QUEEN.
OTHER-WISE—
HOLD ON, MISTER HATTER.
SOMETHING'S NOT RIGHT.
WHAT IS IT NOW?
IT'S A LITTLE LATE TO BE SAYING YOU CAN'T KILL HIM......
I CAN'T KILL HIM ......
HUNH?
HOW COME ......?

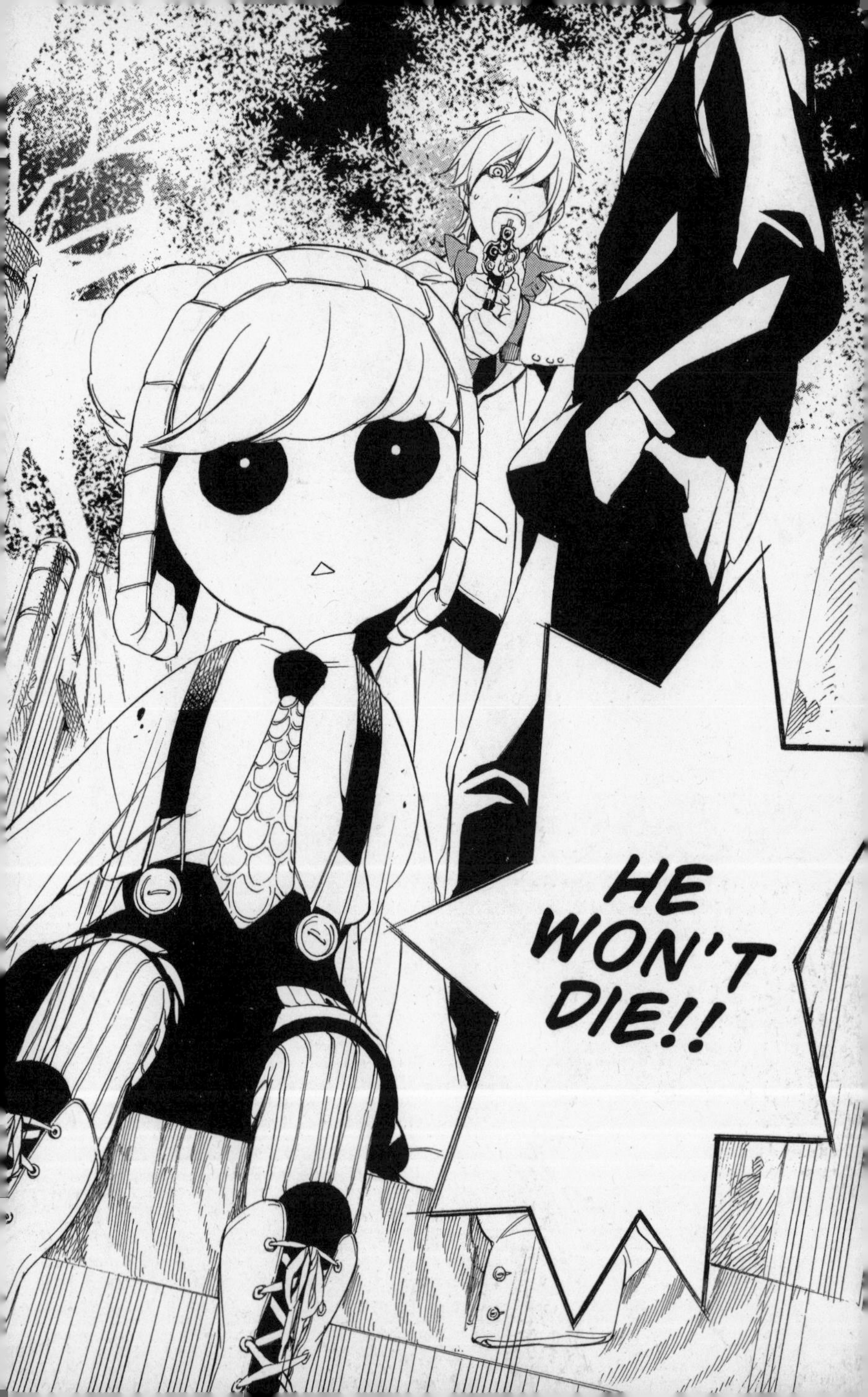
HE WON'T DIE!!

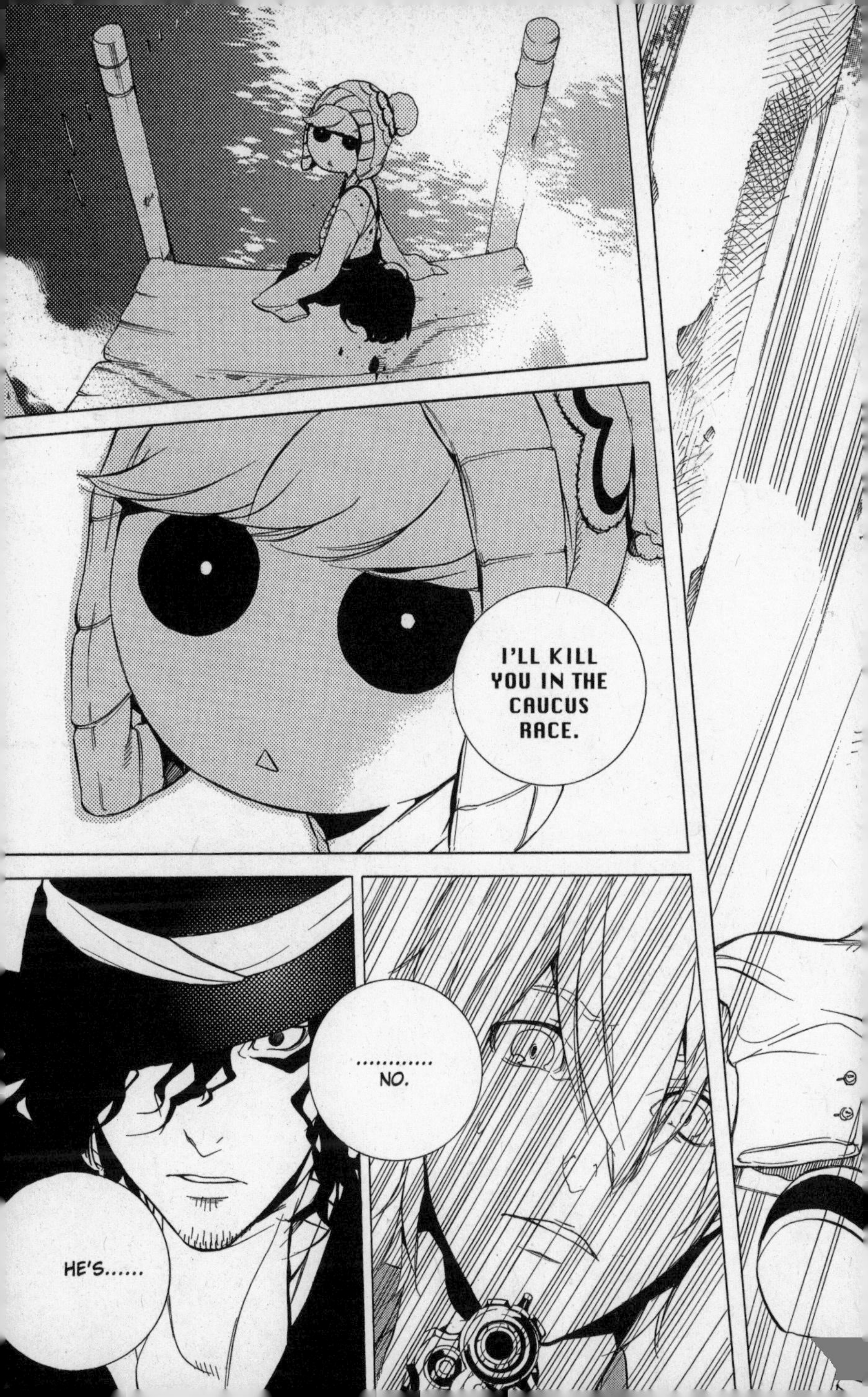
I'LL KILL YOU IN THE CAUCUS RACE.
.... NO.
HE'S......

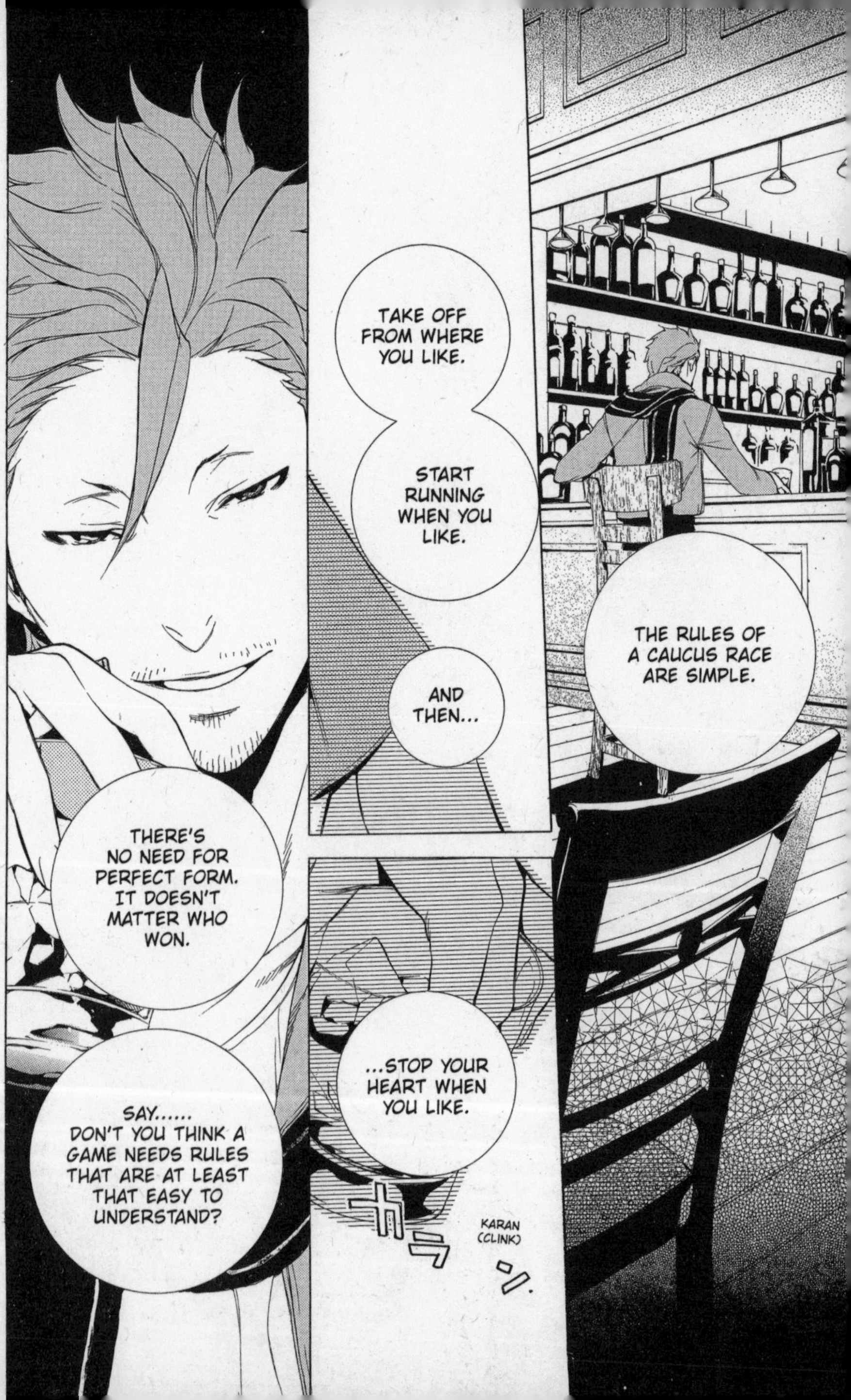
THE RULES OF A CAUCUS RACE ARE SIMPLE.
TAKE OFF FROM WHERE YOU LIKE.
START RUNNING WHEN YOU LIKE.
AND THEN...
...STOP YOUR HEART WHEN YOU LIKE.
KARAN (CLINK)
THERE'S NO NEED FOR PERFECT FORM. IT DOESN'T MATTER WHO WON.
SAY...... DON'T YOU THINK A GAME NEEDS RULES THAT ARE AT LEAST THAT EASY TO UNDERSTAND?

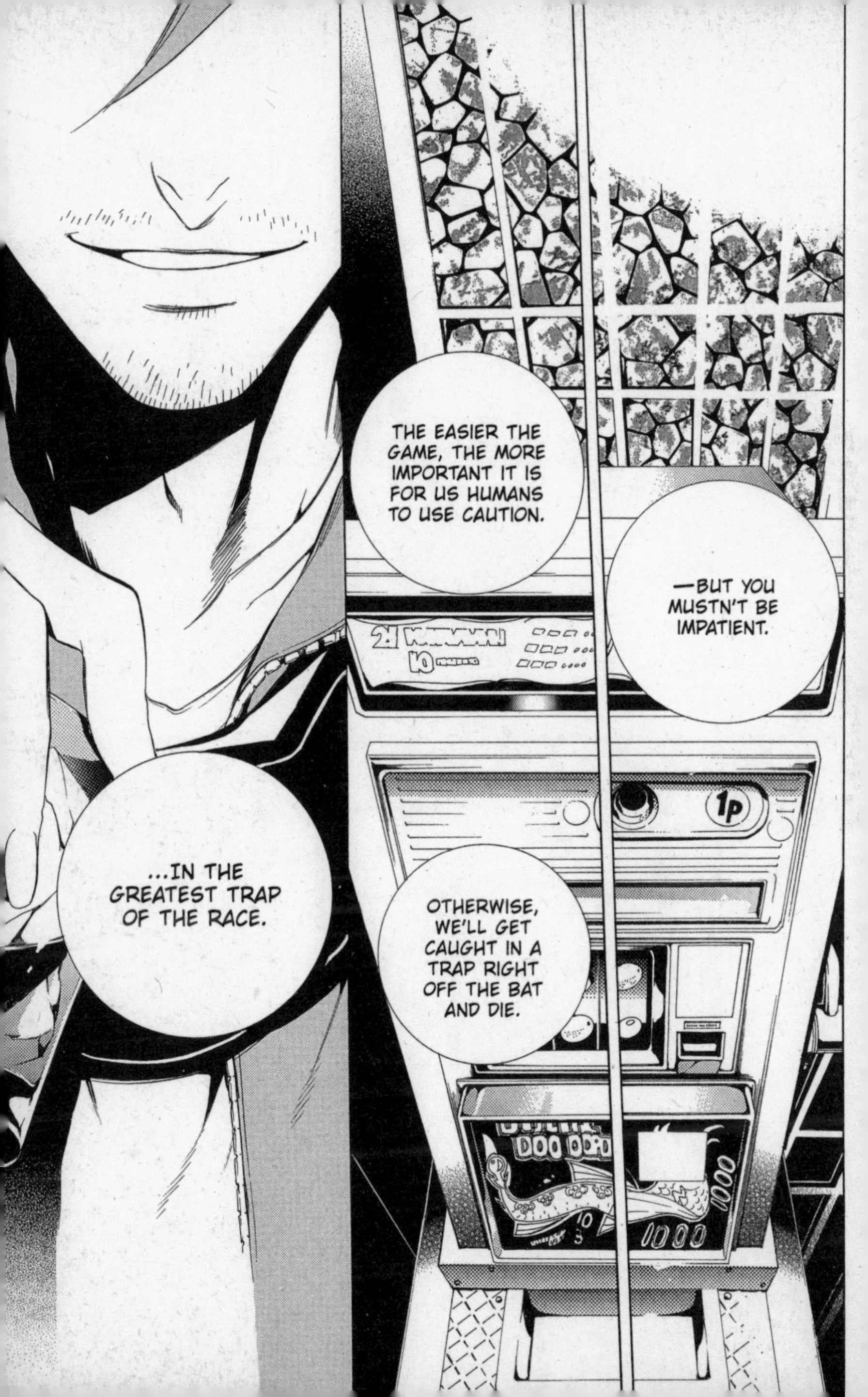
THE EASIER THE GAME, THE MORE IMPORTANT IT IS FOR US HUMANS TO USE CAUTION.
—BUT YOU MUSTN'T BE IMPATIENT.
OTHERWISE, WE'LL GET CAUGHT IN A TRAP RIGHT OFF THE BAT AND DIE.
...IN THE GREATEST TRAP OF THE RACE.

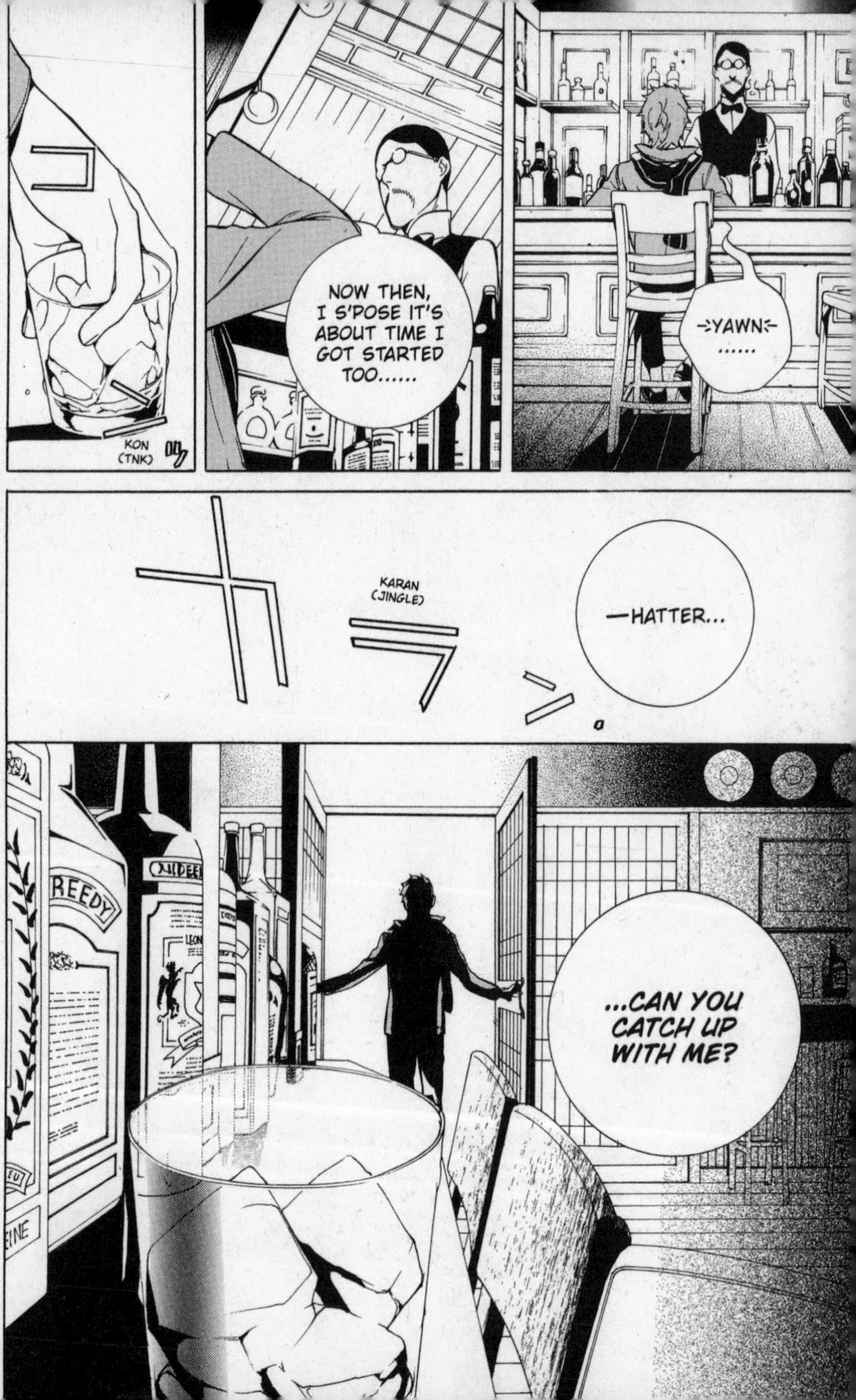

-YAWN- ......
NOW THEN, I S'POSE IT'S ABOUT TIME I GOT STARTED TOO......
KON (TNK)
—HATTER...
KARAN (JINGLE)
...CAN YOU CATCH UP WITH ME?

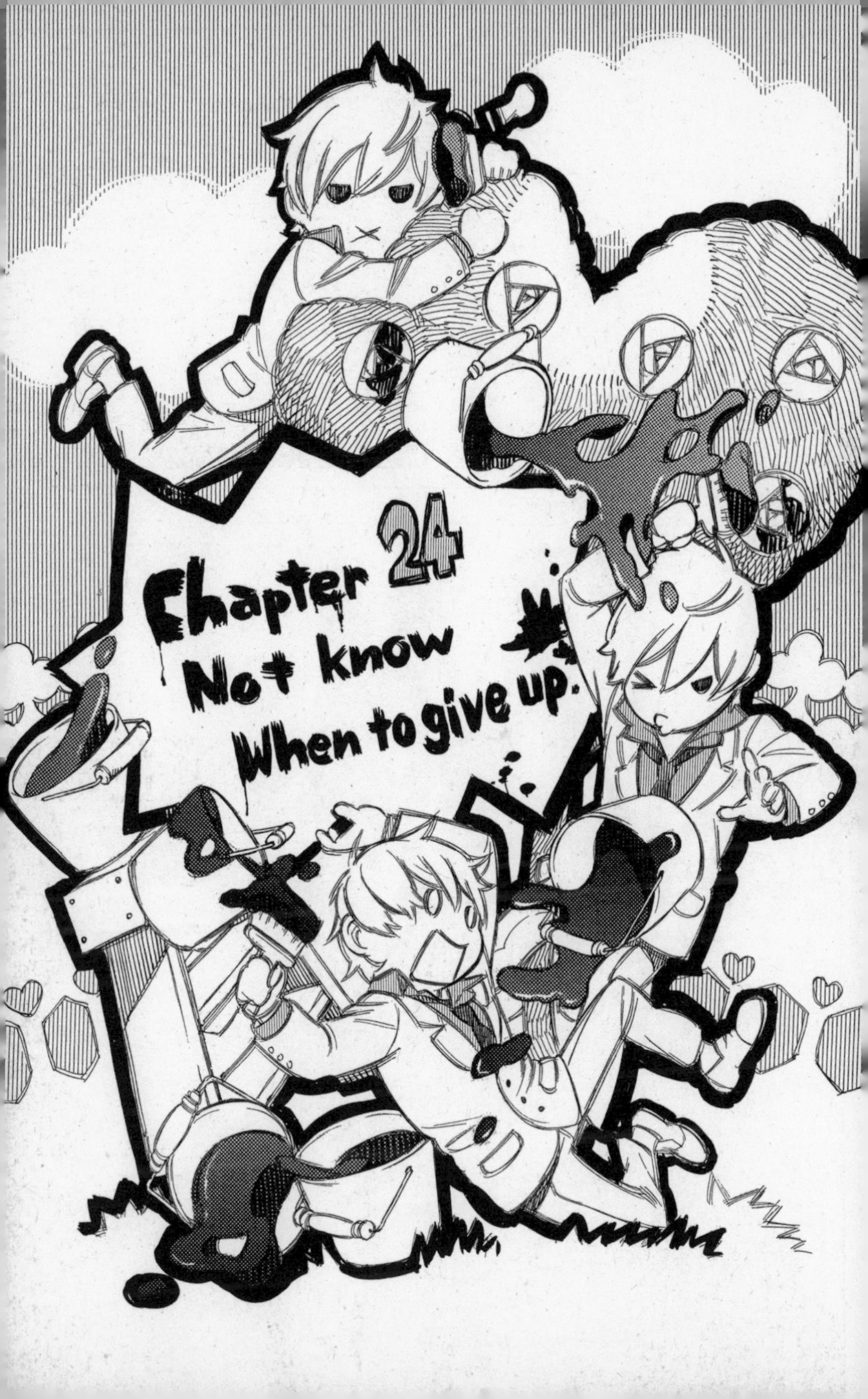
Chapter 24
Not know
When to give up.

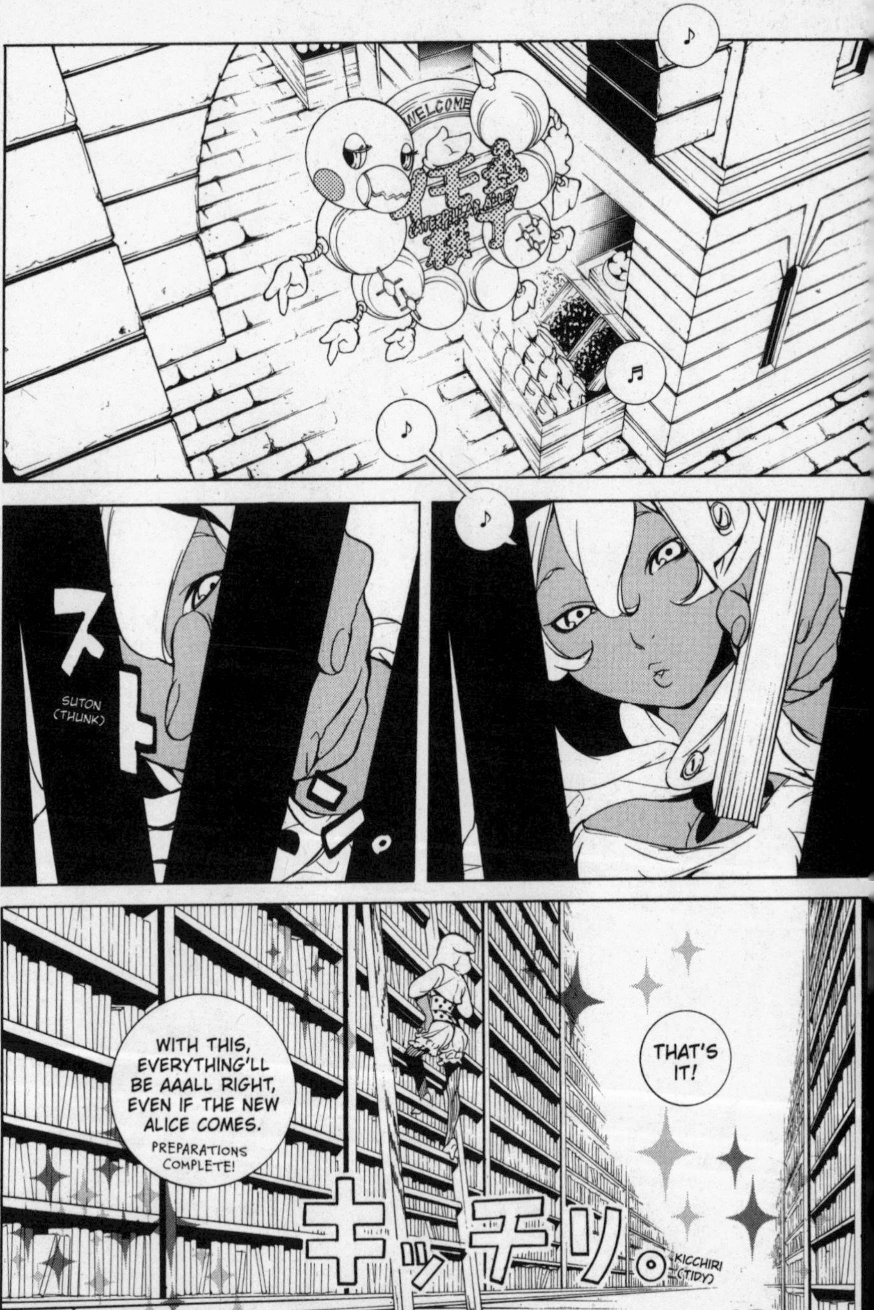
♪
WELCOME
CATERPILLAR ALLEY
♬
♪
♪
スト
SUTON (THUNK)
THAT'S IT!
WITH THIS, EVERYTHING'LL BE AAALL RIGHT, EVEN IF THE NEW ALICE COMES.
PREPARATIONS COMPLETE!
キッチリ。
KICCHIRI (TIDY)

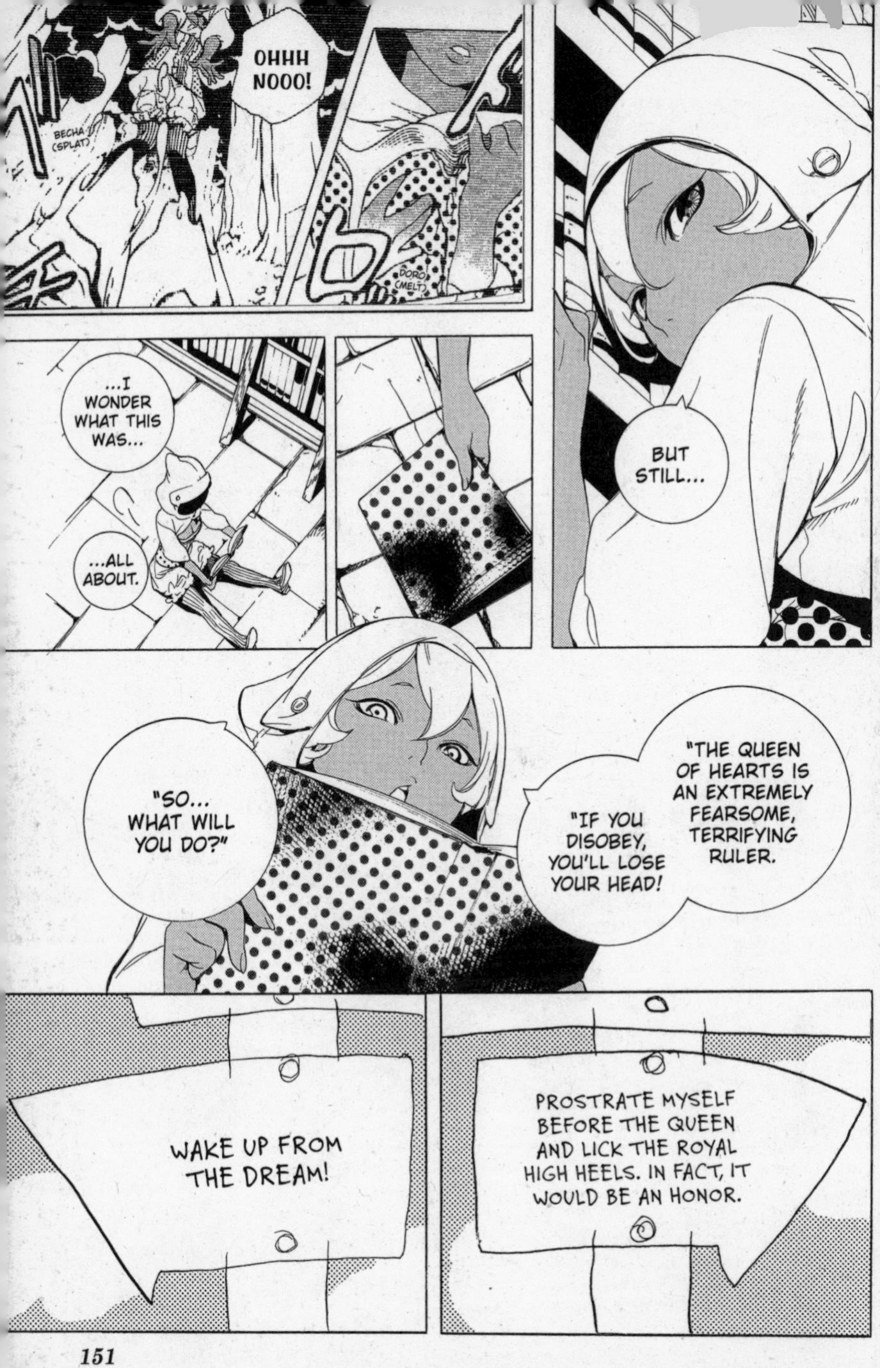
BUT STILL...
DORO (MELT)
OHHH NOOO!
BECHA (SPLAT)
...I WONDER WHAT THIS WAS...
...ALL ABOUT.
"THE QUEEN OF HEARTS IS AN EXTREMELY FEARSOME, TERRIFYING RULER.
"IF YOU DISOBEY, YOU'LL LOSE YOUR HEAD!
"SO... WHAT WILL YOU DO?"
PROSTRATE MYSELF BEFORE THE QUEEN AND LICK THE ROYAL HIGH HEELS. IN FACT, IT WOULD BE AN HONOR.
WAKE UP FROM THE DREAM!

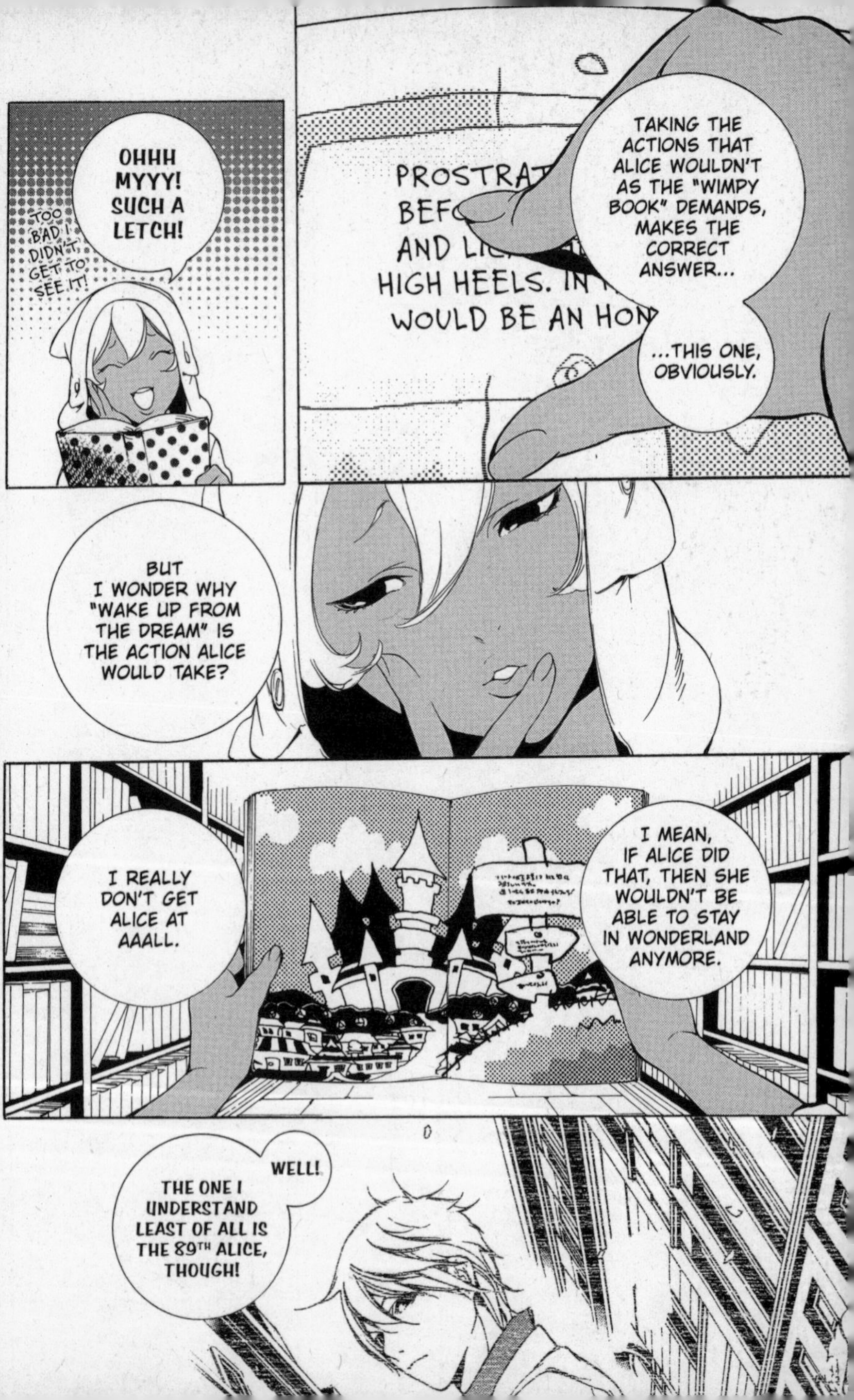
TAKING THE ACTIONS THAT ALICE WOULDN'T AS THE "WIMPY BOOK" DEMANDS, MAKES THE CORRECT ANSWER...
PROSTRAT
BEFO
AND LI
HIGH HEELS. IN
WOULD BE AN HON
...THIS ONE, OBVIOUSLY.
OHHH MYYY! SUCH A LETCH!
TOO BAD I DIDN'T GET TO SEE IT!
BUT I WONDER WHY "WAKE UP FROM THE DREAM" IS THE ACTION ALICE WOULD TAKE?
I MEAN, IF ALICE DID THAT, THEN SHE WOULDN'T BE ABLE TO STAY IN WONDERLAND ANYMORE.
I REALLY DON'T GET ALICE AT AAALL.
WELL!
THE ONE I UNDERSTAND LEAST OF ALL IS THE 89TH ALICE, THOUGH!

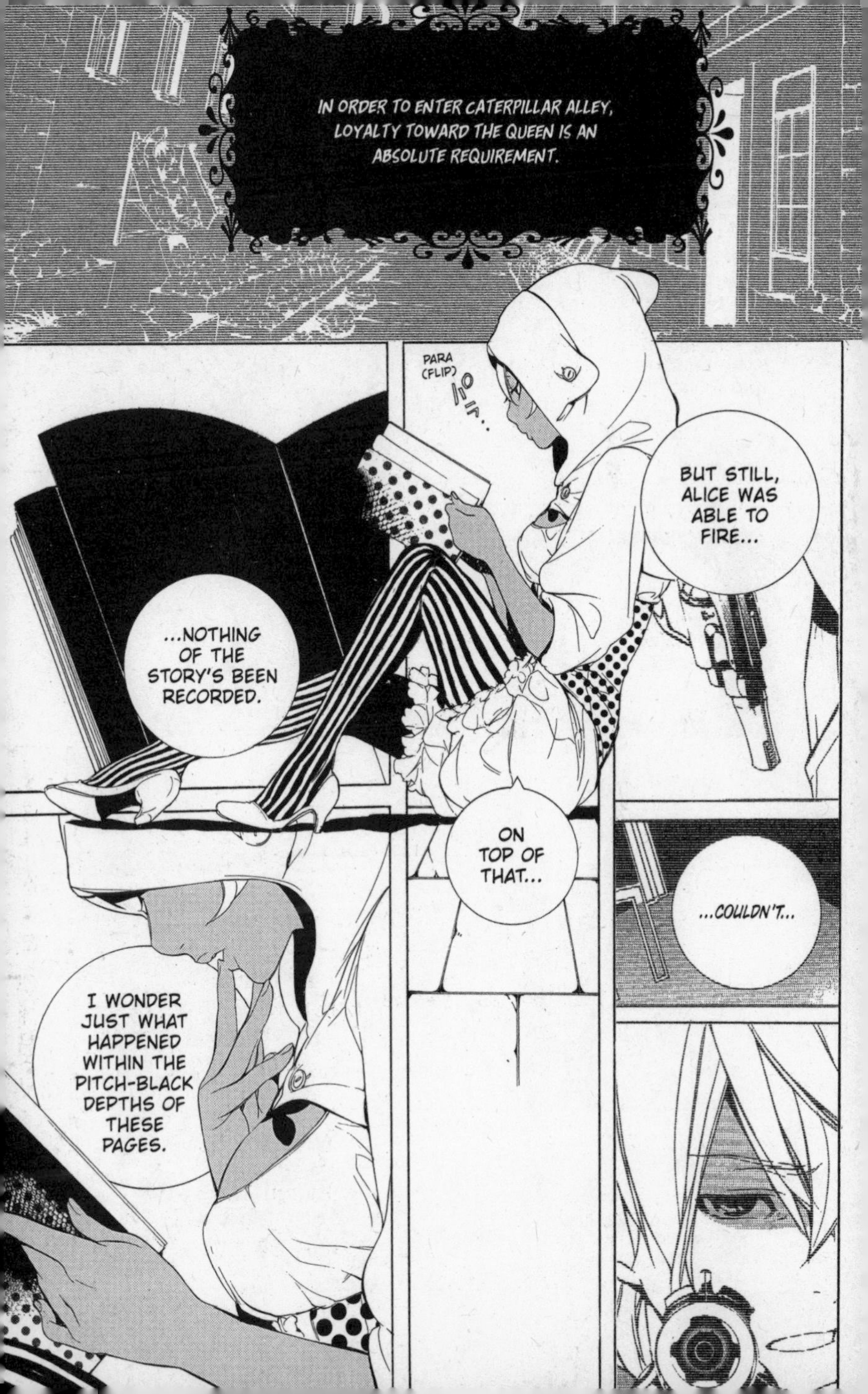
IN ORDER TO ENTER CATERPILLAR ALLEY, LOYALTY TOWARD THE QUEEN IS AN ABSOLUTE REQUIREMENT.
BUT STILL, ALICE WAS ABLE TO FIRE...
PARA (FLIP)
...NOTHING OF THE STORY'S BEEN RECORDED.
...COULDN'T...
ON TOP OF THAT...
I WONDER JUST WHAT HAPPENED WITHIN THE PITCH-BLACK DEPTHS OF THESE PAGES.

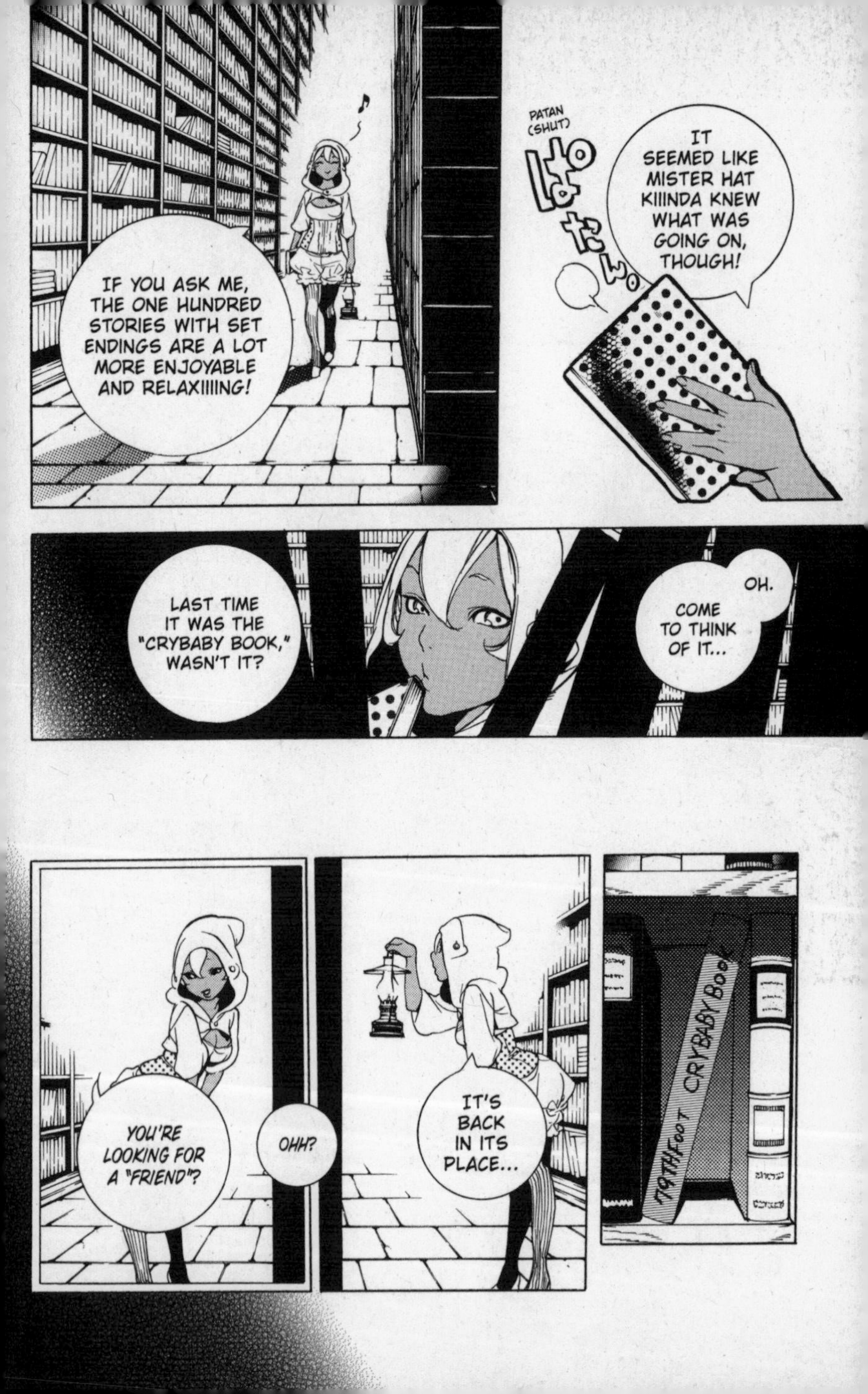
PATAN (SHUT)
IT SEEMED LIKE MISTER HAT KIIINDA KNEW WHAT WAS GOING ON, THOUGH!
IF YOU ASK ME, THE ONE HUNDRED STORIES WITH SET ENDINGS ARE A LOT MORE ENJOYABLE AND RELAXIIIING!
OH.
COME TO THINK OF IT...
LAST TIME IT WAS THE "CRYBABY BOOK," WASN'T IT?
79THFoot
CRYBABY Book
IT'S BACK IN ITS PLACE...
OHH?
YOU'RE LOOKING FOR A "FRIEND"?

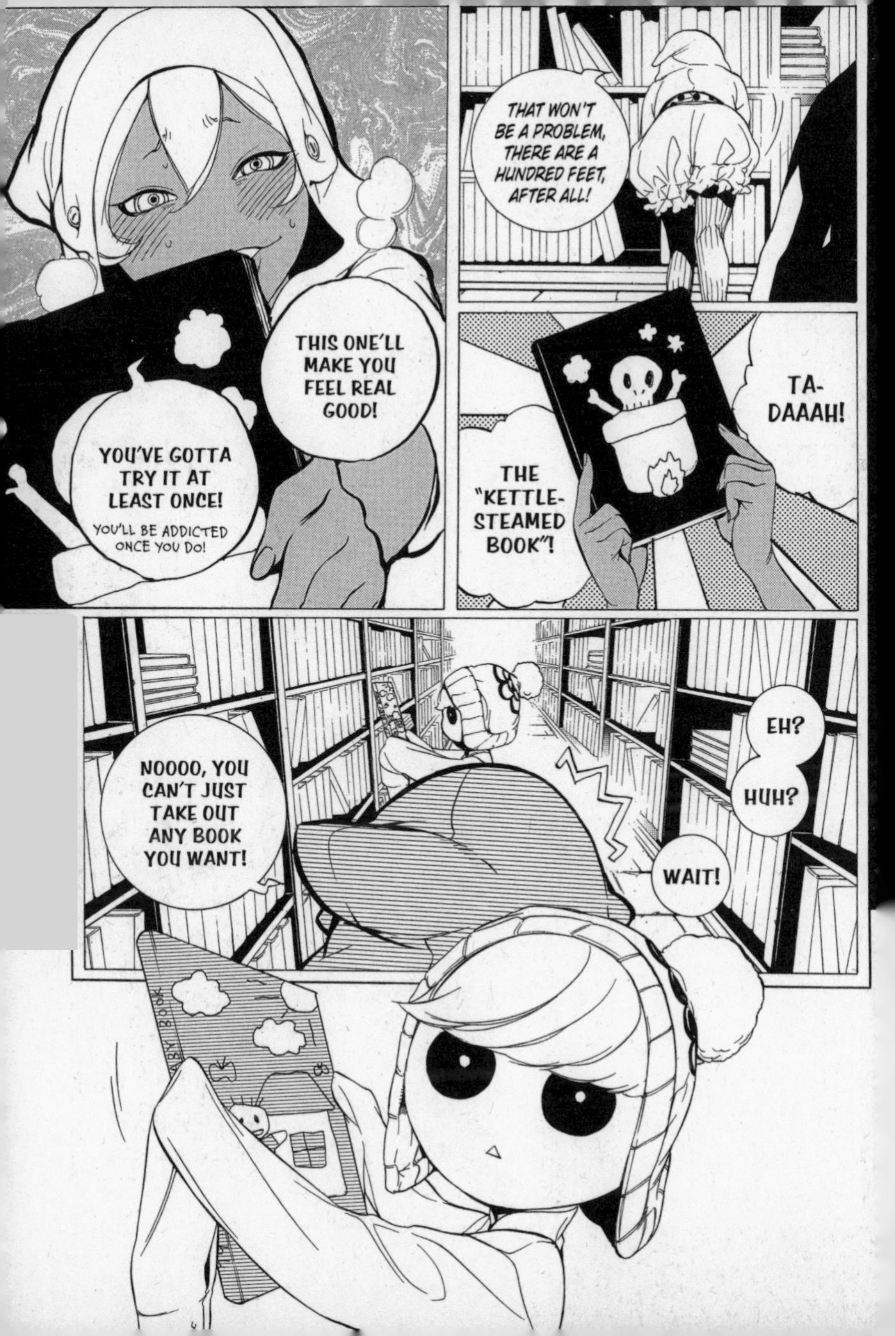
THAT WON'T BE A PROBLEM, THERE ARE A HUNDRED FEET, AFTER ALL!
TA-DAAAH!
THE "KETTLE-STEAMED BOOK"!
THIS ONE'LL MAKE YOU FEEL REAL GOOD!
YOU'VE GOTTA TRY IT AT LEAST ONCE!
YOU'LL BE ADDICTED ONCE YOU DO!
EH?
HUH?
WAIT!
NOOOO, YOU CAN'T JUST TAKE OUT ANY BOOK YOU WANT!

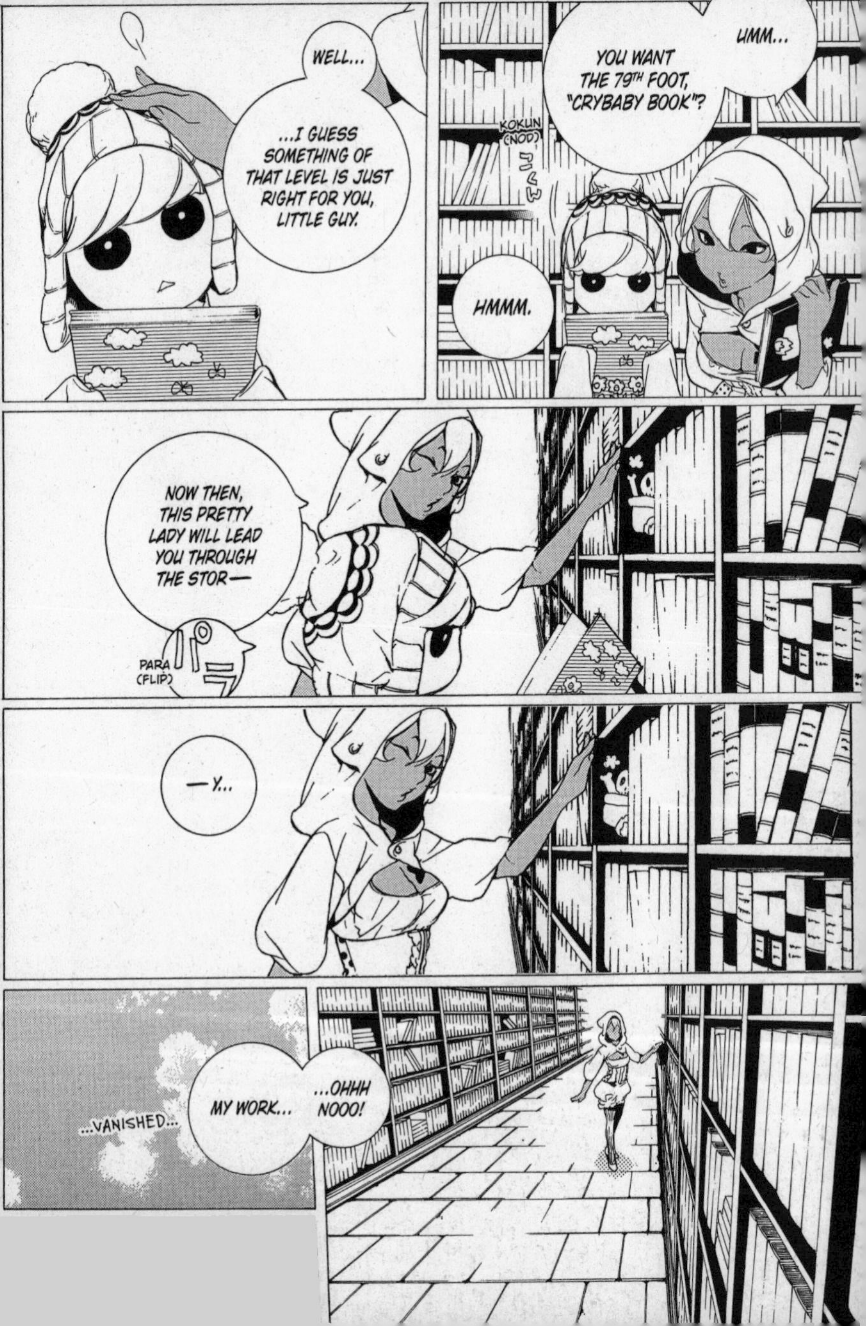
UMM...
YOU WANT THE 79TH FOOT, "CRYBABY BOOK"?
KOKUN (NOD)
HMMM.
WELL...
...I GUESS SOMETHING OF THAT LEVEL IS JUST RIGHT FOR YOU, LITTLE GUY.
NOW THEN, THIS PRETTY LADY WILL LEAD YOU THROUGH THE STOR—
PARA (FLIP)
—Y...
...OHHH NOOO!
MY WORK...
...VANISHED...

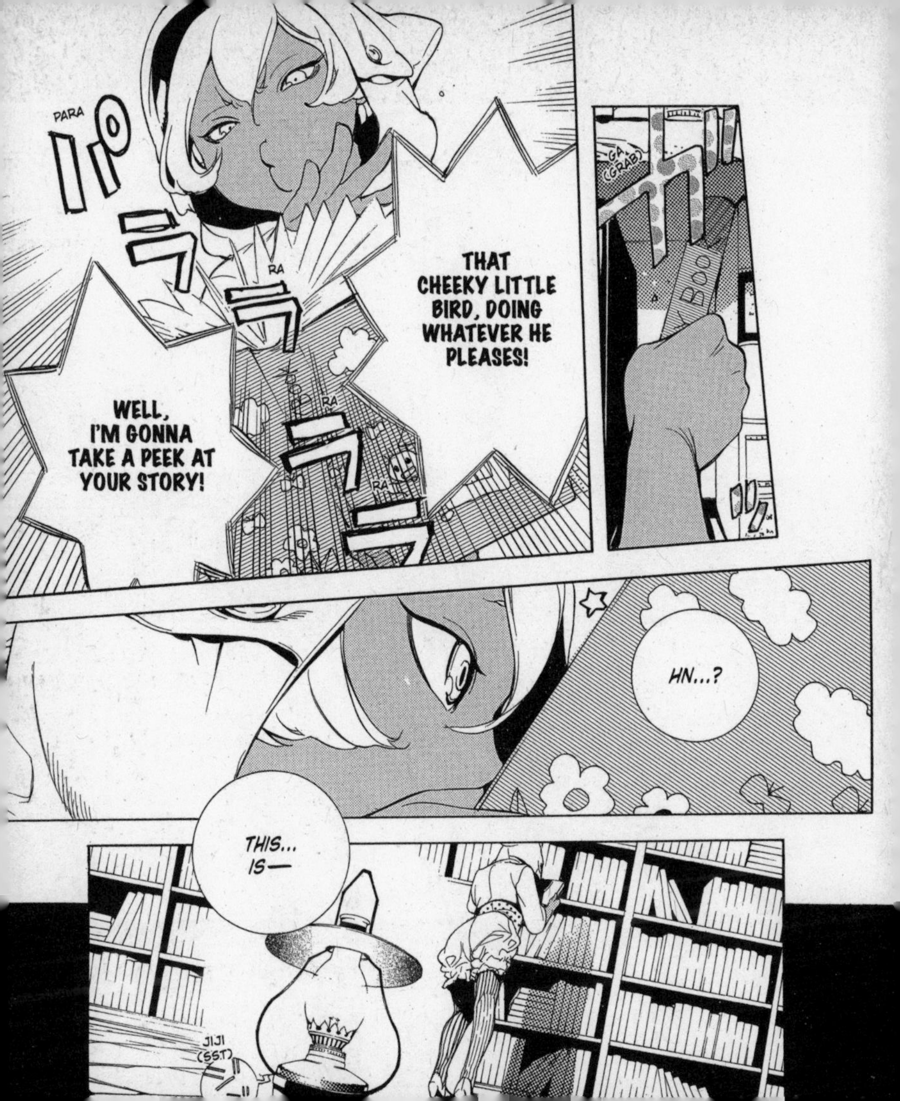
GA (GRAB)
PARA
THAT CHEEKY LITTLE BIRD, DOING WHATEVER HE PLEASES!
RA
RA
RA
WELL, I'M GONNA TAKE A PEEK AT YOUR STORY!
HN...?
THIS... IS—
JIJI (SS.T)

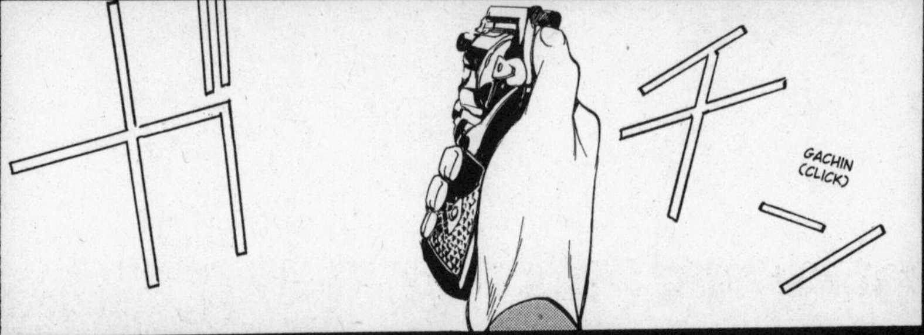
GACHIN
(CLICK)

*AHH, IT'S SO ANNOYING.
IT'S REALLY IRRITATING.*

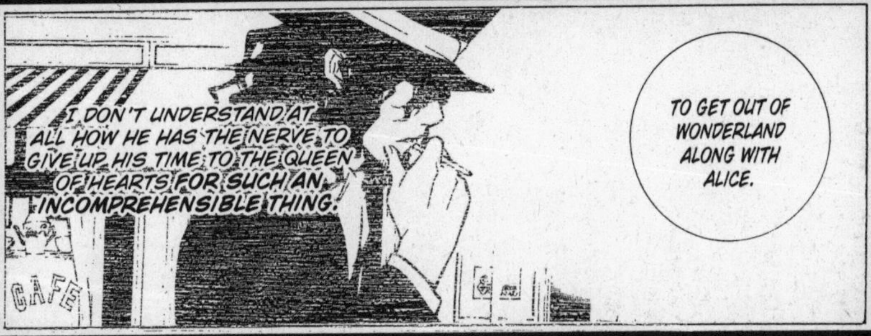
TO GET OUT OF WONDERLAND ALONG WITH ALICE.
I DON'T UNDERSTAND AT ALL HOW HE HAS THE NERVE TO GIVE UP HIS TIME TO THE QUEEN OF HEARTS FOR SUCH AN INCOMPREHENSIBLE THING.
CAFE

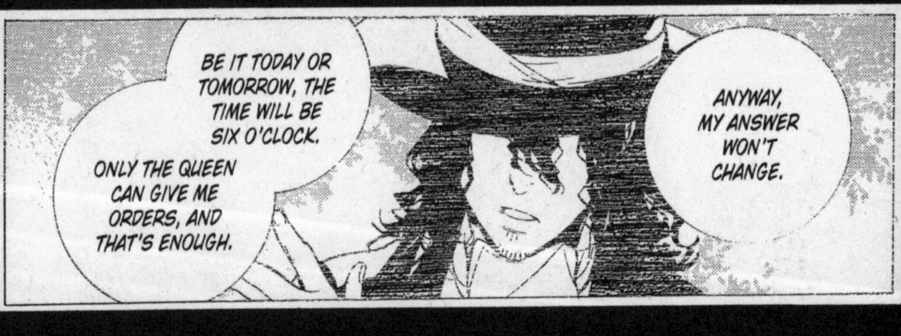
ANYWAY, MY ANSWER WON'T CHANGE.
BE IT TODAY OR TOMORROW, THE TIME WILL BE SIX O'CLOCK.
ONLY THE QUEEN CAN GIVE ME ORDERS, AND THAT'S ENOUGH.

*AND WITH HIS ARROGANT WAY OF SAYING SELF-IMPORTANT THINGS,
DOES HE REALLY INTEND TO CHANGE "SOMETHING" AT ALL?*

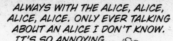

ALWAYS WITH THE ALICE, ALICE, ALICE, ALICE. ONLY EVER TALKING ABOUT AN ALICE I DON'T KNOW. IT'S SO ANNOYING...

'COS I'M GONNA BECOME ALICE IN WONDERLAND.

I'M GONNA, RIGHT NOW.

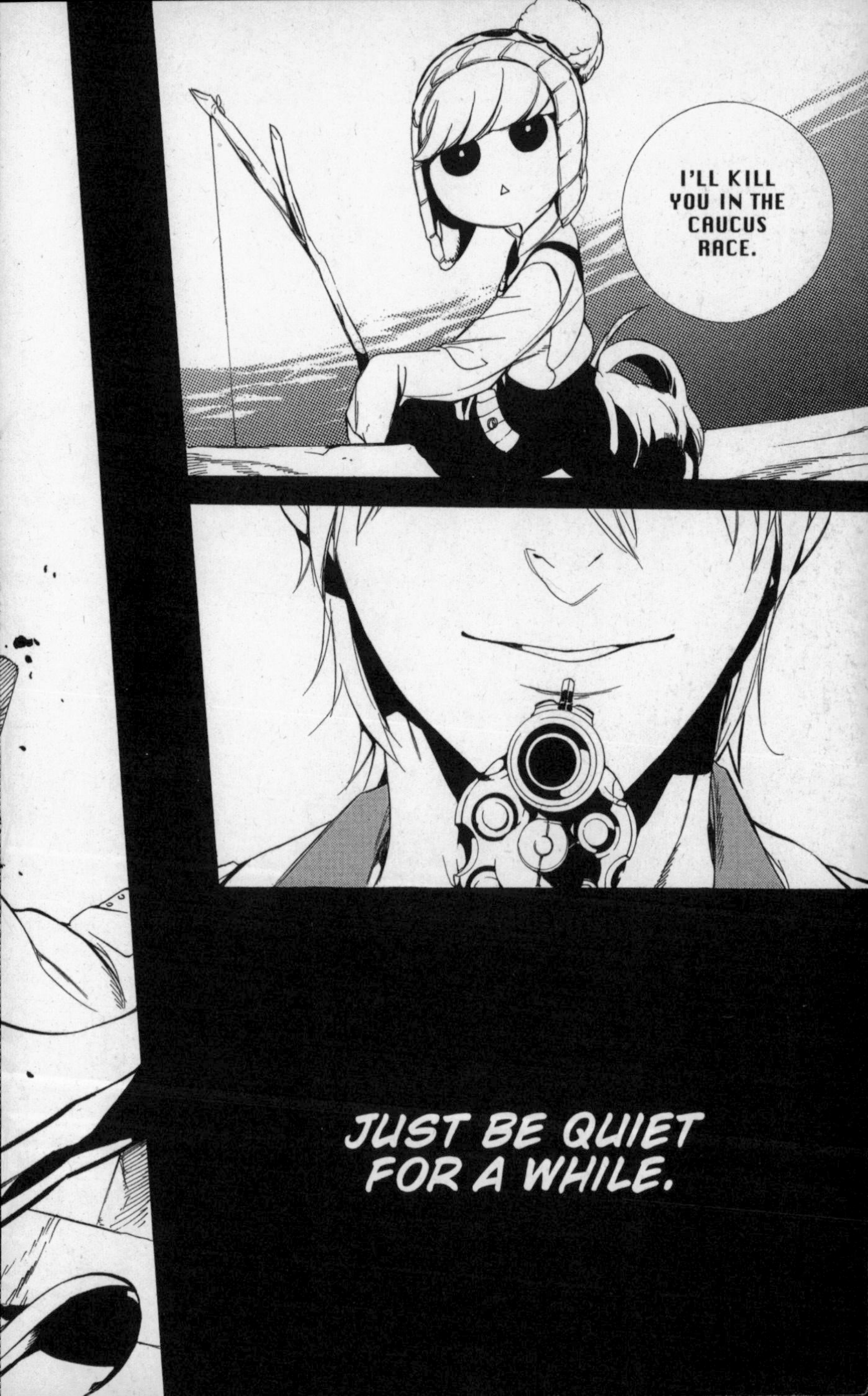
I'LL KILL YOU IN THE CAUCUS RACE.
JUST BE QUIET FOR A WHILE.

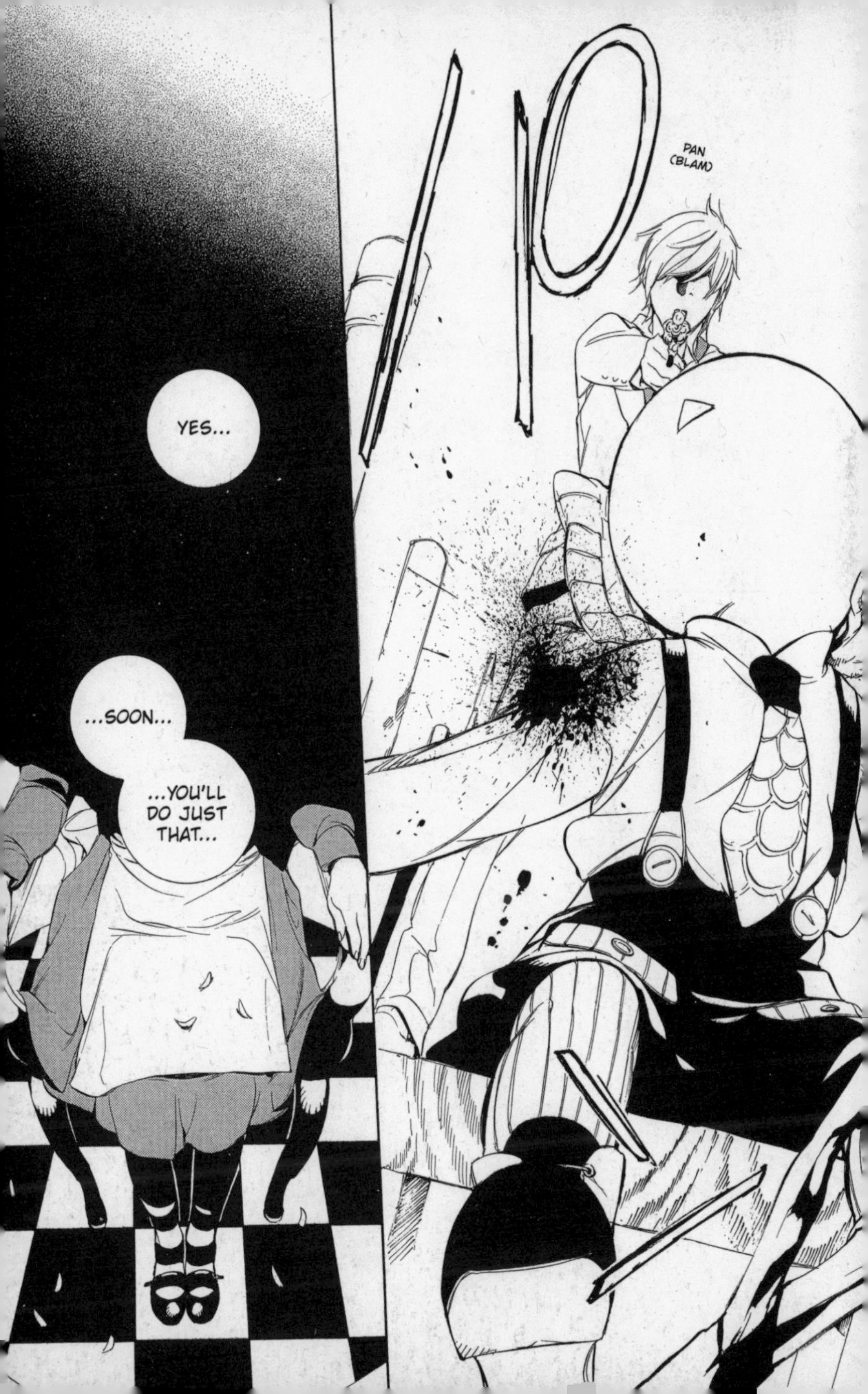
PAN (BLAM)
YES...
...SOON...
...YOU'LL DO JUST THAT...

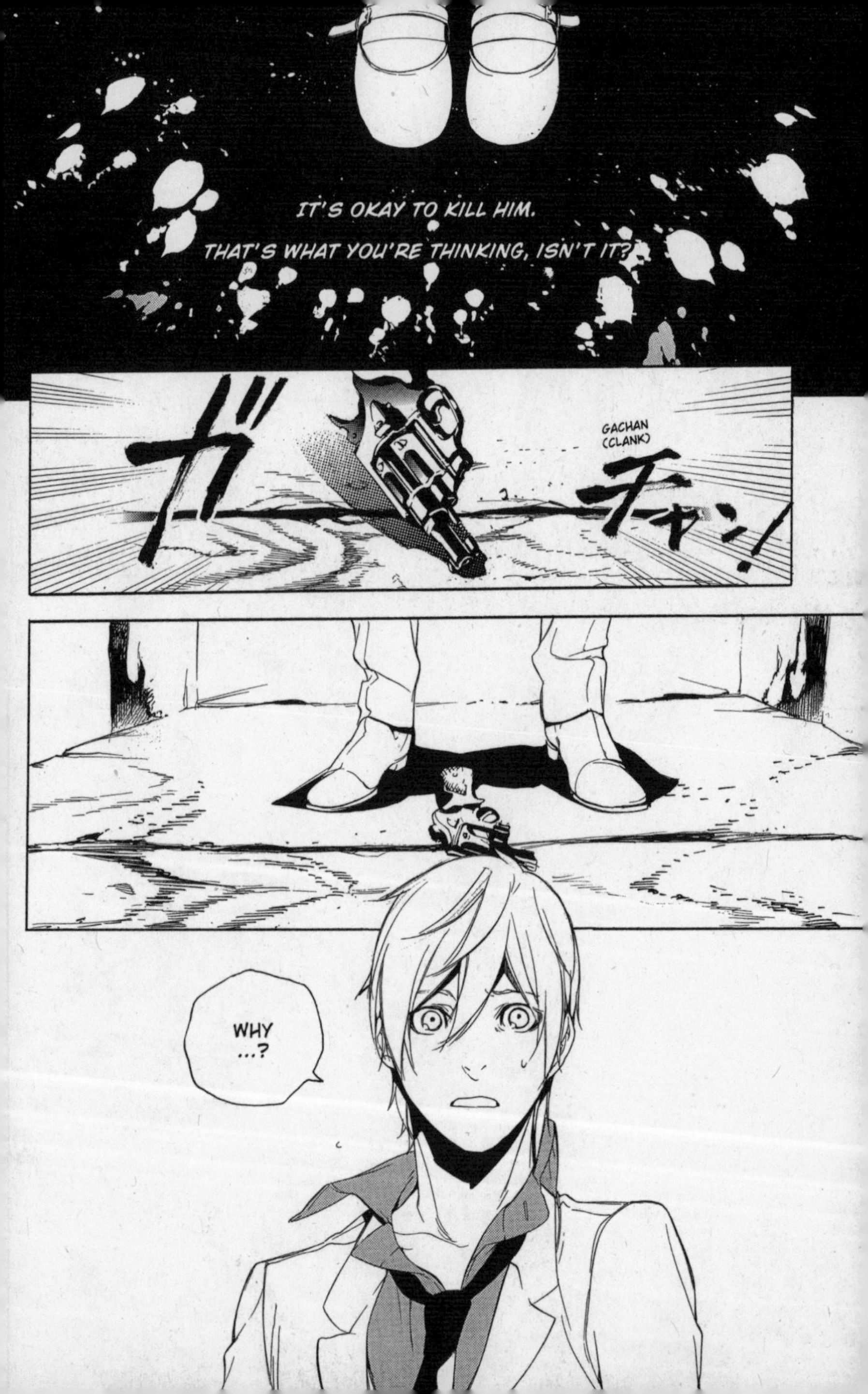
IT'S OKAY TO KILL HIM.
THAT'S WHAT YOU'RE THINKING, ISN'T IT?
GACHAN (CLANK)
ガチャン!
WHY ...?

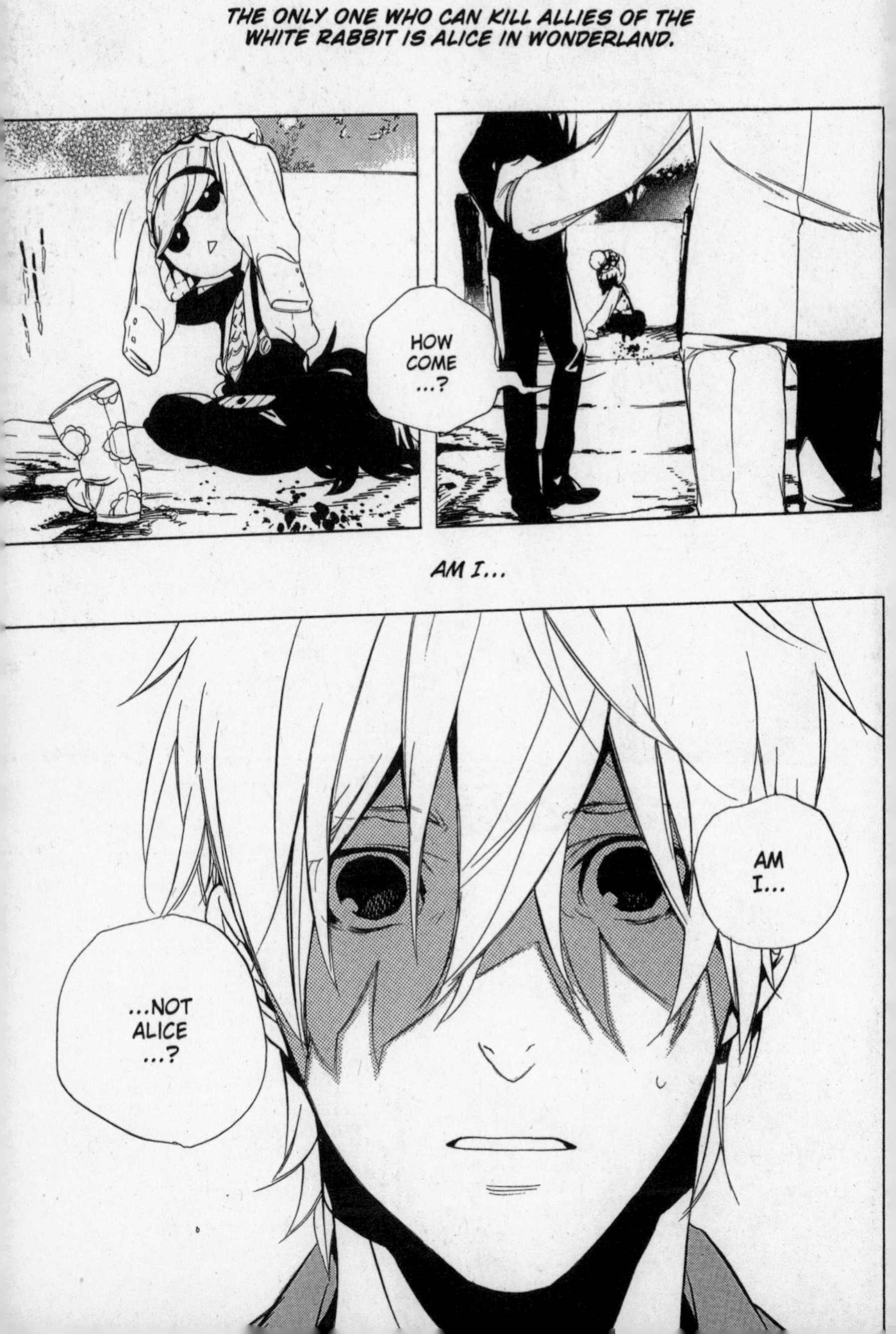
THE ONLY ONE WHO CAN KILL ALLIES OF THE WHITE RABBIT IS ALICE IN WONDERLAND.
HOW COME ...?
AM I...
AM I...
...NOT ALICE ...?

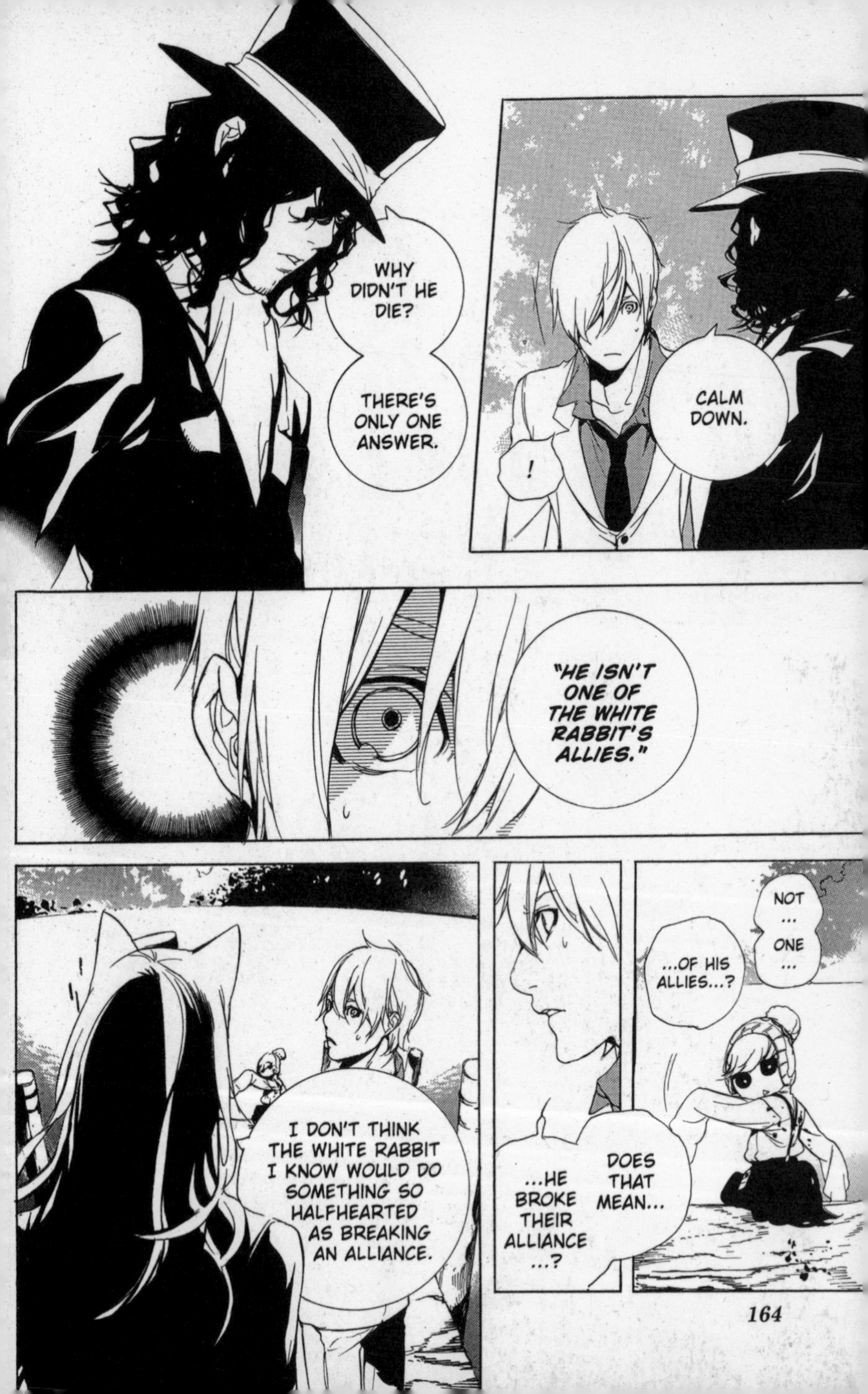
CALM DOWN.
!
WHY DIDN'T HE DIE?
THERE'S ONLY ONE ANSWER.
"HE ISN'T ONE OF THE WHITE RABBIT'S ALLIES."
NOT ... ONE ...
...OF HIS ALLIES...?
DOES THAT MEAN...
...HE BROKE THEIR ALLIANCE ...?
!
I DON'T THINK THE WHITE RABBIT I KNOW WOULD DO SOMETHING SO HALFHEARTED AS BREAKING AN ALLIANCE.

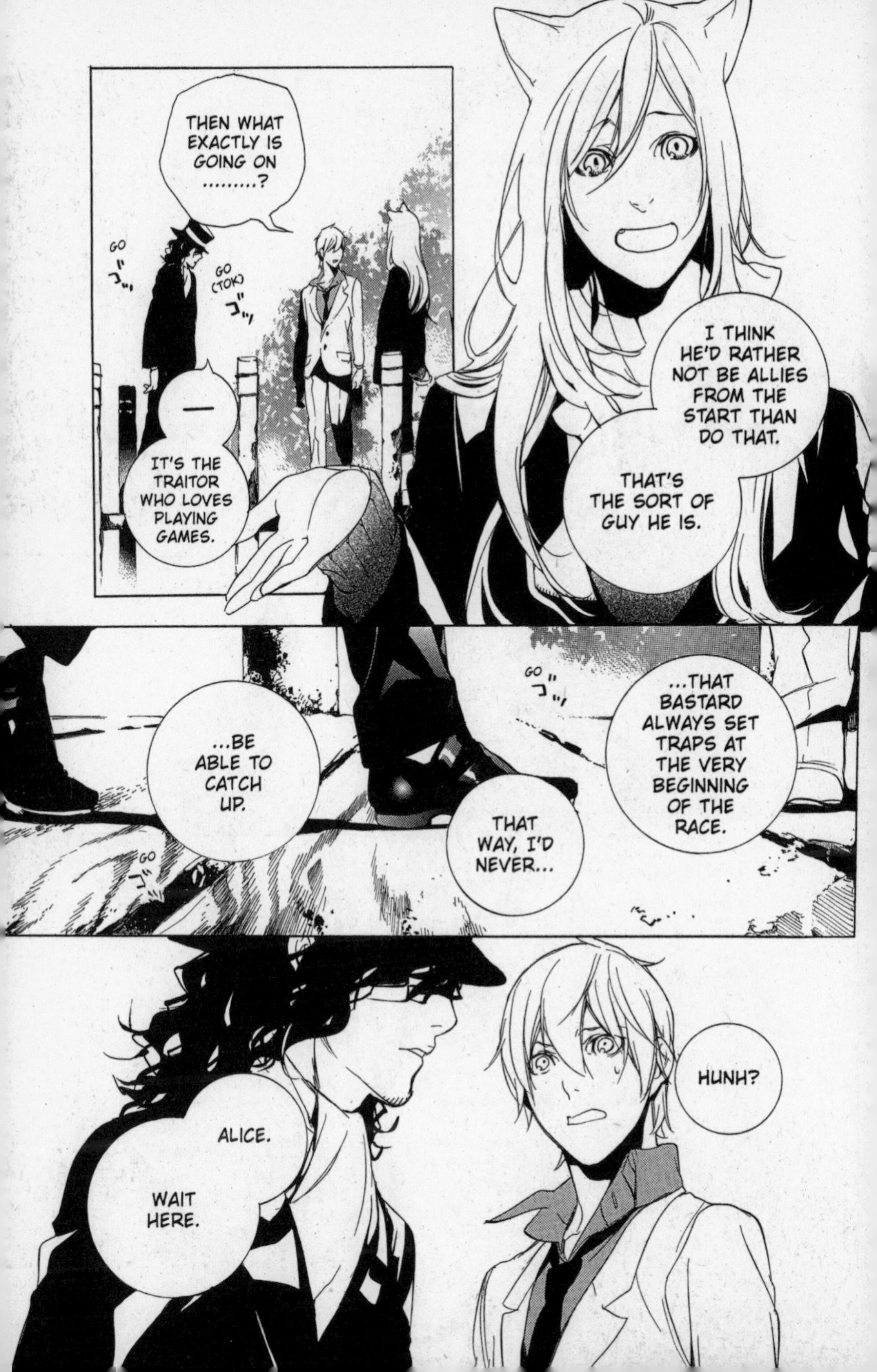
I THINK HE'D RATHER NOT BE ALLIES FROM THE START THAN DO THAT.
THAT'S THE SORT OF GUY HE IS.
THEN WHAT EXACTLY IS GOING ON ....?
GO
GO (TOK)
—
IT'S THE TRAITOR WHO LOVES PLAYING GAMES.
GO
...THAT BASTARD ALWAYS SET TRAPS AT THE VERY BEGINNING OF THE RACE.
THAT WAY, I'D NEVER...
...BE ABLE TO CATCH UP.
GO
HUNH?
ALICE.
WAIT HERE.

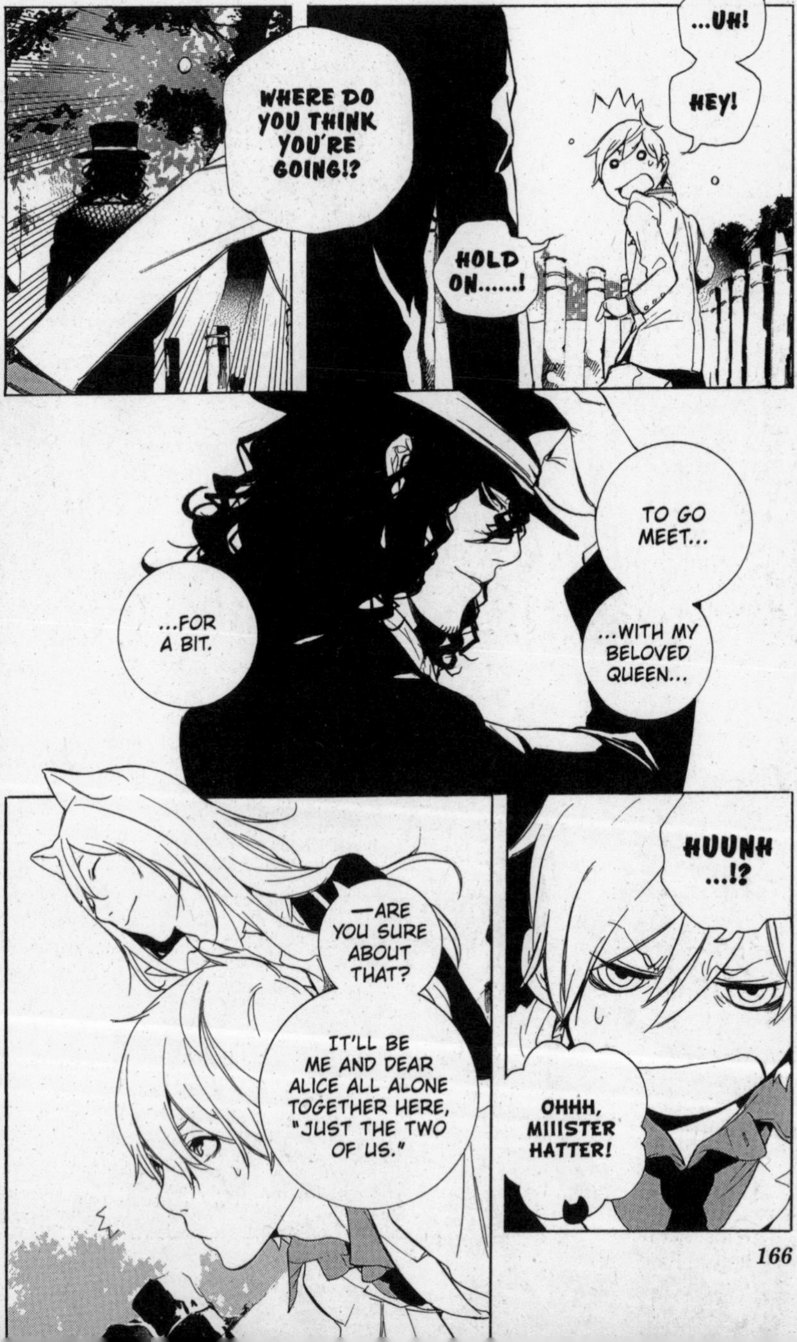
...UH!
HEY!
HOLD ON......!
WHERE DO YOU THINK YOU'RE GOING!?
TO GO MEET...
...WITH MY BELOVED QUEEN...
...FOR A BIT.
HUUNH ...!?
OHHH, MIIISTER HATTER!
—ARE YOU SURE ABOUT THAT?
IT'LL BE ME AND DEAR ALICE ALL ALONE TOGETHER HERE, "JUST THE TWO OF US."

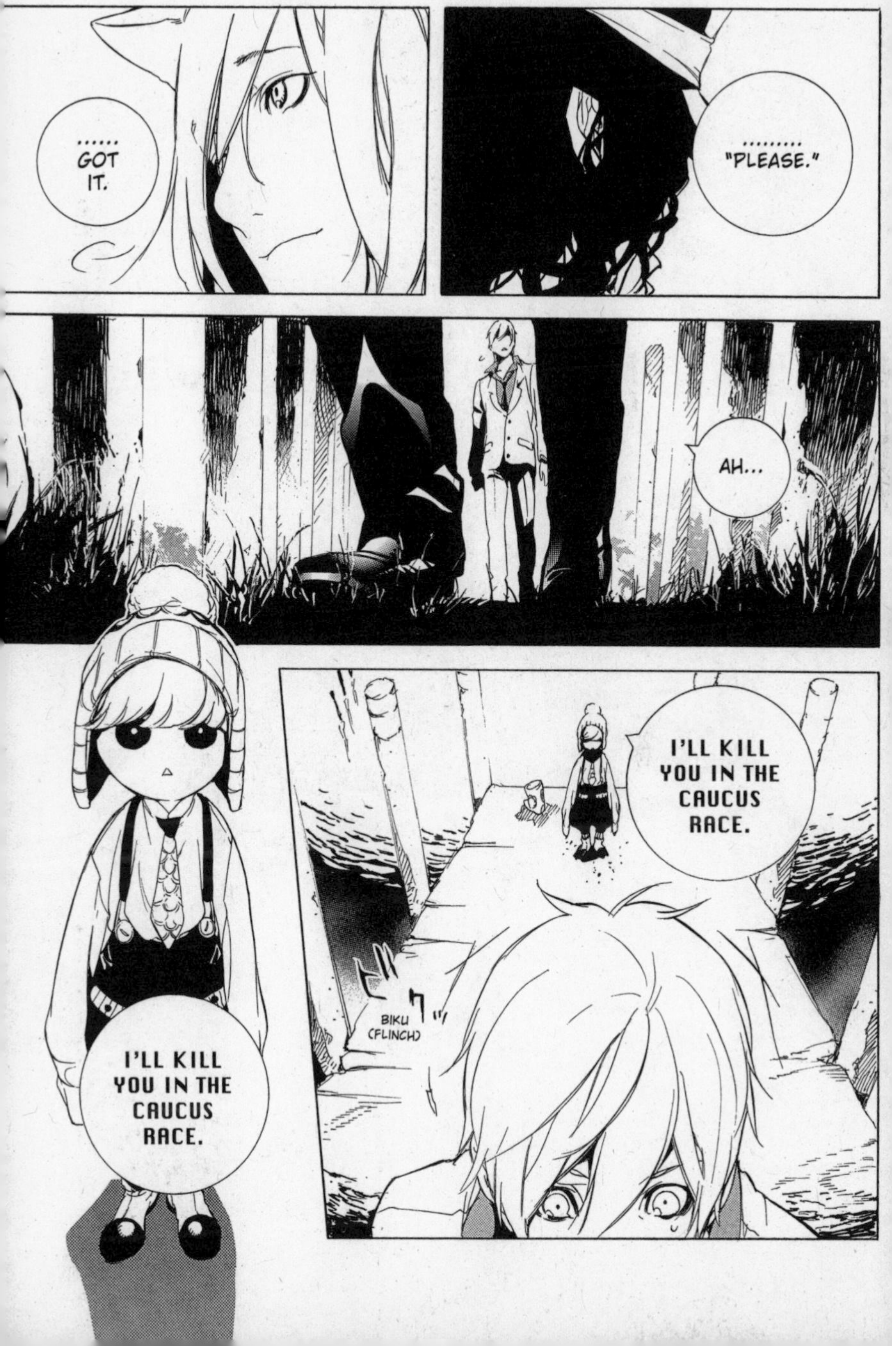
.... "PLEASE."
...... GOT IT.
AH...
I'LL KILL YOU IN THE CAUCUS RACE.
BIKU (FLINCH)
I'LL KILL YOU IN THE CAUCUS RACE.

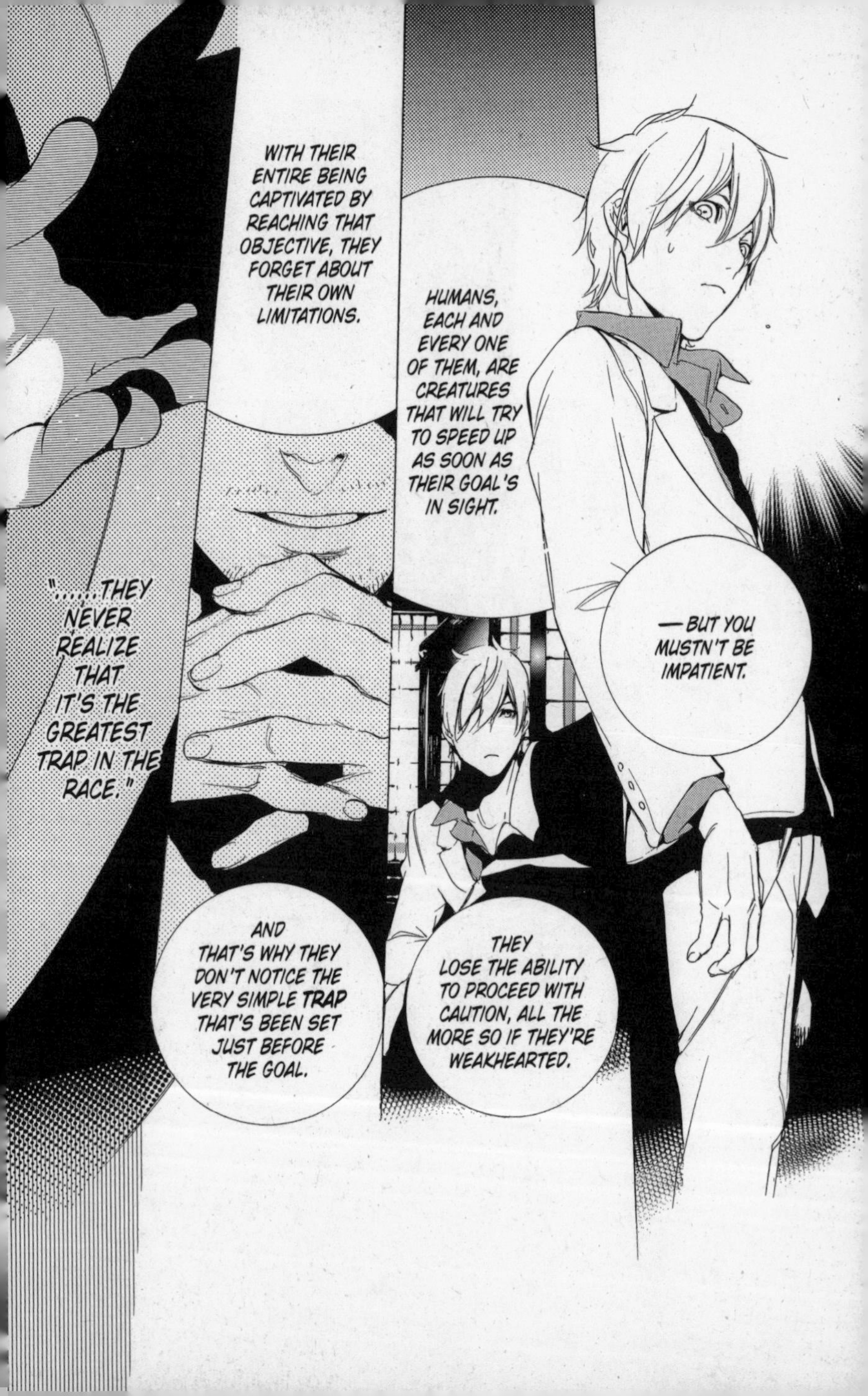
HUMANS, EACH AND EVERY ONE OF THEM, ARE CREATURES THAT WILL TRY TO SPEED UP AS SOON AS THEIR GOAL'S IN SIGHT.
—BUT YOU MUSTN'T BE IMPATIENT.
THEY LOSE THE ABILITY TO PROCEED WITH CAUTION, ALL THE MORE SO IF THEY'RE WEAKHEARTED.
WITH THEIR ENTIRE BEING CAPTIVATED BY REACHING THAT OBJECTIVE, THEY FORGET ABOUT THEIR OWN LIMITATIONS.
AND THAT'S WHY THEY DON'T NOTICE THE VERY SIMPLE TRAP THAT'S BEEN SET JUST BEFORE THE GOAL.
"......THEY NEVER REALIZE THAT IT'S THE GREATEST TRAP IN THE RACE."

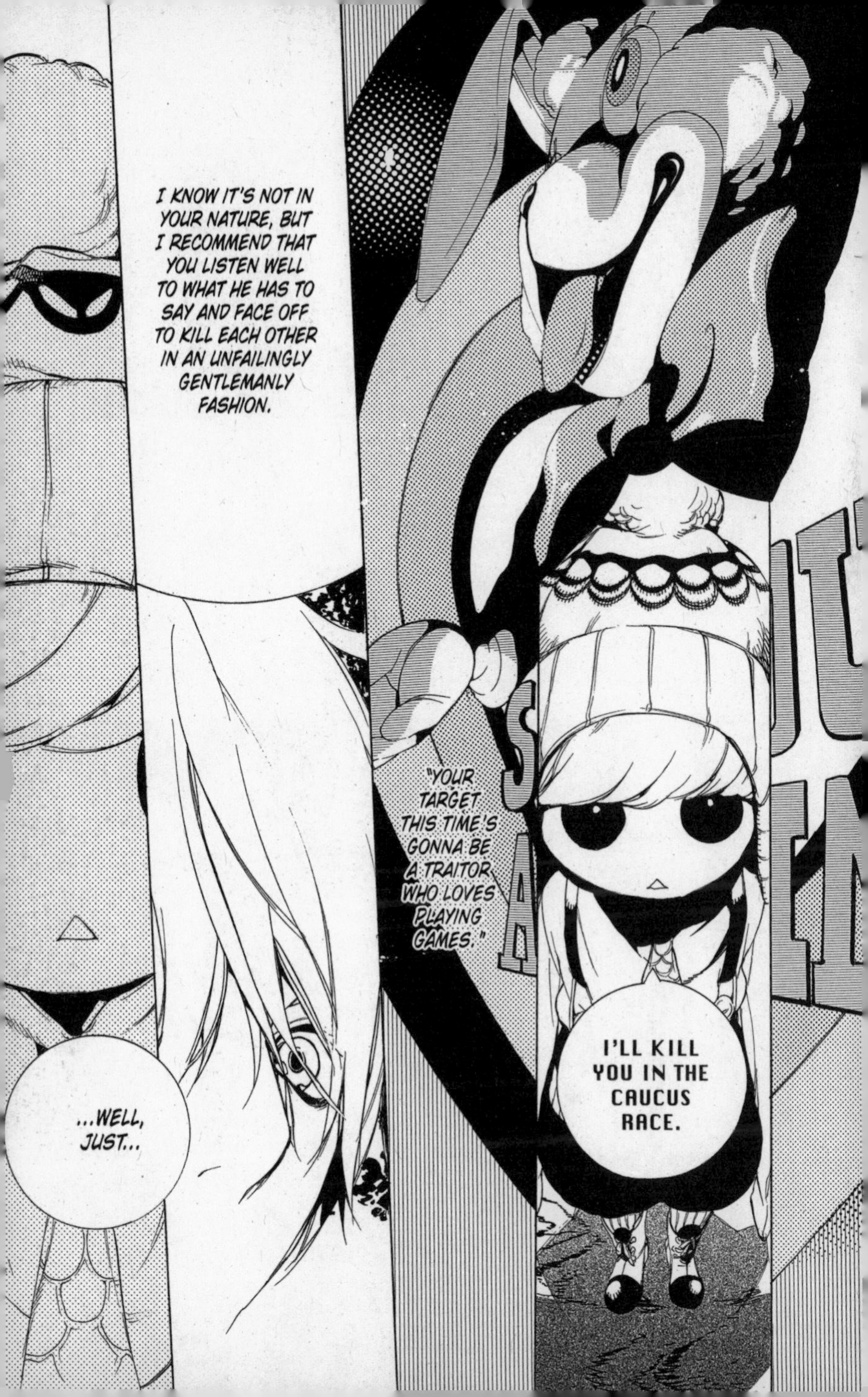
"YOUR TARGET THIS TIME'S GONNA BE A TRAITOR WHO LOVES PLAYING GAMES."
I'LL KILL YOU IN THE CAUCUS RACE.
I KNOW IT'S NOT IN YOUR NATURE, BUT I RECOMMEND THAT YOU LISTEN WELL TO WHAT HE HAS TO SAY AND FACE OFF TO KILL EACH OTHER IN AN UNFAILINGLY GENTLEMANLY FASHION.
...WELL, JUST...

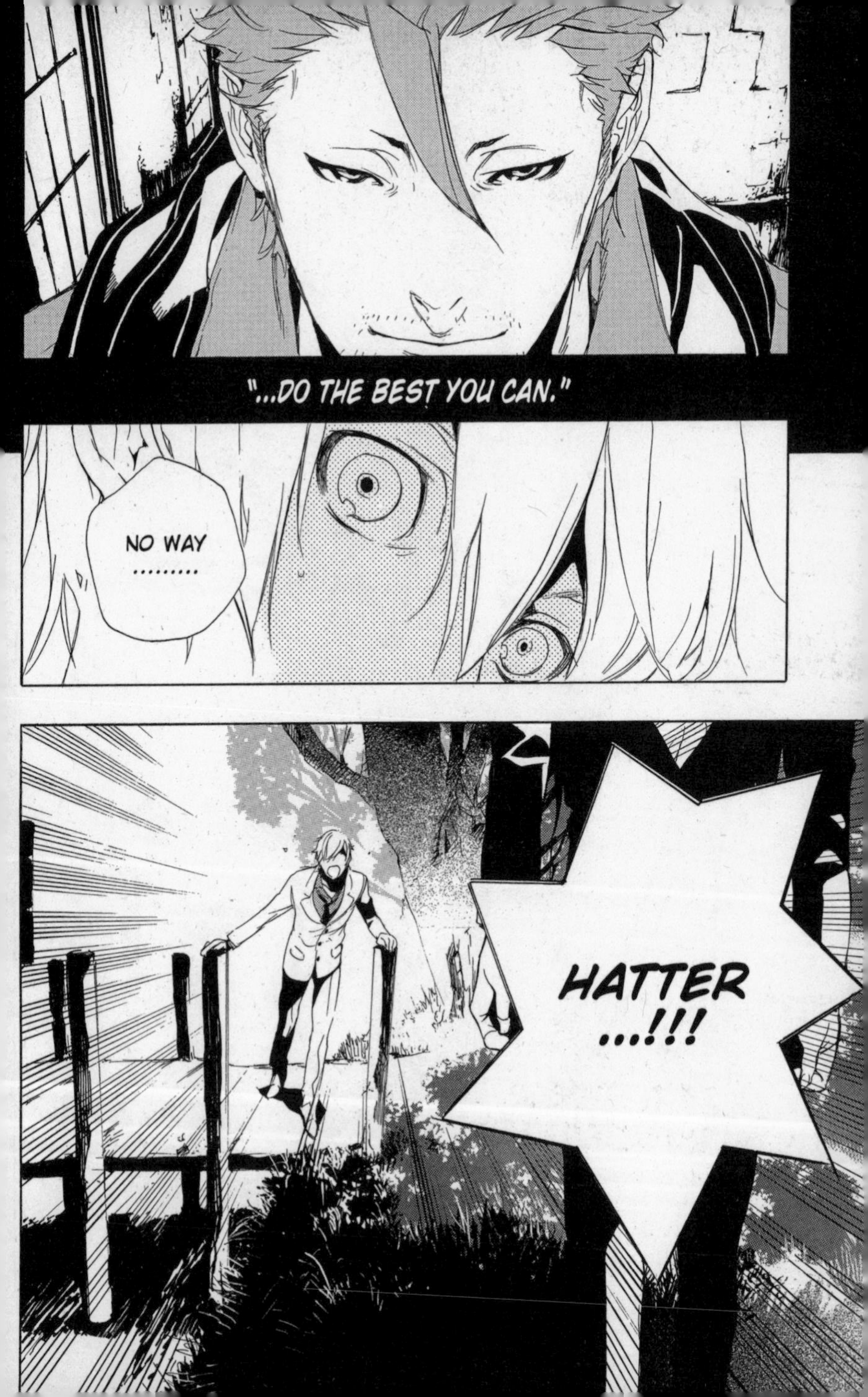
"...DO THE BEST YOU CAN."
NO WAY ....
HATTER ...!!!

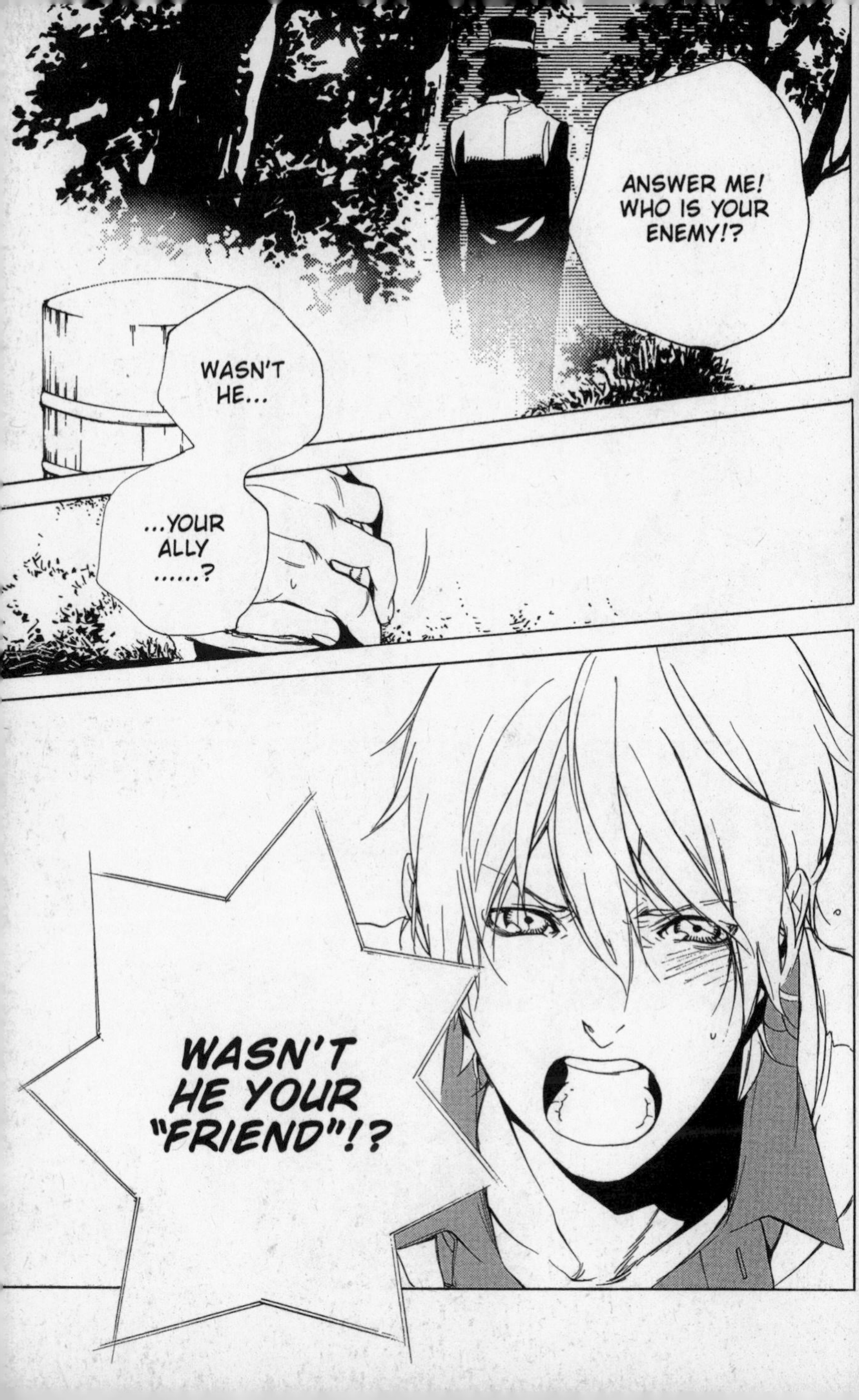
ANSWER ME! WHO IS YOUR ENEMY!?
WASN'T HE...
...YOUR ALLY ......?
WASN'T HE YOUR "FRIEND"!?

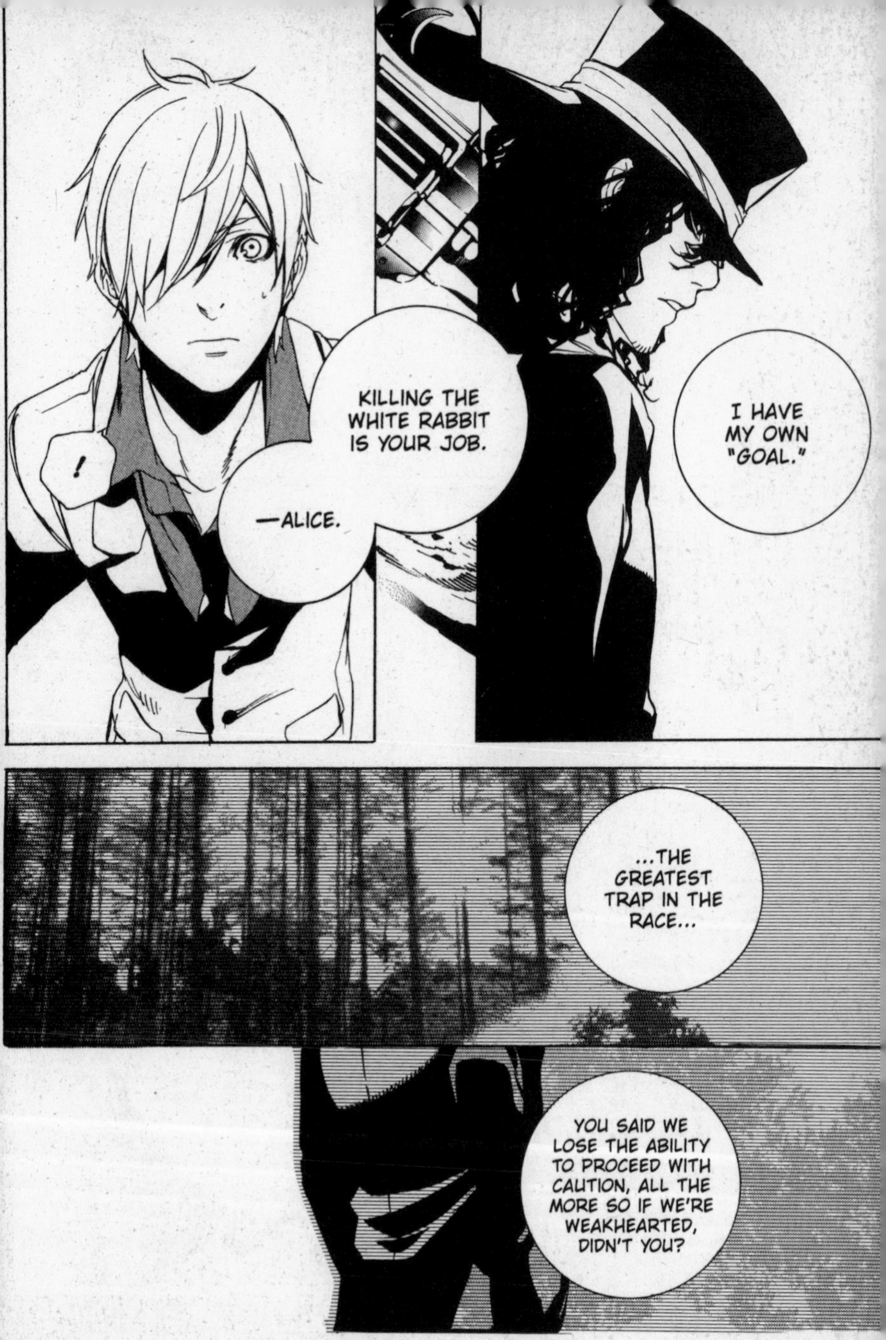
I HAVE MY OWN "GOAL."
KILLING THE WHITE RABBIT IS YOUR JOB.
—ALICE.
!
...THE GREATEST TRAP IN THE RACE...
YOU SAID WE LOSE THE ABILITY TO PROCEED WITH CAUTION, ALL THE MORE SO IF WE'RE WEAKHEARTED, DIDN'T YOU?

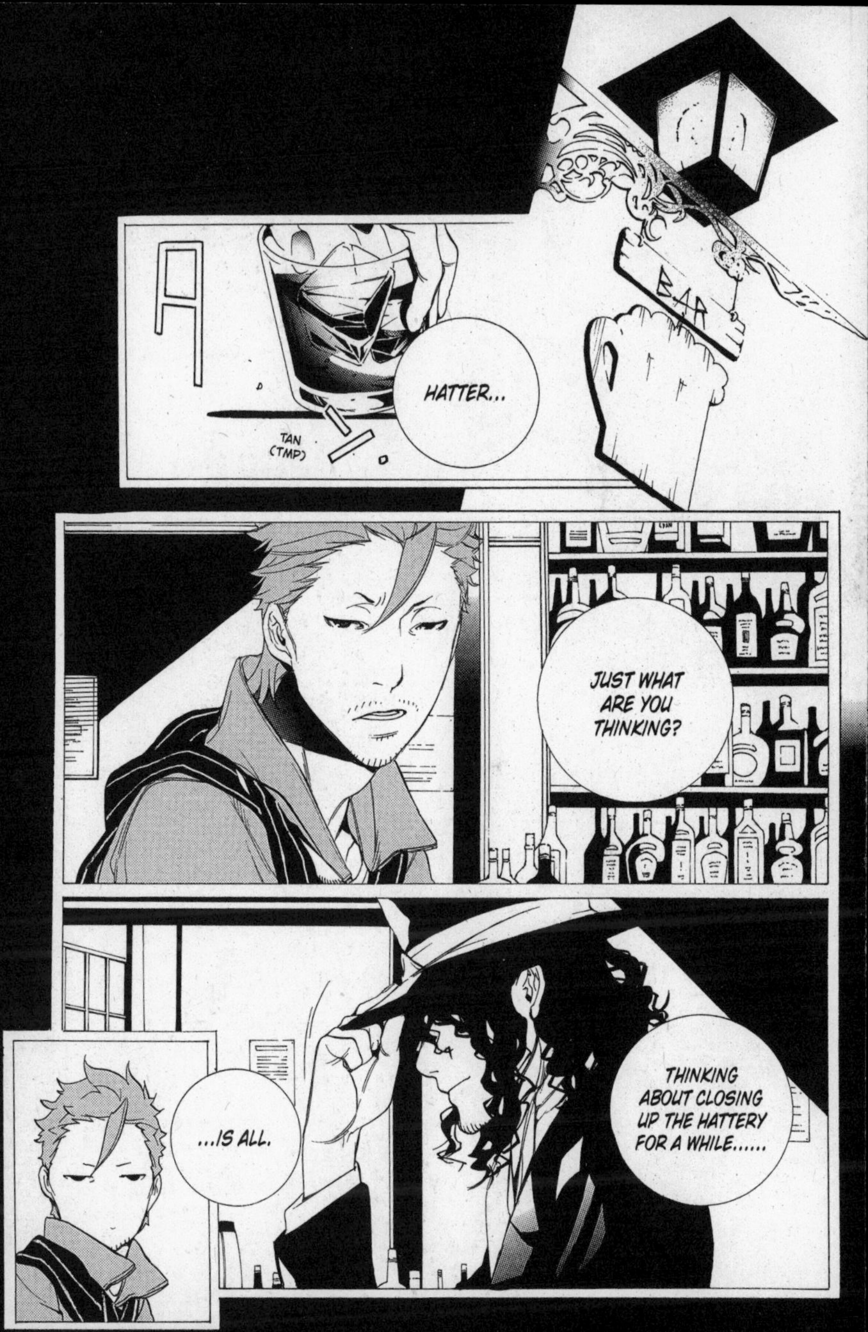
BAR
HATTER...
TAN (TMP)
JUST WHAT ARE YOU THINKING?
THINKING ABOUT CLOSING UP THE HATTERY FOR A WHILE......
...IS ALL.

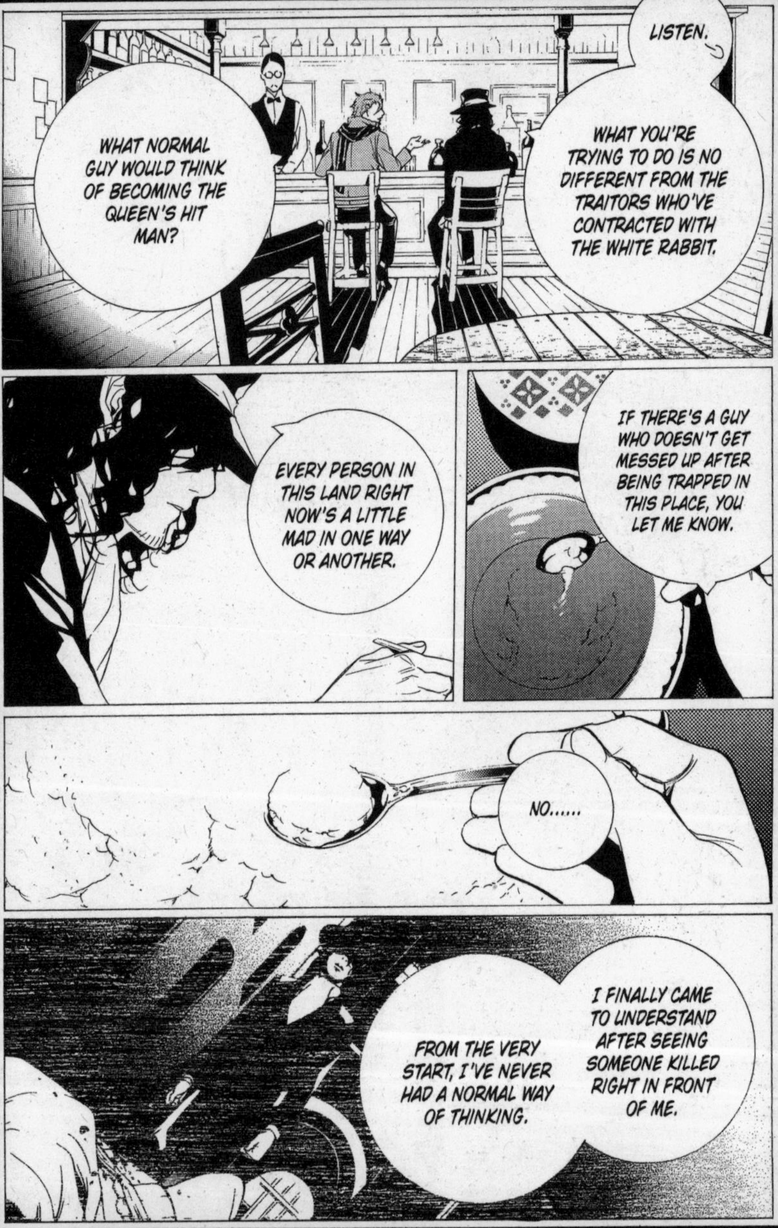
LISTEN.
WHAT YOU'RE TRYING TO DO IS NO DIFFERENT FROM THE TRAITORS WHO'VE CONTRACTED WITH THE WHITE RABBIT.
WHAT NORMAL GUY WOULD THINK OF BECOMING THE QUEEN'S HIT MAN?
IF THERE'S A GUY WHO DOESN'T GET MESSED UP AFTER BEING TRAPPED IN THIS PLACE, YOU LET ME KNOW.
EVERY PERSON IN THIS LAND RIGHT NOW'S A LITTLE MAD IN ONE WAY OR ANOTHER.
NO......
I FINALLY CAME TO UNDERSTAND AFTER SEEING SOMEONE KILLED RIGHT IN FRONT OF ME.
FROM THE VERY START, I'VE NEVER HAD A NORMAL WAY OF THINKING.

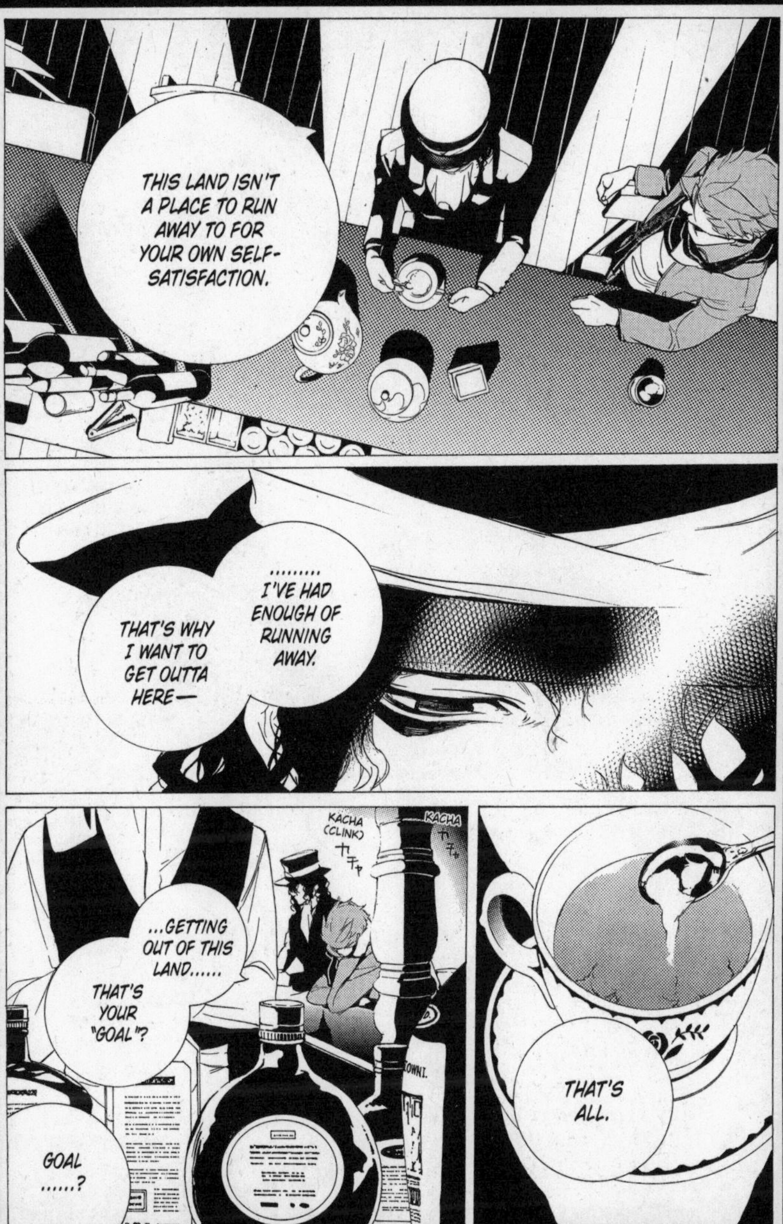
THIS LAND ISN'T A PLACE TO RUN AWAY TO FOR YOUR OWN SELF-SATISFACTION.
.... I'VE HAD ENOUGH OF RUNNING AWAY.
THAT'S WHY I WANT TO GET OUTTA HERE—
THAT'S ALL.
KACHA
KACHA (CLINK)
...GETTING OUT OF THIS LAND......
THAT'S YOUR "GOAL"?
GOAL ......?

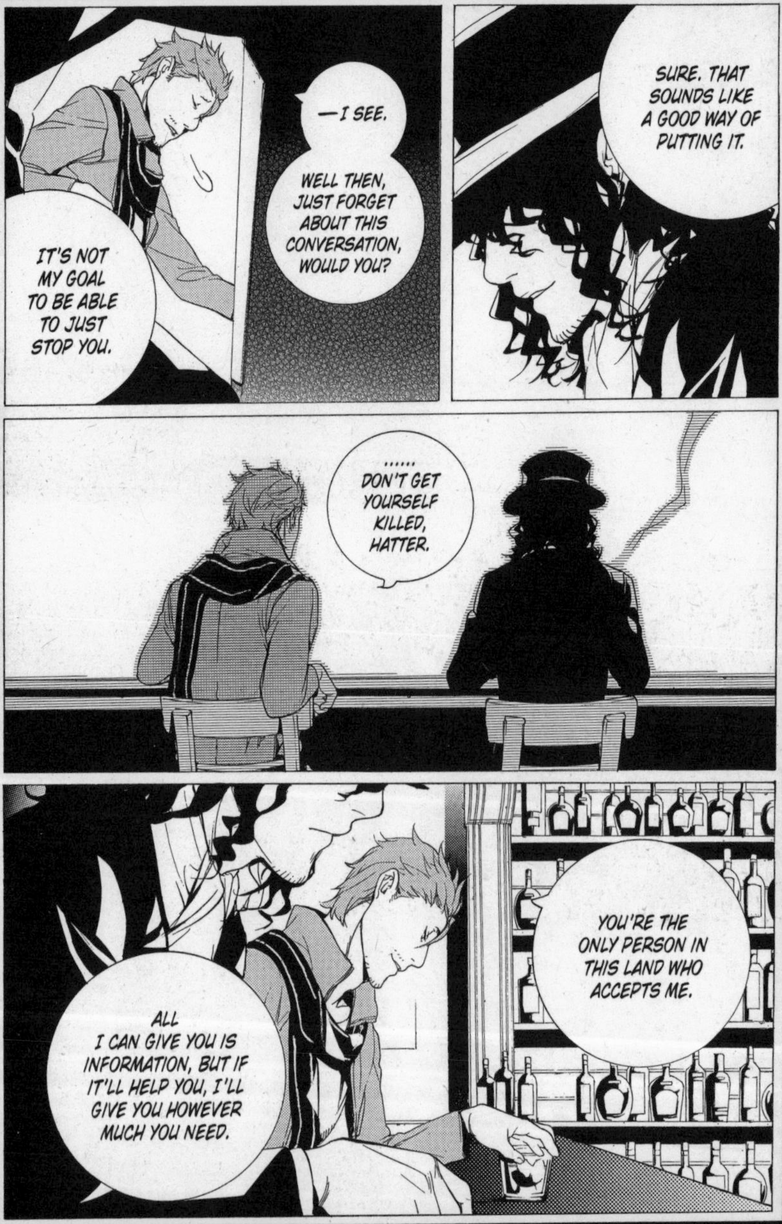
SURE. THAT SOUNDS LIKE A GOOD WAY OF PUTTING IT.
—I SEE.
WELL THEN, JUST FORGET ABOUT THIS CONVERSATION, WOULD YOU?
IT'S NOT MY GOAL TO BE ABLE TO JUST STOP YOU.
...... DON'T GET YOURSELF KILLED, HATTER.
YOU'RE THE ONLY PERSON IN THIS LAND WHO ACCEPTS ME.
ALL I CAN GIVE YOU IS INFORMATION, BUT IF IT'LL HELP YOU, I'LL GIVE YOU HOWEVER MUCH YOU NEED.

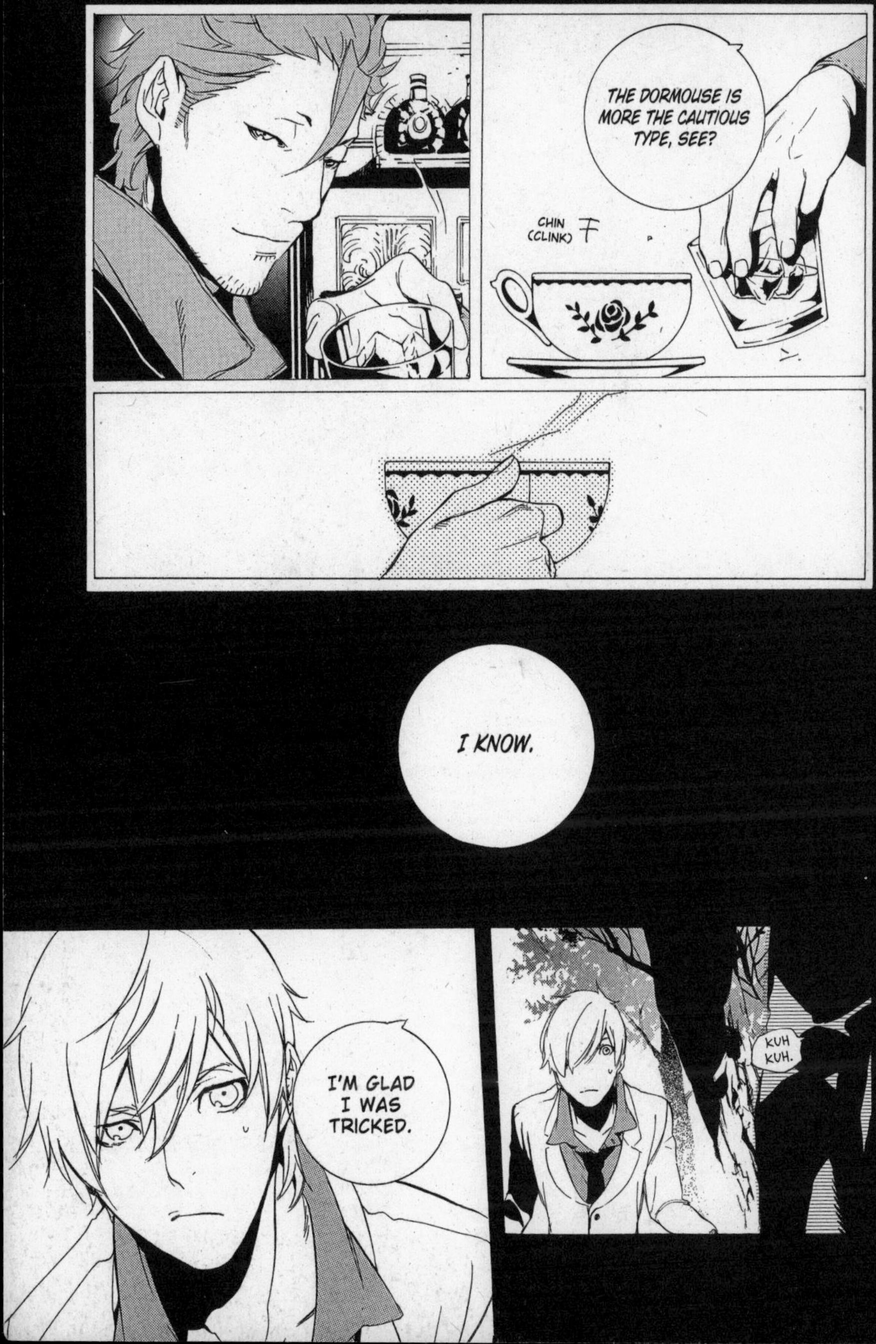
THE DORMOUSE IS MORE THE CAUTIOUS TYPE, SEE?
CHIN (CLINK)
I KNOW.
KUH KUH.
I'M GLAD I WAS TRICKED.

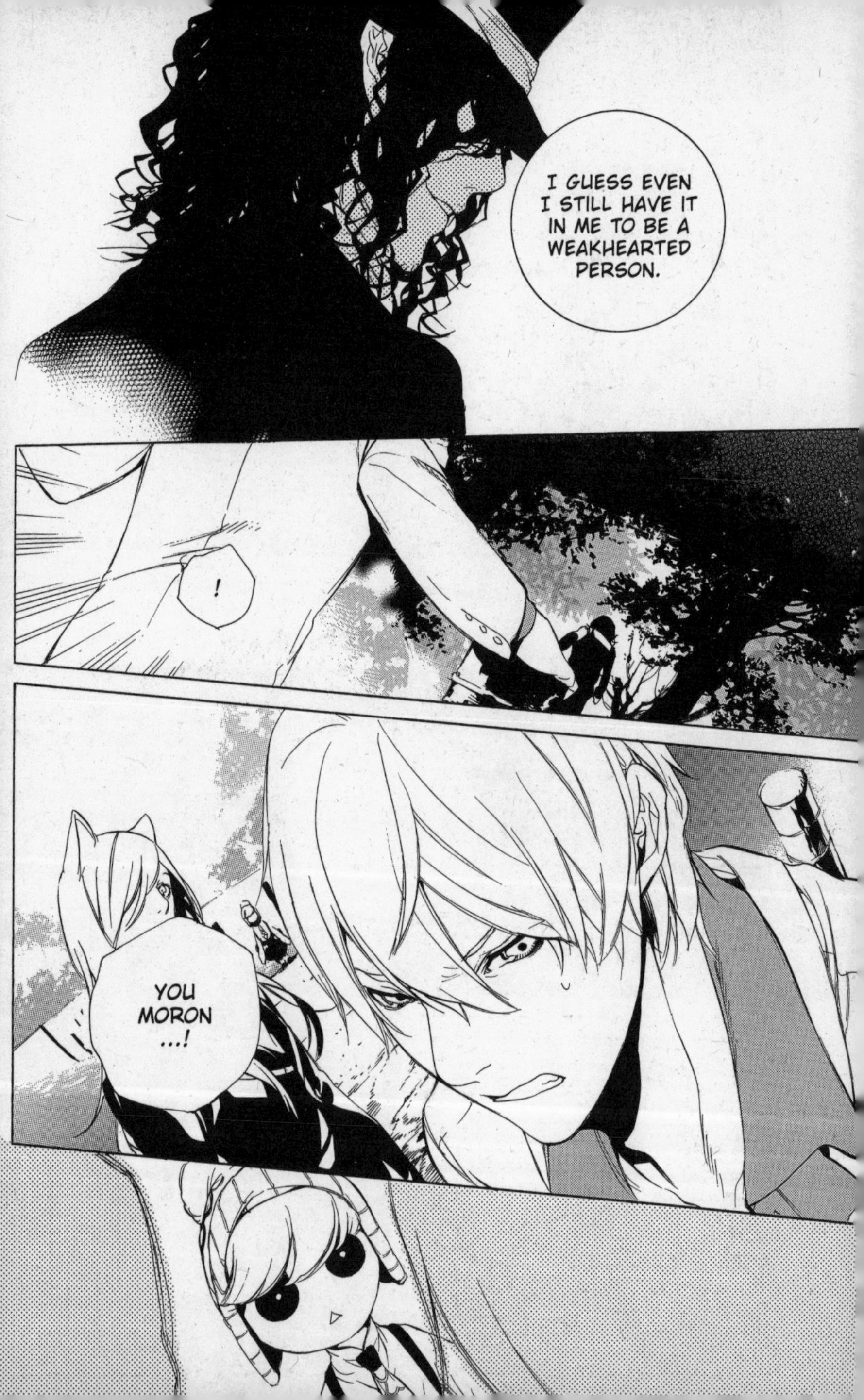
I GUESS EVEN I STILL HAVE IT IN ME TO BE A WEAKHEARTED PERSON.
!
YOU MORON ...!

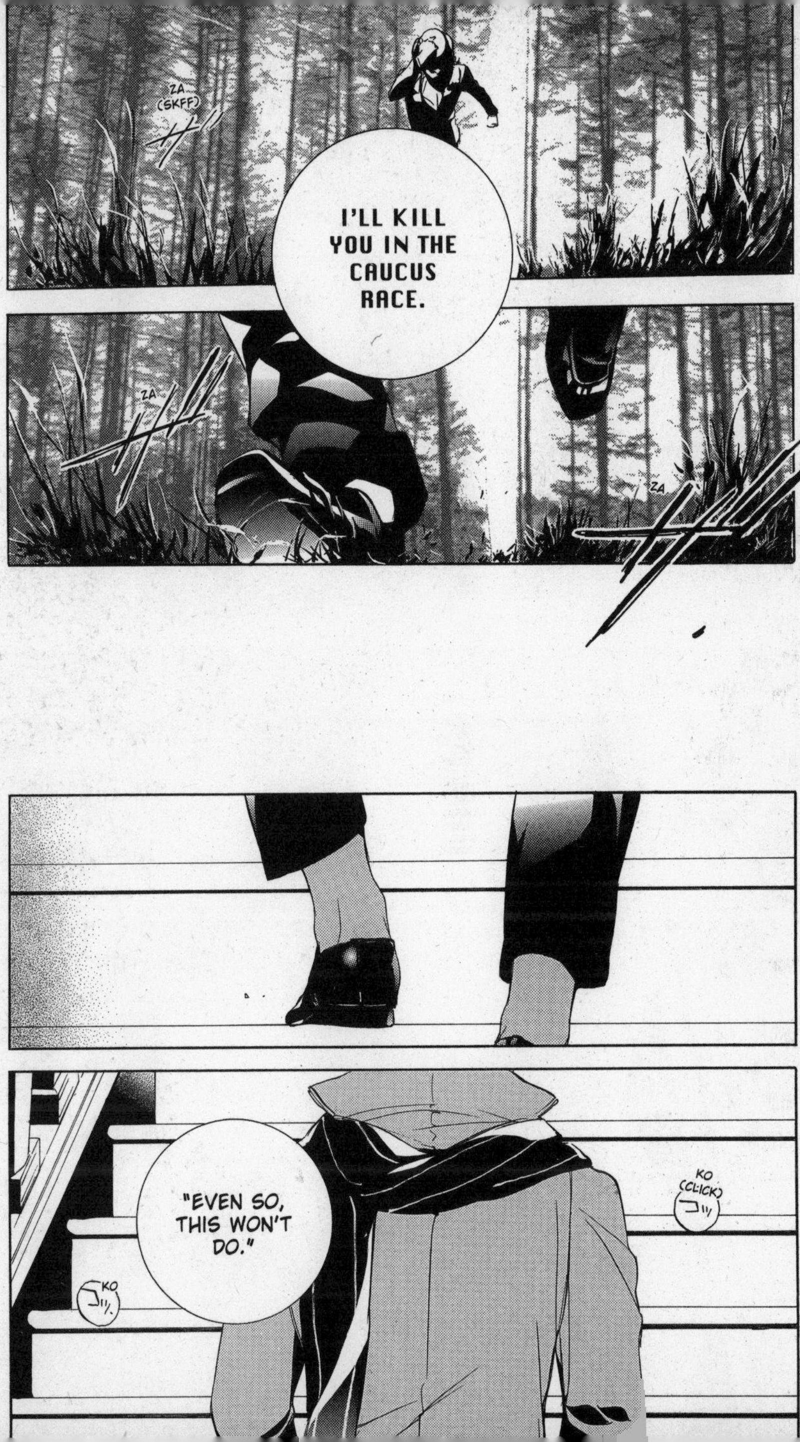
ZA (SKFF)
I'LL KILL YOU IN THE CAUCUS RACE.
ZA
ZA
KO (CLICK)
"EVEN SO, THIS WON'T DO."
KO

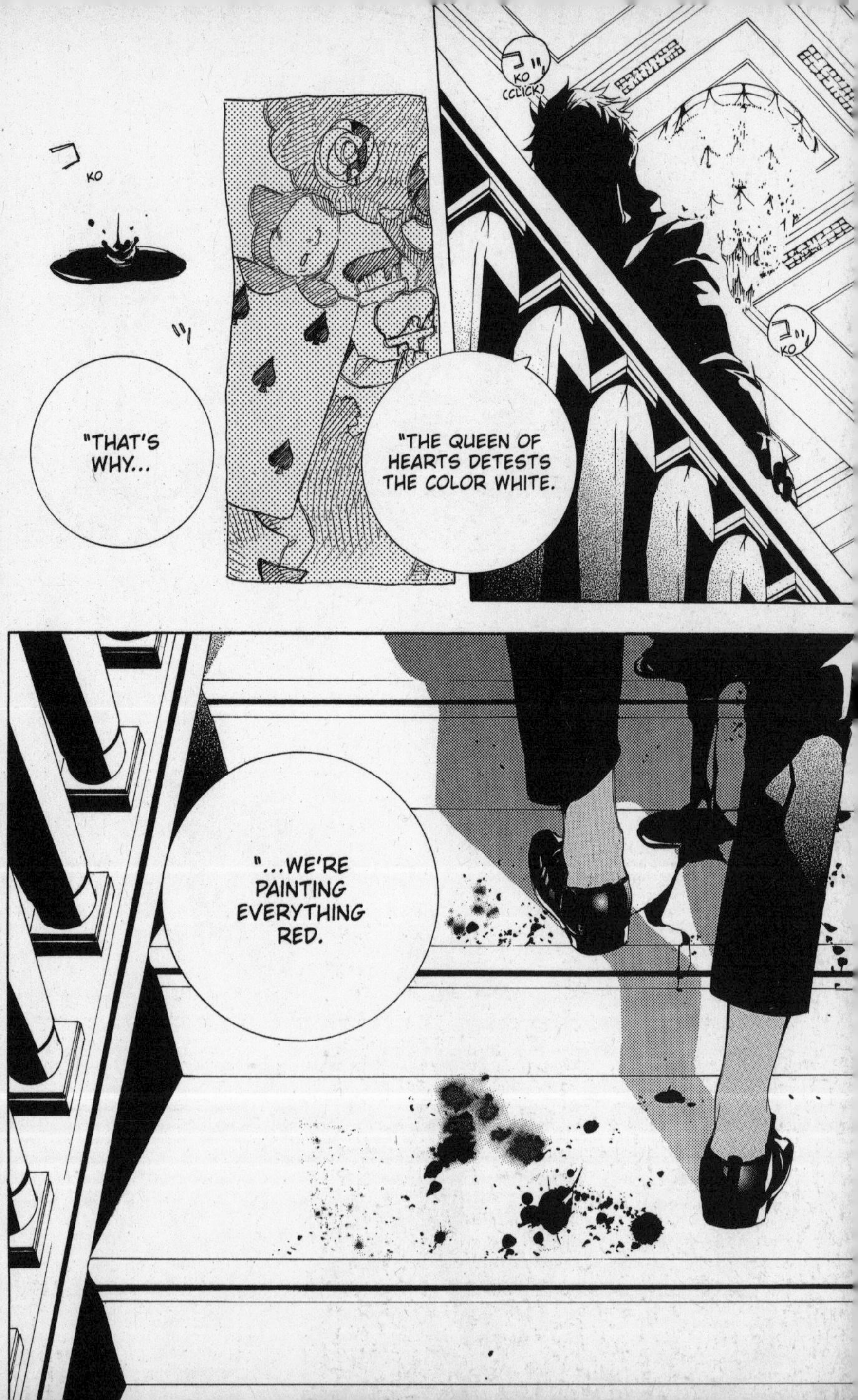
KO (CLICK)
KO
"THE QUEEN OF HEARTS DETESTS THE COLOR WHITE.
KO
"THAT'S WHY...
"...WE'RE PAINTING EVERYTHING RED.

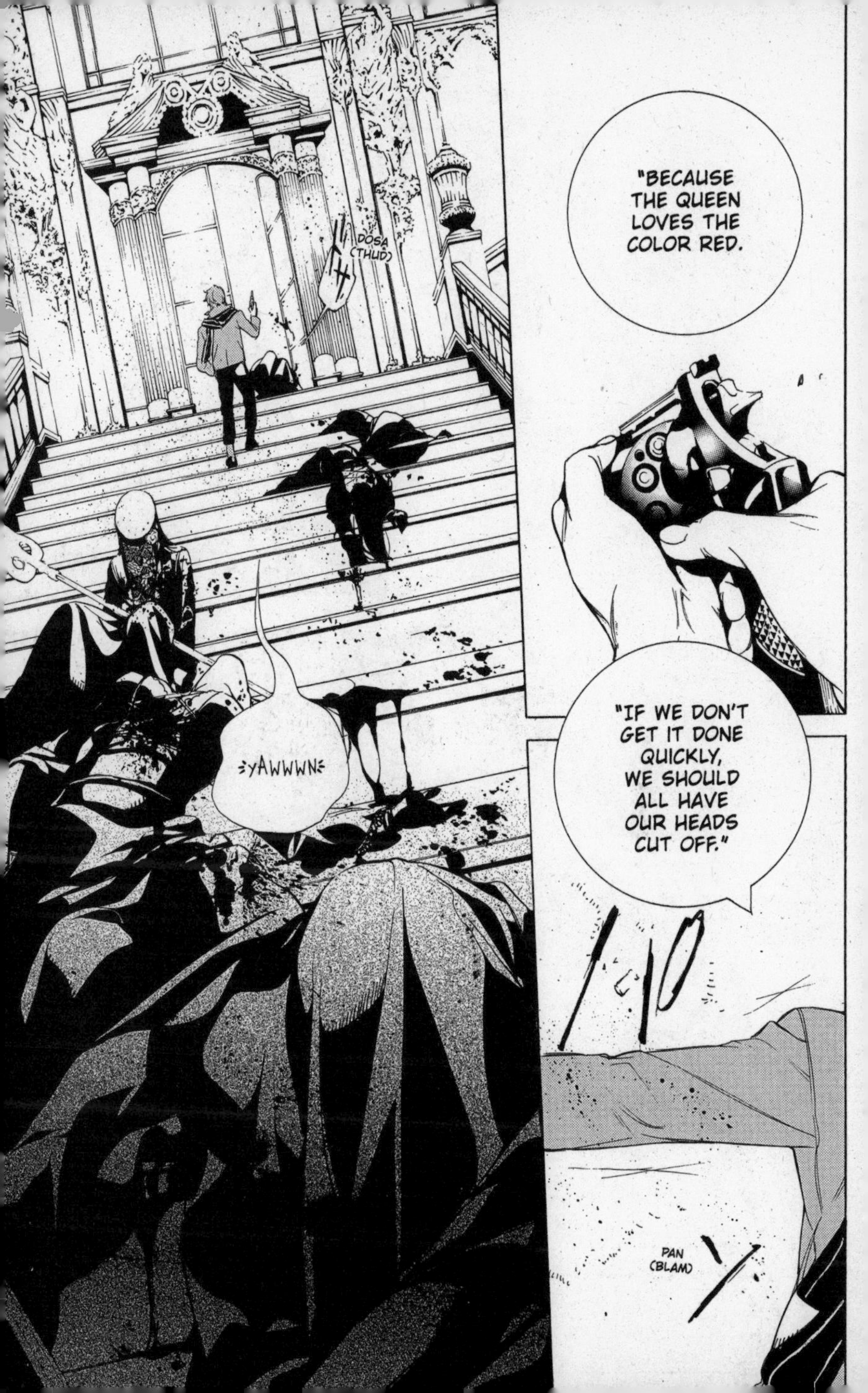
"BECAUSE THE QUEEN LOVES THE COLOR RED.
"IF WE DON'T GET IT DONE QUICKLY, WE SHOULD ALL HAVE OUR HEADS CUT OFF."
PAN (BLAM)
DOSA (THUD)
yAWWWN

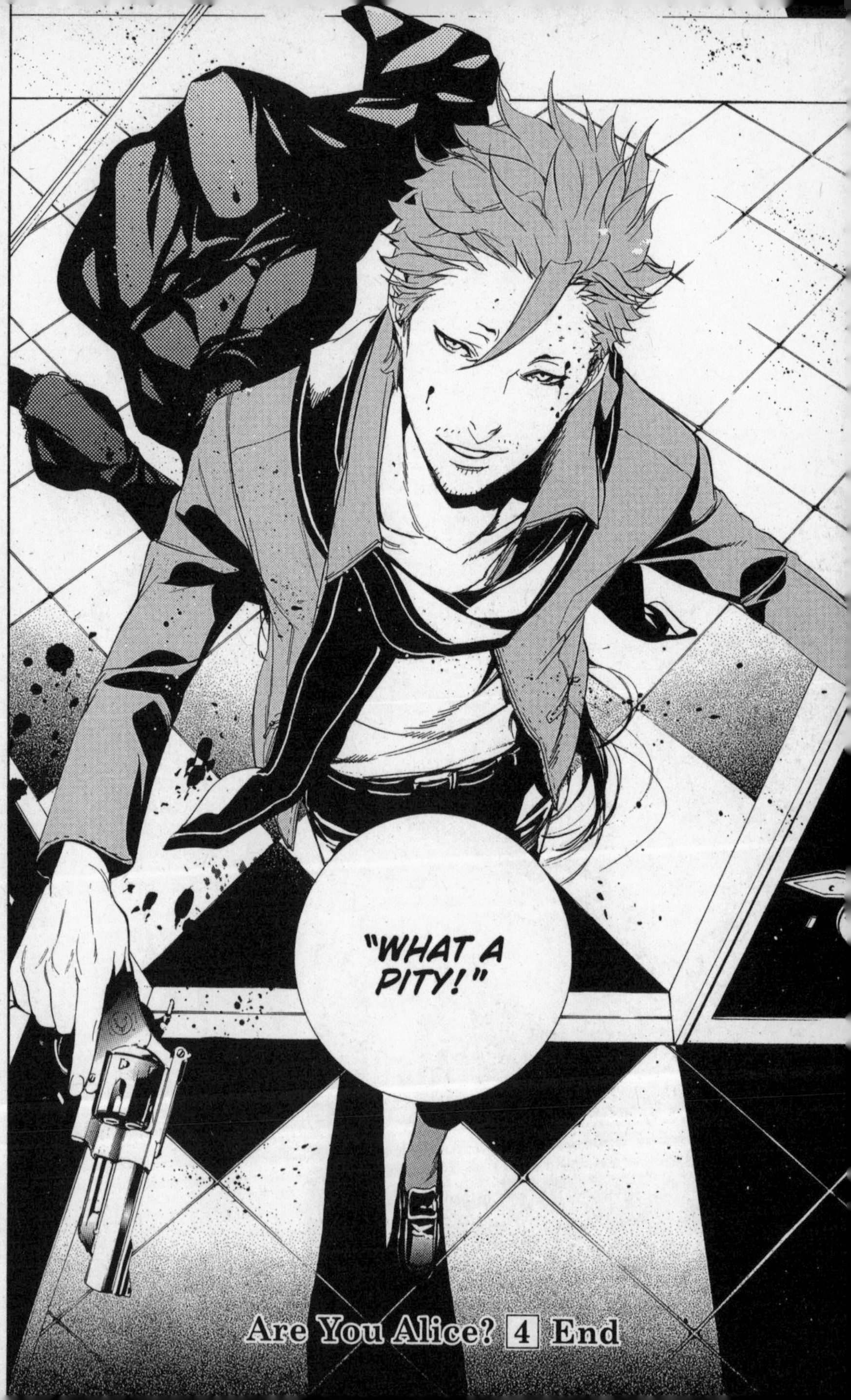
"WHAT A PITY!"
Are You Alice? 4 End

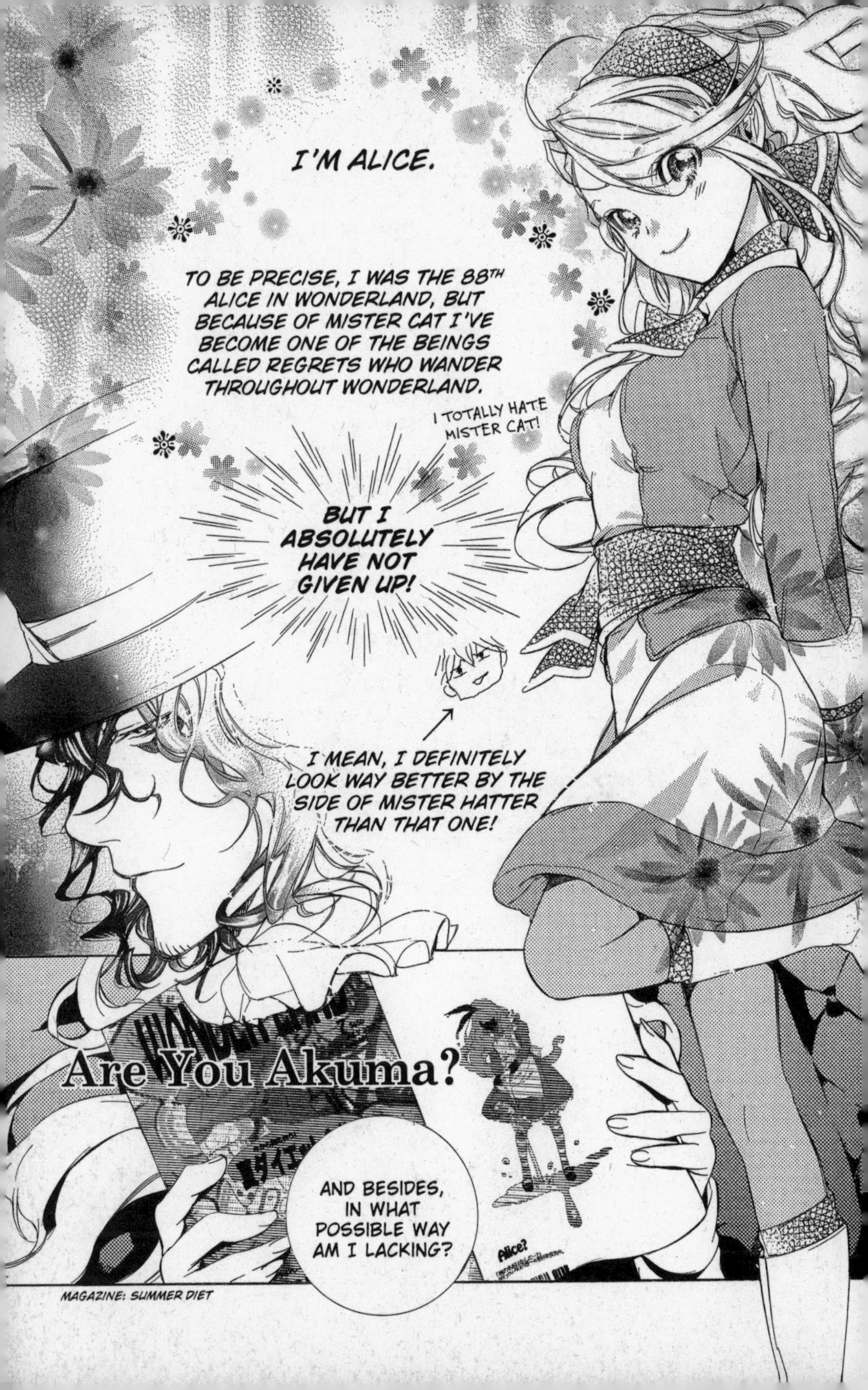
I'M ALICE.
TO BE PRECISE, I WAS THE 88TH ALICE IN WONDERLAND, BUT BECAUSE OF MISTER CAT I'VE BECOME ONE OF THE BEINGS CALLED REGRETS WHO WANDER THROUGHOUT WONDERLAND.
I TOTALLY HATE MISTER CAT!
BUT I ABSOLUTELY HAVE NOT GIVEN UP!
I MEAN, I DEFINITELY LOOK WAY BETTER BY THE SIDE OF MISTER HATTER THAN THAT ONE!
Are You Akuma?
AND BESIDES, IN WHAT POSSIBLE WAY AM I LACKING?
Alice?
MAGAZINE: SUMMER DIET

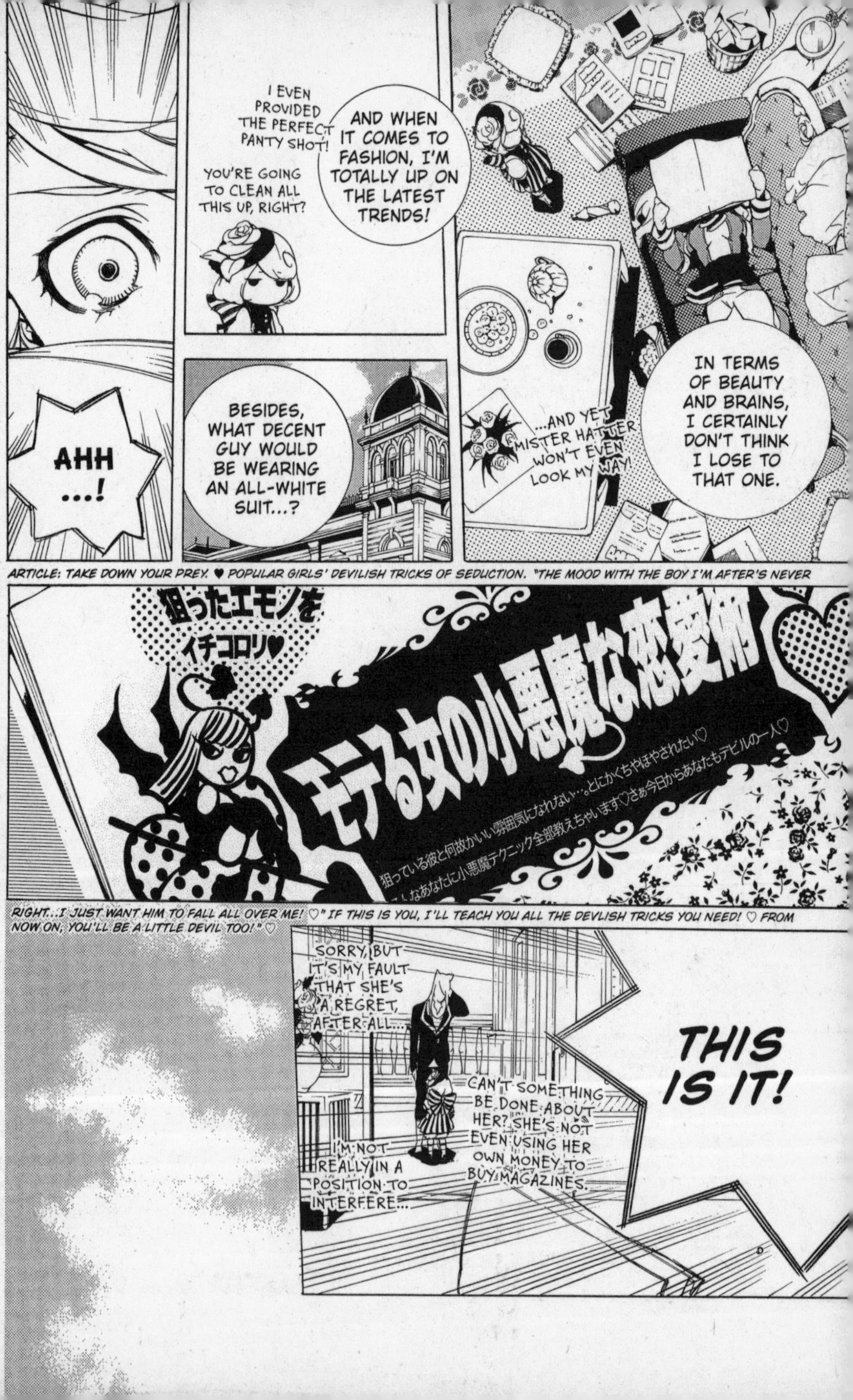
IN TERMS OF BEAUTY AND BRAINS, I CERTAINLY DON'T THINK I LOSE TO THAT ONE.
...AND YET MISTER HATTER WON'T EVEN LOOK MY WAY!
AND WHEN IT COMES TO FASHION, I'M TOTALLY UP ON THE LATEST TRENDS!
I EVEN PROVIDED THE PERFECT PANTY SHOT!
YOU'RE GOING TO CLEAN ALL THIS UP, RIGHT?
BESIDES, WHAT DECENT GUY WOULD BE WEARING AN ALL-WHITE SUIT...?
AHH ...!
ARTICLE: TAKE DOWN YOUR PREY. ♥ POPULAR GIRLS' DEVILISH TRICKS OF SEDUCTION. "THE MOOD WITH THE BOY I'M AFTER'S NEVER RIGHT...I JUST WANT HIM TO FALL ALL OVER ME! ♡" IF THIS IS YOU, I'LL TEACH YOU ALL THE DEVLISH TRICKS YOU NEED! ♡ FROM NOW ON, YOU'LL BE A LITTLE DEVIL TOO!" ♡
狙ったエモノをイチコロリ♥
モテる女の小悪魔な恋愛術
狙っている彼と何故かいい雰囲気になれない…。とにかくちやほやされたい♡
なあなたに小悪魔テクニック全部教えちゃいます♡さあ今日からあなたもデビルの一人♡
THIS IS IT!
SORRY, BUT IT'S MY FAULT THAT SHE'S A REGRET, AFTER ALL...
CAN'T SOMETHING BE DONE ABOUT HER? SHE'S NOT EVEN USING HER OWN MONEY TO BUY MAGAZINES.
I'M NOT REALLY IN A POSITION TO INTERFERE...

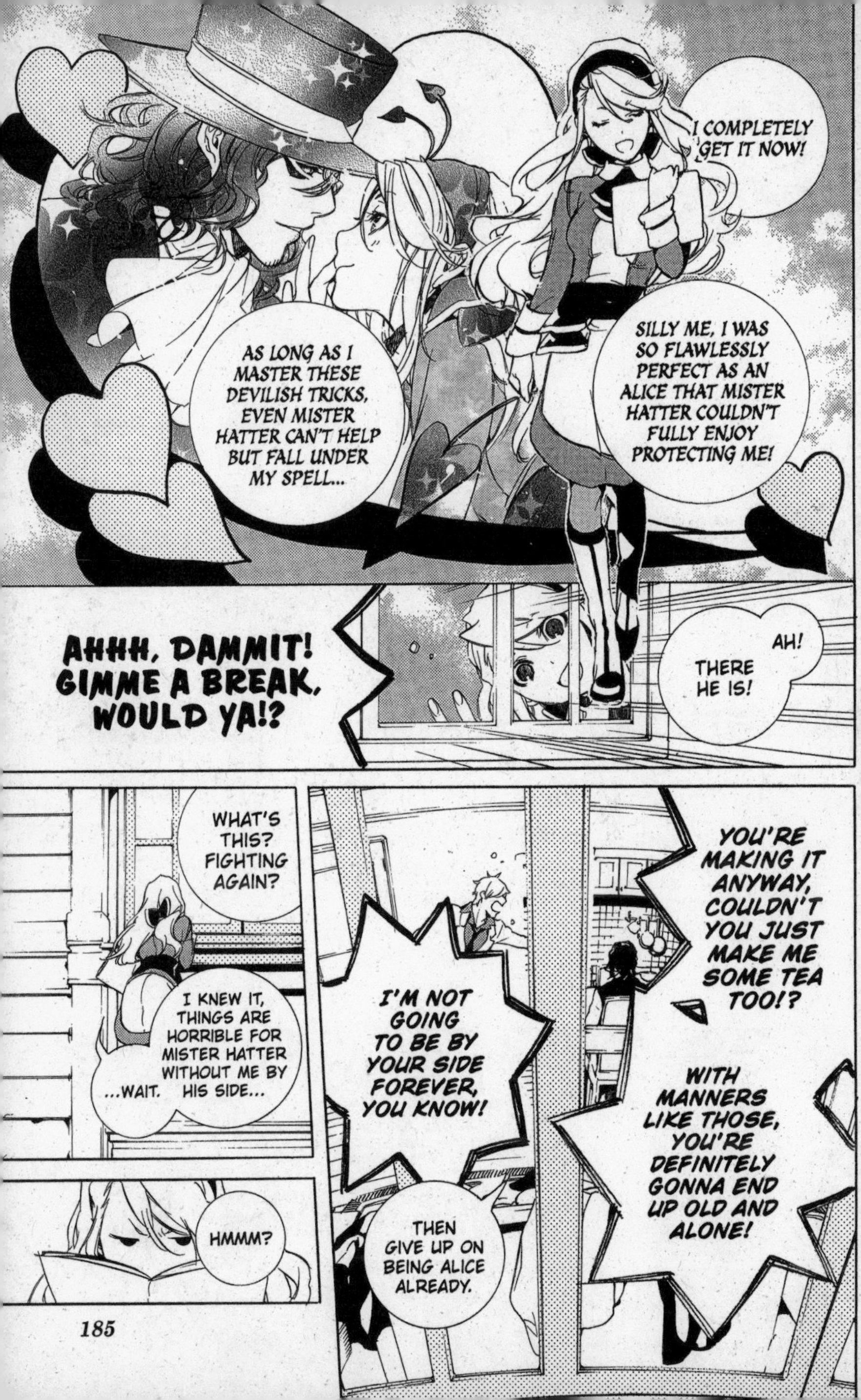
I COMPLETELY GET IT NOW!
SILLY ME, I WAS SO FLAWLESSLY PERFECT AS AN ALICE THAT MISTER HATTER COULDN'T FULLY ENJOY PROTECTING ME!
AS LONG AS I MASTER THESE DEVILISH TRICKS, EVEN MISTER HATTER CAN'T HELP BUT FALL UNDER MY SPELL...
AH!
THERE HE IS!
AHHH, DAMMIT! GIMME A BREAK, WOULD YA!?
YOU'RE MAKING IT ANYWAY, COULDN'T YOU JUST MAKE ME SOME TEA TOO!?
WITH MANNERS LIKE THOSE, YOU'RE DEFINITELY GONNA END UP OLD AND ALONE!
I'M NOT GOING TO BE BY YOUR SIDE FOREVER, YOU KNOW!
THEN GIVE UP ON BEING ALICE ALREADY.
WHAT'S THIS? FIGHTING AGAIN?
I KNEW IT, THINGS ARE HORRIBLE FOR MISTER HATTER WITHOUT ME BY HIS SIDE...
...WAIT.
HMMM?

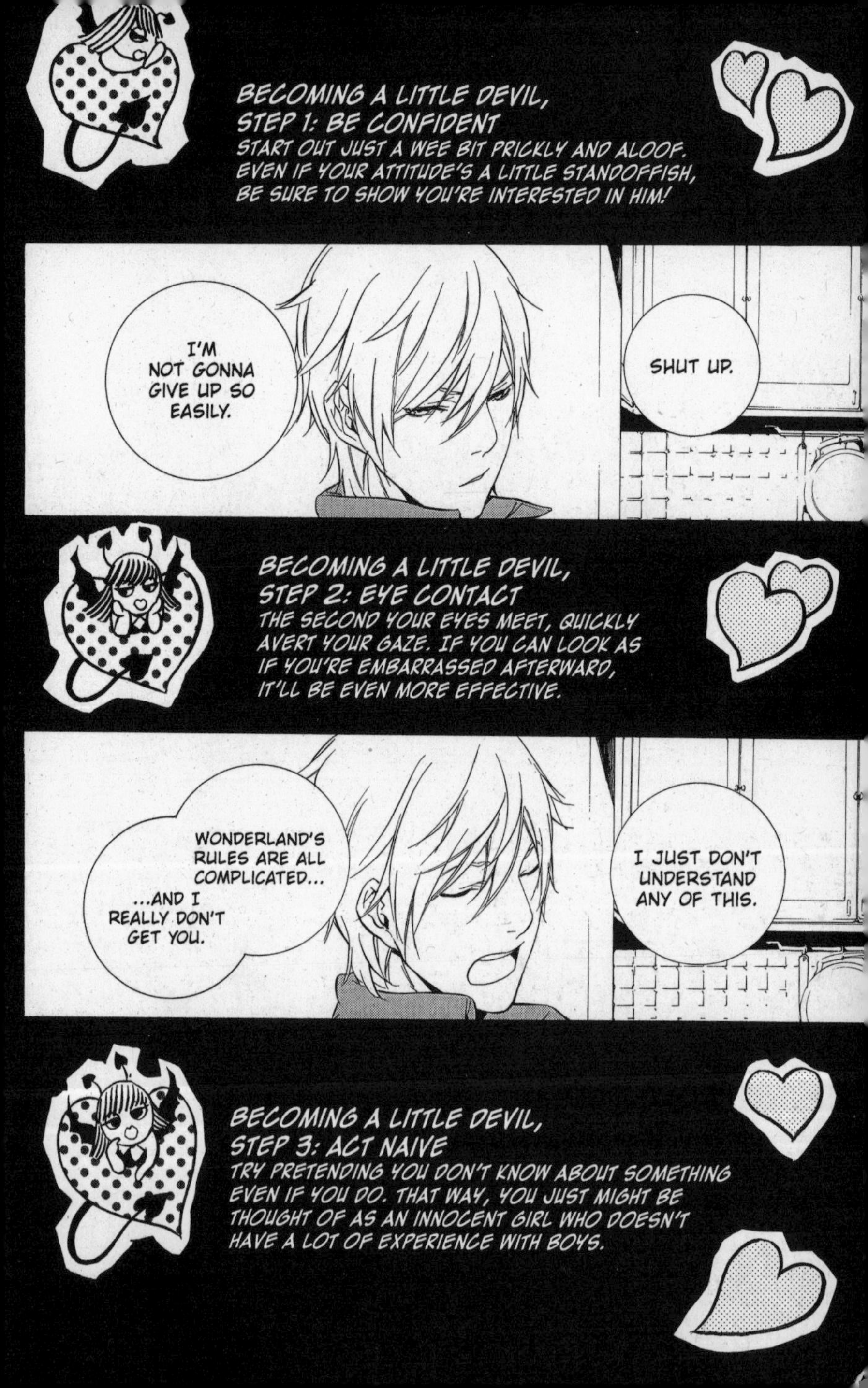
BECOMING A LITTLE DEVIL,
STEP 1: BE CONFIDENT
START OUT JUST A WEE BIT PRICKLY AND ALOOF. EVEN IF YOUR ATTITUDE'S A LITTLE STANDOFFISH, BE SURE TO SHOW YOU'RE INTERESTED IN HIM!
SHUT UP.
I'M NOT GONNA GIVE UP SO EASILY.
BECOMING A LITTLE DEVIL,
STEP 2: EYE CONTACT
THE SECOND YOUR EYES MEET, QUICKLY AVERT YOUR GAZE. IF YOU CAN LOOK AS IF YOU'RE EMBARRASSED AFTERWARD, IT'LL BE EVEN MORE EFFECTIVE.
I JUST DON'T UNDERSTAND ANY OF THIS.
WONDERLAND'S RULES ARE ALL COMPLICATED...
...AND I REALLY DON'T GET YOU.
BECOMING A LITTLE DEVIL,
STEP 3: ACT NAIVE
TRY PRETENDING YOU DON'T KNOW ABOUT SOMETHING EVEN IF YOU DO. THAT WAY, YOU JUST MIGHT BE THOUGHT OF AS AN INNOCENT GIRL WHO DOESN'T HAVE A LOT OF EXPERIENCE WITH BOYS.

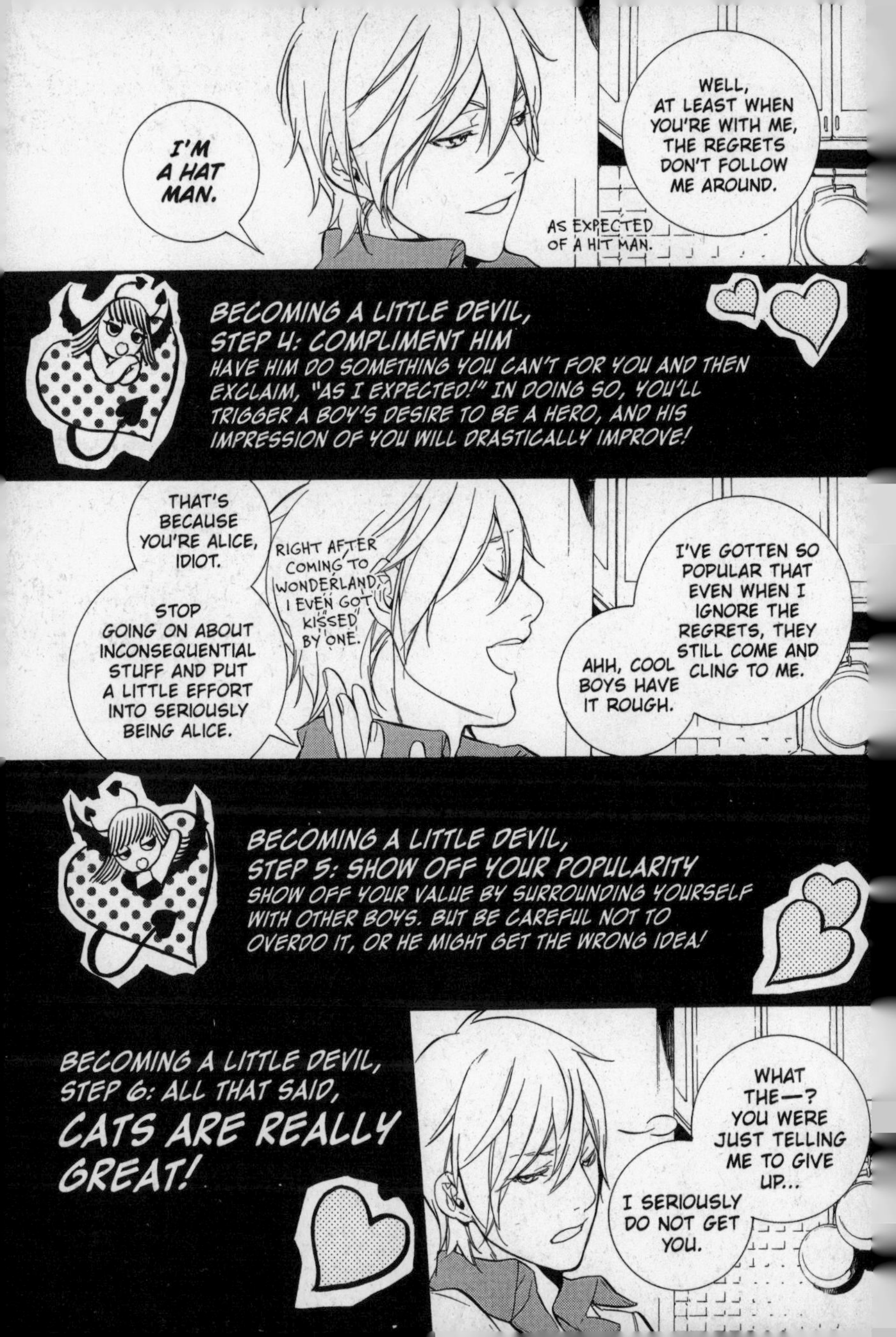
WELL, AT LEAST WHEN YOU'RE WITH ME, THE REGRETS DON'T FOLLOW ME AROUND.
AS EXPECTED OF A HIT MAN.
I'M A HAT MAN.
BECOMING A LITTLE DEVIL, STEP 4: COMPLIMENT HIM
HAVE HIM DO SOMETHING YOU CAN'T FOR YOU AND THEN EXCLAIM, "AS I EXPECTED!" IN DOING SO, YOU'LL TRIGGER A BOY'S DESIRE TO BE A HERO, AND HIS IMPRESSION OF YOU WILL DRASTICALLY IMPROVE!
I'VE GOTTEN SO POPULAR THAT EVEN WHEN I IGNORE THE REGRETS, THEY STILL COME AND CLING TO ME.
AHH, COOL BOYS HAVE IT ROUGH.
THAT'S BECAUSE YOU'RE ALICE, IDIOT.
STOP GOING ON ABOUT INCONSEQUENTIAL STUFF AND PUT A LITTLE EFFORT INTO SERIOUSLY BEING ALICE.
RIGHT AFTER COMING TO WONDERLAND, I EVEN GOT "KISSED" BY ONE.
BECOMING A LITTLE DEVIL, STEP 5: SHOW OFF YOUR POPULARITY
SHOW OFF YOUR VALUE BY SURROUNDING YOURSELF WITH OTHER BOYS. BUT BE CAREFUL NOT TO OVERDO IT, OR HE MIGHT GET THE WRONG IDEA!
WHAT THE—? YOU WERE JUST TELLING ME TO GIVE UP...
I SERIOUSLY DO NOT GET YOU.
BECOMING A LITTLE DEVIL, STEP 6: ALL THAT SAID, CATS ARE REALLY GREAT!

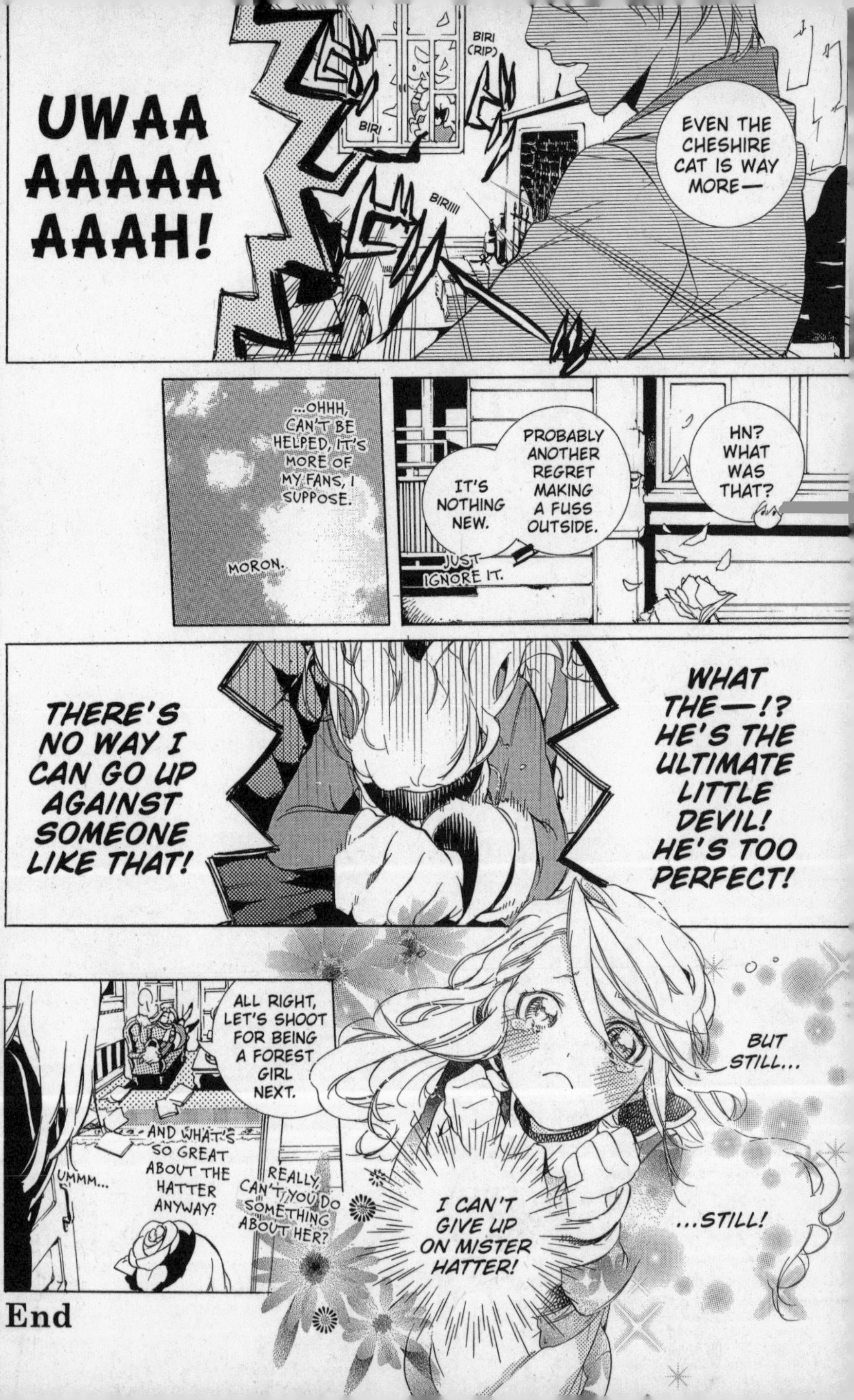
EVEN THE CHESHIRE CAT IS WAY MORE—
BIRI (RIP)
BIRI
BIRIIII
UWAA AAAAA AAAH!
HN? WHAT WAS THAT?
PROBABLY ANOTHER REGRET MAKING A FUSS OUTSIDE.
IT'S NOTHING NEW.
JUST IGNORE IT.
...OHHH, CAN'T BE HELPED, IT'S MORE OF MY FANS, I SUPPOSE.
MORON.
WHAT THE—!? HE'S THE ULTIMATE LITTLE DEVIL! HE'S TOO PERFECT!
THERE'S NO WAY I CAN GO UP AGAINST SOMEONE LIKE THAT!
BUT STILL...
...STILL!
I CAN'T GIVE UP ON MISTER HATTER!
ALL RIGHT, LET'S SHOOT FOR BEING A FOREST GIRL NEXT.
AND WHAT'S SO GREAT ABOUT THE HATTER ANYWAY?
REALLY, CAN'T YOU DO SOMETHING ABOUT HER?
UMMM...
End

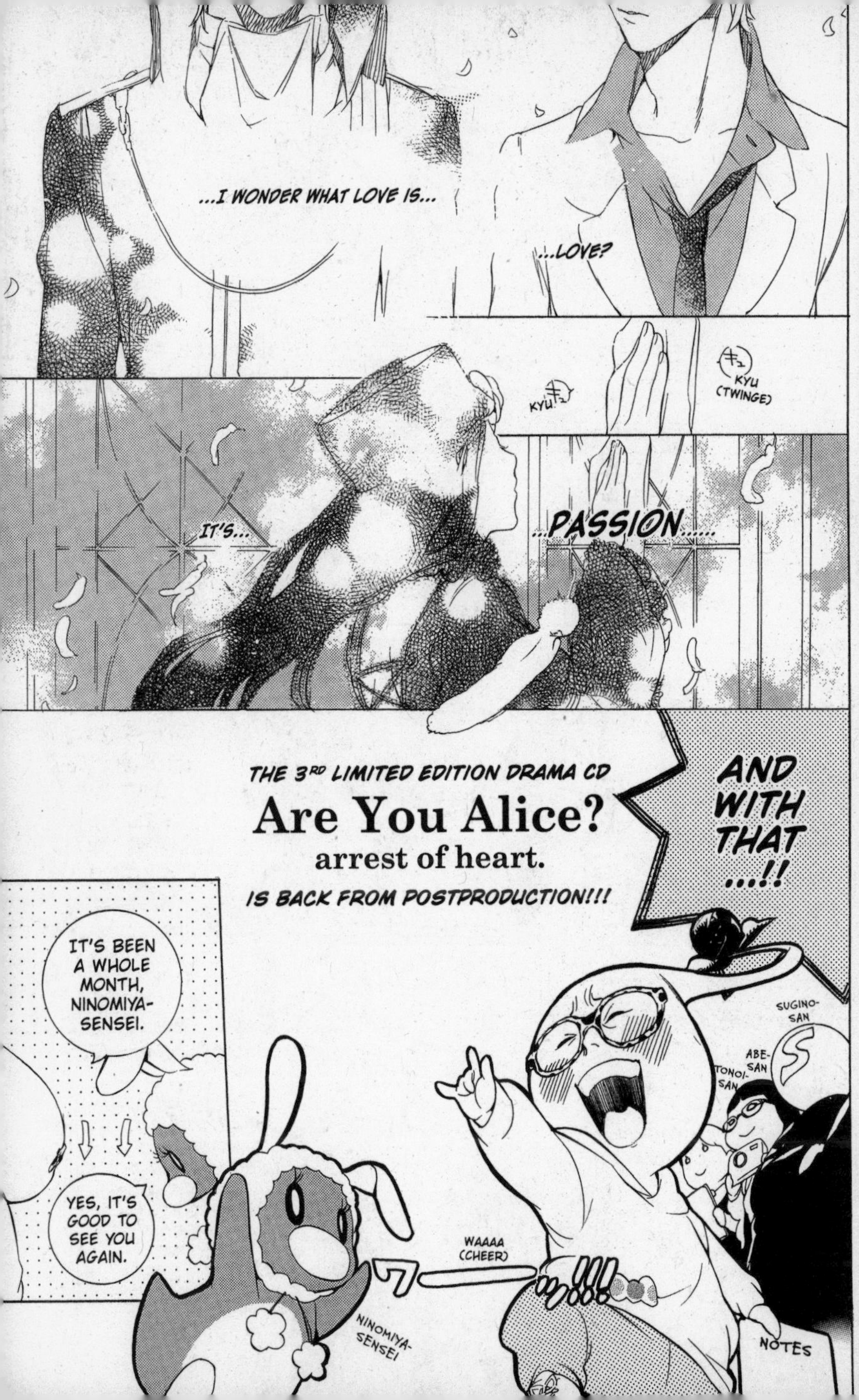
...LOVE?
...I WONDER WHAT LOVE IS...
KYU (TWINGE)
KYU
IT'S...
...PASSION......
AND WITH THAT...!!
THE 3RD LIMITED EDITION DRAMA CD
Are You Alice?
arrest of heart.
IS BACK FROM POSTPRODUCTION!!!
SUGINO-SAN
ABE-SAN
TONOI-SAN
WAAAA (CHEER)
NOTES
NINOMIYA-SENSEI
IT'S BEEN A WHOLE MONTH, NINOMIYA-SENSEI.
YES, IT'S GOOD TO SEE YOU AGAIN.

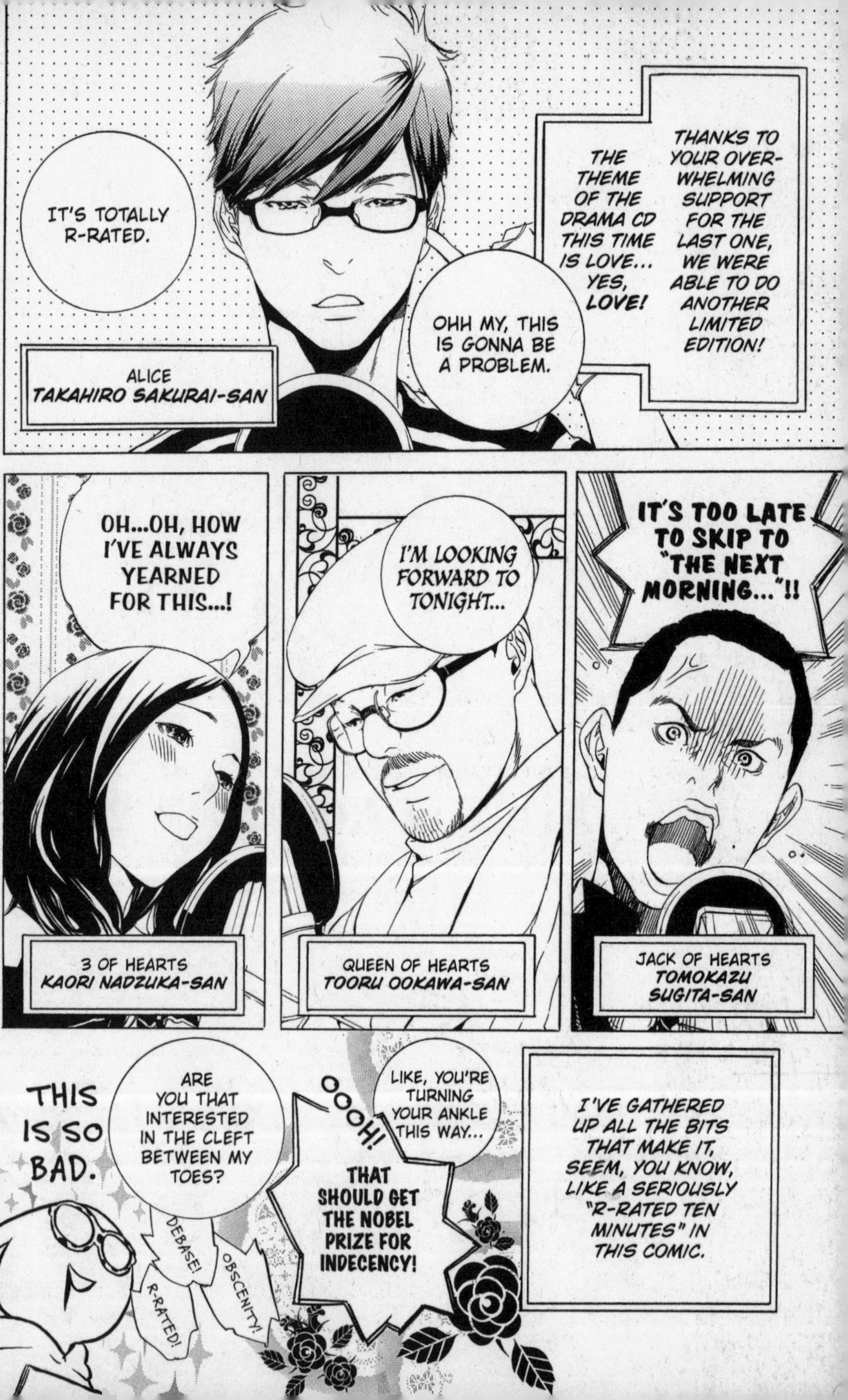
THANKS TO YOUR OVER-WHELMING SUPPORT FOR THE LAST ONE, WE WERE ABLE TO DO ANOTHER LIMITED EDITION!
THE THEME OF THE DRAMA CD THIS TIME IS LOVE... YES, LOVE!
OHH MY, THIS IS GONNA BE A PROBLEM.
IT'S TOTALLY R-RATED.
ALICE
TAKAHIRO SAKURAI-SAN
IT'S TOO LATE TO SKIP TO "THE NEXT MORNING..."!!
JACK OF HEARTS
TOMOKAZU SUGITA-SAN
I'M LOOKING FORWARD TO TONIGHT...
QUEEN OF HEARTS
TOORU OOKAWA-SAN
OH...OH, HOW I'VE ALWAYS YEARNED FOR THIS...!
3 OF HEARTS
KAORI NADZUKA-SAN
I'VE GATHERED UP ALL THE BITS THAT MAKE IT, SEEM, YOU KNOW, LIKE A SERIOUSLY "R-RATED TEN MINUTES" IN THIS COMIC.
LIKE, YOU'RE TURNING YOUR ANKLE THIS WAY...
OOOH!
THAT SHOULD GET THE NOBEL PRIZE FOR INDECENCY!
ARE YOU THAT INTERESTED IN THE CLEFT BETWEEN MY TOES?
THIS IS SO BAD.
OBSCENITY!
DEBASE!
R-RATED!

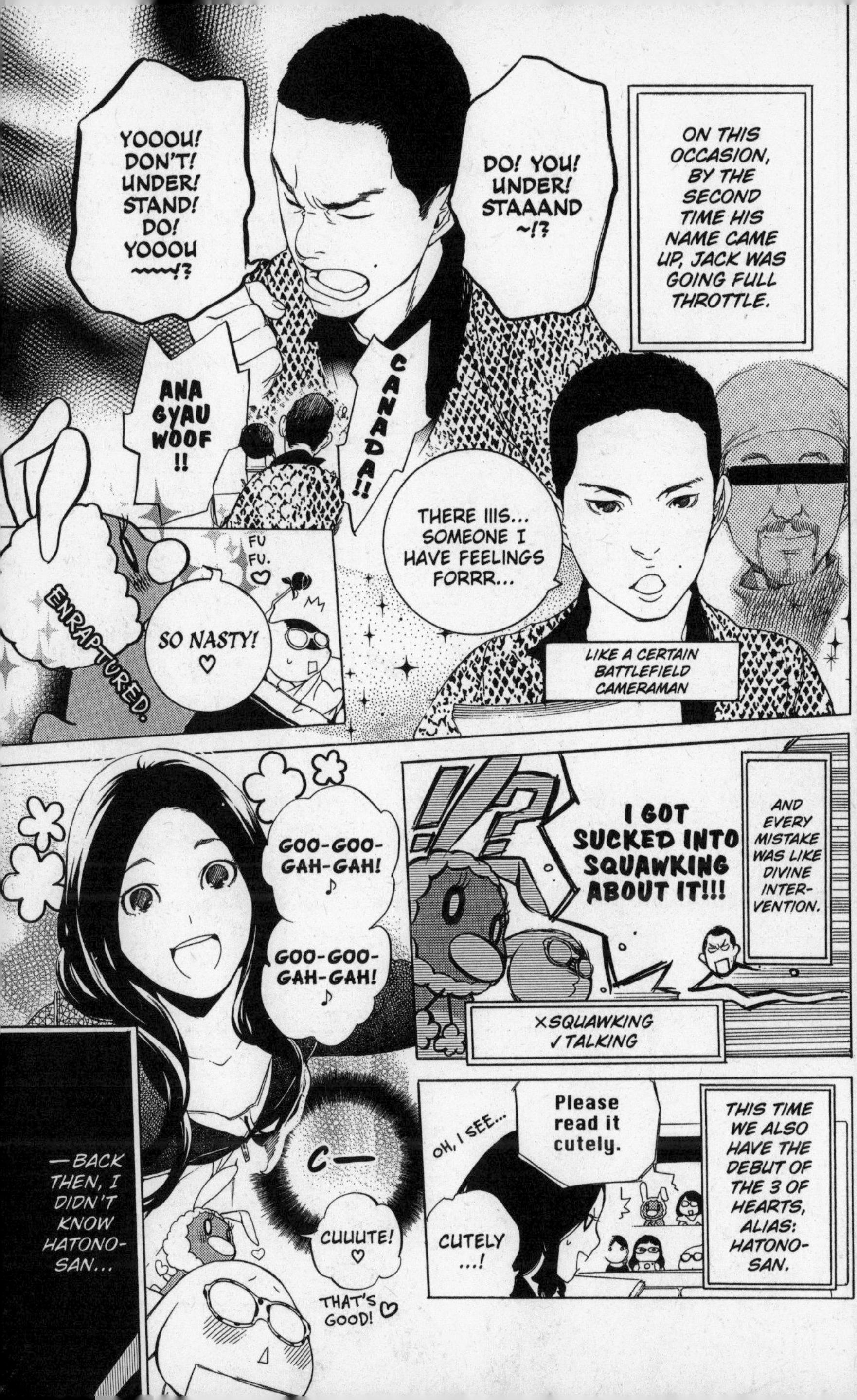
ON THIS OCCASION, BY THE SECOND TIME HIS NAME CAME UP, JACK WAS GOING FULL THROTTLE.
DO! YOU! UNDER! STAAAND ~!?
YOOOU! DON'T! UNDER! STAND! DO! YOOOU ~~~!?
CANADA!!
ANA GYAU WOOF !!
THERE IIIS... SOMEONE I HAVE FEELINGS FORRR...
LIKE A CERTAIN BATTLEFIELD CAMERAMAN
FU FU. ♡
SO NASTY! ♡
ENRAPTURED.
AND EVERY MISTAKE WAS LIKE DIVINE INTER-VENTION.
!?
I GOT SUCKED INTO SQUAWKING ABOUT IT!!!
×SQUAWKING
✓TALKING
THIS TIME WE ALSO HAVE THE DEBUT OF THE 3 OF HEARTS, ALIAS: HATONO-SAN.
Please read it cutely.
OH, I SEE...
CUTELY ...!
GOO-GOO-GAH-GAH! ♪
GOO-GOO-GAH-GAH! ♪
C—
CUUUTE! ♡
THAT'S GOOD! ♡
—BACK THEN, I DIDN'T KNOW HATONO-SAN...

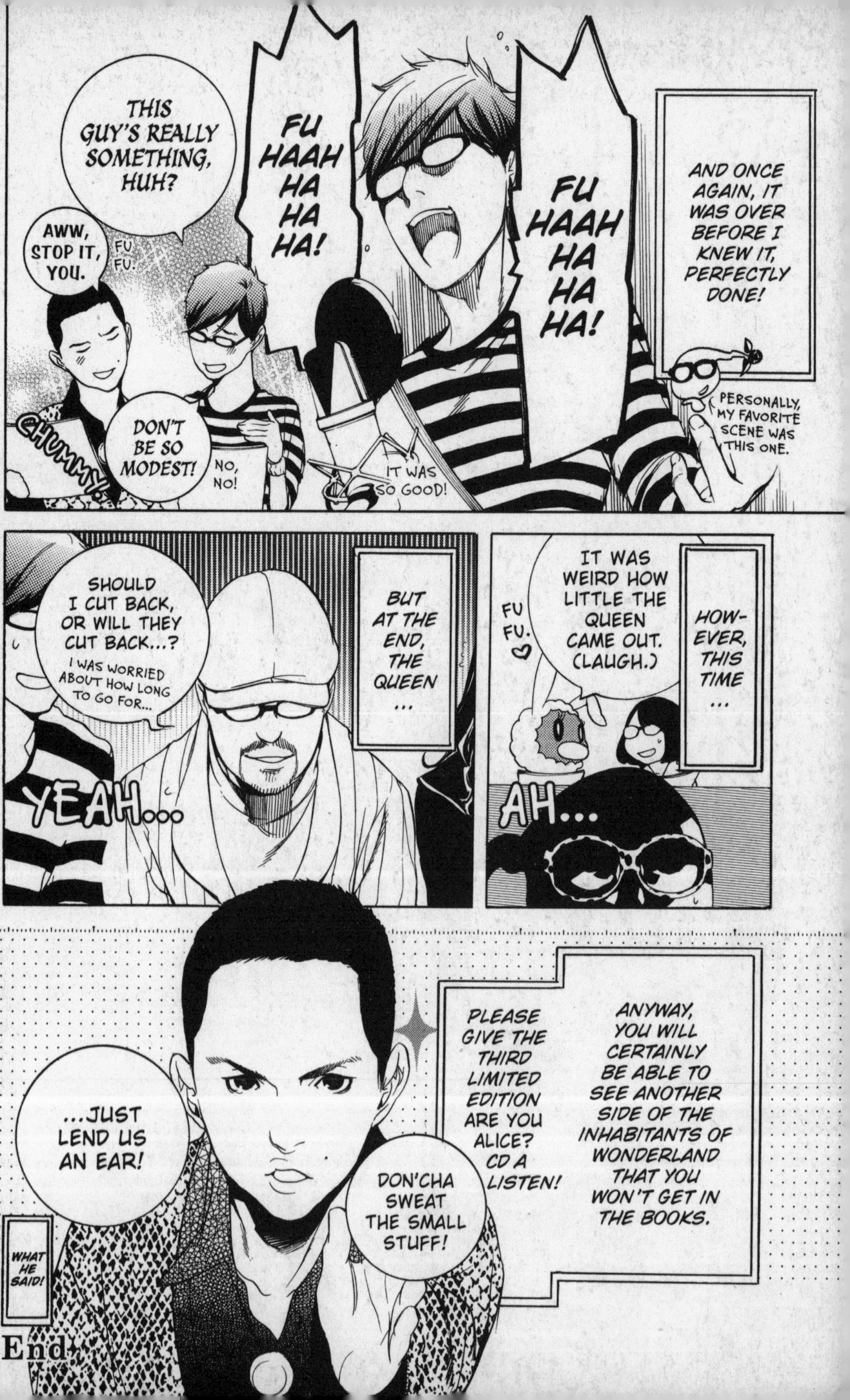
AND ONCE AGAIN, IT WAS OVER BEFORE I KNEW IT, PERFECTLY DONE!
PERSONALLY, MY FAVORITE SCENE WAS THIS ONE.
FU HAAAH HA HA HA!
FU HAAAH HA HA HA!
IT WAS SO GOOD!
THIS GUY'S REALLY SOMETHING, HUH?
FU FU.
AWW, STOP IT, YOU.
NO, NO!
DON'T BE SO MODEST!
CHUMMY.
HOW-EVER, THIS TIME...
IT WAS WEIRD HOW LITTLE THE QUEEN CAME OUT. (LAUGH.)
FU FU.
AH...
BUT AT THE END, THE QUEEN...
SHOULD I CUT BACK, OR WILL THEY CUT BACK...?
I WAS WORRIED ABOUT HOW LONG TO GO FOR...
YEAH...
ANYWAY, YOU WILL CERTAINLY BE ABLE TO SEE ANOTHER SIDE OF THE INHABITANTS OF WONDERLAND THAT YOU WON'T GET IN THE BOOKS.
PLEASE GIVE THE THIRD LIMITED EDITION ARE YOU ALICE? CD A LISTEN!
DON'CHA SWEAT THE SMALL STUFF!
...JUST LEND US AN EAR!
WHAT HE SAID!
End

The story of Alice and everyone
reaches Volume 4 at long last.
The highlight of this volume
was Caterpillar, characterized
by the Ninomiya triple-threat:
tan skin, hooded, and breasts.

Katagiri-sensei's taken to
calling this popular lady
"Cater-girl" and so she's
accidentally had Alice and the rest
call her Cater-girl a few times too,
it was a close call (laugh).

Cater-girl plays a big role in the
new Limited Edition Mini-Drama CD
too, so I truly hope you enjoy it.

And of course there's that
feast of bearded old men
that mustn't be overlooked!
Oh, where did our main
character go?

Ai Ninomiya

Translation Notes

Page 22
To go with *imomushi*, the Japanese word
for "caterpillar," the names of the books all
include the Japanese word for "bug" (*mushi*)
in them. "Living Idly" is *suiseimushi*.

Page 75
Number One
Caterpillar is talking as if she works in a hostess
club, where women pour drinks for customers
and are ranked by popularity with clients.

Page 188
Forest Girl
The term the 88th Alice uses is "mori girl," which
is a style typified by natural looks, vintage
clothing, and a sweet, innocent demeanor.

Page 190
The Next Morning
The phrase used is *asachun* (literally "morning
chirping") which refers to when a show or
manga abruptly ends a scene that's getting
steamy and skips ahead to the next morning
(often with birds chirping) to indicate that
the characters had sex without showing it.

Page 191
**"Do you understand?
You don't understand, do you~"**
This phrase is a reference to a famous gag by
comedic storyteller Chitose Shokakuya.

ARE YOU ALICE? 4

IKUMI KATAGIRI
AI NINOMIYA

Translation and Lettering: Alexis Eckerman

Are you Alice? © 2011 by Ai Ninomiya / Ikumi Katagiri. All rights reserved. First published in Japan in 2011 by ICHIJINSHA. English translation rights arranged with ICHIJINSHA through Tuttle-Mori Agency, Inc., Tokyo.

Translation © 2014 by Hachette Book Group, Inc.

Yen Press
Hachette Book Group
237 Park Avenue, New York, NY 10017

www.HachetteBookGroup.com
www.YenPress.com

Yen Press is an imprint of Hachette Book Group, Inc. The Yen Press name and logo are trademarks of Hachette Book Group, Inc.

First Yen Press Edition: March 2014

ISBN: 978-0-316-25280-5

10 9 8 7 6 5 4 3 2 1

BVG

Printed in the United States of America